THE NEW ENGLAND HANDCRAFT CATALOG

*The reason we honor the
label* handmade *is not because it evokes
a technological relationship between
producer and product,
but a social relationship between
producer and consumer.*

—*Marvin Harris,*
Psychology Today,
August 1981

KENNETH A. SIMON

THE NEW ENGLAND HANDCRAFT CATALOG

OLD CHESTER ROAD · CHESTER, CONNECTICUT 06412

Copyright © 1983 by Kenneth A. Simon
All rights reserved.
No part of this work may be reproduced or transmitted
in any form by any means, electronic or
mechanical, including photocopying and recording,
or by any information storage and retrieval system
without permission in writing from the publisher.

Library of Congress Catalog Card Number: 83-48191
ISBN: 0-87106-916-4

Manufactured in the United States of America
First printing

Cover photograph by Sean Kernan
Cover design by Barbara Marks
Book design by Tom Goddard

133 X

CONTENTS

INTRODUCTION 1

SHOPS/GALLERIES 5

ARTISANS 67

   Clay 71

   Fiber 113

   Glass 161

   Jewelry 181

   Metal 193

   Mixed 205

   Wood 229

FAIRS 263

SCHOOLS 275

GLOSSARY/INDEX 289

FOR SAM AND FANNIE

ACKNOWLEDGEMENTS

My deep thanks to the hundreds of craftspeople, administrators, and shop and gallery owners throughout New England who generously granted interviews and responded to mail inquiries.

I would especially like to thank Carol Sedestrom of American Craft Enterprises for her contributions, including permission to use their glossary of craft terminology. Special thanks are also extended to Richard Fitzgerald and Kathleen Soldati of the League of New Hampshire Craftsmen, Ann Roth of the Vermont State Craft Center at Frog Hollow, Loring Stevens with the New England Buyers Marketplace, and Kathy Downs of Directions, The Professional Craftspeople of Maine.

The onerous task of research and correspondence was greatly eased by the assistance of Maggie Sternik. Gail Egan and Roberta Shorthouse flawlessly typed the manuscript, often on a tight deadline. My thanks also for the contributions of Karen Anderson, Nancy Ledderhose, Suzanne O'Sullivan and Elena Szuc.

The jurying process, which helped to determine the craftspeople who appear in this book, benefitted from the expertise of jurors Susan Banner, Laverne Barile, Roger Gandelman, Joyce Simon and Nancy Stevens. My appreciation also to Dana Gracey, Nancy Moskin and the East Haddam Public Library for their help.

I am also grateful for the sensitivity and expertise of Globe-Pequot's Linda Kennedy and Kevin Lynch. Their insights and encouragement are reflected throughout the book.

Finally, my gratitude to my parents for their support, and to Judy for her patience.

If you would like information on how to apply for inclusion in the next edition of *The New England Handcraft Catalog*, please send a self-addressed, stamped envelope to: *The New England Handcraft Catalog*, PO Box 459, Moodus, Connecticut 06469.

Be sure to specify whether you are a craftsperson, a shop or gallery owner, school administrator, or fair promoter.

<u>All shops and galleries in this book were personally visited and selected by the author. All products were juried for quality by the author and a panel of professional artisans and gallery managers. No one pays or is paid to be included in this book.</u>

Introduction

The Age of Technology is fully upon us. And yet each year the public's appreciation for contemporary handcrafts continues to grow. Thousands of craft professionals across the country find self-fulfillment and financial sustenance through their work, which has a ready market in hundreds of craft shops and galleries and a growing number of gift, jewelry, clothing and department stores. Major craft fairs attract hundreds of thousands of people annually, while universities, craft centers and schools provide both emerging and established artisans with an ever more sophisticated education. Just as importantly, millions of people have discovered the joy that working with handcrafts on an amateur level can bring.

The craft tradition in New England has been a particularly strong one. The first craftsmen sailed over on the Mayflower and in the years to follow, it was the basic craft skills and the small industries emerging from them that helped create a strong, self-reliant economic foundation for the struggling colonies.

In colonial days, everyone was to some extent a craftsman or craftswoman, weaving, sewing, making and fixing tools, building shelter. In addition to the "household manufactures," community needs were met by respected village artisans who specialized in work not easily or efficiently done in one's own home. The smithy, the cooper, the potter, the cabinetmaker, the glassblower — all added immeasurably to the quality of life in the colonies.

From the making of textiles to the making of iron nails, this country was initially built with the labor of skilled hands practicing their craft. Sometimes, respected craftsmen and women contributed in other ways to the country's heritage. Witness one Paul Revere, a well-known silversmith who was also active in community organizing. Or Betsy Ross, who as one observer noted, "did some interesting patchwork."

My introduction to crafts was in 1969, just after I had started a weekly newspaper in Syracuse, New York. During my weekly advertising solicitation rounds, I usually spent time at a leather shop called Down Under, chatting with its owner, Chuck, while he turned out sandals, belts and vests. I followed the Central New York craft scene with interest over the following years, attending fairs, meeting area craftspeople and profiling many of them in my papers. In 1977, my involvement with crafts intensified when I cofounded with other members of my family a craft facility on our family farm in Connecticut.

What exactly are fine handcrafts? They are not, as far as this book is concerned, rope belts or silk flowers, calico, decoupage or kits. Those are handicrafts. With the "i."

Noted potter Charles Counts has defined handcrafts as well as anyone: "Articles predominantly produced by hand rather than assembly-line techniques. This means that there is maximum control of the design and process by the craftsman, with the finished product exhibiting a special quality of individuality as a result of the method of production. A true craft object reflects the time, the place, the personality and the character of the craftsman, the method by which it was made and its use."

Usually made from materials of the earth such as clay, glass, fiber, wood and metal, a fine handcrafted object may be either functional or purely decorative. But it is always a direct result of the craftsperson's intellect, inspiration and technical proficiency. The final piece, notwithstanding differences in taste and style exhibits a sort of visual rhythm whose components are design, color, form and texture. A finely designed, handcrafted item is an effective medium of communication between the maker and the user or viewer, giving comfort and joy to both.

And, I should add, comfort and joy to many. According to Carol Sedestrom, who runs the country's largest crafts fairs for the American Craft Council, the finished craft business in the United States is a $2 billion industry, with the growth curve pointing up. It is also, happily, one industry that cannot be exported to Hong Kong.

This emergence of crafts as a major industry is a relatively recent phenomenon. The craft tradition in the United States had been in a long decline beginning in the early 19th century and continuing into the 20th. Although there are parts of New England, Southern Appalachia and other areas where the basic craft skills have always remained alive, the industrialization and later "massification" of America generally made these skills superfluous to modern living.

Mass production, mass marketing and mass communications had enabled the objects of everyday life to be made more cheaply and distributed more widely than ever before. A new type of person — the consumer — was born and a dizzying array of products was sold ever more efficiently and impersonally.

Then came the Sixties, and a new phenomenon: mass alienation. Many people rejected what they saw as technological, commercial and societal excesses. They yearned for a more "natural" way of life. New movements — self-reliance, natural foods, back to the land, the human potential field — gained converts.

Some people turned to craft work, producing items such as leather belts, clay mugs and silver jewelry. The frazzled consumer, discovering these things in a studio, local craft fair or one of the few craft shops, was charmed. Here was something personalized, of real human value, and made by an honest act of caring and creativity.

Soon the objects became more varied and sophisticated as craftspeople gained more experience and more trained artisans entered the field. There was an explosion of creativity in redefining everyday objects, and a new generation of shops, galleries and craft fairs began marketing handcrafts to a growing craft-buying public. It became, in the words of *Time* magazine in the early Seventies, "a crafts revolution."

The revolution has clearly been successful. Although we are still beleaguered by the commercial, the impersonal, and the trashy, the professional craft field continues to benefit from a desire to embrace individualized things of quality, beauty and charm. The faster the pace, the more people appreciate crafts as a counterpoint.

Today, New England continues its heritage of excellence in crafts:

In New Hampshire, the League of New Hampshire Craftsmen has for fifty years provided extraordinary marketing and educational opportunities for the state's craftspeople. Its ten retail shops, a popular fair and a year-round program of classes, among other activities, expose tens of thousands of people to handcrafts each year.

For more than 100 years, Rhode Island has been home to one of America's most influential art and design schools, the Rhode Island School of Design, which has trained hundreds of outstanding craftspeople in its strong multi-disciplinary program.

In Massachusetts, two of this country's seminal craft organizations, the Society of Arts and Crafts in Boston and the Worcester Craft Center, continue to serve their constituencies with a variety of educational and marketing programs. Starting in 1984, the state will also host in Springfield the American Craft Council's premier craft fair, the world's largest.

Maine has a vigorous group of retail craft-producer cooperatives throughout the state, as well as one of the country's most respected summer craft schools, Haystack Mountain School of Crafts.

Within Connecticut's borders lie some half dozen craft centers and guilds, which provide studio space to artisans while offering a full range of marketing and educational activities.

And in Vermont, where the dollar amount of handcraft production is greater than that from their famed maple syrup, the country's first state-recognized craft centers provide a strong focal point for Vermont crafts.

These places and organizations are just part of the thriving New England craft community. Hundreds of craft producers work with a support structure of shops, galleries, centers, fairs and schools to contribute vigorously to both the region's cultural and economic health.

This book is your guide to the best of that unique community.

Shops/Galleries

Southern New England

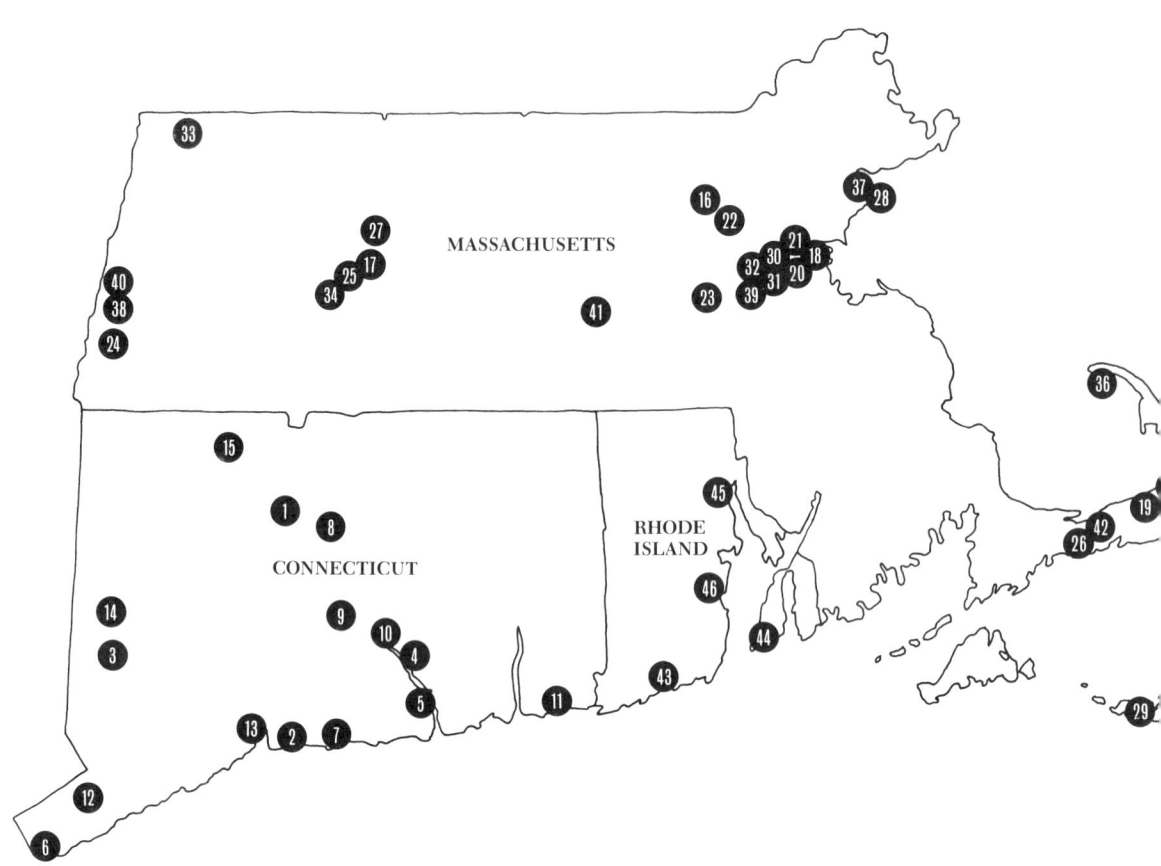

6 · SHOPS/GALLERIES

SOUTHERN NEW ENGLAND

CONNECTICUT

Map No.		Page No.
1.	Avon, The Fisher Gallery	11
2.	Branford, Bittersweet Handcraft Village	12
3.	Brookfield, Aufrichtig's	12
	Brookfield, Brookfield Craft Center	12
4.	East Haddam, Connecticut River Artisans Cooperative	13
5.	Essex, Limited Editions	13
6.	Greenwich, The Elements	13
	Greenwich, The Greenwich Art Barn	14
7.	Guilford, Evergreen	14
	Guilford, Guilford Handcrafts Center	15
8.	Hartford, Old State House	15
9.	Middletown, The Shop at Wesleyan Potters	16
10.	Moodus, Down on the Farm	16
	Moodus, A Touch of Glass	18
11.	Mystic, The Company of Craftsmen	18
12.	New Canaan, Silvermine Guild Galleries	19
13.	New Haven, Endelman-Kraus Galleries	20
14.	New Milford, Atelier Studio/Gallery	20
	New Milford, The Silo	20
	New Milford, Voltaire's	22
15.	Riverton, Contemporary Crafts Gallery	22

MASSACHUSETTS

16.	Acton, Handworks	32
17.	Amherst, The Leather Shed	32
	Amherst, River Valley Crafts	32
	Amherst, Silverscape Designs	32
18.	Boston, Alianza	33
	Boston, Artisans Cooperative	33
	Boston, Signature	34
	Boston, The Society of Arts and Crafts	34
	Boston, Vermont Imports	35
	Boston, Whippoorwill Crafts	35
	Boston, Wild Goose Chase	36
19.	Brewster, The Spectrum	36
20.	Brookline, Marion-Ruth	36
21.	Cambridge, Journeyman	37
	Cambridge, Ten Arrow	37

Map No.		Page No.
22.	Concord, Perceptions	37
23.	Framingham, Danforth Museum Shop	38
24.	Great Barrington, Wonderful Things	38
25.	Hadley, Skera	38
26.	Hyannis, Signature	39
	Hyannis, The Spectrum	39
27.	Leverett, Leverett Craftsmen and Artists, Inc.	40
28.	Marblehead, Quaigh Designs	40
29.	Nantucket, Artisans Cooperative	40
	Nantucket, The Spectrum	41
30.	Newton, Limited Editions	41
31.	Newton Highlands, The Potters Shop	41
32.	Newton Center, Jubilation	42
33.	North Adams, The Corner	42
34.	Northampton, Don Muller Gallery	42
35.	Orleans, The Ethel Putterman Gallery	43
	Orleans, The Artful Hand	43
	Orleans, New Horizons	43
	Orleans, Tree's Place	44
36.	Provincetown, The Ellen Harris Gallery	44
	Provincetown, Metamorphosis	44
	Provincetown, Whaler's Wharf	45
37.	Salem, The Spectrum	45
38.	Stockbridge, Holsten Galleries	45
39.	Wellesley, The Gifted Hand	46
40.	West Stockbridge, Design Works	46
41.	Worcester, The Prints & The Potter	47
	Worcester, Redwing Craft Cooperative	47
	Worcester, Worcester Craft Center	47
42.	Yarmouthport, Northside Craft Gallery	48

RHODE ISLAND

43.	Charlestown, Small Axe Productions	56
44.	Newport, The Spectrum	57
45.	Providence, Lily G. Iselin	57
	Providence, The Spectrum	57
46.	Wickford, Different Drummer	58
	Wickford, J. W. Graham	58

7 · SHOPS/GALLERIES

Northern New England

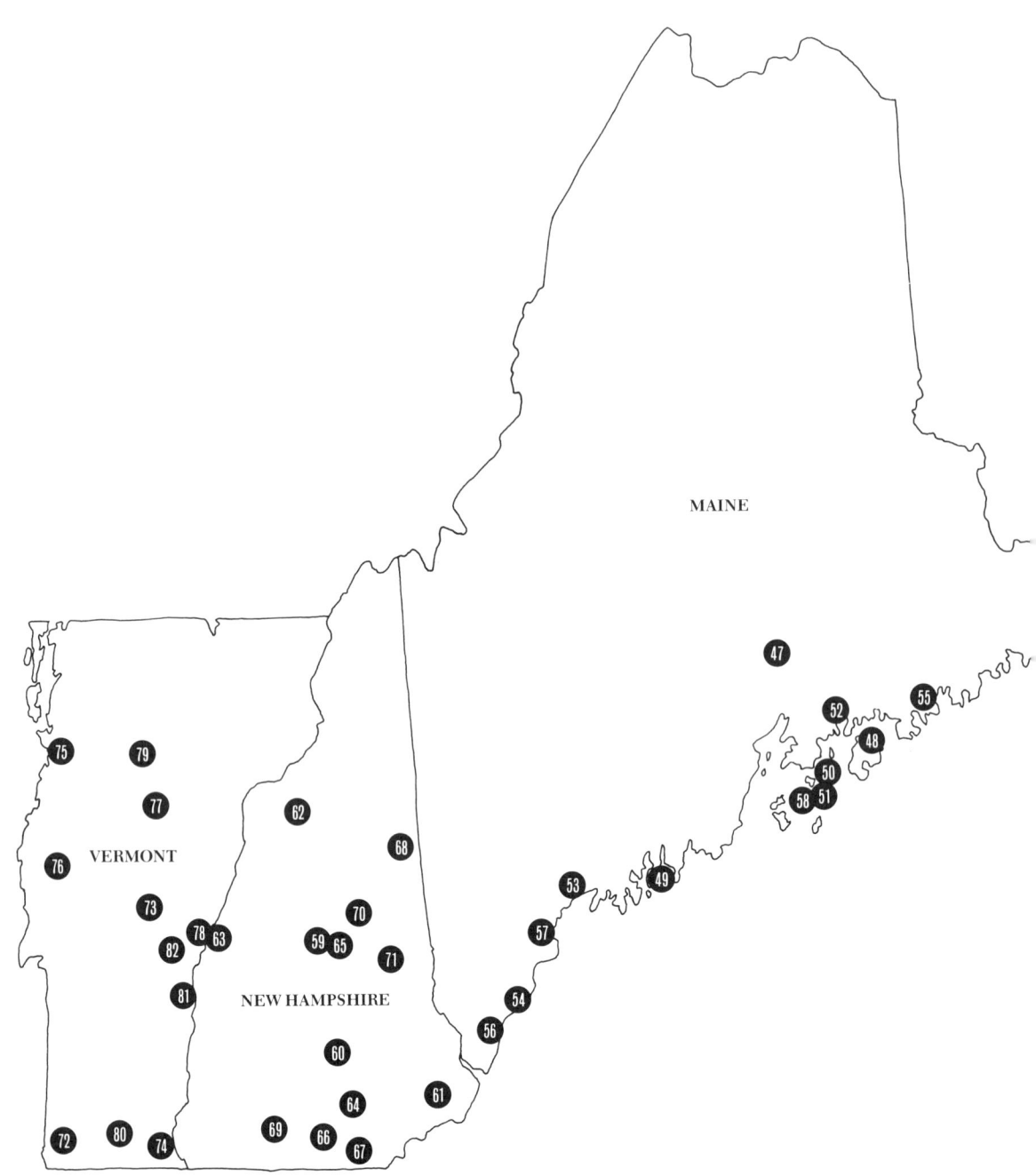

NORTHERN NEW ENGLAND

MAINE

Map No.   *Page No.*

47. Bangor, Chosen Works 23
48. Bar Harbor, Caleb's Sunrise 23
    Bar Harbor, Island Artisans, Inc. . . 23
49. Boothbay Harbor, Mung Bean 24
50. Brooklin, Brooklin Crafts
    Cooperative 24
51. Deer Isle, Gateway Gallery 25
    Deer Isle, Timeless Designs 25
52. Ellsworth, Hands On! 26
    Ellsworth, Strong Craft Gallery ... 26
53. Freeport, Praxis 27
54. Kennebunkport, Plum Dandy 27
55. Milbridge, Eastern Maine Craft
    Co-op 28
56. Ogunquit, Maple Hill Gallery 28
57. Portland, Handcrafters Gallery ... 29
    Portland, Maine Potters Market .. 29
    Portland, The Marketplace, Inc. ... 30
58. Stonington, Eastern Bay
    Cooperative Gallery 30

NEW HAMPSHIRE

59. Ashland, Artist Express Depot ... 49
60. Concord, Concord Arts & Crafts .. 49
    Concord, Concord Gallery 49
61. Exeter, Exeter Craft Center 50
62. Franconia, Franconia League of
    New Hampshire Craftsmen 50
63. Hanover, League of New
    Hampshire Craftsmen 50
    Hanover, The Artifactory 51
64. Manchester, Shop at the
    Institute 51

Map No.   *Page No.*

65. Meredith, Meredith-Laconia
    Arts & Crafts 52
    Meredith, Rainbow's End 52
66. Milford, The Golden Toad 52
67. Nashua, Artisans East 53
68. North Conway, League of New
    Hampshire Craftsmen 53
69. Peterborough, Tewksbury's 54
    Peterborough, Sharon Arts
    Center 54
70. Sandwich, Sandwich Home
    Industries 54
71. Wolfeboro, Schoolhouse Shop 55

VERMONT

72. Bennington, Hawkins House 59
73. Bethel, The Silk Purse & The
    Sow's Ear 59
74. Brattleboro, L.J. Serkin Co. 60
75. Burlington, Designers Circle 60
76. Middlebury, The Vermont
    State Crafts Center at Frog
    Hollow 61
77. Montpelier, The Artisans' Hand .. 62
78. Norwich, Trillium Fine Crafts 62
79. Stowe, Samara 62
    Stowe, The Stowe Pottery 63
80. Wilmington, Craft-Haus 63
    Wilmington, Klara Simpla 63
    Wilmington, Quaigh Design
    Center 64
81. Windsor, The Vermont State
    Craft Center at Windsor House ... 64
82. Woodstock, Unicorn 65

9 · SHOPS/GALLERIES

INTRODUCTION

A few months ago I set out in pursuit of New England's best outlets for professional crafts. Four thousand miles later, here are the results of that search. Housed in old mills and new malls, in the Maine woods and downtown Boston, in rehabbed barns and slick new stores, these are the finest places in New England to see, hold and purchase contemporary American handcrafts.

Only those places maintaining a permanent and substantial inventory of contemporary crafts made by fulltime craftspeople have been included. Those that feature only sporadic displays, colonial reproductions, amateur, ethnic or foreign crafts have been screened out.

Although the style and ambiance of these places vary widely, I can assure you that they all emphasize fine contemporary work made both in New England and across the country. None will display their crafts next to junk. A few, however, sell fine paintings, prints, or commercially made design items and housewares in addition to crafts.

Generally, the character of a craft shop or gallery is affected by its location. For instance, the more urban the area, the more designed and experimental the crafts. A shop in Greenwich, Connecticut, is not likely to resemble one in rural Vermont. And like New England itself, as you move farther north, the crafts tend to become more rugged.

Many of the craftspeople featured in this book are well-represented in the listed shops and galleries. A visit will often allow you to see a good-sized grouping of their work. This is highly recommended as even the best black-and-white photographs can't compare to the real thing. If you're looking for a specific artisan's work, don't hesitate to ask the person who's tending shop. In fact, don't hesitate to ask them anything regarding crafts or the people who make them. They are quite knowledgeable about the field and will gladly share that knowledge with you.

Another advantage of visiting a shop or gallery is the opportunity to see a wide selection of work not easily seen elsewhere. Some places specialize in a collection of crafts from their own state or region, others in a particular style or medium. Most try to keep a nice selection of an artisan's work on hand. Also, craftspeople will often give preference to those places that "discovered" or supported them early in their careers. Consequently, when an artisan becomes popular and the demand for their work outstrips production capacity, those places will remain supplied with new work.

Craft shops and galleries are also excellent places to order specially commissioned work. Their owners and managers have expertise in a variety of media and contacts among a broad group of craftspeople. Take advantage of it. You'll get good advice and in many ways, commissioning work through a shop or gallery is easier than going directly to the craftsperson.

A few words on terminology.

I've used the terms, "shop," "gallery," "gallery/shop," and "retail gallery" to characterize the different kinds of craft outlets. Perhaps a word of explanation is in order.

A traditional gallery features periodic exhibitions of primarily "museum quality" and one-of-a-kind work. There are usually no permanent displays of crafts. Although there are fewer pieces on display than at other types of outlets, those that are there are often striking and will interest even the most experienced craft connoisseur. The work on display is usually nonfunctional and its prices reflect its value to serious collectors.

A craft shop will often display substantial groupings of mostly production and limited edition work, along with some one-of-a-kind pieces. The craft objects here tend to be more functional and less in the realm of "art for art's sake." However, at the level of virtuosity with which we're concerned, there is artistry in even the most humble mug. Shops will usually feature regularly scheduled special exhibits.

The retail gallery or gallery/shop has some of the display sensibilities of a traditional gallery, but shows groupings of work at all levels, from production to museum quality. Also, to appeal to the wider craft buying public, there will usually be at least as much functional as nonfunctional work here. These places often have periodic special exhibits of work featuring top-end crafts.

All information in the listings is accurate at the time of this writing. But things do change, so before you pile the family into your car to visit that great-sounding shop several hundred miles down the road, call ahead to confirm hours and days open. Incidentally, the word "daily" is used to signify that a place is open Monday through Saturday and closed Sunday.

Although I've made an attempt to include all the region's finest contemporary craft outlets, new places periodically open and I may have missed some others. If you have a candidate for inclusion in the next edition of this book, please write me and I'll check it out.

So what are you waiting for? Go explore New England's fine array of craft shops and galleries. Happy craft hunting!

CONNECTICUT

THE FISHER GALLERY
Farmington Valley Arts Center
Avon Park North
Avon, Connecticut 06001
(203) 678-1867

In 1971 a group of local artists and craftspeople banded together to establish studios here in a handsome 19th-century brownstone factory building once used for the manufacture of explosives. The location was ideal: woodsy and quite idyllic, yet close by the bustle of greater Avon and nearby population centers.

One thing led to another and with the help of involved area residents, the Farmington Valley Arts Center has developed into a respected cultural center emphasizing fine craft work. Besides managing the working studios, the nonprofit center runs an educational program and mounts shows in a gallery space that features ten exhibits each year in visual arts and craft.

The intimate gallery, located next door to the studios, shows contemporary works of art in all media, but concentrates on "craft as an art form, within the functional tradition." Eighty percent of the exhibits are of the fine crafts of invited individual artists and group shows. Most work is for sale at prices from $10 to $2,000. "There is an emphasis on fine craft not usually seen in this area," notes center director Betty Friedman.

A few steps from the gallery sits a sturdy, two-level factory building, which houses twenty working studios connected to each other by covered porches. A cooperative of twelve potters occupies two of the studios and more than two dozen artists and craftspeople pursue their respective muses in the others. There are among them a furniture maker, a stained-glass artist, a leatherworker, a paper marbler, a basketmaker, a jeweler, a photographer, painters and printmakers. There's also a chair-caning studio here.

Although many studios are often open to the public, their occupants don't keep regular hours. It's suggested that you call the center to make arrangements to see a particular artist.

Besides its schedule of more than 200 classes and workshops each year, the center sponsors regular demonstrations, art tours, films and lectures.

Hours: Tuesday through Saturday 11 A.M. to 4 P.M.; Sunday 1 A.M. to 4 P.M.
Directions: From I-84 West, take Exit 30 and follow Route 4 West to Route 10. Take Route 10 North to Route 44 in Avon. Turn left and go about two miles. After crossing the railroad tracks, look for Avon Park North on your right.

The Fisher Gallery

11 · SHOPS/GALLERIES

CONNECTICUT

BITTERSWEET HANDCRAFT VILLAGE
779 East Main Street
Branford, Connecticut 06405
(203) 488-4689

More than thirty-five artisans and shopkeepers sell everything from candy, nuts and herbs to painting and graphics, to amateur and professional handcrafts, on this recycled, 150-year-old farm that abuts heavily traveled Route 1.

About twenty artisans work on the farm, doing work that ranges from undistinguished to nationally recognized fine craft. Although the artisans come and go here and there's more than one hobbyist at work, the craft connoisseur will find at Bittersweet a good selection of professional crafts in a variety of media.

Among the professionals here are: Bittersweet Glassworks, a hot glass studio where several glassblowers have achieved national recognition; a four-person pottery cooperative that has been here since 1973, the year that Bittersweet Village was established; and a basketmaker, a weaver, a leatherworker, and a husband-and-wife woodcarving team.

Also occupying space on the farm are Country Gardens, a well-stocked herb and spice shop; the Back Porch Restaurant, which serves lunch and Sunday brunch; a framing shop; and a gift shop. There is also a shop selling antiques and collectibles and one that specializes in interior design and accessories.

Hours: Tuesday through Saturday, 11 A.M. to 5 P.M.; Sunday, noon to 5 P.M. Individual shop and studio hours may vary.
Directions: Take Exit 56 off I-95 and follow north to Route 1. Take a right on Route 1. Bittersweet will be on your right near the Guilford town line.

AUFRICHTIG'S
837 Federal Road
Brookfield, Connecticut 06804
(203) 775-1015

Just around the corner from Brookfield Craft Center, Dana and Norma Aufrichtig run a rustic craft shop in their early 19th-century house. Established in 1971, the shop features Dana's functional stoneware pottery, which fills one small room near the front of the shop.

Besides Dana's work, there is also on display the work of about two dozen jewelers and an equal number of primarily New England craftspeople working in media such as stained and blown glass, leather accessories, wood and metal. Prices start at a few dollars and rise to $1,000, with most pieces in the $10 to $75 range.

Hours: Monday through Friday, 10:15 A.M. to 5:30 P.M.; Saturday, 10 A.M. to 5 P.M.
Directions: Take new Route 7 to the last exit, which is Federal Road. The shop is approximately one-half mile north on Federal Road.

BROOKFIELD CRAFT CENTER
Route 25
Brookfield, Connecticut 06804
(203) 775-4526

Since its founding in 1954 as a nonprofit school for craft education, the Brookfield Craft Center has grown into a significant craft-oriented cultural center offering more than 180 classes a year for all levels, from basic craft techniques to workshops for the expert craftsperson.

A restored 18th-century grist mill is the centerpiece of this campuslike setting on the

Brookfield Craft Center

banks of the Still River. The mill and three buildings house well-equipped studios for the study of weaving, ceramics, woodworking, metalsmithing, stained glass and more.

The center also has a 600-square-foot gallery space in the old mill, which shows six exhibitions a year of the work of invited individuals and groups as well as themed shows. Recent shows have included handmade paper, pewter, and wearable art.

The center's retail craft shop is located in a nearby farmhouse that once housed the miller and his family. The 19th-century structure now contains a 450-square-foot consignment shop in two of its rooms for the display of the work of more than 100 craftspeople. About twenty-five percent of the crafts on sale here

CONNECTICUT

were made by professional craftspeople who belong to the center. The rest of the crafts are made by the center's amateur members and students. Work shown includes both production and one-of-a-kind work in clay, glass, fiber, metal and wood. Prices range from $1.50 to $500, with most items under $50.

Hours: Gallery open daily 10 A.M. to 4 P.M. and Sunday 2 P.M. to 5 P.M.; shop is open Wednesday through Sunday noon to 5 P.M.
Directions: From I-84 take Exit 9 to Route 25 North. Follow to Brookfield Craft Center, which is on the left just before you reach a junction at Route 7 and 202.
From I-95, take Exit 15 to Route 7 North and follow to Brookfield. Take a right onto Route 25 and you'll find the center ahead on your right.

CONNECTICUT RIVER ARTISANS COOPERATIVE
Goodspeed Landing
East Haddam, Connecticut 06423
(203) 873-1661

"Not only do we have a fine place to sell our work," says weaver Carol Clifford, founder and director of the Connecticut River Artisans Cooperative, "but everybody cares about everybody else. You just kind of pull for each other. When you're on duty and someone else's stuff sells, you're just as happy as if it were yours."

Established in 1980, the co-op is collectively owned by about two dozen part- and full-time craftspeople. The shop occupies the first floor of a vintage clapboard building just a few steps from the Goodspeed Opera House. In three display rooms totaling 800 square feet, the co-op shows pottery, woven rugs and apparel, baskets, stained glass, woodcarving, leather accessories, painted silk clothing, jewelry, barnwood furnishings, antique dolls, soft sculpture and folk art. Prices run from about $1 to $300, with the average work priced at $20 to $30.

"We try to carry a range of crafts so people can appreciate what we have on different levels," Carol told me. "You can find things affordable for a child and things for the collector." All craftspeople are juried by a nine-member panel for quality, originality and workmanship before they are accepted into the co-op.

Hours: Summer, Tuesday through Saturday, 11 A.M. to 6 P.M. and Sunday, 1 P.M. to 5 P.M.; Winter, Thursday through Saturday, 11 A.M. to 5 P.M. and Sunday, 1 to 5 P.M.
Directions: From Route 9, take Exit 7 and follow the signs to the Goodspeed Opera House.

LIMITED EDITIONS
59 Main Street
Essex, Connecticut 06426
(203) 767-1071

In 1978, Ann and Doug Soper had finally found a suitable apartment to rent right on Main Street in one of the dozens of restored historic buildings in this old shipbuilding town. But there was a problem: The landlord wouldn't rent out the second-floor apartment without also leasing the vacant store downstairs.

As it turns out, Ann and Doug had been attending professional craft fairs for the previous four years, selling their line of rope furniture. They thought that maybe a contemporary craft shop in this popular tourist town would have a good chance of success. They decided to give it a try and signed on the dotted line.

According to Ann, they started the store primarily on a barter system, trading their furniture for the work of craftspeople they had met at the fairs. Today their four-room 800-square-foot shop displays the work of about 110 craftspeople who create blown glass, rugs, weaving, baskets, pottery, jewelry, leather accessories and clothing. The Sopers' rope furniture is also on display here. Prices range from $20 to $1,700, with the average estimated at about $40.

Hours: Daily, 10 A.M. to 5 P.M.; Sunday, noon to 5 P.M.
Directions: From I-95, take the Route 9 exit to Exit 3. Go to the traffic light and follow signs to Essex Center. Limited Editions is halfway down Main Street on the left.

THE ELEMENTS
14 Liberty Way
Greenwich, Connecticut 06830
(203) 661-7988

This respected showplace for fine crafts is housed in an old livery stable just behind Greenwich's main shopping street. Since its opening in 1973, The Elements has displayed the work of some of this country's best craftspeople "whose work shows a clear standard of design and artistic vision." The partners here also run The Elements in New York City's Soho district, an area known as an artistic hotbed.

The stable's whitewashed brick walls, cement floor and beamed ceiling form a fitting backdrop for the display of both contemporary and more traditionally influenced work by some 350 craftspeople.

"We try to attract a broad mix of people," says managing partner Emily Toohey. "We don't have the way-out stuff that the New York place has."

The 1,800-square-foot gallery/shop has an especially fine selection of ceramics and art glass, and there are about a dozen cases that display a large variety of gold and silver jewelry. Wood and fiber are also represented. There are many larger pieces in the shop and prices start at $10, rising to $1,500.

"Things here tend to be more functional than nonfunctional," notes shop manager Barbara Wood. "Even if the customer will never use it, they want to feel that they can."

The Elements is noted for its showings of both themed exhibits and the work of invited artists. You'll usually find a show in progress.

Hours: Tuesday through Saturday, 10 A.M. to 5 P.M.
Directions: From I-95, take Exit 3 to Arch Street, which dead ends at Greenwich Avenue. Cross Greenwich Avenue and turn left at the first light (Mason Street). Turn left at second light (Elm Street) and then right again. In the middle of the block, turn into the parking area. Liberty Way is in the middle of the lot.

THE GREENWICH ART BARN
143 Lower Cross Road
Greenwich, Connecticut 06830
(203) 661-9048

The Greenwich Art Barn was founded by a group of Greenwich residents in 1962 as a nonprofit center for the visual arts and crafts. The center has grown to include a large gallery space, a craft shop and three floors of studios for the teaching of weaving, ceramics, printmaking, painting and drawing, among other arts and crafts.

The gallery is the site for monthly invitational and juried shows of both crafts and two-dimensional art. Among the annual scheduled shows are exhibitions featuring painting and sculpture, prints and drawings, a members' exhibition, photography, and the Holiday Handcraft Show and Sale.

The craft shop, which is located in the oldest part of the barn (built in 1747), displays and sells the primarily functional work of 300 craft professionals. You'll find pottery, woven goods, furniture, glass, wood, dolls, toys, clothing, quilts and antique and contemporary folk art at prices ranging up to $2,500.

The craft shop moves into the gallery each November and December for an expanded show and sale. Demonstrations by craftspeople are presented throughout the show.

Hours: Tuesday through Saturday, 10 A.M. to 4 P.M.; Sunday, 1 to 4 P.M.
Directions: The Barn is two miles north of the Merritt Parkway. Take Exit 32 in Greenwich and follow the signs.

EVERGREEN
1310 Boston Post Road
Guilford, Connecticut 06437
(203) 453-4324

Just as there are many professional craftspeople who have changed careers to concentrate on their craft work, so too are there more than a few retailers who left their jobs or professions behind to enter the craft field.

Diane Robinson and Sharon Silvestrini, the partners in the newly opened Evergreen, fit that description.

"We really enjoyed the crafts and hated working in corporations. And the best part is I get to be with this every day," Diane told me, indicating the array of high-caliber craft work displayed around her.

"When we tell people what we do now," says Sharon, "they often think that it's sewing or artsy-crafty things." Those people, I can assure you, would be very wrong.

Sharon and Diane have on display within their 650-square-foot, gallery-style store a fine grouping of crafts from 45 craftspeople. They plan to have increased that to about 75 craftspeople by the end of 1983.

"I like to think of the crafts we have here as functional in an art sense," says Diane. Among the limited-edition and one-of-a-kind work you'll find an excellent collection of blown glass, pottery, woodenware, jewelry, fiber work, leather accessories and enamels. The partners emphasize that they don't carry any of the work seen down the street at the Guilford Handcrafts Center. Prices run from $10 to $600, with most pieces between $50 and $100.

Hours: Daily, 10 A.M. to 5 P.M.; Sunday, noon to 5 P.M.

CONNECTICUT

Directions: Take Exit 57 from I-95. From New Haven, turn right onto Post Road; from Providence, turn left onto Post Road. Follow about three-quarters of a mile to the shop, located in the Strawberry Hill Shopping Complex.

GUILFORD HANDCRAFTS CENTER
Route 77
Guilford, Connecticut 06437
(203) 453-5947

This organization is best known for its popular annual Handcrafts Exposition, held each summer on Guilford's historic town green. In fact, this nonprofit group got its start in 1957 when a group of Guilford residents organized their first fair on the green.

Today the Center is housed in an old lumber mill, which has been rehabbed into a craft shop, an exhibition gallery space and a complex of studios used year round for classes and workshops in various crafts, painting and graphics.

The retail shop shows the work of about 150 craftspeople, sixty percent of whom are professional; the rest polished amateurs. There is pottery, glass, fiber, wood, toys, clothing, jewelry, metal in a price range of $1 to $300. The average item is estimated at $20. Special exhibits of an individual craftsperson's work are often held in the 700-square-foot space.

The nearby Mill Gallery holds between eight and ten themed shows a year of primarily professional work from across the country in crafts and other art. Occasionally the 1,900-square-foot gallery will play host to a show sponsored by other local arts organizations. Work shown here is usually for sale at prices from $25 to $1,500.

Hours: Daily, 10 A.M. to 4 P.M.; Sunday 1 to 4 P.M.
Directions: Take Exit 58 from I-95. Continue north on Route 77 for approximately 200 yards. The center is on your right.

OLD STATE HOUSE
800 Main Street
Hartford, Connecticut 06103
(203) 522-6766

Since its restoration and subsequent rededication in 1979 as a public museum, Hartford's Old State House has offered a wide variety of programs and exhibitions of art and artifacts from the early days of the republic to the present.

In 1982, more than 250,000 people visited this stately example of federal architecture, first used in 1796 as the State Capitol and later, until 1920, as Hartford's City Hall.

"It is not a building frozen into the 1700s," Executive Director Jay McLaughlin recently said. "What has happened in this building has

Old State House Museum Shop

15 · SHOPS/GALLERIES

always been linked to contemporary culture. In 1796, Joseph Steward, an American painter and portraitist, displayed his work here. He set the precedent."

Accordingly, the Old State House has consistently stressed the importance of Connecticut's present-day cultural and artistic heritage, with special support given to the state's craftspeople. Juried exhibitions, an annual craft show, workshops and demonstrations have all contributed to the museum's growing reputation as an important center for crafts.

Connecticut-made crafts also play an important part in the Museum's gift shop. Shop manager Nancy Stevens has chosen high-quality, moderately priced work from 100 Connecticut craftspeople, which is displayed alongside an inventory of gifts, books and souvenirs relating to both historic and contemporary Connecticut.

Neatly displayed on pedestals, display tables and shelves are traditional and contemporary work including ceramics, pewter, weaving, glass, jewelry, baskets, wood, leather, toys and quilts.

One area of the fully stocked, 750-square-foot shop features a changing display of work by members of the Society of Connecticut Craftsmen, a statewide group with 500 members.

Prices for the crafts in the shop range from $5 to $300, with an average range of $10 to $25.

Of special interest is the annual Connecticut Craft Sale, a successful and enticing showing of juried craft work from 100 craftspeople that takes place each year from Thanksgiving to Christmas. The show occupies three exhibition rooms upstairs and, notes Nancy, is the largest showing of exclusively Connecticut crafts anywhere.

Hours: Daily, 10 A.M. to 5 P.M.; Sunday, noon to 5 P.M.
Directions: From I-91 North, take Exit 32, turn left at the light and right at the next light.
From I-91 South, take Exit 31 and follow State Street to the Old State House.
From I-84 East, take Exit 52 to Columbus Boulevard. Turn right, go three blocks and turn right on State Street.
From I-84 West, take Exit 54 across the Founders Bridge. Follow State Street to the museum.

THE SHOP AT WESLEYAN POTTERS
350 South Main Street
Middletown, Connecticut 06457
(203) 344-0039

Wesleyan Potters is a nonprofit cooperative guild founded in 1948, when a group of Wesleyan University wives got together with the goal of learning how to pot.

The group was informally organized until 1954, the year that professional potter Mary Risley arrived in town with her husband, who had taken a position in the Wesleyan Art Department. Mary had extensive pottery experience and was knowledgeable about the workings of craft guilds. The group accepted her offer to teach and help organize and things accelerated from there.

Today, Wesleyan Potters offers about two dozen classes each season in pottery and other media, along with a schedule of lectures, exhibits, demonstrations, films and professional workshops. The group also holds a popular annual show in late November, which exhibits the work of about 200 New England craftspeople in a variety of media.

Most recently, the fifty working members of the group voted to open a permanent retail shop in the front of their studio and classroom building, a former Venetian blind tape factory that they had purchased in 1971. In 1982 the shop opened with 500 square feet of display space for crafts.

More than 100 craftspeople are represented with work that has been juried by a four-person board of professional craftspeople. You'll see pottery, weaving, jewelry, basketry, soft sculpture, prints, stained and blown glass and sculpture at prices from $5 to $500.

Special exhibits of the work of individual artists are regularly scheduled.

Hours: Thursday through Sunday, 1 to 5 P.M.
Directions: From Route 9, take the exit for Route 17 South. At the traffic circle, pick up South Main Street. After the second light, look for the pottery building on your left.

DOWN ON THE FARM
Banner Road
Moodus, Connecticut 06469
(203) 873-9905

"At one time we used to have over 50,000 chickens here," recalls Max Simon of the farm he started in 1938. "Today there's only about 10,000. But there's all these crafts."

CONNECTICUT

Max is referring to the work both on display and in production at Down on the Farm, a growing craft center situated in two large buildings on his family farm.

Once described by a newspaper reporter as "a showplace crafted from a chicken coop," this craft facility is one of my favorites. But that's not surprising — I cofounded Down on the Farm in 1977 with my parents and brothers. Max is my father.

What we did was rehabilitate space in two unused chicken coops for use as a retail gallery/shop and artisans' studios. The split-level, beamed gallery, managed by my mother, Joyce, is housed in a two-story building once occupied by flocks of Rhode Island Reds. Today it is the home for the work of about 300 craftspeople from across the country, with the majority from New England and neighboring states.

The crafts on display in the 2,500-square-foot space include blown and stained glass, wooden accessories and furniture, stoneware and porcelain, leather accessories, fiber (weaving, quilting, soft sculpture, batik, patchwork, silkscreen), basketry, metal and notecards.

Prices range from under a dollar for the cards to about $350, with some furniture running higher. Most of the crafts are in the $25 to $35 range. Exhibits are scheduled regularly.

Visitors to the gallery are often pleasantly surprised by the availability of freshly baked pastries, which regularly emerge from the ovens in Max's nearby bakeshop. Cookies, danish, cakes and croissants are among the goodies in his repertoire. I've tasted them all and can assure you that they're delicious.

In another large coop across the parking area, Andrew Simon (my younger brother) works with two associates in his woodworking studio, where he builds custom interiors, furniture, and a line of clocks, lamps and other accessories. The artful display fixtures in the gallery were designed and built here.

Next door, glassblowers Roger Gandelman and David Boutin operate Rainbow Glass, one of the state's few glassblowing studios. The studio is usually in operation sixteen hours a day, with Dave and Roger creating work for both the farm gallery and more than 100 other shops and galleries around the country.

We've recently rehabbed some more space for use as additional studios and have begun a search for suitable artisan-occupants.

I think that you'll find the farm to be a pleasant place to visit, and I invite you to do just that. We're located on a hilltop across the road from a golf course and just a few miles from the town's popular Goodspeed Opera House.

Hours: April and May, open Thursday through Sunday, 11 A.M. to 5 P.M.; June through mid-January, open Tuesday through Sunday, 11 A.M. to 5 P.M.; closed from mid-January to the end of March.

Directions: From Route 9, take Exit 7. Go left at the end of the exit, take your first right at the light and cross the river. Pass the Goodspeed Opera House and bear left onto Route 149 North. Follow for four and one-third miles to Moodus Center and take a left at the flashing light (Mobil station). Follow for four-fifths of a mile, take a left and go up the hill. The farm is on your right at the top of the hill.

From Route 2, take Exit 16 and follow Route 149 South to Moodus Center. Take a right at the flashing light (Mobil station) and follow four-fifths of a mile. Take a left and go up the hill.

Down On The Farm

17 · SHOPS/GALLERIES

CONNECTICUT

A TOUCH OF GLASS
North Moodus Road
Moodus, Connecticut 06469
(203) 873-9709

There is probably no more fitting place from which to sell stained-glass artwork than the old church in Moodus that houses A Touch of Glass.

The 150-year-old Methodist church went up for sale in 1972 after being used since the early Thirties as a Jewish community center. At the time, A Touch of Glass partner Michael Axelrod was working as the manager of a bar at a nearby resort and living in cramped seasonal quarters on the resort grounds. Michael thought the church offered a world of spaciousness, seemed suitable to his style of living, and the price, $12,500, looked right. As he remembers, he "thought about it for about ten minutes" before deciding to buy the church for his home and a possible business site. He moved in and began to restore the building, eventually spending nearly what he had to purchase it.

Michael hadn't been thinking about selling stained glass when he first started living in the church. It wasn't until after he had used some stained-glass lamps when redecorating his bar that he became intrigued with the art and started collecting some pieces. His collection steadily grew until, in 1979, Michael and partner Paula Moriarty decided to make what had been an avocation into their full-time occupation and A Touch of Glass was born.

The sales area—a former Sunday School classroom—displays the works of about twenty stained-glass artists. There is a fine assortment here of hanging, floor and table lamps, window panels, mirrors, mobiles, and boxes in a variety of styles and at prices ranging from $10 to $500.

Adjacent to the salesroom is the main church area, which now serves as Michael and Paula's living space as well as a showroom for a large collection of their favorite lamps and panels. The 28-foot-by-60-foot, pineboard-panelled room boasts a 15-foot ceiling from which hang six Tiffany-style lamps. The room itself is eclectically furnished with a charming mix of old furniture, a bevy of happy plants—some fourteen feet high—and numerous stained-glass pieces.

At one end of the room there is a stage constructed over the old altar, which serves as Michael's and Paula's bedroom, complete with a heavy, faded green stage curtain.

The collection of stained glass on display in this old church would be an interesting one anywhere. But in this unusually warm and most appropriate setting it is a real treat.

Hours: Tuesday through Sunday, 1 to 5 P.M.; Monday by chance.
Directions: From Route 2, take Exit 16 and follow Route 149 South to Moodus Center. Turn right at the light and watch for the church on your right at a sharp curve.

From Route 9, take Exit 7 and follow Routes 149 and 151 east to Moodus Center. Turn left at the light and watch for the church on your right.

THE COMPANY OF CRAFTSMEN
43 West Main Street
Mystic, Connecticut 06355
(203) 536-4189

"There's isn't anything here that I wouldn't have in my home," says Kathryn Stuart Steel of the exemplary collection of fine crafts displayed in her Mystic store.

The fine selection of crafts and the tasteful contemporary environment in which they're displayed are the results of the meshing of Kathryn's talents—she was a ceramics major in college and had worked in retailing—with those of her husband Jack, a professional sculptor, metalworker and woodworker whose work is periodically displayed in the store. They renovated the old building themselves before opening the shop in late 1980. "This used to be a pet store," notes Kathryn, "When we were rebuilding it we found a petrified cat in one wall."

The cat is gone now, but displayed in the 1,000-square-foot space is a selection of pottery, woodenware and small furnishings, blown glass, rag and woven wool rugs, wrought iron, some sculpture and painting. Prices range from $5 to $750, with the average price at about $30.

Much of the work displayed in the tin-ceilinged store is by craftspeople not often seen in area shops and galleries. "I spend a great deal of effort in finding craftspeople who haven't been overexposed," Kathryn told me.

Hours: Summer, open daily 9:30 A.M. to 5:30 P.M.; Sunday, noon to 4 P.M.; winter hours, daily 10 A.M. to 5 P.M.
Directions: From I-95, take Exit 90 to Route 27 South. Follow to Route 1 and turn right. After crossing the drawbridge, look for the store at the end of the street on the left.

CONNECTICUT

SILVERMINE GUILD GALLERIES
Silvermine Guild Center for the Arts
1037 Silvermine Road
New Canaan, Connecticut 06840
(203) 966-5617

The Silvermine Guild, long recognized as a vigorous and prestigious center for the arts, is a cooperative of artists and arts patrons that runs a gallery and studio complex on an idyllic, six-acre site in the midst of some of Connecticut's prettiest countryside.

The twenty exhibitions of contemporary art that are mounted annually are widely known for both their diversity and high level of quality; its thriving art school offers year-round instruction for adults and children; and there is a comprehensive program of lectures, trips, seminars, studio tours, a chamber music series and other special events.

The oldest guild in the country, Silvermine traces its ancestry back to 1895, when sculptor Solon Borglum settled in the area, attracted by its picturesque landscape, historic homes and meandering country roads.

It seems that Solon Borglum had a lot of artist friends who soon began moving to the area and started to gather regularly in his studio barn to socialize and criticize each other's work.

The Knockers, as they were called, held the first of many public exhibitions of their work at the turn of the century, meeting with great success and attracting people from as far as New York City.

The following years saw great success for the group. As one local art observer wrote, "The Silvermine area was the Vermont of the Twenties."

In 1922 the group incorporated as the Silvermine Guild of Artists, with the goal "to encourage art appreciation and cultural growth in the community." They purchased a barn in which to paint, give lessons and hold exhibitions. That original building is used today as the main exhibition gallery.

More than sixty years after its founding, the Guild is still a strong nonprofit cooperative association of artists, patrons and students. There are 350 working artists, primarily New Englanders, who have been juried into the membership based on the quality of their work. About 250 of these are active members; about 35 are craftspeople.

Applicants for membership are stingently juried by present Guild artists. Less than ten percent of the more than 150 artists who apply for membership each year are accepted into the Guild.

The impressive gallery complex consists of three exhibition spaces that total 5,000 square feet, as well as a sculpture garden and a small craft shop.

Most of the twenty exhibits held each year are one-person and group shows of member artists' work. There are also major juried and invitational shows featuring the work of artists of note outside the membership. There are occasional one-person and themed exhibits of craft, but the majority of shows are of two-dimensional art and sculpture. All exhibits usually run four weeks or longer.

It is in the Guild's craft shop, unfortunately, where their reputation for excellence has been tarnished. The work of their 35 member craftspeople has been displayed under cramped cir-

Hays Hall, Silvermine Guild Galleries

19 · SHOPS/GALLERIES

cumstances in a small room that is a glaring contrast to the spacious and handsome gallery spaces adjoining it.

Lotte Calnek, the gallery manager, told me that the Guild recognizes the problem and is planning to triple the space devoted to the crafts. The refurbished space is to be called "Members' Gallery." Notwithstanding all this, the collection of crafts here is a good one, including art glass, pottery, painted and woven fiber, basketry and jewelry. Prices range from $5 to $1,000.

Hours: Tuesday through Sunday 12:30 to 5 P.M.
Directions: From I-95 take exit 15 and head north on Route 7 connector. Take a right onto Route 123 and after one block a right onto Silvermine Avenue. Go two-and-one-half miles to Silvermine Road and the center.

ENDLEMAN-KRAUS GALLERIES
981 State Street
New Haven, Connecticut 06511
(203) 624-7114

"Contemporary fine crafts for the discerning collector," is how this retail gallery, established in December 1982, bills itself. This time, the advertising slogan matches the reality.

Located in the heart of the State Street antique area, the 500-square-foot gallery shows a collection of the most advanced forms of craft from about twenty-five craftspeople.

There are highly designed, sophisticated pieces here in clay, art glass, gold and silver jewelry and apparel. Prices range from $15 to $5,000.

Every six weeks, an exhibit featuring either an individual's work or a group show is mounted in the gallery space.

Hours: Tuesday through Sunday, noon to 5 P.M.
Directions: Take the Trumbull Street exit from I-91. Go right on Orange Street for five blocks, then right onto Edwards Street for one block. The gallery is directly in front of you at the light.

ATELIER STUDIO/GALLERY
17 Church Street
New Milford, Connecticut 06776
(203) 354-0453

When Beth Collings rented her first studio in 1980 it was to have a place to make and display her copper-enameling work. Although the space in the third floor attic of a restored New Milford firehouse was tiny, she soon invited six artists and craftspeople to exhibit their works there. They accepted, and customer traffic started to increase.

Each month a few more works were added and a few more people came. Before long, Beth found herself with little time to do her enameling due to the requirements of running her growing studio.

In April 1983, Beth moved next door into a corner of the Bell, Book & Candle bookstore, doubling her space to about 400 square feet and gaining street-level visibility.

About forty craftspeople are represented here with pottery, jewelry, enamel, wood, batik, baskets, leather, fused and stained glass, weaving, porcelain and pewter. There is also original art and photography. Prices range from $2 to $1,000. "I like most to have people who are just beginning to be aware of themselves," says Beth.

Hours: Tuesday through Saturday, 10 A.M. to 5 P.M.
Directions: Take Route 7 to New Milford Village Center. The shop is one-half block from the green opposite the police station.

THE SILO
Upland Road
New Milford, Connecticut 06776
(203) 355-0300

There are dozens of restored old farms around New England that are seeing a vigorous second life as craft facilities, art galleries, book barns, restaurants and the like. It is safe to say that few have done as complete or ambitious a renovation job as have Ruth and Skitch Henderson with their beautiful 200-acre Hunt Hill Farms.

Here, in 1972, the Hendersons renovated the farm's large old hay and cow barns into a complex called The Silo, which consists of a kitchenware and gourmet-food store, a cooking school and a gallery for the visual arts.

The Country Kitchen Store carries a large assortment of sophisticated kitchenware and equipment, which is displayed throughout the 3,000-square-foot space, punctuated by a collection of functional dining and kitchen-oriented crafts from about forty craftspeople. You'll find pottery, basketry, woodenware, weaving and blown glass at prices that start at $20 and go to $400. Everything here — commercially made, imported craft or American craft — is in fine taste and well displayed throughout the store, which includes two renovated silo spaces.

Upstairs is a fully equipped cooking school and a gourmet food selection. More than 1,000 classes, ranging from brief workshops to five-day cooking seminars, have been held here since 1972.

Adjacent to the school is a 3,000-square-foot gallery space under a 35-foot ceiling in the old hay barn. From March to December, monthly, changing exhibits are posted in a full range of crafts and arts. Shows are usually one-person shows and have included painting, sculpture, furniture, pottery, basketry, paper, rugs, weaving, photography and sculpture. About eighty percent of the shows are craft-oriented. Monthly receptions for new exhibits are open to the public and are often combined with such events as wine tastings.

Hours: Tuesday through Sunday, 10 A.M. to 5 P.M.

Directions: From I-84 westbound, take Exit 15 (Route 67) and proceed northwest to New Milford and the junction with Route 202. Go about four-and-one-half miles east on Route 202 to Upland Road. The farm is one-half mile up on the right.

From I-84 eastbound, take Exit 7 and follow Route 7 north to the traffic circle at New Milford bridge. Go five miles on Route 202 east to Upland Road.

The Silo Gallery

CONNECTICUT

VOLTAIRE'S
Route 7
New Milford, Connecticut 06776
(203) 354-4200

Voltaire's, founded in 1957 by Alice Voltaire and her late husband Paul, was one of the first "design stores" in the East, Alice told me, offering both commercial and handmade objects. Paul Voltaire, a jeweler, sculptor and inventor, designed and built much of the present building, expanding it six different times as the need for more space arose.

Today, Alice and husband John Seymour, a stoneware sculptor, are the proprietors of 2,300 square feet of retail and gallery space stocked with contemporary manufactured home and personal accessories, two-dimensional art and the work of about 125 craftspeople.

"We are only interested in excellence of design and quality of workmanship and materials," Alice told me. "If the piece is functional, it should serve that function well and the price should reflect reasonably its materials, workmanship and uniqueness."

Alice believes in showing crafts and art in situations similar to that in which they'll ultimately be viewed and used. Consequently, throughout the spacious and attractive store, commercially produced housewares and accessories are displayed together with artwork and fine crafts. "It's not so forbidding a way to display crafts," she notes.

In the 600-square-foot gallery, a more formal arrangement for display is utilized. Changing collections of art and craft are displayed under the gallery's 20-foot ceiling with at least two craft shows a year scheduled at Christmastime and during the spring.

Voltaire's inventory of crafts includes jewelry, weaving, leather, wood, glass, basketry, ceramics and metal. Prices range from a few dollars to $2,000 with the average range between $35 and $150.

The crafts presented here are, says Alice, "of a gentler design. We're not interested in esoterica, because there are better places to present that. All of the things that we display are of a piece with the shop as a whole."

Hours: Daily, 10 A.M. to 5 P.M.
Directions: The store is on Route 7, three miles north of the New Milford traffic circle at the intersection of Route 37.

CONTEMPORARY CRAFTS GALLERY
Route 20
Riverton, Connecticut 06065
(203) 379-2964

Pewtersmith James Gagnon and his wife Ann established this shop/gallery in 1978 in the tiny village of Riverton. Located in their Victorian house on Main Street, the store features Jim's pewter along with the work of about fifty other craftspeople, "most of whom we know personally," notes Ann.

In addition to the large display of pewter, there is blown glass, pottery, wooden accessories, fiber work, jewelry and graphics here at prices from $6 to $3,000.

Riverton is a delightful town that has been essentially unchanged since the early 19th century. It used to be called Hitchcocksville, named after Lambert Hitchcock, whose original chair "manufactory" is still operating down the street.

Main Street has some dozen businesses, all housed in enchanting Victorian houses. There are several well-stocked antique stores, a wonderful old inn, a country store and more. The shopkeepers and proprietors will greet you like an old friend. You will be charmed.

Hours: Tuesday through Saturday, 11 A.M. to 5 P.M.; Sunday, noon to 4 P.M.
Directions: Pick up Route 44 west of Hartford. Take a right onto Route 181 outside of New Hartford and continue to Riverton.

Voltaire's

22 · SHOPS/GALLERIES

Maine

CHOSEN WORKS
35 Central Street
Bangor, Maine 04401
(207) 947-3418

Chosen Works was started in 1971, making it the oldest continuously operating craft cooperative in the state. After operating out of Camden for a while, the seven founding craftspeople decided to move the co-op to Bangor to take advantage of the larger population and the year-round nature of the marketplace there.

But, as the song says, "it don't come easy." After finding a suitable downtown location and spending much time and labor fixing it up, disaster struck in the form of a fire that totally destroyed the shop before they could move their craftwork into it.

Not a group to fret for long, however, they found another spot and soon opened for business. The fates have since been kinder and the co-op has continued to grow. In 1979 they moved into their present location, a triangular 700-square-foot store with ample space to show an array of work from the co-op's eighteen members.

There is pottery, stained and etched glasswork, jewelry, weaving, quilts, knitted wear, leatherwork, ornamental iron, silkscreening, calligraphy and notecards. Prices range from $1 to $500.

In the rear, a small gallery space is the scene for well-respected, monthly exhibits of painting and sculpture.

The shop is staffed by co-op members who will be happy to answer your questions.

Hours: Daily from 10 A.M. to 5 P.M.
Directions: From I-95 take Exit 45A (Bangor/Route 395). Follow Main Street into town until you reach a major intersection with a fork in the road ahead of you. Bear right, take your first two lefts and Chosen Works will be on your left.

CALEB'S SUNRISE
115 Main Street
Bar Harbor, Maine 04069
(207) 288-3102

Leatherworker and co-owner Leah Rae Donahue's attractive leather handbags dominate one wall of her store in beautiful Bar Harbor. She told me that she and her husband Mike started the store seven years ago because "I wanted to have a wonderful place to sell my friends' work."

On display in this 700-square-foot shop is the work of about 150 craftspeople, half from Maine, most of the rest from New England. "I try to concentrate on producers who work on a small production scale," she told me, "People who are trying to make craft their life and their business."

Three-fourths of the crafts here are production work, the rest one of a kind. There is an emphasis on functional objects, "well thought through designs which serve their intended function." A large collection of wood and leather work and a nice assortment of pottery is displayed as are woven shawls, scarves and blankets, and work in glass and metal. There are also some graphics for sale. Prices range from $2 to $300, with the average price $20.

The Donahues note that the work in their store must be "technically right, and well executed."

"We try to have our functional things also be beautiful. So many people, until they own a stoneware mug, can't understand why it's more pleasant to drink coffee from something that's handmade and beautiful," Leah Rae told me.

Hours: Open May through October seven days a week from 9 A.M. to 11 P.M.
Directions: Take Route 3 south into the center of Bar Harbor. The shop is on Main Street.

ISLAND ARTISANS, INC.
99 Main Street
Bar Harbor, Maine 04609
(207) 288-4214

This is another cooperatively owned craft shop that has done very well for itself since it was established eight years ago. Last winter the co-op bought the building that contains this 900-square-foot store to better market their work from a more prominent location.

"The people in the co-op are really serious about their craft and earning a living," co-op member Jean Rappaport told me.

The long, narrow store was gutted and renovated by the members and features a high, wavelike ceiling that is a reflection of the design and construction talents within the group.

As with most co-ops, you'll generally find a large amount of work from each of the craftspeople represented. Everything in the store is locally made on Mount Desert Island and the surrounding area and very often reflects the influence of the beautiful environment around them. Work includes stoneware pottery,

MAINE

etched glass, weaving, batik, forged iron, silkscreening, jewelry, handquilting, custom furniture, handspun yarn, watercolors and embossed notecards. The work is priced from a few dollars up to $1,500. Co-op members staff and operate the store.

Hours: May through October daily from 10 A.M. to 10 P.M. Shorter hours are kept in early spring and late fall.
Directions: Take Route 3 to Bar Harbor. The shop is across from the First National Bank.

MUNG BEAN
55 Townsend Avenue
Boothbay Harbor, Maine 04538
(207) 633-5512

Established in 1973, Mung Bean offers the work of more than eighty craftspeople, all of whom are New Englanders.

The 600-square-foot shop sells porcelain and stoneware, wooden toys, sweaters and other woolens, small wrought-iron pieces, metal sculpture, woodenware, mobiles, jewelry and notecards. Prices range from $1 to $250.

Hours: Open during the season seven days a week, 9 A.M. to 5:30 P.M.
Directions: From Route 1 in Wiscasset, take Route 27 South for twelve miles. When you get to the business district, take a left at Depositors Trust. The shop is up about one-and-one-half blocks on the right.

BROOKLIN CRAFTS COOPERATIVE
Route 175
Brooklin, Maine 04616
(207) 359-2124

The site of the Brooklin co-op, the old grange hall in the tiny village center, had sat empty for thirty years until Jean and Doug Hylan bought the wreck about five years ago with the desire to set up a cooperative retail craft outlet. "It was a total derelict," remembers Jean, a silk-screen and batik artist. "Every window was broken."

Today the place shows the pleasing results of Doug's skills as a carpenter. He is also the resident potter at the co-op, working with local clay in a studio adjacent to the craft shop.

Inside the shop's 600-square-foot retail space, whitewashed plank walls and grey floors nicely offset the pine and oak displays showing the work of the six co-op members and four consigned craftspeople. Pottery, ironware, woven clothing and rugs, silkscreens, batik and knitted goods are among the crafts for sale in the four-year-old co-op. Prices range from 50 cents for notecards up to $1,000. The average price is about $25.

All the work here is from craftspeople who work in the Down East area and, notes Jean, "co-op members take turns tending the store, so there is always informed sales help."

Two points of interest: The shop sells some marvelous homemade jams and jellies such as strawberry/rhubarb and wild blueberry. And be sure to say hi to Spanky, the co-op's offical greeter. Everybody in town knows this half blue-tick hound/half sheepdog. He's a friendly critter and he'll welcome you with open paws.

Hours: June to September, Tuesday through Saturday from 10 A.M. to 5 P.M.; from October to December, open on Friday and Saturday only from 10 A.M. to 5 P.M.
Directions: From Route 1 take Route 175 all the way south through scenic Blue Hill. Follow the signs to Brooklin. The shop will be on your left.

Brooklin Crafts Cooperative

24 · SHOPS/GALLERIES

MAINE

GATEWAY GALLERY
Haystack Mountain School of Crafts
Deer Isle, Maine 04627
(207) 348-6946

"Off the beaten track" is not a strong enough expression for this internationally famous school for craftspeople. It is truly on another track altogether. As the center's brochure states, "Forget easy access. Think 'pilgrimage.'"

Since 1951 Haystack has played host to thousands of craftspeople from novice to world-class master who come to this isolated center to further their abilities, impart to others their insights and skills, and to absorb some of what's referred to as "Haystack magic."

The gallery at the center shows the work of the school's faculty, who are drawn from the ranks of the world's leading craftspeople. Exhibits change with each of the five summer sessions and the amount of work shown varies. At the end of each session there is also a short exhibit of the students' work.

The work, which is not for sale, varies by media and in quantity each session. Depending on when you visit, you'll see creations in glass, clay, wood, fiber, metal, paper or prints.

Visitors are encouraged to explore the compound and observe the activity in the studios, which have large windows through which one can watch the students and faculty at work.

Additionally, most evenings public slide lectures are presented by the faculty and staff. Topics range from a showing of an individual's work to theme shows such as "ecology and crafts."

It's a long ride to Haystack and you never know what you'll see in the gallery when you get there or what the slide show will be that evening. But not to worry. It's worth the time and gas just to see this extraordinary place, its gorgeous coastal vistas, and to feel, however briefly, the spirit of the center.

For decades craftspeople have made the pilgrimage to Haystack for "refreshment of soul" as well as intensive immersion in their craft. A visit to the center will clearly show you why this is so. Gazing out across Jericho Bay from the wooden steps or a perch on the rocks is guaranteed to lower anyone's pulse rate.

Hours: Haystack is open from June to September. Visitors are welcome Thursday through Sunday from 10 A.M. to 4 P.M. Please sign in at the administrative office upon arrival.
Directions: From Route 1 in Orland, take Route 15 south for forty-five miles through Deer Isle Village. Turn left at Twin's Sunoco and follow the Haystack signs six miles to the school.

The last mile, over a gravel road through the woods, is aptly described by M. C. Richards in a Haystack brochure as "an heroic lift to another level of everything: consciousness, landscape, vista, ambiance."

TIMELESS DESIGNS
Deer Isle, Maine 04627
(207) 348-6051

Owner Jane Weiss Adams has created this charming craft shop in a beautifully renovated barn next to her home in Deer Isle. "It cost me more to fix up the barn than to buy the property," she told me. Jane opened the shop five years ago after having been in the craft business in Cleveland, Ohio, for the previous fifteen years.

There is an effective contrast here between the contemporary craftwork and the dark barn wood, a contrast that is accentuated by an original overhead beam running the width of the building that explodes in the middle into a free-form, mirrored and polished wood sculpture.

Eighty craftspeople are represented in the 600-square-foot barn with mostly functional crafts such as weaving, pottery, blown glass, wood and other media. Prices range from $1 to $1,000. Consistent with Jane's belief that it's best to use beautiful crafts in your house on a daily basis, you'll also find a small stock of commercial items for the kitchen and house.

In a small gallery space in an adjacent building Jane puts on three shows each summer. Themes may range from craftwork that she has gathered during her off-season trips abroad to one-person, two-person and group shows in mixed media.

Hours: Open mid-June to mid-September, Monday through Saturday from 10 A.M. to 6 P.M.; Sunday from 1 to 5 P.M.
Directions: Take Route 15 south from Route 1 and follow to Deer Isle Village. Turn left at the Post Office and look for the Timeless Designs sign about 100 feet on the left opposite the Bar Harbor Bank and Trust building.

25 · SHOPS/GALLERIES

MAINE

HANDS ON!
112 Main Street
Ellsworth, Maine 04605
(207) 667-7089

Hands On! was opened in May, 1983, by the same folks who own the ten-year-old Eastern Maine Craft Co-op in Milbridge. "We wanted to start a year-round location," co-op member and quilter Carol Shutt told me. "Ellsworth is changing its character and we thought that it would be a good area for us."

The shop location is marked by a wonderfully done, multicolored sign. Inside the newly renovated store is the work of the co-op's eleven members and another eight non-members who have been juried into the shop as consignors. Carol notes that the co-op's intention is "to grow and change" and that they will be jurying more craftspeople's work into the shop on a monthly basis.

The store's 750 square feet (soon to be enlarged to 1,000) are utilized with a series of gallery-type displays that show each person's work to its best advantage. Displays are rotated regularly. "Each piece is thought about before we design the display," Carol explains. "People come here and they really notice the details."

Craftwork on display includes pottery, weaving, quilts and quilted clothing, hand-smocked clothing, jewelry, blown glass, stained glass, metalwork, woodwork, hand-spun yarns and wooden toys among others. Prices range from $5 to $800, with the average price $25.

Hours: Daily from 9:30 A.M. to 5:30 P.M.
Directions: Coming up the Maine coast on Route 1 you will come right through Ellsworth on Main Street. The co-op is on the left in the center of town.

STRONG CRAFT GALLERY
Bar Harbor Road
Ellsworth, Maine 04605
(207) 667-2595

When Roslyn and Harris Strong decided to move their thriving wholesale wall-art business from the South Bronx to Maine in 1970, they found a fine location in Ellsworth with a building that had some extra space. As Harris remembered in a recent *Maine Life* article, "it was much too big for our offices, so we thought, 'we've been basically in crafts all our lives, we have lots of friends and contacts—how about a craft gallery?'"

Thirteen years later the Strongs preside over one of the most extensive collections of contemporary American crafts shown in one location in New England. On two floors comprising 5,000 square feet, they have collected the diversified work of about 250 craftspeople with an emphasis on work produced in Maine and New England.

According to Roslyn, the work displayed here must be of "good design, good workmanship and good materials. We also tend to drop suppliers who expand and become very commercial."

Some of the craftspeople whose work is carried here have been represented in the store for more than ten years. The generous displays of each craftsperson's work are labeled with his or her name and include pottery, jewelry, blown and stained glass, woodwork, leather bags and belts, metalwork, clothing, scarves, placemats, rugs, musical instruments, greeting cards, rugs and ceramic lamps.

Upstairs there are prints, paintings, posters and etchings. There's also a sale room where selected work can be purchased at reduced prices.

Prices for the craft items range from $1 to $800, with an average price estimated to be from $20 to $30.

"The market is growing," notes Roslyn. "The average customer will come here for, say, a wedding gift rather than buying a toaster. This wasn't so when we first opened."

During the summer season, exhibits featuring mostly one- and two-man shows and sometimes group or theme shows are mounted every two weeks.

Hours: Open year-round Monday through Saturday from 9 A.M. to 5 P.M.; July and August, Monday through Friday 9 A.M. to 9 P.M., Saturday 9 A.M. to 6 P.M., Sunday 11 A.M. to 6 P.M.
Directions: From Route 1 in Ellsworth, take Route 3 south about four miles on the Bar Harbor Road. Strong's is on the right just past The Cheese House on your left, which you can't possibly miss—it's shaped like a giant cheese wheel topped by a person-sized mouse sculpture.

MAINE

PRAXIS
136 Main Street
Freeport, Maine 04032
(207) 865-6201

Freeport is fast becoming a Mecca for factory-outlet store addicts. The venerable L. L. Bean store has recently been joined by outlets for Cole-Haan shoes, Bass shoes, Hathaway shirts and Dansk housewares. This all bodes well for the fourteen craftspeople who cooperatively own and operate Praxis, a shop and gallery that has been located down the street from Bean's since 1977.

"When the shop opened virtually no one knew that anything existed north of Bean's except the Post Office and the bank," says a founding member of the co-op. "Five years later, and the tide seems to have turned."

Housed on the first floor of an attractive old New England house, this is one of the best-stocked and well-presented craft cooperatives in the state. Altogether there are nineteen craftspeople represented here with large collections of their best production and one-of-a-kind work. Besides the fourteen co-op members, there are another five craftspeople whose work has been accepted by the group for sale on consignment.

"Each of the members has enough room to display a good representative group of their work, and inventory is almost always high because members are often reviewing their stock and replacing sold work," co-op member and potter Melody Bonnema told me. Although there is a manager who generally tends the store, Melody told me that a shopper often will be waited on by one of the craftspeople and "can ask specific questions about work in the store or the process that was involved with its creation."

There are five rooms comprising 1,600 square feet in the house. The rooms are generally arranged by media: There is a pottery room, weaving room, rug room, lamp room and the main room with mixed media. Here you'll find jewelry, canvas and leather bags, stained and blown glass, woodwork, forged iron, notecards and candles. Prices start at a few dollars and go up to $300. One nice touch is the color portfolio of members' commissioned and one-of-a-kind work.

"Our strength comes from the sum of our parts, from the cumulative energy of our members, from the diversity of our backgrounds and the blending of our ideas."

Hours: Summer hours are seven days a week from 10 A.M. to 6 P.M.; in winter the shop is closed on Sunday and open daily from 10 A.M. to 5 P.M.

Directions: Take the Freeport exit off I-95 or follow Route 1 into town. Praxis is on Main Street two blocks north of L. L. Bean.

PLUM DANDY
Dock Square
Kennebunkport, Maine 04046
(207) 967-4013

Notwithstanding the quite pretty dried-flower arrangements and the very gift-shoppy look that this store has at first glance, a closer look will reveal a respectable collection of some very nice craftwork mixed in with the commercial craft items here.

"Cute" is an apt word for many of the crafts displayed downstairs in the nine-year-old shop. Owners Linda and Tom Haydock cater to both the tourist trade and the locals and you'll find everything from "little pick-up items" like hand-dipped incense and one-inch pottery containers that say things like "egg money" all the way up to more substantial craftwork priced up to $700. Most of the finer crafts are displayed upstairs, which is reached by a distinctive, helixed oak stairway.

Explaining that she won't handle the "made at home crafts," Linda emphasizes that all the crafts here are handcrafted to "standards that are high with a broad base appeal." "I want to make the place fun and exciting to shop here," she told me. "It's not a snooty place. I don't want to put people off."

In the shop's 850 square feet, you'll find

MAINE

work from 150 mostly New England artisans, including functional and art pottery, a nice collection of handwoven and hand-appliqued clothing, sterling and porcelain jewelry, batik, small stained-glass pieces, enamels, metal, wood and soft sculpture, and photographs, watercolors and prints. Beads are also on sale. Prices start at ten cents for the beads and go to $700 for the top crafts.

The plum theme is carried out throughout just about everything: price tags, wrapping paper, wall colors, the display pedestals, even the clerks are decked out in plum.

Hours: January through March, open Saturday from 10 A.M. to 5 P.M.; April, open Friday and Saturday from 10 A.M. to 5 P.M. and Sunday from noon to 5 P.M.; May through December, open daily from 10 A.M. to 5 P.M. and Sunday from noon to 5 P.M. Longer hours are kept in July and August.

Directions: Take Route 9 east from Route 1 in Wells to Kennebunkport. After crossing the bridge into town, take the first left into the municipal parking lot. The shop faces the lot overlooking the Kennebunk River.

EASTERN MAINE CRAFT CO-OP
Route One
Milbridge, Maine 04658
(207) 546-2063

The Eastern Maine Craft Co-op consists of a group of eleven Down East craftspeople who have been cooperatively selling their crafts in this coastal village for more than ten years.

It is one of the oldest craft co-ops in the state and their long experience shows in the well-done shop. "We have a reputation, which we strive to uphold, of selling high-quality work in a very attractive setting," notes metal sculptor and co-op member Peter Weil.

The co-op is housed on the first floor of a charming century-old house right on the gateway route to some of both Maine's and the Canadian Maritimes' most attractive areas. This is Maine as you imagine it to be, the coastline deeply embayed with many fine harbors and handsome, small fishing villages. Wonderful examples of Victorian architecture abound and there are many inland lakes and hills to explore. The co-op member on duty will be happy to help you with your trip or answer any of your questions.

The shop atmosphere is relaxed and uncrowded and the work on display by the seventeen craftspeople (eleven co-op members and six non-members) is displayed with special concern and care. According to Peter, for a craftsperson's work to be accepted for display in the shop, it must be "technically competent, show imagination and skill in design."

Crafts on display include stoneware and porcelain pottery, handwoven and handsmocked clothing, gold and silver jewelry, metal sculpture, quilts, bells, woodenware, blown glass and Maine-spun yarn. Prices range from $10 to $800, with the average price about $25.

Hours: Open from June to September, 10 A.M. to 5:30 P.M. daily.
Directions: The shop is on Route 1 on the western edge of town in Milbridge. It is thirty miles up the coast from Ellsworth, on the main route to the Maritime Provinces of Canada.

MAPLE HILL GALLERY
Perkins Cove
Ogunquit, Maine 03907
(207) 646-2134

Maple Hill Gallery has been on the docks of Perkins Cove for the past nine years. With its wood-and-white decor and its high, peaked ceiling providing a suitable background, the retail gallery regularly displays sophisticated and innovative crafts chosen by owner Nancy Lee from among the ranks of both American and foreign craftspeople.

In order for a person's work to be considered by Nancy, the work must show a "high quality, creative approach to media, superior design and sense of color and uniqueness." Previously the sculpture studio for the Ogunquit Art School, the 800-square-foot store shows the one-of-a-kind and limited-edition work of several dozen craftspeople working in clay, fiber, glass, wood and jewelry. There is also a fine selection of notecards.

"I've put a lot of effort into finding craftspeople that others aren't carrying," notes Nancy, who was a potter before the demands of running the store ate up her time. Prices for the strictly contemporary work shown range from $18 to $1,500, with the average piece costing $40. The gallery has regular exhibitions.

Perkins Cove is a charming complex of harborside shops. The carved wood sign for the Whistling Oyster restaurant is terrific.

Hours: Seven days from 10 A.M. to 10 P.M. during the summer season.
Directions: Take Route 1 into Ogunquit center. Follow Shore Road to Perkins Cove.

MAINE

HANDCRAFTERS GALLERY
44 Exchange Street
Portland, Maine 04101
(207) 772-4880

Handcrafters Gallery, now in its eighth year, offers to the crafts connoisseur higher-end limited editions and one-of-a-kind, museum-quality craftwork. It is the biggest and finest collection of "New York style" contemporary crafts in Maine and is a must for those interested in seeing an excellent collection of crafts in a pleasant and well-designed setting.

"We're looking more for design things that are unusual," explains manager Georgie Fides. She and her assistants, Elizabeth Prior and Pamela Boudreau, along with the other staffers, will be happy to answer questions about any of the work on display in the two-level store's 2,200 square feet.

"It's really exciting to see the work that's been produced and to sell really nice crafts," Georgie told me. "Our purpose is to display high-quality crafts that are unusual and to promote an interest in contemporary crafts. We try to educate customers and let them know what it is that they're looking at."

The retail gallery has an especially fine collection of gold and silver jewelry. "We don't go in for anything that's faddish in jewelry," notes Georgie, adding, "our local clientele is more conservative."

There is also a well-chosen collection of blown-art glass, ceramics, woodwork, weavings and metalwork. Altogether there are about 200 craftspeople represented here at prices that range from $7 to $3,700. Jewelry prices average $100 and up; other crafts average about $75.

The gallery holds one jewelry show and one in another medium each month, generally spotlighting an individual's work in one-person shows.

Handcrafters Gallery is located in the middle of the prospering Old Port Exchange on Portland's waterfront. The once-decaying area owes much to the foresight and vision of area craftspeople, who moved here early on along with other like-minded artists attracted by the area's natural appeal and cheap rents. The area has a wonderful sense of place and its human scale is highly consistent with the nature of handcrafts. The craft explorer could easily spend many hours just browsing.

Hours: Open year-round, daily from 9:30 A.M. to 6 P.M. and Sunday from 11 A.M. to 5 P.M. During the summer season, open Monday through Tuesday from 9:30 A.M. to 9:30 P.M. and Friday through Sunday from 9:30 A.M. to 11 P.M.
Directions: Take I-95 north to Route 295 north. Follow into Portland area. Take the Franklin exit and follow Franklin Street to Middle Street. Take a right on Middle and follow to Exchange Street. Another left on Exchange will take you to the gallery which is on the right in the middle of the block.

MAINE POTTERS MARKET
9 Moulton Street
Portland, Maine 04101
(207) 774-1633

At a 1977 meeting of the Maine Potters Guild, the question was raised as to why Maine's potters couldn't band together to open their own cooperative store. The answer, developed over the next year, was "why not?" And "when enough people and capital was gathered," the Maine Potters Market got off to a "faltering" start in 1978 in Boothbay Harbor. "This was very much an experimental period for us," says one founding potter, "but, bolstered by modest success, we decided to take the plunge and open a year-round store in Portland in 1979."

Located in the heart of bustling Old Port Exchange, fourteen members of the cooperative sell their work and strive "to educate the public in the ways of handmade pottery."

"Chances are that the person behind the desk is a real flesh-and-blood potter. If you have any questions about pots or potting ask away."

Within the 500 square feet of the store, the co-op's members have put on display one of the largest selections of handmade pottery in New England. Displays are arranged by potter, and both stoneware and porcelain are well represented. There is tableware, dinnerware and objects for home decorating such as oil and electric lamps. The average price is $25 and prices range from $1 to $100.

The members come from all over the state. One member, Mary St. John, travels 360 miles each way for her monthly stint behind the counter. Hailing from St. Francis at the tip of Maine, Mary calls herself, accurately, "Maine's northernmost potter." The co-op has on hand a brochure listing brief backgrounds on members.

Hours: Daily from 10:30 A.M. to 5:30 P.M.
Directions: From I-95 take Exit 6A/Route 295 to Franklin Street. Exit at the waterfront and take a left on Moulton. The shop is on your right, in the Old Port Exchange.

MAINE

THE MARKETPLACE, INC.
101 Exchange Street
Portland, Maine 04101
(207) 774-1376

"I believe in the handmade person-to-thing relationship," says Ellen Higgins, owner of this eleven-year-old craft shop in the Old Port Exchange. "If you have to spend money," she observes, "you might as well spend it on something that you can relate to."

Ellen has put together in her 800-square-foot shop a large variety of media by some 190 craftspeople, about 125 of them from Maine and most of the rest from New England. "I try to stick to useful objects that can be used daily. If you break it, it's okay. It's not so much an art object."

Over the years Ellen has gotten to know well many of the craftspeople whose work is carried in her shop. "They are the most wonderful, incredible, talented people. We're personalizing an object when we sell it. We try to convey that element to the purchaser," she told me, adding, "If I don't support Maine and New England craftspeople, who will?

"Rainbows from California make me sick," she says, although she does bring in a few things here from other areas "to show people what's happening."

Ellen emphasizes that all work in her shop must have an "excellence of design and execution and must have a function—either utilitarian or whimsical." She carries pottery, blown and leaded glass, wood, fibers, metals, paper, leather, wax, acrylics, basketry and apple dolls. Prices range from $2 to $200, with a $15 to $20 average.

"These are things to be picked up, felt and enjoyed," she says.

Hours: Daily from 10 A.M. to 5 P.M. Summer hours are longer.
Directions: Take I-95 to Exit 6A. Follow Route 295 to Portland. Take the Franklin arterial exit toward the waterfront. At the fifth light, turn right on Middle Street. Follow parking signs to the Temple Street garage. The back entrance of the garage opens onto Exchange Street.

EASTERN BAY COOPERATIVE GALLERY
Main Street
Stonington, Maine 04681
(207) 367-5006

This picturesque coastal fishing town is the perfect setting for one of those romantic slice-of-life coffee commercials. The town's well-preserved turn-of-the-century architecture, its narrow streets, the terrific view of eastern Penobscot Bay, and the bustling harbor all comprise a picture-perfect Down East scene.

Co-op member and potter Lynn Duryea told me that the gallery/shop, now in its third location in nine years, is pleased to have recently moved to their new location in the middle of town. Inside the eighty-five-year-old building, a centrally located window perfectly frames a view of Stonington Harbor and the Deer Isle Thoroughfare. The classic harborscape is nicely complemented by the work of forty craftspeople artfully displayed throughout the space.

Almost all of the work shown here is produced in Maine with the focus on artists who live and work in the Penobscot Bay region. The 800-square-foot shop features a fine selection of functional and sculptural ceramics, quilts, weaving and knitting, wood, jewelry, glass, prints, collage, photography and painting. Prices range from 25¢ postcards up to $500. The average is estimated to be $25 or $30.

Work by the seven-co-op members is regularly exhibited in both one- and two-person shows with theme shows involving the work of all forty juried craftspeople held periodically. A co-op staffer on duty will be happy to answer your questions regarding the work, the artists or the area.

To sum up: The view is marvelous, the village charming, the co-op professional and its crafts enticing. And to top everything, the scenic drive to Stonington is alone worth the trip.

Hours: May to September, open daily from 9:30 A.M. to 5:30 P.M. Shorter hours are kept from September through Christmas.
Directions: From Route 1 in Orland, take Route 15 all the way south to the end of the island and the town of Stonington. The co-op is on the left across from the Town Hall. Haystack Mountain School of Crafts is nearby in the town of Deer Isle and should not be missed if you're in the area.

Maine

Eastern Bay Cooperative Gallery

MASSACHUSETTS

HANDWORKS
452 Great Road
Acton, Massachusetts 01720
(617) 263-1707

"Quality is always Number One when we buy for the gallery," says Ken Singmaster, owner of this six-year-old shop/gallery. "Design, color and texture are taken into consideration." More than 200 craftspeople are represented here, carefully shown on attractive free-standing displays.

The work includes both functional and decorative crafts in fabrics, wood, ceramics, jewelry and basketry. There is a nice collection of clothing on display and an emphasis on art glass and jewelry. "We offer very unique pieces of art—all price ranges for many different tastes," says Ken. Prices range from $5 to $1,000.

Hours: Daily, 10 A.M. to 5:30 P.M.
Directions: From Route 495, take Route 2A East into Acton. The store is on Route 2A.

From Route 128, take exit 46B. Follow Route 2 to Route 2A.

THE LEATHER SHED
199 North Pleasant Street
Amherst, Massachusetts 01002
(413) 253-9604

Leatherworker Dick Muller started this store nearly twenty years ago to market his line of leatherwork along with other crafts of design and quality. Today his brother Don, who started helping in the store in 1970 and later bought it, runs the shop as well as a more extensive craft gallery and shop in nearby Northampton.

Dick works on his leather full time and the fruits of his labors can be seen displayed along one wall of the store. Leather bags, belts and other accessories are shown in the small shop along with crafts by fifty other craftspeople who work in gold and silver jewelry, blown glass and ceramics. Prices range from about $20 to $200.

Hours: Daily 10 A.M. to 5:30 P.M.
Directions: From I-91, take Exit 9 and follow route 9 to Amherst. Turn left at Pleasant Street. The shop is several blocks ahead on your right.

RIVER VALLEY CRAFTS
236 North Pleasant Street
Amherst, Massachusetts 01002
(413) 253-7919

Dianne Magee started her first craft shop in 1972 in the living room of her Holyoke house. Things went well and in 1979 Dianne and her mother, Ginny Perkins, who had become her partner, established a large shop in the early 19th-century house they now occupy.

The six rooms and 1,500 square feet of this old underground railroad stop are filled with a variety of mostly production crafts from about 300 craftspeople. Each room is themed with craft displays organized with a clear sense of order and a balanced design.

The Amherst Room has a light and airy feel, showing a preponderance of New England crafts—mostly glass, pewter and porcelain; the Public Room is all in earth tones, with a decidedly masculine feel and items like desk accessories in wood, metal and stoneware; the Safari Room contains a selection of handmade and commercially made clothing as well as leather handbags and accessories; the lobby holds several cases of jewelry; the Garden Room shows larger pieces such as wrought iron, lamps and wall hangings; and finally the Collector's Room has all museum-quality work from nationally known artists, with an emphasis on fine jewelry.

Prices for the crafts at River Valley start at $5 rising to $3,500 and occasionally higher. The average item is between $20 and $40.

Hours: Daily, 10 A.M. to 5:30 P.M.; Sunday 1 to 5 P.M.
Directions: From I-91 take Route 9 East to Amherst. At the Commons, take a left and go through two lights. River Valley is two blocks from the second light on your left.

SILVERSCAPE DESIGNS
264 North Pleasant Street
Amherst, Massachusetts 01002
(413) 253-3324

The bright-yellow Victorian house that is the home of Silverscape Designs contains what owner/jeweler Denis Perlman says is the largest selection of handmade jewelry in the area.

There is a fine collection of jewelry from the hands of some seventy-five craftspeople who work in a range of styles and with a variety of metals and semiprecious and precious stones. Another seventy-five craftspeople produce the

32 · SHOPS/GALLERIES

MASSACHUSETTS

other fine crafts on display here, including blown and stained glass, woodwork and pottery.

Denis, a working goldsmith, still gets excited about the nature of the business that he started here seven years ago. "Most of this is a symbol of love, which I feel good about," he told me. "There is a transference of energy from the artist to the recipient. I like the nature of that transferal."

According to Denis, "clean design, fine execution and quality-to-endure" are the primary elements that he looks for when selecting the craftwork that he sells in his 1,000-square-foot store. Prices range from $3 to upwards of $3,000 for some of the jewelry. The average price of the jewelry is $60 to $100; non-jewelry averages $75. Repairs and restoration work for jewelry are done on the premises.

Annexed to the crafts shop is a charming little cafe, which Denis told me he was planning to expand with the addition of a greenhouse area.

Hours: Daily from 10 A.M. to 6 P.M.
Directions: From I-91 take Route 9 East. Go seven miles to Amherst center, take a left on Pleasant Street, pass through two lights. The shop is one block farther on the left.

ALIANZA
140 Newbury Street
Boston, Massachusetts 02116
(617) 262-2585

When you enter the dramatic entryway at Alianza with its wrought-iron gate, high ceiling, imposing fireplace and white tile floor, you can sense a vaguely Mediterranean ambiance, a reminder of the store's earlier incarnation when it specialized in foreign-made crafts.

Shortly after opening in 1966, owner Karen Rotenberg switched the emphasis to contemporary American crafts that are "innovative in conception and use of materials."

The store sells the work of more than 100 craftspeople, including a large selection of jewelry in sterling, gold and mixed metals, contemporary quilts, decorative and functional pottery, woodwork, and stained and blown art glass. The work is often displayed on Spanish colonial furniture, another holdover from Alianza's earlier days. Prices start at $5 and go to $1,000. There are many larger pieces here, perhaps because of the area's sophisticated art tastes. Newbury Street is the art street of Boston, with many fine galleries and related businesses located there.

Hours: Daily from 10 A.M. to 6 P.M.; open Wednesday until 8 P.M.
Directions: Located one block from Copley Square in Boston's Back Bay.

ARTISANS COOPERATIVE
175 K. Faneuil Hall Marketplace
Boston, Massachusetts 02109
(617) 743-0938

Artisans Cooperative was organized by its present director, Deirdre Bonifaz, in 1973 in Chadds Ford, Pennsylvania. The not-for-profit organization was created to stimulate the growth of professional craft skills in rural areas and to provide alternative marketing opportunities to rural craftspeople while giving them more control over their source of livelihood. As part of its activities, the co-op operates a technical assistance program that helps members with business and design problems as well as aiding groups with special projects such as helping set up training programs to pass on traditional craft skills.

The Faneuil Hall store is one of five retail outlets in Massachusetts and Pennsylvania operated by the cooperative, which also publishes a full-color mail-order catalog of members' work. Each retail outlet is stocked with fine-quality crafts chosen from among the 1,000 member artisans, who set policy through majority control of the cooperative's board of directors.

The 865-square-foot Faneuil Hall store is filled with the work of 200 craftspeople. The craftwork is displayed and arranged logically—clothing, toys, quilts, etc. all effectively grouped together—with the result being balanced displays that clearly highlight the individual craft items.

There is an emphasis on traditional design quilts from crib to king size, many of them made by the co-op's first member group, the Freedom Quilting Bee Co-op in Wilcox County, Alabama. There is also a good selection of textiles, including woven and handsewn clothing, placemats, rugs, napkins and the like. Also displayed here are porcelain and stoneware pottery, stained-glass mirrors, blown glass, woodenware and basketry, jewelry, soft sculpture, batik and toys. Prices range from $2 to more than $700.

Hours: Open seven days a week from 10 A.M. to

MASSACHUSETTS

6 P.M. or later depending on the season.
Directions: The shop is located in the upper level of the South Market of Faneuil Hall Marketplace, Boston's revitalized waterfront area.

SIGNATURE
One Dock Square, North Street
Boston, Massachusetts 02109
(617) 227-4885

Established in 1981, this Signature location is the second one opened by brother and sister Arthur Grohe, Jr., and Gretchen Keyworth. As with their Hyannis location, they have on display here a varied collection of high-level, professional work "from local studios to major museum-type work."

For a new craftsperson's work to be added to their collection, Gretchen notes that it must show a "balance of expert craftsmanship, aesthetics, truth of materials and innovative ideas."

"We try to feel as good about a well-made tea set as we do our top-quality, innovative glasswork," Gretchen told me. The artfully designed 1,100-square-foot retail gallery shows the work of 250 craftspeople displayed on museumlike pedestals and display fixtures. Sixty percent of the work is made in the Northeast.

Every five or six weeks they change the displays, always grouping together a generous selection of each artist's work and keeping a resumé on display nearby. "We feel strongly about promoting the people," Gretchen notes. "It gives an additional warmth to the artwork and we like to educate our customers."

They show a lot of fine work and they show it well, including flat and blown glass, pottery and nonfunctional ceramics, gold and silver jewelry, woodwork, metalwork, enamels, leather and some fiber. Prices start at $10 and range to as high as $3,000. Gretchen estimates the average price to be about $45.

Signature presents three themed or artist shows a year in October, May and February.

Hours: Monday through Saturday from 11 A.M. to 8 P.M. (sometimes 9 P.M.); Sunday from noon to 6 P.M.
Directions: From I-93 north, take the Dock Square exit and make a right onto North Street. Signature is across from Faneuil Hall.

From I-93 south, take the Callahan Tunnel exit, bear right under the overpass and follow to North Street.

THE SOCIETY OF ARTS AND CRAFTS
175 Newbury Street
Boston, Massachusetts 02116
(617) 266-1810

This is the granddaddy of them all: The Society is the oldest nonprofit crafts organization in the United States, eighty six years old, with a distinguished history, and still an active support organization.

In 1897 the newly established Society mounted the first exhibition of crafts in a major American city since the days of the Industrial Revolution. Three years later, continued growth led the Society to open its first "handicraft shop."

After enduring some bad times and several moves in the Fifties and Sixties, the Society bounced back as the new American craft movement took hold. It moved into a beautiful bowfront in the heart of Boston's art-gallery district, from which it operates today.

The Society's activities include the management of an exhibition center and retail craft gallery, educational programs for both individuals and groups, an extensive, historic reference library, and a referral and counseling service for craft artists and apprentices.

Six to eight shows, either themed or one- and two-person, are mounted in the two exhibition rooms upstairs, while in the downstairs space you'll find the highest quality crafts by more than 200 craftspeople whose work has been accepted by the Society's jury.

"It's a shop with a gallery attitude; it's a gallery with a shop attitude," is how Society Co-President Hoerta Loeser characterizes this contemporary craft showcase.

You'll find an exceptional range of both functional and nonfunctional crafts displayed here, "selected on their merit rather than commercial popularity." There is an emphasis on contemporary furniture and a comprehensive collection of jewelry in fine metals; handmade clothing occupies the back room and large fiber hangings adorn the walls. There are also ceramics, glass, metal, wood and leather represented here. Prices start at $10 and go up to $5,000, with a large selection in the $25 to $50 category.

Hours: Daily from 10 A.M. to 5:30 P.M.
Directions: Newbury Street is right off Copley Square and the Massachusetts Turnpike in Boston.

MASSACHUSETTS

The Society of Arts and Crafts

VERMONT IMPORTS
Faneuil Hall North Market
Boston, Massachusetts 02109
(617) 367-6482

This is a touch of Vermont within Boston's major tourist attraction. Forty-five professional Vermont craftspeople have their production work displayed here, mixed with things like candy, maple syrup, Vermont calendars and magazines.

"It's an interesting combination of textures, a little sample of quality crafts from Vermont displayed in one space," shop manager Marilyn Gillespie told me. "We have fine American crafts for foreign visitors to take back to their loved ones. Many are stamped 'Made in America.'"

Included in the 500-square-foot shop is pottery, woodenware, some quilts, soft sculpture mobiles, toys, blown glass and pewter. Prices range to $300, with the average price about $20.

This shop definitely caters to the tourist and the items tend to be smaller and very commercial. But if you can't get to Vermont, you might find something interesting here.

Hours: Monday through Saturday, 10 A.M. to 9 P.M.; Sunday from noon to 6 P.M.
Directions: The shop is on the second floor of the North Market in Faneuil Hall Marketplace.

WHIPPOORWILL CRAFTS
126 South Market Building
Faneuil Hall Marketplace
Boston, Massachusetts 02109
(617) 523-5149

Karen Chrobak, the owner of the Whippoorwill Crafts, is an avowed fine-craft lover who, understandably, has to cater to the tourist food-and-trinket crowd that mobs the Quincy Market restoration. Nevertheless, she's managed to display some good quality, handcrafted production items in her three-year-old store.

"I would like to have a gallery," she told me. "I try to buy things with a difference so that people who like crafts have something to see, but I also have to cater to people who don't understand crafts. I enjoy crafts with humor, fanciful, with a creative twist."

So, mixed in with the pottery, blown glass, paperweights, soft sculpture, woodenware, metalwork, and batiked T-shirts from about 80 craftspeople, you'll find some very commercial craft items in this 750-square-foot shop. Prices range from under a dollar to $300, with most items under $20.

Karen's a sharp buyer and you're apt to discover some real finds here.

Hours: Daily from 10 A.M. to 6 P.M.; Sunday, noon to 6 P.M.
Directions: From I-95 South, take the Haymarket exit; from I-93 North, take the State Street exit.

35 · SHOPS/GALLERIES

MASSACHUSETTS

WILD GOOSE CHASE
1429 Beacon Street
Boston, Massachusetts 02146
(617) 738-8020

This craft shop and gift store grew out of the owner's quilting business. When it was first opened, the store concentrated solely on American crafts, but was later expanded to noncraft items. "We carry a very broad selection of crafts and gift merchandise which allows our shoppers in the community to find things for all occasions—both large and small," says manager David Duddy.

About 90 craftspeople make the handcrafts, which are displayed in the front of the store. The rear of the shop is devoted to gift items such as toys, soap, frames and cards.

Crafts for sale include jewelry, porcelain and stoneware, weaving, leather goods, blown glass, clothing, stained-glass panels and quilts. Prices start at $6 and range to $600.

Hours: Monday through Saturday from 10 A.M. to 6 P.M. Open Thursday until 9 P.M.; Sunday from 1 P.M. to 5 P.M.
Directions: Take Storrow Drive to the Kenmore Square exit. Follow Beacon Street to Brookline.

THE SPECTRUM
369 Old King's Highway
Brewster, Massachusetts 02631
(617) 385-3322

The Spectrum of American Artists and Craftsmen began in 1966 when two Rhode Island School of Design graduates, craftsmen Robert Libby and Addison Pratt, established the first Spectrum location in a nineteenth-century schoolhouse in Cedarville, Massachusetts. Today Addison, Robert and a third partner, Bud Heidebur, manage the largest privately owned retail craft business in New England.

The Brewster location, which was designed and built in 1970 and 1971, is the largest of their six retail shops and galleries, all of which are in Massachusetts and Rhode Island. It serves as the headquarters for the chain and is their showcase space.

"We are interested in bringing the work of the American craftsman to the attention of the public, encouraging them to buy American crafts, and thereby support the crafts movement in this country," Bud told me. In addition to its retail locations, The Spectrum also is the purchasing agent of American crafts for the mail-order catalog, *The Horchow Collection*.

Although all Spectrum locations show a wide selection of crafts, Brewster has the most depth, with something for almost every taste. The work of more than 200 craftspeople is displayed in the three rooms and two courtyards of this 3,600-square-foot facility, which was built especially for the display of handcrafts. You'll see fine collections of ceramics, jewelry, weaving, wood, enamels, leather and glass. There are some pieces of contemporary furniture on display along with large-scale wall art. "We are always looking for new innovative work," says Bud. Prices range from $5 to $2,500.

Hours: Open seven days a week. Summer hours, 9:30 A.M. to 6 P.M.; off-season, 10 A.M. to 5 P.M.
Directions: From Route 6 (Mid-Cape Highway) take Exit 9. Turn left onto Route 134 and head to Route 6A (about four miles). Turn right on 6A at the set of lights and small shopping plaza. The Spectrum is about one-and-one-half miles down 6A on the left.

MARION-RUTH
1385 Beacon Street
Brookline, Massachusetts 02146
(617) 734-6620

Marion-Ruth was started thirty years ago by a woman who was an early patron of crafts. As present owner Jerry Kalman remembers, when he bought the store "the craftsmen came with it."

Everything at this exceptionally well-done houseware design store, whether it be commercially made dinnerware and housewares or fine handmade crafts, is of "pure design and quality construction." The shop successfully integrates distinguished craftwork with the finest of commercially produced work, much the way they would be displayed in your house. It's like a Conrans, but without furniture and with crafts.

The store is spacious, well lit, well maintained and nicely fixtured, with about one quarter of the 3,000-square-foot display area used for showing one-of-a-kind and limited-edition work from about 150 craftspeople.

Jerry takes justifiable pride in the clarity of the displays and the large collections of each craftsperson's work available here. "I don't censure what someone makes," he told me. "We show a complete collection and stock in depth. Everything looks fresh and full."

36 · SHOPS/GALLERIES

MASSACHUSETTS

Noting that he moves "an obscene amount of merchandise," Jerry says that he has the "pick of the litter" of professional craftspeople because of the large amount of crafts purchased by the store and the good treatment given their work.

"Our best-selling items are functional items. We're a tabletop shop," he says. The store carries work in ceramics, blown glass, woodwork, fiber and baskets in a price range of $10 to $1,000.

"This store is like a Broadway play in an Off-Broadway location," Jerry says, hinting that he plans to open a second, larger store in the near future somewhere in downtown Boston.

Hours: Daily from 10 A.M. to 6 P.M.; Thursday open until 8:30 P.M.
Directions: The store is one-and-one-half blocks west of the intersection of Harvard Street and Beacon Street. Brookline is south of Cambridge and west of Boston.

JOURNEYMAN
55 Boylston Street
Cambridge, Massachusetts 02138
(617) 876-0170

This craft shop in the Galleria complex specializes in smaller production craftwork, in which all materials are natural and no animal products are used in the fabrication.

The twelve-year-old shop displays mostly pottery, jewelry, wooden items and accessories, blown glass, mirrors and ceramic lamps. The shelves are crowded with rows of items selling from $5 to $100.

Everything here is well-made with a clean finish and good lines. The specialized inventory is a good representation of the type of functional crafts meant to be used daily.

Hours: Monday through Friday from 10 A.M. to 9 P.M.; Saturday from 10 A.M. to 6 P.M.; Sunday from noon to 5:30 P.M.
Directions: To get to Cambridge, take Exit 46A from Route 128 onto Route 2 East. Follow to the end. At the rotary, get onto Route 16, which is the Alewife Brook Parkway. At Massachusetts Avenue turn right and follow into Harvard Square.

TEN ARROW
10 Arrow Street
Cambridge, Massachusetts 02138
(617) 876-1117

Ten Arrow was the first contemporary gallery and shop in the Boston area to show exclusively American crafts. "When I opened ten years ago," recalls owner Betty Tinlot, "people were amazed at what we had, especially the glass. They thought it was Italian."

Today the diverse mix of people in the Cambridge area continues to come to Ten Arrow to search out the original, innovative and finely made crafts from 150 craftspeople that are shown in the 900-square-foot gallery and shop space near Harvard Square.

The gallery space holds four to five exhibits a year and features one- and two-person and themed shows of the finest in American crafts. "We try to avoid showing work shown elsewhere in the Boston area," notes manager Mary Lynch. There is considerable wood and furniture shown and work from emerging artists is sought out. "We like to find people who are just entering the field," Betty told me.

The work in the shop, which ranges from functional production to one of a kind, is chosen to appeal to the nearby academic and professional community and the area's working people. Although innovative, it is, Betty emphasizes, "conservative and not way out."

There is a nice collection of blown glass, ceramics, wood, metalwork, and metal and nonmetal jewelry in the shop. Prices range from $1 to $4,000. "We try to get as interesting as possible in the lower price range," says Betty. The average price is estimated at $40 to $50.

Hours: Daily from 10 A.M. to 6 P.M.; Thursday open until 9 P.M.
Directions: From the Massachusetts Turnpike, exit at Cambridge/Allston and cross the Charles River to Memorial Drive in Cambridge. Go west on Memorial Drive to Kennedy Street. Take a right on Kennedy, and then right on Mount Auburn and a sharp left onto Massachusetts Avenue. Arrow Street is the first street on the left.

PERCEPTIONS
67 Main Street
Concord, Massachusetts 01742
(617) 369-6797

"We try for an innovative mix of crafts, jewelry and clothing," says one of the partners at Perceptions, a ten-year-old store in Concord center.

Most of what's displayed here is elegant clothing and related accessories with about sixty percent of the fashions made by hand, in-

37 · SHOPS/GALLERIES

MASSACHUSETTS

cluding handsewn raw silk, woven, quilted and batiked apparel. Mixed in with the clothing is a modest selection of crafts, primarily pottery, blown glass and jewelry in silver, gold, brass and clay. There is also a selection of antique ethnic jewelry, some wall hangings, pillows, small rugs, prints and posters to complete the eclectic display in this sophisticated store.

Hours: Daily from 9:30 A.M. to 5:00 P.M.
Directions: Take exit 45 off I-95 onto Route 2A and follow to the center of Concord.
From I-495, take Route 111 to Route 2 and follow signs to Concord.

DANFORTH MUSEUM SHOP
123 Union Avenue
Framingham, Massachusetts 01701
(617) 620-0050

The Danforth Museum mounts a continuing exhibition program in its six galleries showing works of art in all media and in a variety of periods and styles.

As part of its activities, the Danforth operates a museum shop devoted to the display and sale of contemporary, high-quality crafts.

The small shop has one or two art-oriented or functional pieces from each of the approximately seventy-five craftspeople who display here. Media include glass, wood, clay and fiber and there's a small selection of jewelry. Also here are original prints and notecards.

Prices range from $1 to $350, falling mainly in the $10 to $50 category.

Hours: Wednesday through Friday from noon to 4:30 P.M.; Saturday and Sunday from 1:00 to 4:30 P.M.
Directions: From the Massachusetts Turnpike, take Exit 13 to Route 30 West. Get on Route 126 South to Framingham. Take a right onto Lincoln Street and your first left to Pearl. The museum is on the right at the corner of Pearl and Union Streets.

WONDERFUL THINGS
232 Stockbridge Road
Great Barrington, Massachusetts 01230
(413) 528-2473

What happens when a professional modelmaker, an industrial arts instructor and an occupational therapist get together to operate a craft-oriented shop? The answer is, in this case anyway, Wonderful Things, a ten-year-old department store of craft supplies, kits and instruction books that also sells the work of 200 professional craftspeople.

"Fourteen Rooms Full—Six Shops in One," reads their brochure. The finished crafts are displayed in three upstairs rooms where you'll find production and limited-edition crafts in stoneware, glass, weaving, leather, and wood as well as silver jewelry. Prices range from $8 to $1,000 with most items costing from $45 to $75.

The other eleven rooms contain a yarn and needlework shop ("materials and kits for any handwork project or fabric project you have in mind"); a model and hobby shop ("kits for beginners and kits to meet museum standards"); doll houses, miniatures and accessories ("your complete home center for that dream house in miniature"); and art supplies ("materials for painting, sculpting, sumi, printmaking and other techniques, and frames for the finished piece"); and craft supplies ("supplies, kits and books for every craft, including the largest variety of beads in the area").

All told, according to co-owner William Tanguay, there are some 30,000 supplies here for both the hobbyist and the professional.

Hours: Daily from 10 A.M. to 5 P.M.; Sunday from 1:00 P.M. to 5 P.M.
Directions: The shop is on Route 7 in Great Barrington, next to Friendly's restaurant.

SKERA
123 Russell Street
Hadley, Massachusetts 01035
(413) 536-4563

This shop has offered contemporary crafts since 1974. "People can come here and they'll know from experience what they can get," notes manager Carol Banks.

About forty craftspeople are represented here, working in ceramics, wood, weaving, metal sculpture, blown and stained glass, jewelry and enamel. Prices range from $3 to $2,500.

A small gallery space features a different exhibit every four to six weeks.

Hours: Seven days a week, 11 A.M. to 6 P.M.; Thursday and Friday open until 9 P.M.
Directions: Take Exit 19 northbound or Exit 20 southbound from I-91 and follow Route 9 East for two miles. Skera is in the big yellow house directly on Route 9.

MASSACHUSETTS

Signature

SIGNATURE
North Street
Hyannis, Massachusetts 02601
(617) 771-4499

The Hyannis location is the first of the two retail galleries opened by Gretchen Keyworth and Art Grohe Jr., a brother and sister who also own the Boston Signature. Gretchen's background as a production potter and Art's experience as a business executive with Western Union have clearly worked well together. They have put on display a fine grouping of crafts in a refined setting both here and in Boston.

Located in a shopping mall, this 1,200-square-foot shop and gallery carries the same excellent variety, style and quality of crafts as the Boston outlet, although this location tends to carry more wall work than does Boston. The work of more than 250 craftspeople is shown here.

There are some production pieces on display, but one-of-a-kind and museum-quality work predominates. They have an outstanding collection of flat glass panels and blown glass by some sixty artists. "We have probably the best glass collection in the Northeast," Art told me. Other work displayed includes ceramics, woodwork, metalwork, enamels, leather, fiber and jewelry in gold and silver.

Prices range from $10 to $3,000. "People tend to focus on the dramatic," Art notes, "but the average price of the merchandise is less than expected." He says that thirty percent of the crafts are under $30 and the average is $40 to $45.

Featured displays of artists new to the store and themed shows are held regularly.

Hours: Open seven days a week. Summer, 10 A.M. to 9 P.M.; winter, 10 A.M. to 5 P.M.
Directions: Take Route 28 to the airport rotary. Pick up Barnstable Road to North Street. After three traffic lights, look for the Village Market Place in a brick mall on the right.

THE SPECTRUM
433 Main Street
Hyannis, Massachusetts 02601
(617) 771-4554

One of the six respected Spectrum shops and galleries, this downtown Hyannis location shows a nice representation of the craft work available through the chain.

"There's nothing here that I'm not proud to represent," store manager Nancy Toppa-Camish told me. Whether it's "eight or eighty dollars, it's the same quality. There are no rough edges."

MASSACHUSETTS

As with the other Spectrum locations, you'll find displayed here the fine craftwork of more than 200 craftspeople working in all media. Prices start at $5 and go as high as $2,500.

Detailed descriptions of each piece are often displayed next to the work while the effective use of gallery-style displays highlights each grouping for maximum impact.

Hours: Seven days a week. Summer hours, 10 A.M. to 10 P.M.; off-season, 10 A.M. to 5 P.M.
Directions: On Main Street in downtown Hyannis.

LEVERETT CRAFTSMEN AND ARTISTS, INC.
Leverett Center
Leverett, Massachusetts 01054

Joseph Barnes was a Leverett ironmaker who dreamed of establishing a center for arts and crafts in this rural area. Taking the first step toward turning his dream into reality, he bought a plot of land with an old chicken coop, which he intended to turn into studio, classroom and gallery space. He died, however, before it could be renovated.

Fortunately for the community, others had grown to share the ironmaker's dream and continued the work. In 1967, the center was established in the building that it continues to occupy.

Today the Leverett center is a focus of artistic activity in Western Massachusetts. The center runs a full schedule of classes and workshops at all levels and there are eight studios where eighteen resident artists and craftspeople work in various media. Most of the residents are emerging artists, who, according to center director Amy Shapiro, are "given the opportunity to establish themselves at low rent and minimum hassles before moving on." The length of stay depends on the artist's personal situation and progress.

The two large gallery spaces hold monthly exhibits in a variety of media. There is also a retail sales shop, which sells work such as pottery, weaving, wrought iron, furniture, glass, fabric, baskets and woodcuts. Also: painting, graphics, sculpture, photography and notecards are displayed. The work has been juried for display and is made by about 160 professional area artists and craftspeople. Prices range from $3 to $2,000.

Amy told me that they will soon be opening a room for the display and sale of antiques, which she called "old crafts of high design merit, offering a depth of history."

Hours: Tuesday through Sunday from noon to 5 P.M.
Directions: From Route 2, take Route 63 south to Leverett center.

From I-91, take Route 116 to Amherst and follow Route 63 to Leverett.

QUAIGH DESIGNS
Chandlers Row, Spring Street
Marblehead, Massachusetts 01945
(617) 631-4016

As with the original Quaigh Design Center in Wilmington, Vermont, this store, started in 1978, displays both American crafts and imported Scottish woolens.

"We try to buy things that people can use in their everyday life," notes Dorothy Bennett, the shop manager.

There's a good quality of handcrafted work in the 1,000-square-foot store, including pottery, jewelry, woodenware, mobiles, small stained-glass pieces, wrought iron, graphics and lampshades. The work of about seventy-five craftspeople is represented here within a price range of $5 to $250.

Hours: Daily, 10 A.M. to 5:30 P.M.
Directions: From Route 128, take Route 114 to Marblehead. Shop is on Route 114 in town on the corner of Pleasant and Spring Streets.

ARTISANS COOPERATIVE
60 Main Street
Nantucket, Massachusetts 02554
(617) 228-4631

This store and its Boston counterpart are the Massachusetts outlets for this rural craftsperson support organization. The nonprofit organization, which also runs three retail locations in Pennsylvania, represents "skilled artisans throughout this land, from the coast of Maine to the Appalachian Mountains; from the plains of the Deep South and the woods of Minnesota to reservations of Native Americans; and beyond."

Crafts on display here are made by about 200 craftspeople. The organization, established in 1973, serves as a marketing link between its 1,000 members and important markets in affluent areas.

The work on display in this outstanding

MASSACHUSETTS

1813 whaling captain's mansion is similar to that in the Boston store. You'll see quilts, handwoven clothing, blankets and rugs, blown and stained glass, pottery, woodenware, basketry, jewelry, soft sculpture and toys. Prices start at a few dollars and rise to $700 and higher.

Hours: Open seven days a week. April and May, 10 A.M. to 4 P.M.; June and September, 10 A.M. to 6 P.M.; July and August, 9 A.M. to 9 P.M.; October, November and December, 10 A.M. to 4 P.M. Closed January to March.

Directions: Take either the Steamship or Hy-Line ferry from Hyannis to Nantucket (two to three hours).

From the Hy-Line, walk straight ahead to the Pacific National Bank at the top of Main Street. Artisans Cooperative is on your left.

From the Steamship ferry, walk up to the Whaling Museum and take a left. Walk to the end of the street and take a right on Main Street. Follow to the bank.

THE SPECTRUM
26 Main Street
Nantucket, Massachusetts 02554
(617) 228-4606

This is another in the group of six craft stores and galleries owned by the folks at The Spectrum of American Artists and Craftsmen.

Located in a 200-year-old wood-and-brick building in the heart of Nantucket's cobblestoned commercial area, the store, which opened in 1975 and is the third largest in the chain, carries the work of about 200 craftspeople and artists.

Ceramics, jewelry, weaving, wood, enamels, leather, glass, painting, sculpture and prints will be found here in a price range of $5 to $2,500.

Hours: May through December seven days a week from 10 A.M. to 10 P.M.
Directions: Take the ferry to Nantucket. The shop is directly on Main Street.

LIMITED EDITIONS
1176 Walnut Street
Newton, Massachusetts 02161
(617) 965-5474

Now in its eighth year, Limited Editions has effectively integrated the display of quality crafts with gift items and an adjacent gourmet-food area.

In the main part of the store, you'll find commercial gift items for sale alongside a tasteful selection of production crafts. "I try to find functionally beautiful work that's worth the money," shop owner Jo-Ann Issacson told me. There are about 100 craftspeople represented here, including work in pottery, jewelry, silkscreen prints, baskets, blown and stained glass, wooden items and soft sculpture. Prices range up to $500. "I'm not so interested in the big name as I am in someone who does quality work," Jo-Ann notes.

Toute Sweet is a small eating area annexed to the shop. Your food is served on fine handmade porcelain and the menu includes such things as quiches, salads, soups, pastas, croissants and coffee.

Hours: Daily from 10 A.M. to 5:30 P.M.; Thursdays open until 8 P.M.
Directions: From the Boston area take Route 9 West and get off at the Walnut Street exit.

From Framingham area, take Route 9 East to the Woodward Street exit. Take Woodward to Lincoln Street and then take a right onto Walnut.

THE POTTERS SHOP
34 Lincoln Street
Newton Highlands, Massachusetts 02161
(617) 965-3959

If you like to watch potters at work, then you'll love The Potters Shop, a thriving shared workspace, school and retail shop that is now in its seventh year.

According to Steven Branfman, the founder and director of the facility, The Potters Shop started when he realized that there was a need among area potters for suitable studio facilities. So bit by bit he began to enlarge the scope of his own pottery studio, which was housed in cramped facilities next door to the present location.

Two years ago, The Potters Shop moved to its current quarters in the lower level of a commercial village building. Steve has not only created a successful pottery here; he has also put together a notable example of efficient space utilization.

In about 1,500 square feet, there are well-organized common and private workspaces, five electric kilns, classroom facilities, supplies storage and a showroom where the work of about two dozen potters is sold. "I like people to come in and browse around," says Steve. "Visitors can view work being done, classes

MASSACHUSETTS

being taught and meet the potters."

Displayed on the shelves of the retail shop is work in stoneware, porcelain, raku and earthenware in both functional and decorative forms. Prices range from $2 to $600. All work has been made by present and former resident potters and has been juried by studio manager Carol Temkin for adherence to technical standards.

Hours: Monday through Friday 10 A.M. to 9 P.M.; Saturday 9 A.M. to 5 P.M.; Sunday from 11 A.M. to 5 P.M.
Directions: From Massachusetts Turnpike, take Route 128 (I-95) south to Route 9 East. Take a left at the light and a right onto Lincoln Street.

The Potters Shop

JUBILATION
91 Union Street
Newton Center, Massachusetts 02159
(617) 965-0488

The two partners who own Jubilation started their craft-retailing career as the proprietors of a Faneuil Hall pushcart from which they sold fiber crafts. They did well indeed, and in 1978 Elaine Powell and Suzanne Levine took a quantum leap into this well-done corner shop and gallery which displays a good cross section of crafts from about 175 craftspeople.

There is much decorative and sculptural work shown in the 950-square-foot space and a "New York style" sophisticated look predominates. "We're not heavy on functional work," notes Elaine of the store's many avant-garde pieces.

Among the works on display are porcelain, raku and sagger ceramics, blown glass, art jewelry, contemporary quilts, clothes, soft sculpture, leather and wood. There are many one-of-a-kind pieces and prices start at $10 and run to $2,000. The average price is $50 to $100.

Hours: Daily from 10 A.M. to 5 P.M.
Directions: From Route 128 (I-95) take Route 9 East to the Parker Street Bridge in Newton. Take a left onto Parker and follow to Newton Center. Union Street is on your right and the shop is across from the MBTA station.

THE CORNER
19 Holden Street, Berkshire Plaza
North Adams, Massachusetts 01247
(413) 663-3651

The Northern Berkshire Council of the Arts sponsors this craft shop, which carries primarily functional work of seventy-five craftspeople. The majority of the craftspeople represented in this modest shop are professionals, although there is some polished amateur work mixed in. All work is juried into the shop by standards set by the Arts Council.

Tucked away in a corner hideaway behind the Berkshire Bank, the 450-square-foot space is neatly arranged by medium and craftsperson. The craftwork includes soft sculpture, some quilts, smaller stained-glass pieces, wooden toys, stuffed animals, weaving, small fiber pieces, jewelry and photography. Most of the craftwork averages about $10 to $15 with a price range of up to $250.

Hours: Daily 9 A.M. to 5 P.M.
Directions: Take Route 2 West into North Adams. At the second light (Holden Street), take a left and then a right into the Berkshire Plaza parking lot. The store is in front of the Berkshire Bank drive-through window lane.

DON MULLER GALLERY
16 Main Street
Northampton, Massachusetts 01060
(413) 586-1119

Since its opening in 1978, this attractive retail gallery in downtown Northampton has acquired a deserved reputation as the area's finest showcase for contemporary crafts.

Owner Don Muller has collected an exemplary group of production and one-of-a-kind crafts from seventy craftspeople and displayed

MASSACHUSETTS

them against a handsome background of glass-block and red-brick walls. Many of the crafts are displayed on freeform, sculptured wood display fixtures, which are placed throughout the 1,000-square-foot space. Clearly, much effort has gone into the gallery's design and layout with the result being a visually appealing space that's also a comfortable place in which to browse.

Available is blown and stained glass, gold and silver jewelry, ceramics, wood and leatherwork. There is some furniture on display and a large collection of leather. Prices start at $25 and go up to $200 with the average about $40.

About six month-long shows are held in the gallery annually, featuring either an individual's work or a themed exhibit.

Hours: Daily from 10 A.M. to 5:30 P.M.; Thursday open until 9 P.M.
Directions: From I-91 take Route 5 and head north. Then go east on Route 9 for one block.

THE ETHEL PUTTERMAN GALLERY
Route 6-A
Orleans, Massachusetts 02653
(617) 255-5110

Over the past twenty years, The Ethel Putterman Gallery has established a Cape-wide reputation among both artists and patrons for the high quality of the artwork it displays. Started by the late artist, Ethel Putterman, the gallery has been run since her death by her husband, Felix, who has maintained its high standards.

"From two decades of gallery operation," he notes, "we have refined an essential standard that manifests itself in our policy of offering fine creative work at accessible prices. The imagery and craftsmanship are universal and contemporary."

There are about a dozen craftspeople and twenty-five artists whose work is on display in the gallery's four rooms, including a collection of both functional and sculptural "abstract pottery," blown glass, and carving in wood and stone. Also displayed are abstract prints and paintings. Prices range from $25 to $500.

Hours: Daily 10 A.M. to 5:00 P.M.; Sunday from 1 to 5 P.M.
Directions: The gallery is a quarter of a mile from the Orleans rotary on the Mid-Cape Highway. It is approximately 300 feet from where Route 28 and 6-A intersect in Orleans.

THE ARTFUL HAND
Main Street Square
Orleans, Massachusetts 02653
(617) 255-2969

In a town that has its share of fine quality craft shops and galleries, this is one of the best. Joe and Mary Porcari started The Artful Hand in 1980, featuring production and limited-edition crafts, paintings and prints. With the recent addition of a small lofted gallery space, the Porcaris have expanded their display space to nearly 2,000 square feet.

The upstairs gallery hosts regularly scheduled individual and group exhibits of fine flat art and craft. In the two downstairs rooms, the work of 180 craftspeople and 20 fine artists is attractively displayed, clearly labeled with the artist's name and other data. There is good taste at work here and a nice depth and variety of work on display.

Among the mostly contemporary crafts are decorative and functional ceramics, weaving, gold and silver jewelry, quilts, stained and blown glass, wooden accessories and clothing. Joe told me that he plans to add some furniture to his store soon. Prices for the craft work range from $5 to $2,500.

Hours: Daily 10 A.M. to 5:00 P.M.
Directions: From Route 6 take Exit 12 to Orleans Center. Main Street Square is the first left off Route 6A just past the traffic lights where the road intersects Main Street. The Artful Hand is at the end of the plaza.

NEW HORIZONS
Route 28, Peacock Alley
Orleans, Massachusetts 02653
(617) 255-8766

An old sea captain's house provides a fitting environment for this newest addition to the Cape's fine craft shops and galleries.

Established in 1982, New Horizons shows the work of ninety craftspeople in an attractive environment punctuated by whitewashed displays, low ceilings and wide planked floors.

You'll find both traditional and contemporary crafts displayed in the two rooms of this shop, including stoneware and porcelain pottery, ceramic lamps, blown glass, pewter, jewelry, soft sculpture and small fiber work, quilts, woodcarving and woodenware. Prices run from $2 to $500.

New Horizons is part of Peacock Alley, an interesting complex that includes a pottery

MASSACHUSETTS

shop, a leatherworker's shop, a fabric store, an art gallery, a spice shop, an antique store and a clothing store.

Hours: Daily from 10 A.M. to 5 P.M.
Directions: The shop is located on Route 28, a main route in town.

TREE'S PLACE
Route 6A
Orleans, Massachusetts 02658
(617) 255-1330

Tree's Place houses a collection of work by about sixty American craftspeople that is displayed along with a cornucopia of handcrafted imports and commercially made items from all over the world.

Billing itself as "the museum shop without the museum," Tree's has nine rooms and an outdoor sculpture garden filled with merchandise. Altogether, there is 4,000 square feet of retail space and an equal amount of warehoused inventory.

Somehow, with all this space to fill, Tree's has managed generally to avoid tourist ticky-tacky which seems to infest vacation areas. "No gifte shoppe stuffe," reads one of their brochures.

Crafts on display include functional stoneware and porcelain, gold and silver jewelry, blown glass, stoneware and metal sculpture, and unusual items like pentatonic wind chimes and fantasy feather masks.

"We're old hands at finding new things first—at major markets worldwide and back streets in small craft villages," notes owner Julian Baird. Julian is the second generation of his family to run Tree's, which opened in 1961.

Of special note is the extensive display of hand-painted and commercially produced ceramic tiles, which Julian claims is "probably the largest selection of designer tiles in the U.S."

One room has mostly Oriental pieces; yet another is a gallery space with serigraphs, sculpture and one-of-a-kind constructions and collages. There are large displays of such things as Russian lacquer boxes, Thai bronze flatware, Swiss music boxes, tartan wool ties, Japanese antiques.

There have been some good aesthetic choices made here, and everything on sale, whether imported or not, traditional or contemporary, handmade or commercial, is of high quality and in a wide range of styles.

If you like to browse and shop, a visit to Tree's could prove to be most satisfying. Prices for the crafts and other merchandise range from $5 to $5,000.

Hours: Summer, open seven days from 9:30 A.M. to 5:30 P.M.; winter, open daily 10 A.M. to 5 P.M.
Directions: Follow Route 6 to Exit 11, which puts you on Route 6A. Tree's is at the intersection of Routes 6A and 28.

THE ELLEN HARRIS GALLERY
355 Commercial Street
Provincetown, Massachusetts 02657
(617) 487-1414

Ellen Harris has been displaying and selling fine contemporary crafts in her gallery and shop since 1968. Her gallery has long been the only place in town to see a comprehensive collection of fine crafts.

The 500-square-foot space displays the decorative and functional work of about fifty craftspeople as well as a variety of "one-dimensional art," such as painting, graphics and photography.

Included in the crafts are stoneware and porcelain ceramics, basketry, blown glass, stained glass, and sculpture in metal and clay. Prices range from $5 to $2,000.

Hours: From Memorial Day weekend through Labor Day, open daily 11 A.M. to 11 P.M. Call for off-season hours.
Directions: Commercial Street is the town's main street. Provincetown is at the tip of the Cape and is reached by Route 6.

METAMORPHOSIS
237 Commercial Street
Provincetown, Massachusetts 02657
(716) 487-3518

When jeweler Linda Tennyson opened a small shop in the back of Whaler's Wharf in 1976, she named it Metamorphosis because she knew that "it would develop and change over time."

Today, after several moves and expansions, Linda's shop occupies the prime location in the front of a Provincetown craft mini-mall.

Pine displays on both sides of the narrow, zigzagged shop hold a large collection of jewelry in gold, silver and brass and studio art glass primarily in an Art Nouveau style. There are a total of seventy-five craftspeople whose

MASSACHUSETTS

work, mostly jewelry and glass, is represented here. There is also paper collage and metal sculpture. Prices range from $10 to $2,000.

"I like to support men and women who are outstanding artists in their medium," Linda recently said. "I look for those people who put a little more into a piece, designers who create unique items of lasting value."

Hours: During the season, open 10 A.M. to 11 P.M. seven days a week.
Directions: Metamorphosis is in the center of town on the Commerical Street side of Whaler's Wharf.

WHALER'S WHARF
237 Commercial Street
Provincetown, Massachusetts 02657
(617) 487-1966

Provincetown is not an area lacking for tourist-oriented, commercial handcrafts. In the Commercial Street area, I counted seven jewelers and nine leatherworkers operating out of their own stores, and all within a few blocks of each other. My nomination for best-named store? "Leathering Heights."

There's even a two-level mini-mall here — Whaler's Wharf—containing twenty-five stalls where local artists, craftspeople and gift-shop owners sell their stuff. There's crafts to see by about fifty professional and amateur craftspeople in a wide range of work including ivory carving, jewelry, woodcarving, pastel portraiture, coin cutting, embroidery, paintings on wood, stoneware pottery, driftwood constructions, tombstone art, and airbrushed paintings and T-shirts. Prices start at $1 and go to $500.

There is also an awesome collection of seashells on display. Thousands upon thousands of them have been gathered from all over the world and neatly categorized and displayed in dozens of bins. It is, says Whaler's Wharf owner Dale Elmer, "one of the largest shell shops on the East Coast" and I have no reason to doubt him.

Dale is a jeweler who opened his own jewelry store, The Handcrafter, in 1963. Eight years later, he bought the old movie theater next door, did some renovating, connected it to The Handcrafter and established Whaler's Wharf.

Hours: During the season, from 10 A.M. to 11 P.M. seven days a week.
Directions: Provincetown is at the tip of Cape Cod and at the end of Route 6. Whaler's Wharf is in the center of town on the beach side of the street.

THE SPECTRUM
58 Pickering Wharf
Salem, Massachusetts 01970
(617) 745-6171

Opened in 1981, this shop carries a similar grouping of crafts as the other five Spectrum outlets in Massachusetts and Rhode Island.

Chosen for "originality and beauty of design, as well as quality in execution," the craft inventory here includes weaving, jewelry, ceramics, leather, glass, wood and enamel. There are also paintings, sculpture and original prints on display. Prices for the crafts, which are made by about 200 craftspeople, range from $5 to $2,500.

Hours: From Memorial Day to Labor Day, seven days a week, 10 A.M. to 10 P.M.; off-season, open from 10 A.M. to 5 P.M.
Directions: From I-95, take the exit for Route 114 South to Salem, which is north of Boston. The shop is in the newly redeveloped wharf area of downtown.

HOLSTEN GALLERIES
Elm Street
Stockbridge, Massachusetts 01262
(413) 298-3044

Since opening in 1978, Holsten Galleries has acquired a wide reputation for exhibiting the finest in museum-quality "craft-art" and high-quality flat art from artists across the country. The emphasis is on craft, with three-quarters of the artists here in that category.

Sixty craftspeople are represented with work in glass, clay, paper, wood, enamels and jewelry. Prices start at $50 and range up to $10,000.

Hours: Open from June to August seven days a week,10 A.M. to 6 P.M.
Directions: Take Exit 2 from the Massachusetts Turnpike and follow Route 102 West to Stockbridge. Holsten is one-half block off Route 7 past the Post Office and behind the Lee Savings Bank.

MASSACHUSETTS

THE GIFTED HAND
32 Church Street
Wellesley, Massachusetts 02181
(617) 235-7171

This seven-year-old gallery/shop can boast of one of the better collections of contemporary crafts in the greater Boston area. The work of about 130 craftspeople from across the country has been gathered by owners Glenn Johnson and Diane Reede for display in their spacious store.

"We purchase from craftspeople in many parts of the United States in order to be able to offer the highest quality items in each medium," notes Glenn.

You'll find a nicely balanced collection of functional and decorative work on display here, including stoneware and porcelain pottery and sculpture; leather handbags, briefcases and accessories; wearables, woven shawls, afghans, pillows and rugs; blown and stained glass; wooden toys, household items and small furniture; jewelry; baskets; and dolls.

There are additionally about 100 quilts on display, representing one of the largest collections in New England of newly made Mennonite and Amish quilts. Glenn and Diane purchase the quilts primarily from "elderly women in their seventies, eighties and nineties," during their periodic trips to Pennsylvania and Missouri.

Prices for the craftwork here range from $10 to $1,500 with many items in the $30 to $80 range. Résumés are given out with nearly all purchases "so that the buyer or gift recipient will know what the crafted item is all about."

Special exhibits are held two or three times a year, usually a themed show featuring one particular medium.

Hours: Daily from 10 A.M. to 5:30 P.M.
Directions: From Route 128 (I-95), take the Route 16 exit and follow for about three miles through Wellesley Hills to the center of town. Church Street is the first right after Route 16 bears to the left as you enter the town center. The Gifted Hand is at the end of the block.

DESIGN WORKS
Main Street
West Stockbridge, Massachusetts 01266
(413) 232-4235

This tastefully designed gallery-style shop offers primarily functional crafts in a full selection of media from about 175 craftspeople. Owner Ed Hoe, who was a production potter for eight years before opening this store in 1981, notes that he has developed a "trained eye for what's good and what's not" and that technical and design standards must be "extremely high" for work to be carried here.

The 700-square-foot store displays work in wood, pottery, leather, baskets, clothing, toys, jewelry, paper, and blown, stained and etched glass. Prices range up to $700 with the average items between $30 to $35.

Special exhibits of one-of-a-kind work by craftspeople represented in the store are regularly scheduled.

Hours: Wednesday through Monday, open 10 A.M. to 6 P.M.; closed Tuesday.
Directions: From Boston and East, take Exit 1 from the Massachusetts Turnpike. The town is right at the exit.

From New York and West, take the last exit on the New York Thruway Berkshire Extension. Get on Route 22 South, go one-tenth mile to Route 41 East and follow to Main Street.

The Gifted Hand

MASSACHUSETTS

THE PRINTS & THE POTTER
142 Highland Street
Worcester, Massachusetts 01609
(617) 752-2170

The Prints & The Potter traces its roots back nine years to its beginnings as a cooperative of craftspeople who sold their work out of a space that also housed working studios. Today, two moves and many changes later, the now privately owned gallery/shop shows the work of more than 100 craftspeople as well as a selection of prints and posters. There is also a framing operation in the shop.

The well-designed interior of this 750-square-foot store shows the mostly functional crafts on display here to their best advantage. You'll find ceramics, woodwork, leather, blown glass, stained glass, weaving and jewelry in a price range of $5 to $300.

Hours: Monday through Friday 9 A.M. to 5:30 P.M.; Wednesday 9 A.M. to 9 P.M.; Saturday 9 A.M. to 4 P.M.
Directions: From I-290, take the exit for Route 9 West. Follow the route through Lincoln Square, which leads to Highland Street. The shop is at the corner of Highland and West Street.

Redwing Craft Cooperative

REDWING CRAFT COOPERATIVE
51 Union Street
Worcester, Massachusetts 01608
(617) 752-1135

Located on the third level of an old brick factory turned retail complex, the Redwing Co-op comprises twelve local craftspeople who have gotten together to "share rent, time in the store and decisions," says co-op President and potter Barbara Knutson.

Each member has been juried into the group based on the merits of their work and how well their personality meshes with the rest of the co-op. "We look for work that expresses a personal style, with an integrity that conveys zest and celebration as well as usefulness," notes Barbara.

The work on display here includes pottery, weaving, jewelry, ironwork, calligraphy, carved wood decoys, blown and stained glass, prints, photography and fabric art. Prices run from a few dollars up to $500.

As with most craft co-ops, Redwing's members each take their turn at tending shop, allowing for direct contact between the artist and customers.

Hours: Daily 10 A.M. to 6 P.M.
Directions: From I-290 take the Route 9 West exit and follow signs for the Centrum. Union Place is opposite the Marriott Hotel.

WORCESTER CRAFT CENTER
25 Sagamore Road
Worcester, Massachusetts 01605
(617) 753-8183

This superb craft education facility is the oldest institution of its type in the country. The Center is a direct descendant of the Worcester Employment Society, which was established in 1856 to train needy women in sewing and lacemaking skills. In 1951 the Society sponsored the establishment of the Craft Center and in 1958, after a successful community fund-raising drive, the present building was erected, housing studios, exhibition and sales space and a library.

The nondescript brick building looks more like a government research center than the location of a major craft facility. "The building," explains Cyrus Lipsitt, the Center's director since 1979, "was built with an eye to possible conversion to office space if things didn't work out."

Things worked out very well indeed and this

47 · SHOPS/GALLERIES

year the Center completed a $600,000 addition, enlarging the already substantial amount of studio space and creating some more exhibition areas. With the addition, the Center contains 26,000 square feet of studios, gallery space, a craft sales shop, a craft supply shop, a library and offices.

There are three exhibition spaces for the display of craft work. The main gallery posts six major contemporary craft exhibits a year, ranging from invitational exhibits to traveling shows. The 2,000-square-foot space has a classic gallery look—and is a fine place to view the outstanding work shown there. The displayed work is usually for sale at prices that range up to $5,000.

You will also find regular exhibits of craftwork and photography in the Center's two smaller exhibition spaces: the lobby and the 650-square-foot space created when the addition was connected to the original building. There is also an outdoor sculpture courtyard that was being finished at the time of this writing.

The Center's craft sales shop carries the work of about 250 craftspeople from across the country. There is something here in virtually every craft medium with an emphasis on ceramics and jewelry. The work of some instructors and students is represented here and there is also a stock of commercial gift items for sale. Prices range from $10 to $500.

There is also a shop here that sells a wide range of craft supplies for both amateurs and professionals, as well as a selection of craft books.

Hours: Daily 9 A.M. to 5 P.M.
Directions: From I-290, take Route 9 through the rotary at Lincoln Square and take a right onto Grove Street (Route 122A). Watch for Sagamore Road on the left.

NORTHSIDE CRAFT GALLERY
933 Main Street
Yarmouthport, Massachusetts 02675
(617) 362-5291

Barrie Cliff, a business executive turned pewterer, was putting the finishing touches on his new gallery and shop at the time of this writing. He tells me that there will be twenty-five craftspeople, primarily from New England, whose work will be displayed here.

Crafts included are clay, leather, metal, wood and fiber, prices range from $5 to $300.

Barrie, who's president of the Society of Cape Cod Craftsmen, will be regularly featuring exhibits of members of his group in the 1,000-square-foot space.

"I think that the Society of Cape Cod Craftsmen should be as strong as the New Hampshire League," Barrie told me. "It would be nice to let the rest of the world know the mostly high level of production craftsperson living on the Cape."

Hours: Daily, 10 A.M. to 5 P.M.
Directions: Take Route 6 to Exit 8 and head north to Yarmouth/Dennis. At Route 6A take a right toward Dennis. The shop is on the right in Yarmouthport.

Worcester Craft Center

NEW HAMPSHIRE

ARTIST EXPRESS DEPOT
38 Depot Street
Ashland, New Hampshire 03217
(603) 968-3163

With the exception of one outstanding cloisonné artist, the Artist Express Depot represents only noncraft artists—painters, sculptors and collagists.

But it is the gallery concept itself that bears mention here. Several years ago when owner/artist Bill Bernsen, then a deputy Los Angeles sheriff, faced a midlife crisis, he decided to flee the frenetic L.A. scene and set out for New England in his truck. His fantasy was to find an old building in which he could work undisturbed while promoting contemporary art. When a real-estate agent told him about the old Boston & Maine Railroad freight depot in Ashland, his fantasy started to become a reality.

Bill has spent the last three years fixing up the property, a project particularly well-suited for his talents. An artist who creates found-object art—"ready-made aided art"—from mostly wood and metal, he refers to the depot as "my giant sculpture."

The 1849 building, which is now almost fully restored, sits on a seven-foot-thick granite foundation and houses a giant wood stove that holds more than 200 pounds of wood in its burning chamber.

There are fifteen New Hampshire artists whose work is regularly exhibited in the distinctive, 600-square-foot gallery interior. Both one-person and group shows are posted, and work generally sells for between $500 and $10,000.

"The artists shown here must all be full-time and not weekend painters," Bill told me. "There must be a high degree of excellence in both quality and uniqueness. I like to compare the depot to a Fifty-Seventh Street (New York) gallery."

Hours: Tuesday through Sunday from noon to 6 P.M. or by appointment. Closed Monday.
Directions: From I-93, take Exit 24. Take a right off the exit onto Main Street. Go one-half mile to Winter Street and take another right. Another one-quarter mile and you'll come to Depot Street. The gallery is on the corner.

CONCORD ARTS & CRAFTS
36 North Main Street
Concord, New Hampshire 03301
(603) 228-8171

This is one of ten League of New Hampshire Craftsmen-affiliated craft shops throughout the state selling exclusively New Hampshire-made crafts.

Like the other League shops, the Concord outlet carries both the work of craftspeople who have been juried on a statewide basis for sale in all shops as well as local people who have passed a similar local jurying process. The percentage of locally juried crafts in any one store is about twenty-five to fifty percent. Although 500 craftspeople have been approved for sale statewide in all stores, that does not mean that you'll see all 500 in each store. The flavor of each store varies depending on the number and quality of the area's local craftspeople and the strength and nature of each local craftbuying market.

The Concord shop carries the work of about 400 craftspeople and is one of the best examples of the wide range of work in the state, from Shaker influenced to strikingly contemporary work. It is, along with the Nashua outlet, one of the more gallery-like of the shops and has more higher-priced craft work than the others. Prices range from a few dollars to about $1,000. The average item costs about $30.

Hours: Daily from 10 A.M. to 5 P.M.
Directions: The shop is located one-and-one-half blocks north of the central intersection of Main and Pleasant Streets in Phenix Hall.

CONCORD GALLERY
205 North Main Street
Concord, New Hampshire 03301
(603) 224-3375

This gallery space was established in 1974 here at the state headquarters of the League of New Hampshire Craftsmen. A series of four to six exhibits are posted annually, each six to eight weeks duration. Shows may range from regional and national traveling exhibits to exhibits of New Hampshire craftspeople or items from the League's permanent collection.

In the past, shows have been mounted on such subjects as New England quilters, toys, handmade paper, group shows and the yearly Annual Juried Exhibit.

While you're visiting the gallery, stop in at the League's information office to pick up their

NEW HAMPSHIRE

available literature. Among other things, they publish an informative Visual Arts Map, which directs you to the state's art galleries, crafts shops and craftsmen's studios.

The League, founded in 1932, is a statewide organization that has long been of extraordinary help to the state's craftspeople. A paid headquarters staff of ten to twelve people and some 600 volunteers across the state provide marketing services for professional craftspeople along with offering educational opportunities at all skill levels.

Hours: Monday through Friday from 10 A.M. to 4 P.M.
Directions: From I-93, take Exit 15W to Main Street. The building is across the intersection next to Friendly's restaurant.

EXETER CRAFT CENTER
61 Water Street
Exeter, New Hampshire 03833
(603) 778-8282

This is the League of New Hampshire Craftsmen's "seacoast shop." In addition to the influence of the nearby sea, the shop's inventory and style is also shaped by its proximity to Boston. "It's more cosmopolitan, contemporary, sculptural," notes shop manager Nancy Pascucci, adding, "the shop has a very casual and friendly ambiance and a nice view of the Exeter River downtown."

About 200 state-juried and 100 locally juried craftspeople have work on display within the long and narrow store's 1,600 square feet. Under the League system, state and local juries consisting of master craftsmen look for such things as quality, expertise in the field and design skills before accepting a new craftsperson's work for display.

Established in the late Sixties in a location down the street, the Exeter center, like other League shops, holds periodic demonstrations of craft techniques. There is also a "highlighted craftsmen of the month" who is given a special display space in the store.

According to Nancy, the "prolific potters in the area" account for the large stock of pottery in the store. There is also a nice assortment of gold and silver jewelry, stained-glass panels, blown glass, baskets, weaving, wrought iron, leather, knitting, prints, soft sculpture and notepaper for sale at prices up to $500. The shop has recently started to display contemporary furniture and plans are to expand in this area.

Exeter is also a major craft education center, offering a year-round schedule of classes organized by Education Chairman and Assistant Manager Anita Durel. Courses are given in many crafts including pottery, weaving, jewelry, quilting, basketry.

Hours: Daily from 9:30 A.M. to 5 P.M.
Directions: From I-95, take Exit 2 to Route 51. Take a left off the Exeter exit ramp onto Portsmouth Avenue and follow to the T-intersection. Take a right at the intersection, which will lead you to Water Street. The shop is two doors past the movie theater on your right.

FRANCONIA LEAGUE OF NEW HAMPSHIRE CRAFTSMEN
Glaessel Building
Franconia, New Hampshire 03580
(603) 823-9521

This northernmost of the ten League of New Hampshire Craftsmen shops is located in a new ski lodge situated at the foot of Cannon Mountain and near the famed Old Man in the Mountains natural stone sculpture. During the winter season the League packs up its shop for the season and the building reverts to serving skiers.

The bright and airy, three-level shop carries the work of more than 250 craftspeople working in pottery, metal, weaving, wood, leather, jewelry, stitchery and glass, at prices ranging to $1,000. Most pieces are between $10 and $25. There is also a large selection of crafts for children, including clothing and stuffed and wooden toys.

During July and August, craft demonstrations are held at the shop twice weekly.

Hours: Open mid-May through mid-October, daily 9 A.M. to 5:30 P.M.
Directions: Take Route 3 or 93 North through the White Mountain National Forest to Franconia Notch. The shop is opposite the tramway.

LEAGUE OF NEW HAMPSHIRE CRAFTSMEN
13 Lebanon Street
Hanover, New Hampshire 03755
(603) 643-5050

Hanover has had a League outlet since 1946. In the Fifties the League cooperated with local members in designing and building this brick, two-story craft center for the sale of crafts and

New Hampshire

to house classrooms for crafts classes.

The shop was a major step for the League and a far cry from their first sales outlets. As part of its grass-roots organizing efforts during the Thirties and Forties, the League fostered as many as twenty-five shops, which were usually operated by local groups in the front room of a private home or in a borrowed barn. The Hanover building was part of the League's drive during the late Forties and Fifties to get more permanent marketing operations into their own buildings.

The building's brick and whitewashed walls, its natural oak trim, open space and large windows form an attractive background for the effective display of craftwork from both local and statewide artisans working in all media.

There is 2,000 square feet of display space utilized for the sale of crafts. Shelves along one long, white wall hold dozens of ceramic pieces while a brick wall (opposite) displays work in a variety of media. Several cases hold a strong selection of jewelry, and there are large stained-glass panels, blown glass, wrought iron and wood. Upstairs, piles of quilts, weaving, rag and woven rugs, pillows, sheepskin articles and a good selection of prints are displayed. Prices go to $1,000 with the average piece selling for $30.

There is also an exhibit space where large pieces and themed displays are regularly shown.

Jane MacKinnon, shop manager for fifteen years, told me that there is a very active schedule of classes given at the center, including weaving, silk screening, jewelry, stained glass and pottery. There are also periodic demonstrations for the public and advanced workshops for the professional.

Hours: Daily from 9:30 A.M. to 5 P.M.
Directions: From I-89, take Route 120 into Hanover. Bear left at the Co-op Food Store and take a left on Lebanon Street. The center is up a couple of blocks on the left.

From I-91, take the Norwich Street exit to the center of town. Take a right on Main Street and a left onto Lebanon Street. The store is on the right.

The Artifactory
25 Lebanon Street
Hanover, New Hampshire 03755
(603) 643-2277

Co-owner Gordy Thomas is a former stained-glass artist who learned the retail craft business in trying to sell his own work to shop and gallery owners. This shop is Gordy's and wife Pam's third location since they opened for business in 1974. Each move has meant an upgrading of the shop decor and this is the most polished interior yet. The work of the store's seventy-five American craftspeople offers a good alternative to the League's New Hampshire orientation in its center next door.

"Our number-one strength is jewelry," notes Gordy. The store carries jewelry in both precious and nonprecious metals and nonmetals. Many different styles are elegantly displayed in the antique cases, with an emphasis on contemporary design.

The remainder of the 800-square-foot store is stocked with a variety of craft work. Woodwork, pottery and glass are emphasized and there is some leather, decorative ironwork and fiber. "One of my major guidelines is that the craft work be functional," Gordy told me. "That's one reason why there's a lot of containers in different media." Prices range up to $350 with the average about $25.

Hours: Daily from 10 A.M. to 5 P.M.
Directions: The store is a few steps down from the League's shop.

Shop at the Institute
Manchester Institute of Arts and Sciences
148 Concord Street
Manchester, New Hampshire 00104
(603) 623-0313

Incorporated in 1899, the Manchester Institute is a private, nonprofit educational learning center, offering year-round classes in fine arts and crafts, music, dance and language.

As part of its activities, the Institute opened this craft shop in 1979. The work of more than 150 craftspeople, about half of whom are from New Hampshire, is offered here. On display is gold and silver jewelry, wooden items, blown and stained glass, stitchery, stoneware and porcelain ceramics, enamels, wrought iron, basketry, soft sculpture, fiberwork and graphics. Prices range from $5 to $350 with most items under $50.

Hours: Daily, 10 A.M. to 5 P.M.
Directions: From I-93, take Bridge Street exit to Union Street. Turn left on Union and proceed to Concord Street. Turn right on Concord.

51 · SHOPS/GALLERIES

New Hampshire

MEREDITH-LACONIA ARTS & CRAFTS
Route 3
Meredith, New Hampshire 03253
(603) 279-7920

The smallest of the ten retail outlets affiliated with the League of New Hampshire Craftsmen, the Meredith operation is the only shop still in its original building. An example of the cottage-style shop characteristic of the League's early years, it was built for them in the early Thirties and was one of the first outlets opened by the newly founded organization.

The building itself was moved twice over the years before settling in overlooking Meredith Bay on this main access route to New Hampshire's beautiful Lake Winnipesaukee resort area. It's not far from Squam Lake, where some scenes from the movie *Golden Pond* were filmed, and is just south of the White Mountain National Forest.

This cheerful and bright shop sells the work of 150 craftspeople. About twenty-five percent of the artisans come from the local area, the rest from across the state.

"We sell a lot of pottery and jewelry," notes newly appointed manager Chris Ketchum. There is also an assortment of lamps and shades, stained-glass panels, weaving and quilted work. Look for the specially selected crafts and spotlighted craftspeople on the center display table. Prices range from $1 to $500 with an average estimated at $25.

As with other League shops, workshops and demonstrations are held throughout the season.

The Meredith shop is an excellent starting point for a tour of New Hampshire's breathtaking lakes region and the nearby White Mountain foothills. These areas are served by three other historic and nearby shops (Center Sandwich, North Conway and Wolfeboro) and a fourth, Franconia, that is a pleasant jaunt about one hour north through the White Mountain National Forest. Any of the shop's workers will be happy to give you directions and answer questions on the area.

Hours: Open from May 1 to December 31 seven days a week from 9:30 A.M. to 5:30 P.M.
Directions: I-93 to Exit 20. Follow Route 3 to just south of Meredith. The shop is on the right.

RAINBOW'S END
Main Street
Meredith, New Hampshire 03253
(603) 279-6221

There is a general theme of fantasy running through most of the work displayed in this small shop, which is not surprising when you consider that its two owner/craftspeople, silversmith Jack Dokus and fiber artist Bobbi Jo Free, both specialize in that genre. You'll often find one or the other working at their respective craft while tending shop.

There are about twelve craftspeople besides Bobbi Jo and Jack whose work is displayed in the 350-square-foot shop, which they've "built bit by bit" over the past three years. Most of the craftspeople live within a thirty-mile radius of Meredith.

"We encourage everybody to give us their unusual and one-of-a-kind pieces," Jack told me, noting that the work must be "clearly and technically made to a professional finish."

Besides the soft sculpture, jewelry and metal sculpture of its owners, the shop carries pottery, baskets, weaving, stained glass, quilting, woodturning, painting and photography. Prices range up to $500.

Hours: Open during the summer Monday through Saturday from 9:30 A.M. to 5:00 P.M.
Directions: From Exit 20 off I-93, follow Route 3 to the junction with Route 25 in Meredith. Turn left and go up the hill to Main Street. Go a few blocks and you'll find the shop on your left opposite the library.

THE GOLDEN TOAD
65 Elm Street
Milford, New Hampshire 03055
(603) 673-4307

You'll find a little bit of everything in this ten-year-old shop, which houses an eclectic collection of traditional and contemporary crafts on the first floor of a large old house.

As with other non-League shops and galleries in the state, the work of many out-of-state craftspeople is carried here to offer an alternative. "We try to deal with things that you won't ordinarily find in this area," notes manager Kathy McNamara.

A large collection of pottery and kitchenware dominates one room; in another there is a collection of jewelry and glass; one room is set aside for crafts for kids; another for leather items; and another for notecards and station-

New Hampshire

ery. There are also works in metal, wood and fiber. Prices range up to about $300.

"It is always a delight to visit because new ideas are always coming in," says owner Sandra Hammond.

Hours: Daily from 11 A.M. to 5:30 P.M.; Sunday from 1 to 5:30 P.M.
Directions: From Route 3 take Exit 7W in Nashua onto Route 101A West. Continue ten miles, go through the oval in Milford center, continue about one-half mile and you'll find The Golden Toad perched on the right.

ARTISANS EAST
147 Main Street
Nashua, New Hampshire 03060
(603) 882-4171

Artisans East, which was established in 1932 as part of the statewide League of New Hampshire Craftsmen, has occupied this location in the center of downtown Nashua since 1981.

Nashua is a southern New Hampshire urban center and the inventory reflects its location: More contemporary, more experimental, more higher-priced crafts are available here from about 200 craftspeople.

Among the crafts shown in the 1,875-square-foot space are pottery, blown glass, baskets, rugs, jewelry, weaving, fiber, pewter, wrought iron, toys, wooden items, clothes and leatherwork. Prices start at 50 cents and range to $1,000.

Hours: Daily, 9:30 A.M. to 5:30 P.M.; Thursday until 9 P.M.
Directions: Take Exits 3, 4, 5 or 7 East off the Everett Turnpike. The shop is at the corner of Main and Factory Streets in the heart of downtown Nashua.

LEAGUE OF NEW HAMPSHIRE CRAFTSMEN
Main Street
North Conway, New Hampshire 03860
(603) 356-2441

The Conways have had a League of New Hampshire Craftsmen shop since 1932, the year the League itself was founded. According to League records, for the next twenty-four years the shop "shifted from pillar to post," until 1956, when the League purchased the building that has since been occupied by its retail shop.

The homey shop is housed in a wood-frame

The Golden Toad

building at the end of Main Street in a gorgeous ski area and tourist playground.

There are about 300 craftspeople represented here in pottery, wood, glass, iron, gold and silver jewelry, fiber, stained glass, furniture, clothing, baskets and prints. There is an emphasis on North Country items—sheepskins, heavy fibers and the like—and there is a special Maine flavor due to the shop's proximity to the border. (League rules allow out-of-state craftspeople who live within ten miles of the border to be juried for display locally.) Craft items in the 1,200-square-foot shop are priced from 50¢ for a notecard up to $2,200.

Like the other League shops, the Conway group sponsors an active schedule of classes in varied media on levels from novice to professional.

Hours: Open seven days from 9 A.M. to 5:30 P.M.; during July and August open from 9 A.M. to 9 P.M.
Directions: From I-95, take the Spaulding Turnpike to Route 16 and follow north into North Conway. The shop is on Route 16 across from the Congregational Church.

From I-93, take Route 104 to Route 25 to Route 16 and follow to North Conway.

NEW HAMPSHIRE

TEWKSBURY'S
Route 101
Peterborough, New Hampshire 03458
(603) 924-3224

The first day that Ted and Roberta Tewksbury arrived here from Boston fourteen years ago they found for sale a large white house and barn that was to later house their craft shop and gallery. They quickly purchased the property and for the next two years Ted set about renovating the 160-year-old barn.

Today Tewksbury's well-respected craft shop displays the work of sixty craftspeople in the pine-paneled, post-and-beam construction barn. Work includes pewter, woodenware, pottery, handcut crystal, blown glass, weaving, sterling-silver and gold jewelry, soft sculpture, leather and paper. Prices start at $5 up to $800.

Two years ago the Tewksburys established an art gallery in the barn's loft space, where they exhibit paintings and graphics from thirty artists.

"Our standards for buying are as high as for our own past craftwork," Roberta told me. When they opened their shop, Ted was a cabinetmaker and Roberta worked in enamels. "Our growth has forced us to give up our crafts in order to manage our shop," she says.

Hours: January through May, open Wednesday to Saturday from 10 A.M. to 5 P.M.; June to December, open daily from 10 A.M. to 5 P.M. and Sunday from 1 to 5 P.M.

SHARON ARTS CENTER
Route 123
Peterborough, New Hampshire 03458
(603) 924-7256

The Sharon Arts Center is a major southern New Hampshire arts and crafts education center founded in 1947 and situated in the beautiful Monadnock region. Nestled deep in the woods, the tiny town of Sharon (population 160) is dominated by the activity taking place in the center's complex of buildings. More than 25,000 people annually visit the center, which includes nine teaching studios and classrooms for various arts and crafts, a library and administrative office, a respected exhibition gallery and a handcraft shop affiliated with the League of New Hampshire Craftsmen.

The work of 300 New Hampshire craftspeople is represented in the shop, which has operated for more than thirty-five years. All work has been juried by either the local or the state League committees of professional craftsmen. Crafts available here include pottery, quilts, woodenware, jewelry, blown and stained glass, metalwork, fibers, prints and photographs. Prices start at $1 and go as high as $2,400.

The shop features monthly exhibits of either an individual's work or a themed grouping. Regular demonstrations of various craft techniques are also given in the shop.

The gallery, which was built in 1955, mounts year-round exhibits of the work of New England artists, including painting, drawing, prints, sculpture and some crafts.

Hours: Open Monday through Saturday from 10 A.M. to 5 P.M.; Sunday from 1 to 5 P.M.
Directions: The center is located on Route 123, about four miles south of the intersection of Route 101 and 123 in Peterborough.

SANDWICH HOME INDUSTRIES
Main Street
Sandwich, New Hampshire 03227
(603) 284-6831

Although the League of New Hampshire Craftsmen was founded in 1932, its roots can be traced in part back to the mid-Twenties right here to this tiny village in the foothills of the White Mountains.

In 1926 local resident Mary Hill Coolidge worked with the Sandwich Historical Society in organizing a display of hooked and braided rugs made by local craftspeople. That successful outing was followed later that year by the opening of a shop selling local crafts in a small vacant village store.

Around the same time, a group that had started to give craft classes in nearby Wolfeboro joined with the Sandwich group to form a cooperative committee to investigate ways to support a crafts movement statewide.

In 1931 they succeeded in getting the governor to establish and fund the New Hampshire Commission on the Arts, the first state-funded arts commission in the country. One year later the commissioners, which included the Sandwich and Wolfeboro organizers, founded the League "to preserve the state's craft traditions" and to provide much-needed supplemental income in the rural areas. Mrs. Coolidge served as the league's first president until her retirement in 1941.

So it can rightfully be said that the folks in Sandwich have played an important part in the

New Hampshire

birth and growth of the statewide crafts movement. They've been doing this for nearly sixty years, by golly, and judging from the look of their shop, they've got it down exactly right.

The distinguished white Colonial building on the town green is only the third location in the organization's history, having been built in 1934 after a fire wiped out the small, second shop. One hundred twenty craftspeople are represented in its spacious, raftered and pine-paneled rooms. The Industries prides itself on its long history of providing an outlet for traditional local crafts, as well as encouragement to contemporary craftspeople and new techniques. This pride is evident throughout the building's 4,000 square feet, where a variety of traditional and contemporary work is shown from both local communities and throughout the state.

Crafts on sale here include weaving, needlework, embroidery, hooked and braided rugs, pottery, jewelry, woodwork, decorative and functional iron work, enameling, botanical lampshades, sculpture, lithography and calligraphy. Prices run from $5 to $100.

As with the other League shops, a local jury of professional craftspeople approves all work to be sold locally while a state jury passes judgment on crafts from out of the area that are to be sold in the shop.

Craft demonstrations are held in the shop several times a week during July and August and a full schedule of craft classes is supported year round.

Hours: Open Memorial Day weekend to October 15, seven days a week from 10 A.M. to 5 P.M. An outdoor art exhibit is held during mid-August.

Directions: From I-93, take Route 104 to Meredith, then Route 25 to Moultonboro to Route 109 which leads to Center Sandwich.

SCHOOLHOUSE SHOP
South Main Street
Wolfeboro, New Hampshire 03894
(603) 569-3489

The sign welcoming you to Wolfeboro in New Hampshire's scenic lakes region bears the inscription, "The Oldest Summer Resort in America." There could also be a sign that reads, "The Co-Birthplace of New Hampshire's Crafts Movement."

In the Twenties the Wolfeboro Rotary Club sponsored crafts classes organized by A. Cooper Ballantine, a craft educator who

Sandwich Home Industries

worked in the summer-camp field. Mr. Ballantine took his group to Sandwich to explore with a local craft group there, who had opened a small shop, ways to broaden what he thought could be a movement to offer marketing support and technical training to craftspeople statewide.

That initial meeting led to the formation of a cooperative committee that gave birth, with the state's help, in 1932 to the League of New Hampshire Craftsmen. The first two shops in the League were the already existing outlets in Sandwich and here in Wolfeboro.

After being housed in a number of private homes, the Wolfeboro shop moved into its own modest quarters on the town wharf in 1948. The shop was relocated in 1965 when the League purchased from the town a 1901 school building in South Wolfeboro.

Today the schoolhouse, with its old bell still intact, displays the work of more than 250 craftspeople whose work has been approved by either local juries or by the League's state-wide system.

Displayed throughout the 2,000-square-foot space are crafts in all media, including weaving, woodturning, pottery, clothing, knitting, baskets, furniture, stained and blown glass and iron work. Prices start at $1 with the upper end at $500.

The shop offers monthly exhibits during the season and holds an annual craft fair on the lawn in July. The local group also sponsors a year-round series of craft instruction and workshops for beginner to professional.

Hours: Open the first week of May to October 15, seven days a week from 9:30 A.M. to 5:30 P.M.
Directions: The shop is six miles south of Wolfeboro on Route 28.

Rhode Island

Small Axe Productions
The Fantastic Umbrella Factory
Charlestown, Rhode Island 02813
(401) 364-6616

This five-year-old cooperatively owned and run shop is a part of a restored 19th-century farmyard. The building housing the co-op was moved from across the street and used to be the headquarters of Narragansett's Temple of Honor No. 10, a men's temperance society. Today, the place is outfitted with pine displays that nicely show the work of the co-op's five members and seven other Rhode Island craftspeople.

The 550-square-foot space offers stoneware pottery, stained glass, leather bags and belts, musical instruments, weaving and quilting. Prices vary from $2.50 up to $100 with the average price $12 to $15.

The co-op building is one of several on this five-acre farm. A working farm since 1790, it had been abandoned for many years until new owner Robert Bankel, a former art teacher, started renovating it in 1968. The dominant motif here is rusticity—at first glance it seems that there is nary a straight board in the place. Bark-covered post-and-rail fences twist through the farmyard marking the narrow pebble pathways leading to the various attractions outside and in the three main buildings.

The main barn was the first building to be restored. Originally it housed the working studios of several craftspeople. Today it is a wonderful gift shop, full of interesting and odd stuff. The 18th-century building has multiple levels that, observes Bob, "go up and down, here and there." "Duck or Bump" is the good advice given by one sign.

The barn is filled with notecards, candy, toys, paper and party goods, mugs and commercial ceramics, "things to put things in," kites, records and more. Scattered throughout both here and in the other buildings are Bob's collection of antique toys and old jukeboxes.

Nearby, in another part of the barn, a cafe called Salmagundy's offers three meals daily during the season. Chef Dennis Ury, a former architect, makes most everything on the premises. There is seating for two dozen inside or

The Fantastic Umbrella Factory

RHODE ISLAND

you can eat underneath the arbor or in a nearby flower garden.

There are ten flower gardens on the grounds, all cultivated by experienced groundskeeper Patrick Shellman. Depending on the time of year, Patrick makes available cut flowers, dried herbs, pumpkins or decorative gourds.

Across the way, there is a small clothing store that sells an eclectic collection of new-wave, antique and military surplus apparel as well as things like sunglasses and small, whimsical sculpture toys.

Outside, a variety of livestock roam about. Ducks, goats, sheep, geese, peacocks and a horse all call the farm home. There are also penned together some dozen different varieties of exotic and thoroughbred chickens, including a pair of Japanese silkies. These strange birds have the fur and coloring of Angora cats, except that they're chickens.

Hours: The farm is open from June 24 to Labor Day daily from 10 A.M. to 6 P.M.; from September to November, Wednesday to Sunday from 10 A.M. to 5 P.M.; and from Thanksgiving to Christmas daily from 10 A.M. to 6 P.M.
Directions: From Route 1 in Charlestown, take the Ningret Park Wildlife Refuge exit. Go one-half mile. The Fantastic Umbrella Factory is on the right.

THE SPECTRUM
Bannister's Wharf
Newport, Rhode Island 02840
(401) 847-4477

Like the five other Spectrum craft galleries and shops, the Newport location, established in 1976, carries the work of more than 200 craftspeople. As is the style in this sophisticated craft-retailing organization, the crafts are displayed on gallerylike whitewashed pedestals and shelving, which are effectively deployed around this split-level and beamed store in the heart of Newport's wharf area.

The crafts on display include ceramics, weaving, wood, jewelry, leather, enamels and glass, as well as some flat art. Prices range from $5 to $2,500.

Hours: During the summer, open seven days, 10 A.M. to 10 P.M.; off-season, seven days, 10 A.M. to 5 P.M.
Directions: From I-195, take Route 24 South then Route 114 South into downtown Newport.

From I-95 take Route 138 East across the Jamestown and Newport Bridges and follow the signs to downtown. Bannister's Wharf is adjacent to Bowen's Wharf and the Treadway.

LILY G. ISELIN
218 Wickenden Street
Providence, Rhode Island 02903
(401) 272-9769

The two-year-old gallery posts ten shows a year, about half of them craftwork of museum quality and half non-craft art.

Each show exhibits from three to eight craftspeople who owner Lily Iselin chooses for work that is "well-made, innovative, well designed and, hopefully, saleable." In the past, show themes have included glass, ceramics, furniture, tapestry and metalsmithing. The noncraft shows include painting, graphics, sculpture and photography. Craft work is priced from $300 to $2,000.

Lily has retained the slightly funky charm of the old space, whose interior, once a bar, has been whitewashed in typical gallery style.

The 600-square-foot gallery is located on an emerging street in a changing neighborhood. It is flanked by Citywings Bookstore and This & That Antiques and a number of popular bars and cafes are in the area. It is a comfortable gallery on a pleasant street.

Hours: Tuesday through Saturday from noon to 5 P.M.
Directions: From I-95, head east on I-195. Exit at Wickenden Street, turn left at the bottom of the exit and go about a block. The gallery is on the left.

From Route 6, head west on I-195. Exit at Game Street. Go left and jog right onto Wickenden. The gallery is up five or six blocks on your right.

THE SPECTRUM
27-29 The Arcade
Providence, Rhode Island 02903
(401) 273-1590

The experienced folks at The Spectrum chain of craft galleries and shops have managed to squeeze a well-balanced selection from their inventory of high-quality crafts into this smallest of their six locations.

The crafts on display here include jewelry, ceramics, weaving, woods, enamels, leather and glass. The price range is $6 to $1,000 with

RHODE ISLAND

an average of $20 to $100.

The shop occupies 630 square feet at the end of the second tier in The Arcade, a successful restoration project in Providence's financial district. The large Greek Revival building was built in 1827 to house the country's first shopping mall. After many later years of decline, it fell into disrepair until it was renovated in 1980 amid much hoopla. Today the bustling atmosphere is reminiscent of Boston's Quincy Market.

Brightly colored banners festoon the building's open interior, which is marvelously sunlit by the original full-ceiling gable skylight. On the first floor a dozen internationally flavored fast-food places beckon the hungry; on the upper two levels, intricately detailed iron railings mark the terraced walkways leading to the Arcade's many boutiques and shops. This colorful mall is a pleasant diversion for both tourists and natives alike.

Hours: Monday through Saturday from 10 A.M. to 6 P.M.; Thursday open until 8 P.M.
Directions: Take the downtown Providence exit off I-95, The Arcade is in the heart of the financial district on Westminster Street.

DIFFERENT DRUMMER
7 West Main Street
Wickford, Rhode Island 02852
(401) 294-4867

You wouldn't normally find two professional craft shops so close together in a town the size of Wickford. But this quaint quahoging village indeed boasts two such shops just a few minutes walk apart. The shops, both owned by James Graham, each carry a selection of crafts completely different from the other.

Jim started his first shop, Different Drummer, in 1973. "My enthusiasm has not waned in all these years," he notes. Jim told me that he has had an interest in crafts since his days as an undergraduate at the Rhode Island School of Design.

"I wanted to be a potter," he remembers. "One day my advisor asked me if I wanted to make money or be creative. I thought about that and became an industrial designer."

The Drummer is housed in a mid-19th century brick building that used to be the town's fish market. The 600-square-foot shop is quite low key in appearance, using such things as old wooden cable spools as display fixtures.

The crafts here are mostly smaller functional pieces. "I buy the things I like," Jim told me, "and display and sell only the finest quality contemporary work; the standards of craftsmanship are high in all cases."

More than 100 craftspeople are represented here by work that includes pottery, jewelry, mobiles, wind chimes, small stained- and etched-glass pieces and woodenware. There are also a few commercial gift items mixed in with the crafts. Prices range from $5 to $200 with an average price of $10 to $15. The jewelry is mostly sterling silver and is priced from $5 to $50.

Hours: Daily from 10 A.M. to 6 P.M.; Sunday from noon to 6 P.M.
Directions: Take Route 1A directly into Wickford. The shop is located in the center of the village near the intersection.

J. W. GRAHAM
26 Brown Street
Wickford, Rhode Island 02852
(401) 295-0757

Jim Graham didn't intend to open another craft shop just down the street from his first, but the marketplace ultimately dictated the shop's destiny. J. W. Graham was opened in 1980 as a designer furniture store selling high-tech furniture and contemporary manufactured-glass items. That idea didn't work out.

"Competition made me go to what we do best," notes Jim, who converted the bright and airy shop into another craft operation.

This made store manager Susan Smith very happy. "I hated it when we sold furniture," she admits, adding, "Nobody ever came. Now we're nice and busy all the time." Susan told me that the shop's 700 square feet of display space will soon be enlarged to about 1,200 feet.

The look here is decidedly more contemporary and spacious than its neighbor craft shop. A wooden floor and ceiling and polished wood displays highlight the bright space, which displays crafts from more than fifty craftspeople. You'll find rag rugs and fiber wall hangings, stoneware and porcelain pieces including some lamps, blown, etched and stained glass work, pillows, wood, soft sculpture and notecards. Prices range from $2 to $300 with the average estimated to be about $30.

Hours: Daily from 10 A.M. to 5 P.M.; Sunday from noon to 5 P.M.
Directions: Wickford is about twenty miles south of Providence on Route 1A. Look for the blue banner outside the store.

VERMONT

HAWKINS HOUSE
262 North Street
Bennington, Vermont 05201
(802) 447-0488

Ronald and Inga Spivak started their shop/gallery in 1977 at the Hawkins House in nearby Shaftsbury where Inga had her weaving studio. In 1980 they moved to this pleasant-looking two-story brick building, one of the oldest in Bennington. While Inga continues to maintain her studio at the original Hawkins House, Ronald and Debra Fisher, the shop manager, run things here.

The three rooms downstairs and the upstairs space total about 1,500 square feet, which according to Ronald houses the largest collection of professional crafts in southern Vermont. More than 200 craftspeople from the New England area are represented.

Upstairs there's a collection of imported and American clothing handwoven from silks, cottons and wools, including a good representation of Inga's woven pieces. Other fiber work includes traditional and contemporary quilts and crocheted hats and vests.

Downstairs in the front room, an extensive collection of contemporary, classic and antique designs by thirty-five to forty jewelers is prominently displayed in about a dozen display cases. Pottery dominates the second room, with the functional stoneware and porcelain displayed on the pine shelves according to weight and color. In the back room, work in assorted media is displayed. A corner is devoted to "country store items" of inexpensive, strictly production objects of wood, clay and fiber, "fun items that will appeal to the tourists."

The shop also has a fine collection of blown glass, leather handbags and belts, handwrought iron, candles, toys and, say the Spivaks, "whatever else entices and inspires us."

Prices range from $5 to $350 with occasional one-of-a-kind show pieces to $3,500. The average price is $22 with silver jewelry slightly higher.

There are special exhibits held during the summer and the fall featuring individual craftspeople or theme shows.

Hours: Daily from 10 A.M. to 5:30 P.M.; Sunday noon to 5:30 P.M.
Directions: Hawkins House is right on Route 7 at the corner of County Street in the heart of Bennington.

THE SILK PURSE & THE SOW'S EAR
Routes 12 and 107, P.O. Box 169
Bethel, Vermont 05032
(802) 234-5368

This friendly shop is housed in a building that previously was the home of what Silk Purse co-owner Maynard Nelson describes as a "notorious derelict bar" known in these parts for its regular brawls, including the occasional gunfight.

Much to everyone's relief, after the joint finally closed, the building was bought and renovated by Maynard and Donna Nelson, newly arrived from Massachusetts. Maynard, a professional woodworker who did the renovation and built the shop's displays, remembers that the transition six years ago from bar to craft shop was not without its distractions: "One day after we had been open for some time, a biker roared up to our building, came in, took a

The Silk Purse

VERMONT

look, and said, 'Boy, you people have really messed things up,' turned around and left."

The biker was wrong. The Nelsons have successfully created an unpretentious shop containing a nice blend of country and contemporary crafts made by more than 150 local and regional artisans. Donna, who manages the shop, told me that she buys only "well-made, neat and clean crafts—no kits allowed—the overall design must be pleasing to the eye and the soul."

This shop is chockablock with craft items. Among the displays you'll find pottery, quilts, jewelry, handwoven woolens, leather bags, soft sculptures, toys, rag and woven rugs, cards, cushions, candles, and more. Also carried along with the craftwork are some folk and traditional record albums, artwork, New England books, clothes and antique tools.

Ninety percent of the crafts are made by professionals, the rest by local craftspeople, who, according to Donna, are mostly women who supplement their income through their part-time work at their craft. She estimates that the average price of the craft items is about $15 to $20 with a price range of 85¢ to $600.

When I visited the shop, which derives its name from Maynard's skill at restoring old furniture, the Nelsons were preparing to double the shop's display space from its present size of about 400 square feet. They are planning to utilize the new space for the display of some larger pieces and custom furniture.

Hours: Daily from 9 A.M. to 5 P.M.
Directions: From I-89 take Exit 3 and proceed to Bethel. The shop is at the corner of Routes 12 and 107 right by the railroad bridge.

L. J. SERKIN CO.
51 Elliot Street
Brattleboro, Vermont 05301
(802) 257-7044

L. J. Serkin has been the place to go for contemporary professional crafts in Brattleboro for nearly ten years. In 1980 weaver Meg Howland bought the shop where today she displays the work of eighty craftspeople as well as more than 100 varieties of wool, several models of looms and a large selection of prints and selected posters.

Half of the 1,700-square-foot store is used for the display of craftwork that Meg notes is "only the highest quality of work showing excellent design and technique." Well displayed on wood and glass fixtures, most of the work is done by area professionals who, Meg emphasizes, "rank with the national best."

The shop's collection of functional and limited-production crafts includes pottery, weaving, wooden objects, blown glass, jewelry and basketry. Prices range from $5 to $250. Meg does most of the weaving that's on display.

Hours: Daily from 10 A.M. to 5:30 P.M.
Directions: From I-91 take Exit 2 to Route 9 East (Brattleboro). Take a right on Main Street and at the first right, turn onto Elliot Street. Store is on the right.

DESIGNERS CIRCLE
21 Church Street
Burlington, Vermont 05401
(802) 864-4238

The two couples who own and run this basement-level shop/gallery have accumulated many years of experience both as working craftspeople and managers of the respected Craftproducers Markets, organizers of six professional fairs in and around Vermont.

The partners, Riki Moss and Charley Dooley, and Dennis and Judy Bosch, have capitalized on their collective experience and put together an attractively laid out 1,800-square-foot store that represents about 150 New England craftspeople. "We carry the best quality, professional craftwork in New England," Riki told me. "We consider value as well as aesthetics, always looking for new, interesting craftwork in many media." Sixty percent of the artisans represented in the shop are from Vermont, the rest from elsewhere in New England. Riki estimates that the average price for their crafts is about $40 including the higher priced jewelry.

"We feature one-of-a-kind pieces and try to keep a person's work together," she notes. A variety of contemporary displays — shelves, cabinets, chrome and glass displays, cubbyholes and walls are effectively used to show everything "from honey dippers to diamonds." The prices range from $1 to $5,000.

Blown and stained production and art glass are well displayed in front of backlighted translucent Plexiglas panels, which compensate for the store's lack of natural light. A large collection of gold and silver jewelry is displayed in cabinets that are organized by jeweler. Like almost everything else in the store, the jewelry is clearly labeled with the craftperson's name and home town.

Also represented in the store are porcelain

and stoneware, wood accessories "from commercial to exquisite," lamps, scarves, woven and batiked clothing, pewter, wrought iron, soft sculpture and small woven rugs. A few beautiful quilts are displayed upstairs in the entryway display.

The store is located in Church Street Marketplace, which has been heralded nationally as one of the country's outstanding downtown pedestrian malls.

Hours: Daily from 9:30 A.M. to 5:30 P.M. Open Friday until 9:30.
Directions: From I-89 take Exit 14W (University of Vermont). Get on Route 2 West to Main Street, follow signs for parking; walk to Church Street Marketplace. The store is at the far end on the left.

THE VERMONT STATE CRAFT CENTER AT FROG HOLLOW
Middlebury, Vermont 06753
(802) 388-3177

If you want a vivid representation of the nature of Vermont-made professional handcrafts, there are no better places to go than the Vermont State Craft Centers at Frog Hollow and in Windsor.

The center at Frog Hollow was the first facility of its kind in the country, dedicated to the marketing of the state's professionally made handcrafts and, through educational programs, "informing and involving the public in the process and pleasure of crafts."

Frog Hollow opened in 1971 under private sponsorship and was designated a state craft center in 1975. Although both it and its counterpart in Windsor do not receive state funds, the nonprofit center is advised by a board appointed by the Governor and benefits from the state's official recognition. Operating funds are derived from commissions on gallery sales, arts endowments and private and corporate donations. Each year an estimated 35,000 people come to the center to see the work of more than 200 of the state's finest craftspeople and to participate in its educational activities.

Located alongside Otter Creek Falls in downtown Middlebury, the center's collection of crafts is housed in an old mill building, where once spinning-wheel bobbins were produced. A monthly jurying process selects new craftspeople who meet the stringent guidelines for "original design and execution." Once selected, their work is put on display in one of the three large beamed rooms of this 3,000-square-foot gallery.

Whitewashed wood-plank walls, pedestals and other display fixtures combine with thoughtful arrangements of the craftwork so as to impart an open and clean look despite the large amount of crafts being exhibited. "Not junky or cluttered" is how one shop worker accurately put it.

Among the crafts on display here are many examples of pottery, weaving, quilts, jewelry, prints, stained and blown glass, wrought iron, furniture and wooden objects, clothing, sculpture and prints. Prices range from $1 to $3,000 with the average estimated to be $20.

Gallery manager Nancy Dunn does a masterful job of regularly changing the displays in this well-rounded collection of small- and large-scale craft items. Additionally, eight major shows are mounted each year, with the focus on individual work or on a theme show. Past shows have included themes like "winter into spring," folk art, group shows in basketry and tableware and many one- and two-person shows.

In the lower level of the building, studios house three resident craftspeople: a potter, a weaver and a pipemaker. Visitors are encouraged to watch them at work and ask questions. The center also offers some year-round craft classes for both adults and children.

Hours: Daily from 9:30 A.M. to 5 P.M.
Directions: Take Route 7 north or south to Middlebury. Frog Hollow is in downtown Middlebury, just off Main Street by Otters Creek.

Frog Hollow

VERMONT

THE ARTISANS' HAND
7 Langdon Street
Montpelier, Vermont 05602
(802) 229-9492

This cooperatively owned shop/gallery is now in its fifth year of presenting the work of central Vermont's professional craftspeople. Along with the co-op's eighteen members, another forty craftspeople have been juried for display in the two rooms that comprise the shop in this old downtown building. Large windows throughout the corner space allow much natural light into the high-ceilinged shop where handsome oak moldings nicely accentuate the well-done displays of primarily functional crafts.

Included in this 800-square-foot store are pottery, weaving, jewelry, woodwork, blown glass, lamps, puppets, soft sculpture, quilts, leather and cards. The average price is estimated to be about $20 with a range of fifty cents to $300.

One of the advantages of browsing in a co-op craft outlet is that you're likely to be able to talk directly to one of the craftspeople-owners, who rotate shifts behind the counter.

Hours: Daily from 10 A.M. to 5:30 P.M.
Directions: From Exit 8 off I-89, take Route 2 East to Montpelier's business district. Go right at the stop light (Main Street) and take second right onto Langdon Street. The shop is at the end of the street by the Winooski River bridge.

TRILLIUM FINE CRAFTS
The 1820 House
Main Street
Norwich, Vermont 05055
(802) 649-1695

This small shop in a corner of a beautifully restored early 19th-century home is packed with well-made commercial craft items. Not one inch of space is left uncovered here as owner Barbara Tierney Wyckoff has managed to squeeze examples of some 150 artisans' work into her 400-square-foot shop. Although the store has a gift-store feel upon first entering, the crafts connoisseur will, upon a closer look, find some good examples of high-quality work of mostly professional, local and New England craftspeople.

Crafts on display include wooden objects, leather, glass, pottery, handweaving, jewelry, toys, soft sculpture, some apparel and home accessories. Also for sale is a large selection of handmade rubber stamps and some antique furniture reproductions, which like everything else in the store are used for display purposes. Prices range from $1 to $400.

Hours: Daily from 10 A.M. to 5 P.M.
Directions: From I-91 take Exit 13. Take a left and go straight into the center of Norwich. The 1820 House is on the right in the center of town directly across from the Inn at Norwich.

SAMARA
Route 108, P.O. Box 1115
Stowe, Vermont 05672
(802) 253-8318

Samara is the winged fruit of the maple tree. At Samara, says the store brochure, "the name takes on a special meaning, for it is also the seed of an idea ... the celebration of those special people, the Vermont craftsmen whose work is represented here."

The store, which also carries the work of non-Vermont craft professionals, was started nearly eleven years ago. It was later sold to one of its first staffers and the store's present owner, Lynn Miles, an "ex-portfolio analyst and ski bum." Lynn has since developed a wide selection of high quality handcrafted items by 250 craftspeople, "preferably local whenever possible," nicely displayed in the 900-square-foot store.

There's a good selection of quilts, stoneware and porcelain, gold, silver, bronze and brass jewelry, pillows, mobiles, ceramic lamps, stained and blown glass, wrought iron, soft sculpture, candles, woodenware and a selection of whimsical gift-type items.

"People tell me that our shop has a sense of humor," Lynn says, adding, "with crafts becoming slicker, we are still a value-conscious shop." Lynn and Sales Manager K. C. Colt estimate that their average price is $20 with a range of $1 to $250.

"One of the real joys of this business is that I've worked with some of our craftspeople for almost eleven years now," Lynn told me. "They're our friends. It's great; not like dealing with the Sear's catalog."

Hours: Daily from 10 A.M. to 5:30 P.M.; Sunday noon to 5 P.M.
Directions: From I-89 take Route 100 (Exit 10) to Stowe village. Take a left onto Route 108. Samara is two miles north of the village on Route 108 in the West Branch Shops.

VERMONT

THE STOWE POTTERY
Route 108
Stowe, Vermont 05672

"You could make a pretty nice house out of all the old signs of the businesses that have come and gone in Stowe," observes Jean-Paul Patnode, a potter who since 1967 has owned and operated this classic craft shop near the center of Stowe village.

"You have to have some sort of criteria to make it," he told me. "Mine are that the crafts must be the best made, well thought out and well designed." The shop is housed in a 108-year-old building that was formerly a blacksmith shop.

Jean-Paul's pottery wheel is right in the middle of the shop where visitors can watch as he throws his plates, pots, vases and pitchers in a variety of styles. Off to the sides of the main room are the claymaking, glazing and kiln room, also open to visitors.

Besides his own pottery, displayed on pebble-filled wooden tables skirted with burlap, Jean-Paul sells a fine collection of mostly functional crafts from dozens of craftspeople. The craftwork is displayed along the stained wooden walls of the 600-square-foot shop and in several antique display cabinets. You'll find pewterware, ironwork, blown glass, wooden utensils and objects, weaving, wood-block prints and some jewelry, all effectively lit by recycled matte-black painter's lamps.

According to Jean-Paul, the price range is $5 to $300 with an estimated average price of $10 to $15.

Hours: Daily from 9 A.M. to 5 P.M.
Directions: Take Exit 10 from I-89. Proceed on Route 100 about ten miles to Stowe village. Take a left at Route 108, go about 100 yards; the shop is in the red building on the left near the covered bridge.

CRAFT-HAUS
Top of the Hill Road
Wilmington, Vermont 05363
(802) 464-2164

Ursula Tancrel's gold and silver cloisonné jewelry and the work of four or five glassblowers will be of the most interest to craft collectors here. What will be of interest to everybody is the glorious view of Haystack Mountain and Mount Snow from the Craft-Haus, which is located in the downstairs level of Ursula and Ed Tancrel's hilltop house.

The 550-square-foot shop, which displays the work of about eighteen craftspeople, also has pottery, stained-glass shades and oil paintings, watercolors and prints. All work is one of a kind and prices range from a few dollars up to $1,200. Ed also maintains a framing shop in the small space.

"We've been tempted to enlarge," Ursula told me, "but people really like the personal service that we give them." The Tancrels don't advertise their shop very much, primarily depending on the clientele that they've built up over the past seven years. "People are pleasantly surprised when they find us," notes Ursula.

Hours: Open weekends from 10 A.M. to 5 P.M.; weekdays "by good chance or appointment." Closed Wednesdays.
Directions: From either Route 7 to the west or I-91 to the east, take Route 9 to Wilmington. In Wilmington, take Route 100 North to Stowe Hill Road. Proceed up the hill two miles and turn right.

KLARA SIMPLA
10 Main Street
Wilmington, Vermont 06363
(802) 464-5257

According to the guidelines that I established for being listed here, Klara Simpla would ordinarily not be included. But the ambiance of this shop is truly unique and not to be missed if you're in the Wilmington area.

Owner Frances Hollander has over the past seventeen years put together a sort of holistic country store that sells, in her words, "books, food and utile things." You'll have a most pleasant time browsing through the hundreds of items displayed in this 200-year-old former livery stable; it is a treat for the senses, a feast for the mind, and quite possibly a boon to your health. "Klara simpla," incidentally, is Esperanto for "clear and simple."

Although at one time the Vermont Craftproducers Market, now sponsors of six craft fairs, used to have some seventy craftspeople's work on display here, presently there are less than a dozen amateur and professional craftspeople represented with primarily utilitarian, practical objects on display. "This is a place where beginners can get feedback from local people and customers," Frances told me. "However, we do have fine professional work also." Among the craft items are woodenware, flameware, stained and blown glass, soapstone, bas-

63 · SHOPS/GALLERIES

VERMONT

ketry, woven fiber and tinware. Prices range from $5 to $200.

It's the rest of the store, however, that's so fascinating. You'll find a diverse array of items including such things as snowshoes, knapsacks, cooking utensils, natural foods, vitamins, homeopathic medicines, herbal formulas and a large selection of books on crafts, food and nutrition, gardening, psychology, philosophy and religion.

It is said that local doctors occasionally send their patients to Frances for consultation. I don't doubt that she dispenses exactly the right kind of holistic advice; she's that kind of person and you'll know it immediately upon meeting her. This is a must stop. If you miss it, you will miss something very special.

Hours: Daily from 10 A.M to 6 P.M.
Directions: The shop is located near Quaigh Design in Wilmington, which is halfway between Bennington and Brattleboro on Route 9. From I-91 at Brattleboro, take the Route 9 West exit; from Route 7 at Bennington, take Route 9 East to Wilmington.

QUAIGH DESIGN CENTER
West Main Street
Wilmington, Vermont 05363
(802) 464-2780

Quaigh Design was established in 1967 just prior to the beginning of the American crafts resurgence and is one of the older craft shops still around. "Some of our craftspeople have been professionals for twenty years or more," notes owner Lilias Hart.

The name of the shop is derived from the Scottish word for a type of drinking vessel used after the hunt. Along with the 115 craftspeople whose work is displayed in the shop, Lilias has set aside a separate area for a collection of handknit and woven Scottish woolen imports.

Rough-hewn displays and a few antique furniture pieces show some fine examples of contemporary crafts. "The work must be designed by the craftsperson and professionally made and presented," Lilias told me. "We are more interested in functional pieces which are of high quality and good value."

Included here are pottery, jewelry, wooden objects, stained-glass lampshades and small pieces, blown glass, weaving, wrought iron and leather. Prices range from $5 to $250 with the average price $20 to $25.

The building that houses Quaigh Design dates back to 1830. Along with other buildings that comprise the village center, it was transported some time ago down the hill from the old center of town and is worthy of note. Low ceilings, ancient beams and floor joists, exposed pipes that lead nowhere and floors that are hardly level add an architectural note of interest for either the craft explorer or old building enthusiast.

Hours: Daily from 10 A.M. to 6 P.M. except in April when the shop is open only weekends.
Directions: From I-91 take Brattleboro Exit 2. Follow Route 9 West for 20 miles to Wilmington. From the Bennington area and Route 7, take Route 9 East to Wilmington. Quaigh is in the center of the village and is a few doors down from Klara Simpla.

THE VERMONT STATE CRAFT CENTER AT WINDSOR HOUSE
Main Street
Windsor, Vermont 05089
(802) 674-6729

History, handcrafts, architecture and community involvement all converged in the early Seventies to foster the founding of this, the second of two state-recognized craft centers.

Once a major inn on a well-traveled route, the Windsor House, a handsome 1840 Greek Revival building, had deteriorated over the years as modern motels and superhighways enticed travelers away from Windsor. In 1971 the Windsor House was slated to be demolished by a bank that wanted to erect a drive-in-teller branch on that location.

The bank had started to strip the once-proud inn of its furnishings in preparation for demolition when the newly formed Historic Windsor, Inc., a group of concerned local citizens, began its arduous but ultimately successful drive to save the building. The preservation group enlisted the aid of various state and federal agencies along with a couple of competing banks and local support in the campaign to preserve and rehabilitate Windsor House. In 1976 the partially rehabbed building opened with the State Craft Center and Historic Windsor, Inc. as its first two tenants. Today Windsor House also houses a Vermont Public Radio station, the local Chamber of Commerce, several nonprofit organizations and private businesses and is the lynchpin of the town's revival efforts.

Located in the inn's old lobby, the craft center's 1,700-square-foot retail space contains the work of more than 250 Vermont craftspeo-

64 · SHOPS/GALLERIES

VERMONT

ple. Marble-tiled floors, a generous fireplace and deepset arched windows form a fitting background for the display of the mostly contemporary and functional craftwork.

To be accepted for display in the center, the craftspeople's work must pass a jury process that, according to gallery manager Prudence Schuler, is based on "technical excellence, originality of design, creative use of media and marketability."

Virtually all craft media are included here, effectively arranged throughout the expansive space. Many large pieces such as quilts, tapestries, furniture, and stained-glass panels are on display. There is a special strength in pottery and glass, an emphasis on wood and a nice assortment of clothing along with pewterware, jewelry, baskets, prints, toys and sculpture. Prices range from $2.50 to $2,000.

"I like to have people feel that we're in a small village with a comfortable, relaxed and friendly atmosphere," Prudence told me. She or any of the Windsor House staff will be happy to guide you to the many historic and cultural attractions in the Windsor area, known as "The Birthplace of Vermont."

The center holds four major group or theme shows and many minishows throughout the year in an adjacent exhibition space. Visitors are also welcome to observe the pottery and weaving classes that are taught regularly in the Windsor House studios.

Hours: Year-round, 9 A.M. to 5 P.M. daily; June through January also open Sunday, noon to 5 P.M.
Directions: Main Street runs parallel to I-91. Southbound take Exit 9 (Hartland); northbound take Exit 8 (Ascutney). Follow Route 5 to Windsor center. Windsor House is in the middle of town.

UNICORN
15 Central Street
Woodstock, Vermont 05091
(802) 457-2480

Unicorn is a comfortable shop in the center of Woodstock where the basic urge to caress a piece of craftwork is happily encouraged. "I like people to touch my craft items if possible," notes co-owner Jeffrey Kahn, who with his wife and partner Andrea have put on display an enticing collection of handcrafts.

More than seventy-five craftspeople, the majority from the Northeast, have made the primarily functional objects shown here.

Windsor House

There is an emphasis on jewelry, woodwork and pottery. There is also a large stock of notecards, many of them silkscreened or colored by hand.

"People don't realize that your typical neighborhood jeweler casts his pieces by the hundreds," Jeffrey told me. "There's a tremendous value in handcrafted jewelry—a certain quality that comes in part from pleasing lines and the time spent making it." The jewelry pieces, in gold, silver and other metals, are displayed in antique cases that the Kahns found in area barns and restored.

Jeffrey explained to me that he wants to include as many high-quality craftspeople as possible in his store, rather than more extensive collections of fewer people's work. "I'm consistently seeking out new craftspeople who want to get their foot in the door," he says. Prices range from a few dollars up to $500.

Besides the American crafts in the shop, there is a small amount of fine foreign-made crafts, mostly baskets and woven rugs and wall hangings. There is also a stock of intriguing commercially made items chosen for their design, function, uniqueness and quality.

Established in 1978, Unicorn is smack dab in the middle of Woodstock's shops, restaurants and beautiful old architecture. Of special note in the area is the newly opened Woodstock Farm Museum, which exhibits both Victorian and modern-day farming methods side by side.

Hours: Daily from 9:30 A.M. to 5:30 P.M.
Directions: From I-89 take Exit 1 to Route 4 West and follow to the center of Woodstock. Unicorn is near the traffic rotary in town.

65 · SHOPS/GALLERIES

Artisans

INTRODUCTION

Today's professional New England craftsperson is perhaps the prototypical Yankee. Individualistic, proud, self-reliant and creative, they are the inheritors and progenitors of a long tradition. Inspired by the region's seasonal beauty and its supportive environment, they patiently create objects that are destined to become tomorrow's family heirlooms or treasured works of art.

Many might still hold an image of the typical craftsperson as a rough-hewned dropout or a gingham-clad earth mother. However, as the following profiles suggest, the contemporary New England craft professional cannot be easily stereotyped.

Besides being an accomplished artisan and artist, today's craftsperson is also a small businessperson, using the appropriate tools and the techniques of modern society. Often production and marketing schedules are planned months in advance. Although income levels vary dramatically, the contemporary craftsperson finds a large and appreciative market for his or her work. For instance, at just one five-day event, the 1983 American Craft Council Fair at Rhinebeck, the 500 craft exhibitors averaged nearly $11,500 each in wholesale and retail orders.

Advances in technology, the sharing of information through a large and sophisticated network of craft media, schools and organizations, the ease of mobility, and changes in public attitudes about art and craft have all converged to speed up the growth and diversity in the professional craft community.

Freed from the historic role of providing society with its basic necessities, today's artisan has the freedom and knowledge to experiment with techniques, concepts and personal visions.

The results are objects of beauty that speak clearly and forcefully of art and the human soul. Fine crafts are a form of a spiritual truth and a natural connection between maker and purchaser, nature and humanity, past and future. It is these marvelous objects and the diverse group of people who make them that are featured here.

How to order.

Besides being a look at the region's best craftspeople, their creations and their lifestyles, this chapter is also a mail order catalog.

Craftspeople are presented by the medium in which they work: clay, fiber, glass, jewelry, metal, assorted media, and wood. Within each medium, the order is determined alphabetically by state, then town, and finally last name. There is also a general index at the back of the book that lists all craftspeople alphabetically.

It is suggested that you contact the craftsperson before placing an order. The work pictured with each profile is in most cases just a small sample of the items in each craftsperson's line. Many artisans offer brochures that show their complete lines, sometimes in full color. I have indicated when a brochure is available. If one is offered you should request it. You will also often get more product information than space here allows.

Although prices, addresses and phone numbers have been checked for accuracy, these are, of course, subject to change. Once again, it pays to contact the craftsperson before ordering.

Unless otherwise noted, prices do not include shipping costs. As a general rule, you can figure that a shipping charge of from three to ten percent will be added to the cost of each item. This will vary according to size, weight and pricing. Prices also do not include sales tax, which will be added by the craftsperson where appropriate.

Remember, these items are made one at a time. You can except that shipping time will be from two to six weeks in most cases. Also, being made by hand, there are likely to be slight variations in size, shape and design from what is shown in the photographs and described in the captions. This is not sloppiness. It is the essence of handcrafted work.

Most work is signed and dated by its maker. Some is also numbered and registered by the craftsperson in a studio log. Feel free to ask which of the above is done.

The nature of craft work being what it

Introduction

is, you can, if you wish, think of the work pictured in this catalog as a taking off point for specially commissioned pieces that conform to your particular desires or environment. I've noted in each profile whether commissions are available.

Finally, although one of the considerations for being included in this chapter is the reliability of the craftsperson, neither I nor the publisher can take any responsibility for transactions between readers and craftspeople. Please correspond directly with the craftsperson if any problems should arise.

Clay

Elizabeth MacDonald

Box 205
Bridgewater, Connecticut 06752

Elizabeth MacDonald's professional world was the theater before she began working as a potter. "Although the solitude of studio life is a far cry from the public nature of acting," she explains, "it is the communication of feeling that is central to my desire — whether it be on the stage or through an object of clay."

In the twenty years that she has been working in clay, she has explored the medium with a relentless and shifting change of styles, materials and techniques. Her most recent work is an outgrowth of her long-held concern "with a sense of time and timelessness" and her interest in "mystery."

These involvements, coupled with her growing interest in color, have led the forty-seven-year-old artist to create a series of stoneware tile constructions that have been accurately compared to "very serene and painterly ceramic canvases that evoke images of sun-bleached land and seascapes."

By coloring and firing small, square stoneware tiles with torn edges ("much like handmade paper") and assembling them on Masonite substructures, Elizabeth creates alluring layers of color in flowing patterns that are at once calming and exhilarating.

"Wherever I travel, I linger by ancient walls, feeling the ages with a glance; layer upon layer of mingling color, journeys through time revealing the silent marks of human life. And with each tile I make I dream of far places with peeling walls. And with each tile I shape my own."

Elizabeth's work has been featured in numerous solo and group exhibitions. She has received artist's grants from the Connecticut Commission on the Arts in 1978 and 1982 and is a trustee of the Brookfield Craft Center.

Brochure: No.
Commissions: Yes.
Studio Hours: By appointment.
Telephone: (203) 354-0594.

Textured stoneware tile constructions are available in virtually any desired size. While still damp, the 2½-inch torn-edged tiles are painted with colored slip and pressed into pigment. After firing to 2100°, the colors are further fixed with acrylic. The tiles are then arranged into striking patterns of pastel colors and mounted with adhesive on a wooden substructure. $75 per square foot.

72 · CLAY

LOIS CASSEN NADEL

Nadel Design
7 East Liberty Street
Chester, Connecticut 06412

"There's something about working with clay that touches the soul," says Lois Cassen Nadel. "Once you're addicted, you're addicted for life." Lois, who has been a clay addict since she was six years old, specializes in one-of-a-kind work done in fine English porcelain and decorated with crystalline glazes. It is a process that she says allows "the perfect balance" between the porcelain and the glaze.

Crystalline glazes are zinc-saturated glaze formulations that are forced to crystallize during the cooling process in beautiful patterns that have been described as snowflake, sunburst and flower-like designs. The white porcelain allows for a clarity of color that is at once striking or subtle depending on the colorings, which can range from very soft and subtle mauves, greys and yellows to warm or cool whites and bright, pure cobalt blues and intense greens.

The sixteen-hour firing process is exceedingly temperamental and doesn't always work. "It involves a lot of incantation around the kiln," explains Lois. "Just when you think that you're in control, it slaps you in the face and lets you know otherwise. When it works, you turn around and say, 'thank you, kiln.'"

Lois is not interested in producing a regular production line of pottery. "I enjoy making pieces for which there is not a mass market. It's all part of a different attitude. I have one foot in as a craftsperson and one in as an artist. There is not for me a very clear dividing line. No one would tell a fine-arts painter that they have to produce a certain number of paintings each week. Why tell a potter?" she asks.

Lois, forty-one, is a graduate of the Manhattan High School of Music and Art and has a bachelors degree in fine arts from Carnegie-Mellon University. Her pottery has been sold and exhibited throughout the United States and has been featured in *House Beautiful* and *The New York Times*. She is a member of the American Craft Council and the Society of Connecticut Craftsmen, of which she was a member of the board of directors.

Brochure: No.
Commissions: All work is one of a kind and commissionable.
Studio Hours: By appointment.
Telephone: (203) 526-5745.

This wheel-thrown porcelain plate is filled with star patterns of a warm golden white on a white background. Plates may be ordered individually or in sets, from 6 to 12 inches in diameter. This 10-inch plate is $60.

Like all of Lois' pottery, this vase is a one-of-a-kind piece. Made of the finest English porcelain, the crystalline glaze is dark green with clusters of silver crystals. At about 6 inches high, it is priced at $70.

SUSAN FOX

Milkhouse Pottery
Cornwall Bridge, Connecticut 06754

As a small child, Susan Fox was given weekly pottery lessons. "The word 'Wednesday' holds magic for me even now," she notes. Although her pottery showed promise, it wasn't until some twenty-five years later that her early interest in clay was rekindled. Taking a pottery course given by a local craftsmen's guild, she happily realized that "what my head had forgotten, my hands had not." So she bought her own wheel and started to work.

After joining with some friends in the early Seventies in running a cooperative studio and store, Susan started her own studio in 1978 in the barn on her parents' farm in Cornwall Bridge. It is here that she teaches and makes pots, mostly whiteware, redware and sawdust-fired blackware.

Confessing that she's "intimidated by a paintbrush," Susan, forty-five, decorates her pottery with stamps that she's designed and cut herself. "I concentrate on form, which I consider basic," she told me, "and I continue to be fascinated by the qualities of my vanilla-ice-cream clay."

"I like to imagine people sitting down to a table laden with my work," says the largely self-taught potter. "It pleases me, at Christmas time especially, to think about the number of people for whom I've made presents."

Brochure: Yes.
Commissions: Yes, particularly dinnerware.
Studio Hours: By appointment.
Telephone: (203) 672-6450.

These ice-catcher pitchers are designed to keep the ice in the pitcher when pouring, allowing the lemonade, iced tea or sangria to flow smoothly. The pitchers, like all her pieces, are made of white clay with a clear glaze applied over floral patterns. The flowers will vary but all are blue with green stems and leaves. The material is lead free, dishwasher safe and ovenproof. The pitchers pictured here are 12 inches tall, with a "bosomy shape" that, Susan points out, "makes it easy to pour when full." $50 each postpaid.

CHRIS CLARK

PO Box 712
New Haven, Connecticut 06511

Chris Clark has managed with delightful results to combine both her "magical side" and her "utilitarian side" in her craft by building fanciful yet functional castles in clay. Chris designs the castles so that they can serve various functions: Some are used as candleholders, some as birdfeeders, some as aquarium tunnels. She even makes one castle on a mountain that opens up for storage space.

Each castle is made of different individual sections which Chris throws and when leather-hard, pieces together into a finished castle. No two castles are alike in size, shape or configuration. "I put them together as the mood strikes me," the thirty-six-year-old potter says, "arranging the parts differently each time."

While she enjoys the process of creating the castles, what Chris really enjoys is seeing them used, "with candles alight in the midst of a festive supper table, or with chickadees lunching on sunflower seeds from the courtyard of a birdfeeder castle." That, she says, is "what keeps the clay alive for me."

Chris moved to Connecticut in 1982 after ten years as a producing potter in Denver to take the position of resident potter at Guilford Handcrafts School. She is a member of the American Craft Council and Colorado Artist Craftsmen.

Brochure: No.
Commissions: "I've done commissions for specific castles and would love to do more."
Studio Hours: Monday through Friday, 10 A.M. to 4 P.M.
Telephone: (203) 453-5947.

Candle huts hold a votive candle (not included) and are also made in brown stoneware. Height 8 to 9 inches. Chris also makes outdoor birdfeeder castles, aquarium and terrarium castles, fountain and chess set castles — "Anything goes." Candle Huts, $30.

This castle night-light is made of brown stoneware. A candle is placed in the back door to light up the windows. Height is from 12 to 15 inches; $200.

75 · CLAY

Anita K. Griffith

It's Only Mud
PO Box 1054
Madison, Connecticut 06443

"To evoke surprise" is the most important intention of Anita Griffith's ceramic pieces. "I suppose I have always been tickled by flamingoes on the lawn, cow-shaped plastic creamers at truckstops and other colloquialisms of modern America," she told me. She enjoys thinking that one of her ceramic objects could occupy such a whimsical position in its keeper's environment.

It is very important to Anita that her inanimate objects, what she calls "ceramic incidents," have a liveliness, a sense of captured gesture; "What is a facial expression; what about a mouth makes it laugh?" she asks. Indeed when her studio shelves begin to fill up with her anthropomorphic image-objects, the place seems to be delightfully inhabited.

The greatest challenge for Anita in her everyday studio work is "to throw, hand build and slip-cast forms that combine in various plastic states and retain some of the look of wet, plastic clay in the hard, fired ware. She has developed a way to use a coating of thin terra sigillata (clay) that is lightly polished with a soft cloth, creating a surface that is smooth, soft and almost wet-looking.

Anita, thirty, is a member of the American Craft Council and the Society of Connecticut Craftsmen. She teaches pottery at the Guilford Handcrafts Center and New Haven's Creative Arts Workshop and also presently is manager of a small pottery factory that specializes in producing dinnerware for Japanese restaurants. Her long-term goals include the design, development and production of a handmade commercial giftware line, available at reasonable cost to the mass market.

Brochure: No.
Commissions: Will consider, especially custom color options.
Studio Hours: By appointment.
Telephone: (203) 245-2912.

"Tooth pitchers" are wheel thrown in a natural terra-cotta color. White earthenware slip-cast teeth are added to the pitcher and altered to create one-of-a-kind expressions and shapes. Heights vary from 10 to 18 inches and "all grins are designed to be friendly." $60.

"Sneeze box" terra-cotta tissue dispensers are unglazed and coated with a thin slip called terra sigillata, then polished with a soft cloth to achieve a satin finish. One-of-a-kind expression on lips. Available in the natural brick-red color of the clay or in pink with painted deep-rose lips. Specify choice. About 5½ inches square by 7 inches high; $36.

ELLEN MURPHY AND BOBBI SETZLER

MudSlingers Studio
P.O. Box 407
Manchester, Connecticut 06040

"Technology has given us machine-made, dry-pressed, perfect tiles with computer-stamped glazed patterns," says Bobbi Setzler, explaining why she and partner Ellen Murphy recently decided to establish their own studio.

Drawing on their converging talents and training (Bobbi majored in ceramics and graphic design, Ellen in painting) these 1982 graduates of the University of Connecticut's fine-arts program had searched for a medium that would allow them to indulge their deep interest in color. They decided that ceramic art tiles were perfect: They carry color well, make a good permanent surface for painting and there was, they surmised, a market for their work among homeowners, designers and architects.

Firing their tiles at relatively low temperatures allows them to use a broad palette of colors. Occasionally, for enhancement of a piece, they'll use multiple firings to set overglazes that provide "elusive or exotic colors and increased depth."

Their tile paintings can be used as hot plates, set into tables and other furniture, used decoratively around the fireplace, as a framed painting on the wall or even as a floor painting. Since each tile is made by hand, they can control surface texture from heavy textural or modeled relief forms to a very flat surface to use as a more conventional canvas or a giant mosaic puzzle.

"We like doing special design work," Bobbi told me, "where we can push ideas, the clay and the color." They are members of the American Craft Council.

Brochure: None as of this writing, but there should be one ready by date of publication.
Commissions: Yes.
Studio Hours: By appointment.
Telephone: (203) 646-1408.

Mosaic wall piece made from a wet slab of earthenware clay, which was cut into pieces and allowed to dry. After a bisque firing, each piece is colored, glazed and fired again. The pieces are then mounted and grouted. The wall piece pictured here is done in purples and greys and framed with grey tiles. Width 14¼ inches, height 20¼ inches. Similarly sized work is $70.

Chess set consists of an oak-framed board made of blue-and-gold glazed tiles mounted and color grouted. Each chess piece is individually hand-modeled and glazed. This is a one-of-a-kind set, but represents similar work, for $125.

77 · CLAY

MARY LOU ALBERETTI

RFD 3, Box 18
New Fairfield, Connecticut 06810

Mary Lou Alberetti is involved mainly with the raku method of firing, derived from an ancient Japanese process. It is a delicate operation, one that requires close attention at the kiln. The bisque-fired pot is glazed and then fired for about twenty-five minutes at temperatures of up to 2000°F. It is then carefully removed by tongs and placed in a closed container that also contains combustible material such as hay or sawdust, whose burning causes reduction to take place.

"Raku is characterized by softness and freedom that allows for a certain amount of control and repetition," she explains, "yet preventing exact duplication due to the varying elements and conditions." Her raku pieces often have brilliant metallic lusters and crackle finishes enhanced by soft pastel colors that she integrates with the characteristic raku-produced carbon greys.

Mary Lou, forty, also creates large, earthenware platter-paintings, which she decorates with low-fire underglazes in a wide range of colors, and which are sometimes raku-fired.

An Assistant Professor of Ceramics at Southern Connecticut State University, Mary Lou has exhibited her work widely throughout New England and New York in one-person, group and invitational exhibitions. She received her undergraduate art degree from Southern Connecticut State College and a masters in ceramics from Arizona State University. Her work is carried by several Connecticut galleries.

Brochure: No.
Commissions: Yes.
Studio Hours: By appointment.
Telephone: (203) 797-4279.

The platter series incorporates painting on clay using stains in vitreous slip and underglaze. "Impressions and low relief impart sculptural qualities. These works evolved from a wish to combine involvement in color and painting with my works in clay." They are usually fired in oxidation and occasionally a light smoking is used. Each is unique and all are ready for wall mounting. Diameter ranges from 14 to 22 inches; prices from $60 to $200.

Raku pots are wheel-thrown and often altered by paddling. After a bisque firing, tape, ribbon, netting or other materials are used in a resist process with air brushing of vitreous slips containing stains of pastel peach, pinks, blues and greens. Reduction in an organic material imparts soft greys and blacks and a crackle effect. The pot shown here is 7 inches tall. It sells for approximately $45.

John H. Seymour

RFD 2
New Milford, Connecticut 06776

John Seymour has been making stoneware animal sculptures for fifteen years. With one studio in a wooded section of Connecticut and another at his camp in the north Maine woods, John has plenty of opportunity to observe some of the three dozen or so critters that he stylizes in clay. "Elegance of form, balance of form, a natural rhythm of shapes are the self-imposed guidelines for my work," he explains. "If my sculptures are whimsical, that is due to a simplification of form and elimination of nonessential details."

Although John took a "long detour" through the business world, he had always suspected that he would someday be able to regularly work at a craft. Recalling his childhood in a small Hungarian town, he remembers that at one end of his street lived a potter who cranked out small utilitarian pieces that his wife sold "for pennies at the marketplace." At the other end lived a blind basket weaver. John spent most of his free time as a child watching one or the other practice their respective crafts. "The potter, who used to sit barefoot at his kick wheel, gave me my first piece of clay to play with," John recalls.

He describes his forms as "sculptural in design and ceramic in material," which, says the sixty-two-year-old artist, "creates some problems for me, mostly among professionals who have difficulty in categorizing my work." "The collectors, however, appreciate my sculptures simply for what they are," he notes. "They come from all kinds of people, both with simple and sophisticated tastes. This, after all, is the final reward."

Brochure: A lavish brochure showing his entire line is available.
Commissions: Yes.
Studio Hours: By appointment for student groups.
Telephone: (203) 354-4018.

This brown stoneware squirrel is one of a large family of animal sculptures. As with all of John's work, it is made with a slab process, which allows changes in the design. Subsequent pieces will be similar but not exactly identical. All animal sculptures are weather resistant, suitable for both indoor or outdoor display all year round. Height 12 inches; $90. Other sculptures range to 22 inches high and are priced from $60 to $750.

Frances Lee Heminway

LEE-HEM Porcelain
248R Farms Village Road
West Simsbury, Connecticut 06092

When Frances Heminway first marketed her new porcelain tableware, the response was so overwhelming that it was far beyond what she could produce with her existing production system. She spent a year translating her design into a process of slip casting and altering that "retained the feeling and substance of the original but at vastly increased production levels." Today, her striking, satiny finished tableware is available in more than fifty shops and galleries across the U.S.

"The concept of this design was to create shell-like shapes that would be lovely to look at, sensuous to hold and the perfect vessel to hold food," she says. "Each piece, either by itself or grouped together, transmits a sense of union between smooth refinement, subtle irregularities and simple whiteness that enhances the color and variability of foods."

Frances graduated from the Rhode Island School of Design in 1954 with a degree in interior architecture. After working in that field for ten years, she spent eighteen months as a potters' apprentice. Later she cofounded Cherry-Brook Potters, where she began the development of her porcelain tableware. She recently left CherryBrook to produce her tableware in her own studio in West Simsbury.

Frances, fifty, is a member of the Canton Artist Guild, the American Craft Council and the Farmington Valley Arts Center. She won the Best in Ceramic Award at the forty-third annual juried exhibit of the Society of Connecticut Craftsmen, of which she is a member.

Brochure: Her complete line is pictured in a glossy black-and-white brochure sent on request.
Commissions: Yes.
Studio Hours: Daily from 10 A.M. to 4 P.M.
Telephone: (203) 651-0410.

The pieces pictured here are from a line of some thirty items of porcelain tableware. They are all slip cast and altered porcelain finished with a satin matte white glaze. The stacked plates shown are a 10½-inch dinner plate, a 9-inch luncheon plate and a 7-inch dessert plate. Plates cost from $10 to $26. Shown in the second photo are several suggestions for table settings. Four-piece place settings are approximately $65.

GAIL MARKIEWICZ

15 Vernon Court
Woodbridge, Connecticut 06525

It is form that is most important to Gail Markiewicz. In the design of her ceramic vessels, she creates strong and sensual shapes whose fragile, textured surfaces contrast with the strength of the form. "I enjoy the challenge of working this delicately," says the thirty-two-year-old artist, "playing the surfaces against each other, finally culminating in a very fragile edge."

Gail's vessels have been said to reflect both a primitive and a futuristic spirit, a feeling that she feels is due to two elements: the combination of the subtle pastel colors of the exteriors with the dark, iridescent interiors, and the contrast of the crater-like and striated areas with the vessel's smooth surfaces.

Gail graduated in 1978 with a Bachelor of Arts from Bridgewater State College and later received her Master of Arts from Southern Connecticut State College. She has attended Penland School of Crafts and has been a practicing ceramics artist for the last four years. Her work is represented by more than a dozen galleries and regularly exhibited in group exhibitions.

Brochure: In progress at the time of writing.
Commissions: All work is one of a kind; commissions are welcomed.
Studio Hours: By appointment.
Telephone: (203) 397-2609.

Large stoneware urn, one in a series of one-of-a-kind vessels. Exterior pastel colors applied through stains and underglazes with a black interior. Heavily textured surface embellished with colored squares, chevrons, stripes. Porcelain sticks added. Different sizes range from $85 to $475. Pictured piece is 14 inches high by 16 inches wide and is $400.

81 · CLAY

Garret and Melody Dalessandro Bonnema

Bonnema Potters
Main Street
Bethel, Maine 04217

Garret and Melody have been partners in pottery for about ten years, first in Pennsylvania and, since 1974, in Bethel, where they have their studio, showroom and home in a large old Victorian house. "Bethel is beautiful, culturally rich, but Spartan," Melody told me. "Summers and during snow season the population swells, but much of the year Bethel is quiet and most entertainment must be self-generated. This peaceful atmosphere and beautiful natural environment contribute much to our work life."

Color and scale are the most distinctive features of their work, which consumes about 20,000 pounds of clay annually. They decorate their simple, strong shapes using up to twenty-five different glazes, which are applied by pouring, dipping and brushing. Their desire to "color surfaces and make pictures" has led them to do commissioned tile work, anything from commissioned tile murals that cover entire walls to single tiles that are self-contained pictures.

The Bonnemas' goal is to lead an artistic lifestyle that has at its center the making of pottery of long-lasting quality. Their work cycle of twenty kiln loads a year along with the changes of the season governs their time. To keep their busy lives "balanced," Garret, thirty-five, Melody, thirty-six, and their daughter Leah strive for "a healthful way of life that includes cooking and eating well, keeping physically fit and experiencing the environment by running, skiing, garden work and wood handling."

The Bonnemas are members of Praxis Cooperative Gallery, Directions Professional Craftspeople of Maine and the American Craft Council.

Brochure: Nearly two dozen items are illustrated along with samples of color combinations in an excellent brochure.
Commissions: Yes.
Studio Hours: Summer hours everyday 9 A.M. to 5 P.M.; winter hours Monday through Saturday 9 A.M. to 5 P.M.
Telephone: (207) 824-2821.

(Left) Tile quilt consists of nine 7-by-7-inch tiles in a hardwood frame with flush mount hangers. The tiles shown are a sampler of available custom tile. "They are landscape-like murals that accent kitchens, wood stoves and fireplaces." Pictured tile quilt $150. (Center) Hand-thrown stoneware lamp base can be made from the many color combinations shown in their brochure or can be specially matched to a color swatch. Shade not included. Base is 15 inches high; $65. (Right) Stoneware crock has a flat removable lid and is suitable as a seat, table or storage pot either indoors or out. Height is 17 inches; $150.

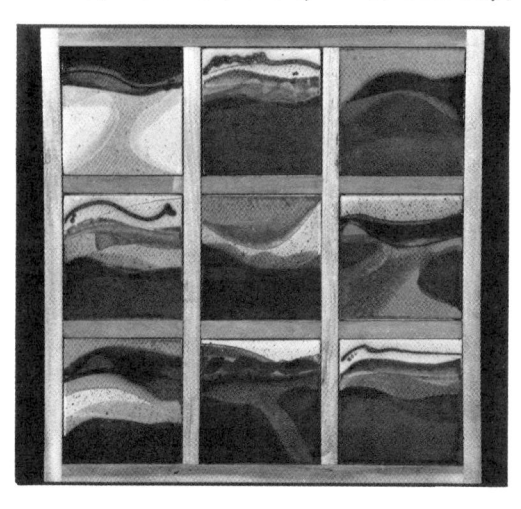

LAURIE V. ADAMS

RR 1, Box 4062
Camden, Maine 04843

Laurie Adams' love affair with clay began in 1962 when an alumnus of the school where she was teaching painting and printmaking donated a potter's wheel to the Art Department. "I was instructed to teach pottery beginning the next day," she remembers. So the following day, both Laurie and her students embarked on a joint learning experience. "Immediately, I knew I wanted to make my own pottery," she told me. "But I had no awareness then of the direction that my life would take because of the clay."

Laurie took classes of her own at a local workshop, went to Haystack Craft School, bought a wheel and in 1964 began selling her work. "As I encountered the handmade work of others, my appreciation grew," she recalls. "I relished a growing awareness that people enjoyed using my pots. My world was becoming very craft-oriented."

In 1965, while working as a part-time lecturer on ceramics at the Boston Museum of Fine Arts, she studied the history of clay, especially enjoying the graceful Sung Dynasty and Korean celadons. Her own work has since developed a clearly Oriental influence.

After moving to Maine in 1971, she "built houses for a while" and then struck out on her own with her two small children to become a potter. While living on Deer Isle, she worked "all too full-time," enjoying the potting process while continuing to develop a personal stylistic direction. Eventually the isolation of island life prompted a move in 1979 to Camden, where she became a member of Perspectives, a cooperative craft gallery. Here she says she has found the freedom to experiment with her own clay growth and to further build her wholesale business.

Stylistically, her work has begun to evolve in a more sculptural direction, combining her dual interest in form and surfaces. "The delicacy of the porcelain challenges me," the forty-four-year-old potter says. "The surface of the porcelain is a wonderful vehicle for subtle color. The decoration is painterly, a reaction to space, intertwining glazes and oxides in abstract patterns."

Brochure: Yes.
Commissions: Yes.
Studio Hours: By appointment.
Telephone: (207) 236-8457.

Porcelain wheel-thrown dinner plate. Pink glaze with a grey wash decoration, copper and iron details. The plate has a light and translucent appearance with a smooth matte-finish glaze. Plates are one of a kind but glazed as to work together visually and complete dinner sets can be ordered. The plate pictured here is 11-inches diameter; $35.

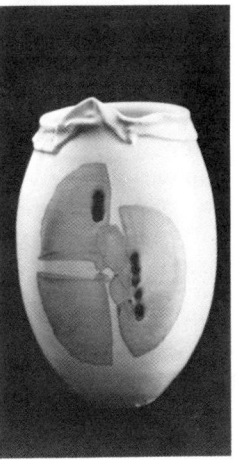

White porcelain vase, wheel thrown and one of a kind. The decoration is a grey wash with copper details; the white glaze has a smooth buttery surface. This is one of a series of vases with rims handformed after the piece is thrown. Height 12 inches; $85.

Lynn Duryea

RFD 105
Deer Isle, Maine 04627

"I find that I am inspired as much by work in other materials as I am in clay," says ceramist Lynn Duryea. "The important thing is to keep looking, keep exploring." Lynn's interest in media cross-pollination is reflected in her successful line of "quilt" plates and bowls, which were inspired by the traditional designs and contemporary colors in some quilts made by a friend.

"Excited and pleased" with the initial plates in her quilt series, Lynn has continued to diversify the line over the past four years. Today, she produces her quilt designs in both one-of-a-kind pieces as well as in sets and larger quantities. Several of her quilt designs were chosen by Tiffany & Co. in 1981 for sale in their New York store.

"These pieces are decorative as well as functional, which is part of their appeal to me," says the thirty-six-year-old artist. "The pattern is most important to me, although they are certainly good, solid pieces of pottery." She notes that "many customers appreciate the plates for both decorative and functional purposes, often buying the plates to hang on a wall. A table set with quilt plates and bowls is striking, whether the patterns match or are different."

In addition to her line of quilt plates and bowls, Lynn also makes small sculptural work, primarily wall pieces, which are raku-fired or smoked in sawdust.

Lynn began working with clay while a graduate student in art history at New York University. Her interest continued after graduation while she was working at the Metropolitan Museum of Art. In 1974, she decided to try pottery full time, moved to Maine and started to work with two other potters who were operating a production studio at the time. Although at the beginning she occasionally had to take part-time jobs to hold things together, things worked out just fine. She now works full time in her own studio in a building that she bought and renovated.

Lynn is a member of the American Craft Council, the Deer Isle Artists Association and a founding member of Eastern Bay Cooperative Gallery in Stonington, Maine. Her work has been shown in one-person and selected group exhibitions throughout Maine and in New York City. She is an alumna and former teaching assistant at Haystack Mountain.

Brochure: Yes.
Commissions: Yes.
Studio Hours: By appointment.
Telephone: (207) 348-6195.

Five basic quilt patterns are available in a wide assortment of colors. Two designs are shown here. The three-piece place setting shown consists of a large plate, 12-inch diameter; small plate, 8-inch diameter; and a small bowl, 7 inches in diameter and 2 inches deep. The individual plate is also 12 inches in diameter. Place setting as shown in your choice of pattern, $150. Individual plate prices range from $45 to $70. Write for flyer and complete price list.

LOUIS & MARJORIE RIZZO

Hollis Center Pottery
RFD 1, PO Box 3
Hollis Center, Maine 04042

When Louis Rizzo returned to Boston in 1967 from a year of study at L'Academia di Bell'Arte in Rome, Italy, he opened an art studio, where he intended to specialize in metal sculpture. One day, while working on a piece, he thought that it could be enhanced by the addition of ceramic shapes. As he remembers: "When I stuck my hand in the clay, I vowed never to take it out."

For ten years after that fateful day, he created all the traditional wares of a potter—plates, mugs, bowls and planters. Finally in 1977 his love for music, sculpture and cartooning combined to spur the creation of a thirty-six piece whimsical orchestra of handsculpted, naked musicians playing eighteen different instruments.

The reception to this stoneware orchestra was encouraging enough that the Rizzos soon expanded their family to include occupational characters and sports figures. Made from specially formulated, reddish-brown clay, each figure possesses a distinct personality, full of humor and attitude. The clay people are made by the Rizzos in their Maine home. Marjorie prepares the clay, which is then formed by Louis into the figures. After the work dries out for a few weeks, Marjorie glazes, fires and ships it out to their customers.

Louis graduated from Massachusetts College of Art. When he and Marjorie are not working on their stoneware caricatures, they are farming or enjoying the woods with their dogs. They belong to Directions, Professional Craftspeople of Maine.

Brochure: Yes.
Commissions: Yes.
Studio Hours: None.
Telephone: (207) 929-4861.

Doctor and nurse in consultation are accented with colored glaze and engobe. Choice of sex for both figures. Height 7 inches, width 2¾ inches. Each $20 plus $2.50 shipping. A complete line of professional figures is available, special orders are welcomed.

Stoneware orchestra of reddish-brown clay musicians with instrument may be purchased individually. Standing figures measure 9 inches high by 2¾ inches wide. Seated figures 7 inches high by 2¾ inches wide. Each is $20 plus $2.50 shipping; timpani player, contrabassist and harpist are $35 each plus $3.50 shipping; conductor is $30 plus $3 shipping.

DOTTIE PALMER

Ceramic Choreography
PO Box 429
South Harpswell, Maine 04079

A big change in Dottie Palmer's life and pottery occurred in 1976 when she travelled to Europe and studied art on a Greek island. "I came in touch with a new spirit of life and of dancing, which later appeared in my clay work," she says. "The little dancing people that now make up my pottery seemed to sprout from my fingers after I returned from Greece. I loved playing with these little people and making them dance with life and love."

"I love folk dance and I love to watch ballet," she told me. "The human body seems most beautiful and alive to me when it is moving to music; and people seem most alive to me when music lights up their souls and sets their bodies in motion."

The pottery that Dottie makes is all handbuilt using pinching, coiling and slab techniques. Each piece is made of high-fired porcelain with a clear glaze. "The sculptor in me much prefers working with each piece by hand and letting the form come through the simple pureness of the white porcelain," she says.

Dottie's studio occupies the whole second story of her farmhouse on the Maine coast. Working at home suits her fine, allowing her to be mother to her young son as well as a creative working person. "I find much satisfaction in running my own business and providing jobs for others in this small fishing community," says the thirty-eight-year-old potter.

Dottie received her undergraduate degree in sculpture from the Rhode Island School of Design in 1967. She is a member of Directions, Professional Craftspeople of Maine and the American Craft Council.

Brochure: Yes.
Commissions: No.
Studio Hours: None.
Telephone: (207) 833-5502.

This votive candleholder is the first piece that Dottie made for her production line of Ceramic Choreography and still remains one of her favorites. When lit, it causes the bottom to glow and sends out shadows of dancing people on the wall. 5½ inches tall. $32 postpaid (includes a votive candle).

"A set of these liqueur cups will make quite a conversation piece during after-dinner drinks." Each hand-pinched cup is held aloft by three small people. 5 inches high. $34 per pair postpaid.

RANDY FEIN

PO Box 1205
Stockton Springs, Maine 04981

Randy Fein could be described as a cartoonist in clay. Fashioning her creations in an animated, whimsical style, she offers an unconditional guarantee that her work will bring a smile to any viewer.

Her building facade pieces—wall sculptures, cookie jars, planters and a "townhouse toothbrush holder" all reflect an imaginative mix of both urban and rural styles, combining "childhood imagery of New York City's Lower East Side with the grandeur of Maine's fine Victorian Captains' homes." In addition to her imaginary facades, she will create a wall-relief sculpture of the facade of your own home or storefront in her distinctive style.

Randy has also spawned a family of hand-built sculptures called Pookey people ("Pookius Peculiaris"). The Pookeys are "extroverted creatures, who mostly sit around and tell elaborate stories all day. They are multilingual and give impeccable advice to the lovelorn."

Randy, thirty, received her art education from the State University at New Paltz, New York. She has been a potter for eight years and is presently Vice President of the Maine Potter's Guild.

Brochure: No.
Commissions: Yes.
Studio Hours: By appointment.
Telephone: (207) 567-4161.

The Pookey couple are handbuilt, beige stoneware figures seated on a natural-color imported wicker chair. "Each Pookey has a different expression with a unique story to tell." These one-of-a-kind sculptures are meticulously hand decorated by the artist. Height 8 inches; $50.

Handbuilt stoneware townhouse container is underglazed with brown tones and yellow highlights and has a gloss finish. Its lid comes off to reveal a smooth, glossy interior glaze. "Perfect for cookies." This is one of a kind but basic motifs, size and color will be similar. 10 inches high; $90.

BETH ANDREWS

Windfall Pottery
33 Spruce Street
Acton, Massachusetts 01720

Beth first studied pottery in high school and college. But it was her later education, first at a Danish school for handcrafts and then as an apprentice to Bob Vermillion, a North Carolina potter, that she credits as the most influential parts of her training. "Each helped me learn that simple, strong lines in a piece are the most pleasing to the eye and will withstand scrutiny through years of use," she told me.

First drawn to pottery by "its enormous possibilities," Beth says that she "was astonished by the endless variations that could be created by using mixtures of different clays, glazes and firing technologies. I was also pleased with the purely physical sensation of throwing clay forms on the wheel. Working with my hands was incredibly therapeutic."

In addition to its pleasures, however, the life of a production potter has presented Beth with some new and unanticipated challenges. "All of a sudden I was playing the role of bookkeeper, manager and salesperson. Yet I was only trained to be a potter."

This soup set includes a 4-quart tureen, six 10-ounce soup bowls and a ladle 14 inches long. It is available in matte white, three earth tones and tomato red/white. "This is a very versatile set for although the tureen is excellent for soup, it may also be used as a casserole. The bowls could be used everyday for cereal, salad or whatever you like." $110 the set.

Despite this challenging aspect of her profession, Beth, thirty-one, finds it all worthwhile. "It gives me the freedom and flexibility I want in my life, especially now that I have a family," she said. "As I feel my skills and my aesthetic sense growing stronger each year, I realize that I've invested my life in something that cannot be taken away from me: my work, my craft, is my own."

Brochure: Yes.
Commissions: No.
Studio Hours: None.
Telephone: (617) 263-9871.

Pair of candleholders are thrown on the wheel with small pieces of clay added to form the leaves. Like all of Beth's work, they are stoneware clay and fired in a reduction atmosphere to 2300° F. Available in matte white glaze only. 8 inches high. $30 the pair.

GREGOR GIESMANN

*Giesmann/Ceramix
270 Amherst Road
Belchertown, Massachusetts 01007*

After a childhood spent in postwar Germany, Gregor Giesmann came to the States in the late Fifties. It was several years later, while an Art Education major at the State University in New Paltz, New York, that he received his first serious exposure to clay and pottery. He was hooked on ceramics after his first course and decided to pursue advanced study at Michigan's Cranbrook Academy of Art, where he was attracted to the work of ceramics instructor Maja Grotell.

"Her work was more in keeping with my own notions about ceramic design, which originate in the European industrial design revolution rather than in the abstract expressionism of painting and sculpture that contributed to the pseudo-Japanese style then evolving in the United States," notes the forty-one-year-old artist.

Although not a believer that form should be determined strictly by function alone, Gregor is concerned that his pieces—all container forms in porcelain or whiteware—are functional as well as aesthetic objects. He considers himself more of a designer than a craftsman. "I am interested in forming concepts and seeing them realized than in the process and mechanics of making pieces," he says, adding that he nonetheless enjoys discovering new techniques in order to realize his ideas. "I use various industrial techniques, that until recently were shunned by craftsmen, including mold-making, slipcasting, jiggering, photo-silkscreening, airbrushing and the use of some commercial glazes."

Gregor has participated in some two dozen major ceramic exhibitions and has been a faculty member or visiting artist at universities throughout the country. "Teaching," he says, "in the creative environment of the classroom situation serves as a catalyst for my work and thinking." He is a member of the American Craft Council.

Brochure: No.
Commissions: Yes.
Studio Hours: None.
Telephone: (413) 323-7651.

*Porcelain teapot is wheelthrown and has white and blue/black marbleized decoration with a clear gloss glaze. Holds one quart; $45.
Porcelain slipcast cup has a semimatte spray glaze in a predominantly mottled dark blue. 3½ by 4 inches, holds eight ounces; $20.
Faceted porcelain vase is thrown and features bands of color stain decoration on white matte glaze. 7 inches high by 9 inches wide; $100.*

J. David Broudo

5 Gary Avenue
Beverly, Massachusetts 01915

One look at his ceramic creations will tell you that J. David Broudo is one who avoids movements and trends in his art. "If prevailing taste dictates what you do," he says, "you are not yourself; you are not an artist."

It is clear from his work and his frank opinions that David knows his way around when it comes to art. And well he should. As chairman of the Endicott College Art Department for more than thirty-five years, he has blended "teaching and creating in a healthy balance." The creating side of his career has focused on clay, "that most magical material."

Inspired by the "sea and rocks, the mountains, the exciting forms and textures that surround us in New England," David produces one-of-a-kind pieces that have found their way into numerous collections around the world. "I do not make multiples," says the sixty-two-year-old artist, "because the needless repetition destroys the spirit of creation." But when he finds an idea that works for him, he will explore it through a series of related objects until he feels that he has exhausted its possibilities.

"I want my work to make life more enjoyable," he notes, "whether the items are functional to hold a plant, or sculptural to hold your eye." Over the past thirty-five years his work has been exhibited in more than 250 exhibits both here and abroad.

Brochure: Yes.
Commissions: Yes.
Studio Hours: By appointment only.
Telephone: (617) 927-0585 ext. 257.

This thrown stoneware vase has been stamped, stained and torn around the top edge. One of a kind from a series. Glazed in white and earth tones. 22 inches high; $350.

LYNN GERVENS

25 First Street
Cambridge, Massachusetts 02141

"People ask me," says Lynn Gervens, "why don't your pots fall apart with all those holes in them?" The answer is, she says, in the delicate strength that is one of the beauties of porcelain.

Lynn began working in porcelain five years ago. Like most potters she had originally learned to work in stoneware. "Porcelain was always such a mystery—the forbidden clay," she says. As her interest in carving developed, she found that "the constant fight against the large particles in the stoneware became too limiting. The fine texture and smoothness of porcelain proved much more suitable for this kind of work."

The patterns that Lynn carves are inspired by Japanese and Persian motifs. They are composed of simple shapes that develop into intricate patterns when placed side by side. "Each angle of a piece yields a different impression—first the shapes that have been cut out, then the latticework structure that remains," notes the twenty-nine-year-old artist.

"I like the quiet elegance of my pots," she told me. "There is a subtle beauty to the blending of the classic forms, patterns and colors. I especially like the chance to combine this uniquely decorative style with functional designs."

Lynn is a member of the Cambridge Art Association, the American Craft Council and Mudflat Pottery, where she teaches.

Brochure: Yes.
Commissions: Yes.
Studio Hours: Monday through Friday from 9 A.M. to 6 P.M.
Telephone: (617) 876-3877.

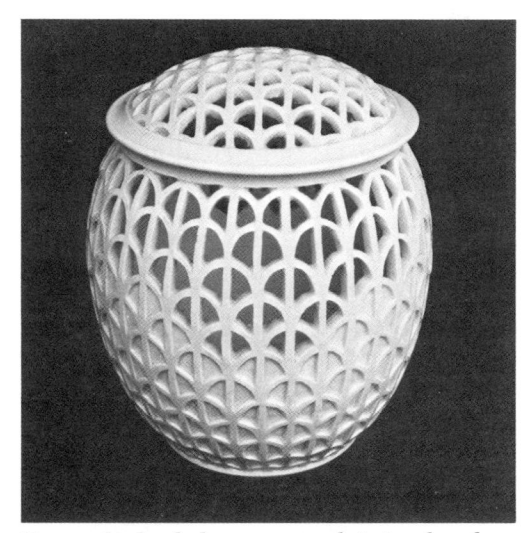

Covered wheel-thrown porcelain jar, hand-carved, with a split-scallop pattern. Each opening is first marked, then cut out with an X-acto knife. Transparent glaze, one of a kind. Height 7 inches, diameter 5½ inches; $400. Other pieces range from $24.

91 · CLAY

Lois Hershberg

*Deer Mountain Pottery
7 Linnaean Street, No. 6
Cambridge, Massachusetts 02138*

When Lois Hershberg walked into Mudflat Pottery School seven years ago, she never dreamt that she would become a full-time potter. "After a masters degree in Community Mental Health and five years as an adolescent therapist, it never occurred to me that I had talent in any other field. But the first time I sat down at the potter's wheel, I knew I had caught the disease," she told me.

Lois hand builds her pieces from slabs of clay, creating simple forms that she uses as a "canvas of self-expression" for her glazes and brushstrokes. She has been greatly influenced by the "Japanese sense of design-simplicity and firing technique." Her pieces are fired by raku, a process developed in Japan. "I am constantly working with hot pots, using tongs to place the pieces into the hot kiln and removing them at precisely the moment that the glaze melts," she explains. When the pots meet the outside air, thermal shock is created, causing the glaze to crackle. The burning pots are then placed into trash cans filled with combustible materials such as sawdust or woodchips. It is at this point that the dramatic patterns of raku emerge: The unglazed portions turn black or smokey gray and the crackle in the glaze becomes a mysterious dark network of black lines.

"This firing process creates a spontaneity and immediacy in my work," she says. "I am constantly working with each pot so that I feel more a part of the process, developing a close relationship with each individual piece."

Lois, thirty-five, is still at Mudflat, only now as a studio potter and instructor. Since the raku process has to be performed outdoors, she has a summer studio on Cape Cod in Cedarville. She is a member of Cape Cod Potters and the American Craft Council.

Brochure: No.
Commissions: Yes.
Studio Hours: None.
Telephone: (617) 876-8793.

Raku vase is hand built from slabs of clay and raku fired. Like all Lois' pieces, this one utilizes a white crackle glaze and copper oxide. Besides the exterior stripe, this piece has the crackle glaze on the inside as well so that it may hold water. "I enjoy the contrast of the white glazed section to the dull black, unglazed portions." 10 inches high by 4 inches square; $55.

Jan Lacoste

Lacoste Pottery
215 Cambridge Turnpike
Concord, Massachusetts 01742

Having been involved with crafts since her college days, Jan Lacoste decided in her mid-twenties to choose pottery making as her career. Leaving her job as a mediator with a Cambridge, Massachusetts, landlord, she took a job at Boston's Museum of Fine Arts, where for two years she was in charge of the manufacture of all ceramic glazes. After a subsequent stint working in a retail design store, Jan went into business for herself in 1977, opening Lacoste Pottery.

Her inspiration comes from many sources. "I especially like antiques and I visit museums regularly. I also go to contemporary design stores and department stores to see what is happening there. From the tradition of clay and ceramics, I am fond of English delft and French porcelains, and the blue-and-white ware of Korea, China and Japan."

Painting with color slips on porcelain allows Jan to achieve a fine, handpainted look. Color is important to her work, especially the challenge of getting a good reduction blue, not always easy to do successfully. She finds that her work appeals "to those who like antiques, the French country look and fanciful things." "The flower motif, often stylized, runs through my work," observes the thirty-six-year-old potter. "But it is the brush stroke itself which is most exciting." Her goal is someday to open a craft gallery featuring her work along with the work of others.

"The business and economic end of things must really be considered and looked after," she told me. "It's possible to make money in crafts, but you must be very careful and adhere to plans and schedules in order to have time for creativity."

Jan is a member of the China Students Club of Boston, the American Craft Council and the Society of Arts and Crafts in Boston, of which she is a member of the board. She received her bachelors degree in fine arts from Tulane University.

Brochure: Yes.
Commissions: Yes.
Studio Hours: By appointment.
Telephone: (617) 369-0278.

Pitcher and bowl of hand-thrown porcelain decorated with underglaze blue painting. "This charming pair may be used together or separately." Like the rest of her line, they are fired at a high temperature, making them strong, nonporous and suitable for eating and drinking. Bowl is 12¼ inches in diameter, pitcher is 8 inches high; $94 for both.

STEVEN BRANFMAN

The Potter's Shop
34 Lincoln Street
Newton, Massachusetts 02159

Steven Branfman works exclusively in raku, a process that he finds "exciting, spontaneous and unpredictable." His forms are large-scale, wheel-thrown vessels.

He has been working clay full time since 1975, teaching, making pots and operating his own studio. "My challenge is to make good pots and in doing so maintain the integrity of the pottery form—not to abandon or stretch the form out of recognition.

"Raku is a process that has allowed me to expand my art experience," he told me. "I approach it with the utmost respect for the technique and its origins. It's as though we are equal partners in the creative process. I can have complete control and do everything right but when the piece is sitting in the smoke, it's out of my hands. It humbles you."

Steve describes the nature of art as "a reflection or portrait of the artist." "I have viewed my work in this light for some time. Work that is honest is the most valid and must come from within the artist," he says. "My most successful work is that which I feel the closest to during its growth. Whether you want to admit it or not, all art is portraiture and some pieces make you look better than others."

Steven, thirty, received his masters degree in fine arts from Rhode Island School of Design in 1975. A professional potter since graduation, he is a faculty member at the Thayers Academy in Braintree, Massachusetts, and owns and operates The Potter's Shop, which provides services for professional and amateur potters, offers pottery courses and retails pottery to the public. He is a member of the American Craft Council, Massachusetts Association for the Arts, and World Craft Council among others.

Brochure: No.
Commissions: Yes.
Studio Hours: Monday through Friday, 10 A.M. to 9 P.M., Saturday 9 A.M. to 5 P.M.; October through April, open Sunday 11 A.M. to 5 P.M.
Telephone: (617) 965-3959.

This vase is an example of a wide variety of raku vessels available from Steve. His work exhibits various surface treatments and glazing combinations varying from glossy, smooth and colorful surfaces to rough, black, raw-looking ones. Decorative techniques often used include impressed designs, altered forms and carved areas. Sizes from 12 inches to over 35 inches high. Prices range from $75 to $600. Pictured vase is 21 inches high and priced at $500.

Barbara Walch

*150 Main Street
Northampton, Massachusetts 01060*

Barbara Walch says she first became interested in pottery while an art student in 1971, although her memories of clay go back much further. "When I was an infant," she recalls, "my father made pots as a hobby and I grew up with a kiln and buckets of clay in the basement."

Her pottery is about as organic looking as can be. "All my life I have picked up shells, leaves, seed pods and other interesting forms in nature," she says. "These have all played a subconscious part in influencing the form that I reproduce in clay."

Barbara has concentrated on hand building, making all her pieces by pinching, rolling and constructing the clay. All her work, which is mainly stoneware, is nontoxic and "impervious to water, although its earthly appearance may lead you to think otherwise." Most of her pieces are glazed only on the inside with a warm-colored, semimatte glaze.

The thirty-two-year-old potter is a member of the Asparagus Valley Potters Guild and the East Street Clay Studio. She has been a practicing potter for nine years. "I enjoy the actual working of the clay in my hands," she says, "as well as the independence and self-reliance that this kind of self-employment gives me."

Brochure: No.
Commissions: No.
Studio Hours: None.
Telephone: (413) 586-4509.

Pair of small serving bowls with serving spoons. Hand built in dark-brown stoneware, the clay is left unglazed except inside, which is glazed a warm orange-beige. All her work is nonporous and nontoxic. Each bowl about 6 inches in diameter; $13 each.

Dinnerware in hand built dark-brown stoneware with an orange-beige glaze on all eating surfaces. Goblet $9, teacup and saucer $16, dinner plate (10-inch diameter) $20, small plate $10.

TOM WHITE

PO Box 145
Northfield, Massachusetts 01360

It's been twelve years since Tom White, then a predental student at St. Peter's College in New Jersey, "stumbled into pottery." Invited over to a friend's house for dinner, he became quite intrigued with the stoneware place settings that adorned the dinner table. His friend, a potter, invited him back for some lessons.

Returning the next day for some rudimentary instruction on the wheel, he remembers that he sat down and made six bowls that very first day. "I thought it was grand. So I started making pots," he told me. "It came extremely easy to me."

Enamored of the potential of pottery, Tom took that fall off to mull over career matters. When he returned to school the next semester he had changed both his major—to fine arts—and his school—to Monmouth College in New Jersey—where he received his fine arts degree.

Like most potters, Tom started working in stoneware. But as his pieces became progressively more complex, involving techniques such as carving and slip decoration, he found porcelain to be more suitable for his work and switched six years ago. Today all of his pieces are of high-fired porcelain and finished in traditional, generally solid glazes.

"I use traditional techniques like slip decorating or trailings and carving," he notes, "and I have a great appreciation of the classical work of Chinese ceramics." "But what I do using these methods is, I think, very personal and contemporary. You want to add to a tradition so that it becomes yours."

"Everything I make is very functional and most definitely made to be used," notes the thirty-five-year-old potter. "But they're also fancy enough so that they can be appreciated as a display piece."

Tom teaches ceramics at Northfield Mount Herman School, a preparatory school in Northfield, Massachusetts. He is a member of the American Craft Council, the League of New Hampshire Craftsmen and the Asparagus Valley Potters Guild.

Brochure: No.
Commissions: Yes, especially large vessels, urns and wall pieces.
Studio Hours: By appointment.
Telephone: (413) 498-2175.

Porcelain platter with a cut rim and slip decoration over a celadon (light green) glaze. 18 inches high; $110. Porcelain teapot has a carved, fluted surface with a celadon glaze. 9 inches high with a cane handle; $45. The small incense box, also made of porcelain with a celadon glaze, can be used as a bureau box or a desk accessory. About 4 inches in diameter by 2 inches high, with a carved, fluted surface; $18.

Porcelain covered box has a copper-red glaze and is decorated with two applied birds; 4 inches in diameter, $22.

RALPH AND SANDY TERRY

The Terry Pottery
32 Walnut Road
Norwell, Massachusetts 02061

The Terry Pottery studio came to life in 1969 when Ralph Terry began winding down his award-winning graphic-and-packaging design business in favor of the "peace of mind and creative freedom" that he found working in clay. He was soon joined by wife Sandy, who, after a short career as an art teacher and an ongoing career as the mother of three boys, began to transfer her painting techniques to Ralph's three-dimensional clay forms.

Today Ralph, forty-nine, continues to concentrate on "perfecting shape and form" in thrown and hand-built stoneware, while Sandy, forty-four, embellishes them with intricate tapestries of coils, lines, textures, inlays and stains. The result is a continuously evolving collection of fine pottery.

The Terrys work in a busy and crowded studio attached to their home, where during rush periods you'll find all the family members pitching in to do "whatever is needed to help out." It is this family unity that the Terrys credit with providing the environment that allows for continued growth of the pottery.

The Terrys' philosophy of their work is simple and direct: "We create pots to be used, to be beautiful, to hold things or just to make people smile."

The Terrys have exhibited at many professional-level fairs and have had a number of individual and group exhibitions. They are represented by more than eighty galleries across the U.S. and have produced specially commissioned pieces for the Springfield and Boston Science Museum.

Brochure: Yes.
Commissions: Yes.
Studio Hours: By appointment.
Telephone: (617) 659-7007.

This vase is also of unglazed white stoneware and shares decorative techniques with the other vessel. It was wheel thrown rather than built by hand. Height 9 inches; $52.

Handbuilt unglazed white stoneware vessel has applied decoration in white and colored porcelain with stains added. The handle is made of multiple reeds with whipping. Height 16 inches including handle; $56.

FRANK OZEREKO

5 Amherst Road
Pelham, Massachusetts 01002

Frank Ozereko's interest in architecture, Third World cultures and totemic and primitive art can be seen in his unique double-walled vessels. The stoneware vessels, which usually have surfaces that resemble ancient metal or stone, are reminiscent of some age-old culture. Yet they are contemporary artifacts, containing their own unspecified sense of history, time and space.

"The building of a piece is a constant surprise to me," says the thirty-four-year-old artist. "Each piece represents constant invention, decision making and discovery, so that after a piece is finished, I would be hard pressed to duplicate it."

Frank suggests that the vessels can work as planters or left empty to emphasize the "interesting relationship between the subdued interior to the more active exterior space." They can also be used, he says, in landscapes, "like a Japanese stone lantern" or as a "decorator's punctuation mark."

Frank is an Assistant Professor at the University of Massachusetts at Amherst. A member of the American Craft Council and the World Craft Council, he has been making clay vessels for seven years and has received study grants from both the Massachusetts State Council on the Arts and the National Endowment for the Arts.

Brochure: No.
Commissions: Yes.
Studio Hours: By appointment.
Telephone: (413) 545-2750.

This vessel has a blue-green to grey-and-white glaze over a brown clay body. A smooth interior contrasts the busier exterior. It can be used for plants, interior design or outdoor landscaping and is 20 inches high by 15 inches across. All Frank's vessels are one of a kind and are priced from $200 to $600.

Martha Winston

*838 East Broadway
South Boston, Massachusetts 02127*

Martha Winston uses clay to create wall pieces that are reminiscent of painting. Having been trained at the Rhode Island School of Design as a painter prior to taking up ceramics, she found that the clay surface offered her many more possibilities than could two-dimensional painting. "The malleability of clay allows for a very versatile surface that combines both painting and sculpture," says the twenty-six-year-old artist.

Her current works deal with the "interaction of figures and figurative elements within a tribal context. By exploring this imagery, I attempt to represent emotional conflict as it occurs in fantasy and reality. Using the tile as a format I can combine and re-order elements of a design to satisfy the intensity of the conflict."

In 1982, while a summer apprentice at the Moravian Tileworks in Pennsylvania, Martha further explored the use of tile and clay in architectural surroundings. "I believe that there is a demand for a new direction in clay/tile as a decorative art," she told me. "Creating one-of-a-kind or site-specific works has special appeal for me because I wish to develop my imagery, not mass-produce it."

Brochure: "Not as yet."
Commissions: All work is by commission.
Studio Hours: By appointment.
Telephone: (617) 787-4177.

"Figurative Fanfare." "The wavelike figures establish a pattern that is enhanced by the depth/relief created by the figure limbs." She has combined terra-cotta with luster on raw clay, with slips and bright tempera colors used to provide a dramatic background. 11 inches long by 23 inches wide by 1 inch deep, mounted on board; $150. Prices vary according to how pieces are mounted.

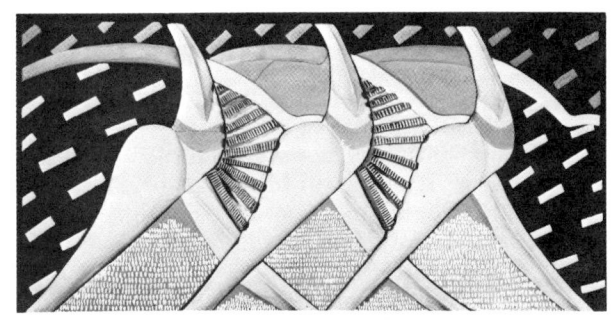

"Tribal Boogie." Utilizing pattern and continuity as the key elements of this multicolored wallwork, Martha assembles the figures according to the structure of the zig-zag background. "The warmth of the terra cotta combined with inlaid, colored clay, incised lines and slips creates a strong surface image." 15 inches long by 22 inches wide by 1 inch deep. Mounted on board, $150.

Laura Shlien

Turning Point Pottery
14 Reservoir Road
Wayland, Massachusetts 01778

Laura Shlien is fascinated by porcelain. "It has an internal glow, a luminosity that is quite seductive." But until the thirty-three-year-old potter had discovered crystalline glazes, she had always felt that the glazing process was inadequate to express the "elusive and enchanting nature of porcelain. The first time that I saw a crystalline glaze I knew all my interests could be unified in the production of pots I consider to be self-sufficient."

With crystalline glazes, crystals grow in the molten glaze as the pot is fired in the kiln to 2400°F and then cooled down. Although one glaze is used to cover the entire pot, colors may separate as the crystals grow so that they appear to float on a background of another color. The crystals may appear in a variety of shapes from starbursts or fan shapes to round, flowerlike forms. It is this unpredictability that excites Laura and makes the opening of the kiln after a firing one of the "special moments" in her work.

Laura's forms tend to be traditional, with simple, flowing lines designed not to compete with the spontaneously formed crystalline effects. Calling her pieces "semifunctional," she explains that "the glaze effects are so rich and varied that the pieces often transcend function."

She often asks customers what they do because she's amused at how many of them turn out to be scientists. "They appreciate the laws of nature that create the crystals and so enjoy the pieces conceptually as well as visually."

Brochure: A brochure with color photos is available.
Commissions: Yes.
Studio Hours: By appointment.
Telephone: (617) 358-7423.

Shown here are, from left, an open round vase, a semiclosed round vase and a bottle form. The forms can be finished in a variety of crystalline glaze colors and effects. Open round vases are 6 to 16 inches high and $50 to $70; semiclosed round vases from 5 to 9 inches high and $50 to $70; bottles from 3 to 12 inches high and $40 to $80. Cylindrical vases (not shown) are 6 to 16 inches tall and range from $40 to $140.

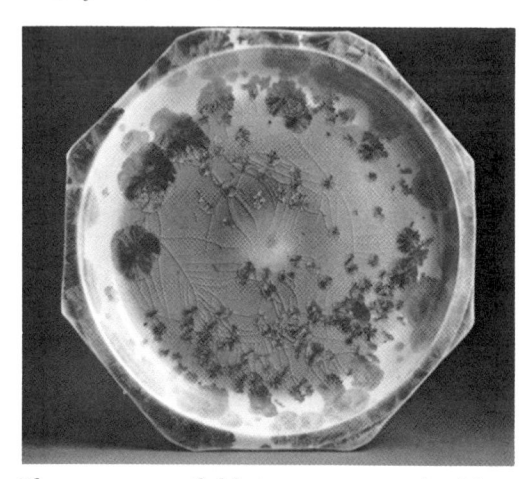

Platters are available in two sizes and in blue/brown, orange or cream colors. Diameter 12 to 14 inches, $50; 14 to 16 inches, $65. All sizes are approximate; the glaze effects and size determine the price.

Nancy Gilson

PO Box 33
Wollaston, Massachusetts 02170

"Frequently in the arts," says Nancy Gilson, "the works themselves tend to glorify the vocation of the artist and to place tremendous emphasis on difference. Attempting to gain popularity and to appeal to the audience's love of the spectacular, younger artists are often enticed to ignore tradition, to put off or simply avoid a long apprenticeship to one's chosen art form."

It is Nancy's hope that what is distinctive about her porcelain blackware will emerge through a mastery of technique. She is convinced that inventive breakthroughs in the arts are "more apt to occur when a person devotes a good deal of time to the careful study of form and to constant experimentation with the material—not wild departures, but subtle change."

Each porcelain piece is wheel thrown and hand trimmed. After burnishing with a smooth stone, a clay slip is applied, the piece is incised and carved and any additional colored clay slips are applied. The bisque firing is done in an electric kiln. The pots are then fired in sawdust for up to forty-eight hours, which removes oxygen from the clay, turning it black in the process. Because of the low firing temperature, the clay is porous and will not hold liquids. The surface patina requires only an occasional buff with a soft cloth to retain its shine.

After graduating in 1972 with a degree in art history from Mount Holyoke College in South Hadley, Massachusetts, Nancy earned her bachelors degree in fine arts from the California College of Arts and Crafts in Oakland. She has been a potter for eleven years and has taught several seminars and workshops in her craft.

Brochure: Yes.
Commissions: Yes.
Studio Hours: None.
Telephone: (617) 698-7177.

Cylindrical container made of porcelain and hand burnished with terra sigillata and colored clay slips. It is then sawdust-fired with a variety of soft and hard woods. Height 5 inches; $55.

Bob Ellis and Teresa Taylor

Salty Dog Pottery
RFD 1, Route 28
Barnstead, New Hampshire 03218

Bob Ellis and Teresa Taylor are practitioners of the increasingly rare art of salt glazing, whose effects can be seen in the rich variety of mottled or "orange peel" surface textures that embellish their work.

Each potter first works individually on their own pieces, then combining them in the kiln for the salt-firing process. When the kiln reaches 2300°F, rock salt is thrown into the kiln through ports. The heat causes the sodium in the salt to fuse with the clay's natural silica and produce distinctive and varying glaze patterns in the tones of blues or browns. Some pieces may have a heavy orange-peel texture from intense chemical reaction while others may have a light, delicate coating where the flame and salt licked by. The potters also fire their kiln with wood, which further adds to the variety of textural subtleties.

"Our work demands this surface," they explain. "It is dependent on it and designed specifically for it. The work is constantly changing, growing-regressing-growing, always on the move. Monday's idea may result in Friday's successful piece. But then again, it may not."

Bob and Teresa, both thirty-one, studied clay at the University of Illinois, graduating in 1973. They are members of League of New Hampshire Craftsmen, Potters Guild of New Hampshire and Boston Society of Arts and Crafts.

Brochure: Although they don't have a brochure due to the changing nature of their work, they will on request send photos and descriptions of sample pieces to interested people.
Commissions: Special orders take up half their time and they'll be happy to produce either functional or decorative pieces.
Studio Hours: Studio and showroom open by appointment.
Telephone: (603) 435-6014.

This stoneware two-quart steamer features the increasingly rare salt-glaze process. It is available in blue or brown tones. The steamer collects vitamin-rich juices that can be used for soup stock or gravy. Instructions for use are included with each steamer. $42 plus shipping.

A saltglazed planter banded with colored clays. In blues or brown tones. Height 5 inches, width 7 inches, $22 plus shipping.

Susan Link

*Five Wings Studio
RFD 293, East Lake Road
Fitzwilliam, New Hampshire 03447*

It was about ten years ago, during a period of study and travel in Japan, that Susan Link became inspired by the "high level" of their arts and crafts, particularly the pottery. "I appreciated how people's lives were enriched by the pottery that they used every day, pottery that was both functional and very beautiful. In my recent work, I strive to use the same standards of beauty, only appropriate for the culture I live in."

Delayed for a while in her pottery career by the responsibilities of raising three small children, Susan began working in her present studio two years ago. Prior to that, she had worked with brush, ink and paper in a form of Japanese ink painting called sumi. "When I began to make pots again," she says, "I found the three-dimensional form and glaze qualities a new and exciting challenge for my brushwork."

Gathering her inspiration from flowers, plants, insects and animals, the thirty-three-year-old potter expresses their "essential nature" with as few brush strokes as possible. "When I use a pattern on a series of pots for a period of time, it becomes very fluid, like a signature," she told me, adding, "I like to continually expand what I do. With every kiln load there is new energy and new designs being added to the standard items."

Susan teaches both pottery and sumi painting to students at Franklin Pierce College and the Sharon Arts Center. "I find this helps keep a balance between the time spent alone in the studio and time spent with new and interesting people," she says.

Brochure: Yes.
Commissions: Yes.
Studio Hours: Monday through Saturday, 9 A.M. to 5 P.M.; Sunday, 1 P.M. to 5 P.M.
Telephone: (603) 585-6682.

Porcelain baskets with blue cobalt decoration in a variety of sizes and designs. "I find this form very exciting: The low, slightly squared bowl enclosing a circle with a free-flowing yet detailed design." Custom made washable handles of ash splits and cane. From left: small basket with orchid decoration, 7-inch diameter, $55; medium basket has camelias, 8½-inch diameter, $75; large basket with wisterias, 9½-inch diameter, $90.

"Daylilies" lamp base of high-fired porcelain and blue-cobalt decoration. The design is wrapped around the base, which features brass fixtures and a three-way switch. The cord can be stored inside the base. Custom-made shade is made of silk and blue grosgrain. Velvet trim nicely sets off the brushwork on the base. Lamp base is 9½ inches high with an 8-foot cord. Shade is 12 inches high with a diameter of 7 inches on top and a 9-inch bottom. Price of base $75. Optional shade $25.

WAYLAND W. BUNNELL

The Color Wheel
71-A Myrtle Street
Manchester, New Hampshire 03104

Wayland Bunnell was one frustrated college student. After three years at the University of New Hampshire he was ready to change majors for the fourth time. "Another fellow in the dormitory was bringing back some pots that he'd made in class and I was bringing back essays, reports and exams," he told me. Deciding that what his friend was doing seemed "more sensible," and seeing an opportunity to indulge his desire to "make things," Wayland decided to major in ceramics.

Fifteen years later, the thirty-five-year-old potter has his own studio, sharing space with a welding studio a few blocks from downtown Manchester. There is sometimes a degree of tension between Wayland and the welders. "Art or craft is not really considered work by most people outside the profession," he says, adding that many within it feel the same way. "I am constantly barraged by the attitude that I am playing." Wayland notes that being a potter doesn't free you from drudgery, no matter how pleasant it might seem. "I use about four tons of clay a year. With all the steps that it goes through to go out the door as finished work, I handcarry that four tons of clay tenfold. That is a lot of work!"

The glazing process is of special interest to Wayland, who has taught several workshops on the subject and completed about 7,000 glaze tests. This interest is one reason that he works in porcelain, throwing simple forms designed "to carry the expression in the glazes."

"Function is the most important consideration when I throw," he told me. "I enjoy pottery and wish others to be able to do the same." His pieces usually have thickened edges and thick walls, all the better to survive daily use. Although he feels that "design is intimately tied to function," Wayland has developed his own style over the last fifteen years, calling it a "natural extension of the personality. As the body gets comfortable moving the clay and handling the glazes," he explains, "beginnings and endings of pots define themselves."

Wayland is a member of the League of New Hampshire Craftsmen and the New Hampshire Potters Guild.

Brochure: Yes.
Commissions: Yes.
Studio Hours: Monday through Thursday from 9 A.M. to 4 P.M. and by appointment. Please call first.
Telephone: (603) 668-5466.

Canister set of four matching pieces. Available in aqua, dark and light blue, brown and beige and cranberry. Largest jar is 11 inches high; $100 plus shipping.

Lamp with handmade cut-and-pierced paper shade. The porcelain base is available in a wide variety of solid colors from Wayland's palette of some twenty glazes. Colors include dark and light blue, beige, blue-beige, aqua, cranberry, green, wheat, brown and white. Lamps include shades of matching paper and ribbon. Overall height 20 to 22 inches; $200 plus shipping.

JEAN SILVERMAN

Plum Tree Pottery
Neal Mill Road
Newmarket, New Hampshire 03857

Jean Silverman came to the craft of pottery through archaeology and the study of classical art. "While writing a doctoral dissertation on Minoan vase painting, I took my first pottery classes to see if the experience of making pots myself would aid my archaeological research," she remembers. "Soon I became wholly involved with the medium of clay."

Jean credits classical and preclassical Greek pottery as having a strong influence on her work. This can be seen particularly in the shapes of her objects, which often tend toward narrow bases and high, wide shoulders. The three-dimensional decoration that she uses is inspired not only by ancient Crete but also draws from Japanese brush painting. "With the decoration," she explains, "I am setting up a tension between the smooth, round surface of the pot and the contrasting texture of the ornament which emerges out of this surface, both disturbing and enhancing the form."

It is porcelain's unique properties that attracted Jean. "Porcelain spans the boundary between clay and glass," she told me. "Since it is compounded of fine-particle white clays, feldspar and flint, when it is fired to its saturation point, it becomes hard, dense and translucent."

Jean, thirty-eight, makes her pieces either on the wheel or from hand-rolled slabs and forms the decoration by hand. No molds are ever used. When the pot has become leather-hard, she trims or smooths the base, sketches a preliminary design on the surface and then begins carving some areas, building on to others. The piece is set aside until it is bone dry, when it then receives its first, low-temperature bisque firing. After firing, it is painted with various glaze stains, dipped in a clear glaze and fired again.

Jean belongs to the League of New Hampshire Craftsmen and the New Hampshire Potter's Guild.

Brochure: Yes.
Commissions: Yes.
Studio Hours: By appointment.
Telephone: (603) 659-2632.

Porcelain dinnerware is wheel-thrown with hand-formed irises and underglaze painting. Colors are a muted purple for the iris, a soft spring green for the leaves on a white background. The teapot may also be ordered white on white. Center: Teapot with relief iris on the side and lid. "My teapot is comfortably round with a side-attached handle, which I think makes it balance better and pour more easily." Height 7 inches; $40. Left: Creamer and sugar bowl with carved and painted iris on creamer and an iris as the handle on bowl lid. Height 3½ inches; $26. Right: Mugs with carved and painted iris under handle. Height 4½ inches; $10 each. Other flower varieties are available.

E. H. WHEELER

*Wheeler Pottery
PO Box 300, Strawbery Banke
Portsmouth, New Hampshire 03801*

E. H. "Bud" Wheeler has been aptly described as a "born-again potter." Dissatisfied with his established career as a biological oceanographer, he decided seven years ago at the age of forty to leave academic life and pursue a career as a potter.

"The first successful pot made the hairs stand up on the back of my neck," he told me, "and that still happens when a superb and lively pot appears." Clearly, the thrill is not gone. "I now stare at pots and go over them inch by inch with my eyes and hands," he says. "Texture and subtle color contrasts on basic container shapes fascinate me."

Bud uses a salt-impregnation technique that provides a surface texture directly related to the firing of the piece. It is, he says, "unpredictable enough to be exciting." "I love the anticipatory tension that builds while the kiln is cooling. It's not unlike waiting to see what comes up in the nets from the deep sea."

Being the full-time potter at Strawbery Banke, an historical museum community near his home, has allowed Bud to sell most of his work from his studio, giving him the financial security from which to grow as a creative potter.

"The life-style is a good one," he says. "I love to make pots, decorate pots, fire pots in the kiln and to sell pots! I would guess that I'll be doing this until I drop."

Bud is a member of the League of New Hampshire Craftsmen and the New Hampshire Potters Guild.

Brochure: No.
Commissions: No.
Studio Hours: Tuesday through Sunday, 9:30 A.M. to 5 P.M.
Telephone: (603) 436-1506.

The contrasting top and handles of these stoneware vases are white stoneware with crackle glaze. The body is unglazed brown stoneware. The interior is glazed. Left: Two handles, 16 inches high, 9 inches wide; $120. Right: Three handles, 14 inches high, 10 inches wide, $120.

Three-handled stoneware vase with crackle glaze on a wrought-iron tripod. "Although these pieces are of my own design, the style is from the past and comfortable to me. The crackle glaze is very soft to the touch — the pot is meant to be picked up and held." Unglazed versions are also available. Height 12 inches, width 7 inches; $75.

JILLIAN BARBER

PO Box 51
Jamestown, Rhode Island 02835

With inspiration from "the light, the beauty of nature, the stories that faces tell," Jillian Barber creates striking and calming ceramic masks. "My work with masks," she says, "combines a love of nature with the fantasy of dreams. In a way, I am creating my own mythology."

Accurately describing her exquisitely colored masks as "in this world but not of it," she speaks of their "mystery, serenity and a deep, meditative calm in the gently closed eyes."

In addition to her series of Oriental masks, Jillian will create individually commissioned portrait masks. "What better way to become immortal," she asks, "than to be cast in clay with an exotic headdress of your own imaginings, to have a real, three-dimensional likeness of yourself?"

Jillian, thirty-seven, works at home, giving herself time for long walks with her dog, Goonah, and "time for just staring out the window at glowing sunsets." "It is a life-style with built-in discipline," she says. "I've developed a philosophical, spiritual outlook on life, readily visible to me in my entourage of work."

Jillian received her fine-arts degree in ceramics in 1968 from the Rhode Island School of Design. Her work has been shown in many exhibitions. She is a member of the the American Craft Council, the Conanicut Island Artists Association and the Mystic (Connecticut) Art Association, among others.

Brochure: Yes.
Commissions: "I am happy to do individual portrait castings by commission. Imagery and personal color preferences are decided before completion of the mask."
Studio Hours: By appointment.
Telephone: (401) 423-2335.

Oriental mask with flowers is hand built of white clay. Various pieces of antique lace are used for the textured impressions of the headdress. Roses, gardenias, lilies, poppies, leaves and peapods frame the Oriental face, which is an original casting. Colors are optional and are delicately applied beneath a shiny transparent overglaze. Height 18 inches, width 14 inches; $425. Smaller size masks available from $110 with prices ranging to $500 and more.

PATRICIA UCHILL SIMONS

Pat's Ceramics
20 Lincoln Avenue
Providence, Rhode Island 02906

When Pat and her family moved to Providence from Wisconsin three years ago, she looked around and saw that "New England had thousands of traditional functional potters." In search of her own niche, she decided to create a line of functional animal sculptures to add to the traditional pottery that she still produces.

"I like to create clay pieces that are earthy, warm and inviting to touch," she explains, adding that her menagerie provides her with the "perfect context for my exploration of textures." Each piece is first thrown on the wheel and then altered into the various animal figures. "I am indebted to the plastic quality of clay which allows me to press textures into the skin or stretch the surface for a pleasing visual pattern and an integration of form and figure," she told me.

Whether it's the elongated forms of the giraffe, the exaggerated features of the camel or llama, the bands and patterns of the armadillo or the cracked surface texture of the elephant and rhinoceros, Pat's animals evoke a sense of humor that attests to the joy felt by their creator in bringing them to life.

"When I worked as a painter or a printmaker," says the forty-six-year-old mother of two, "I found it hard to deal with the pressures of keeping up production. It's very easy, however, to work ten hours a day seven days a week doing ceramics and still look forward to the next day. It's a technical mesmerization."

Pat has exhibited her work across the country and holds an undergraduate degree in design from the University of Michigan, a masters in fine arts from the University of Chicago and a masters in art education from the Rhode Island School of Design.

Brochure: Yes.
Commissions: Yes.
Studio Hours: None.
Telephone: (401) 272-1431.

Stoneware clay rhino candle is 8 inches high, 9 inches long and 4 inches wide; $25. Also available: camel sugar bowl and creamer, mother and child giraffe vases and others. Many pieces are available in either stoneware or porcelain.

ROBERT COMPTON

Robert Compton Ltd.
Star Route, PO Box 6
Bristol, Vermont 05443

Bob Compton's fourteen-year fascination with clay has led him down many paths, from traditional dinnerware to lighting fixtures and furniture to his current work, which is a result of his attempt to "transcend the limits of clay" and effectively integrate with it light, glass, motion and water.

"The sounds and movement of running water have a truly soothing effect upon the human spirit," Bob notes. His desire to evoke that feeling has led him to create his waterfall, cascading fountains and aquariums. He makes the fountains in two styles. Sizes range from 28 inches to 10 feet tall. Each fountain has its own variety of sounds and visual effects.

With his single, double and triple aquariums, Bob manages to again push the clay's limits, making it seem transparent through his use of glass, while using light to illuminate the form.

Bob first throws his pieces on the wheel and then alters the forms into new shapes and functions. Using surface texture as effective enhancement of his shapes, one of his goals is to achieve a purity of form. The thirty-three-year-old ceramicist works in his studio at the foot of Vermont's Green Mountains. "I find living in the country environment gives me immediate access to the outdoors, which I feel I must keep in constant touch with."

Bob's work has been featured at many one-man shows and invitational exhibitions. He first studied clay while attending the University of Vermont and is on the board of directors of the Vermont State Craft Center. He is also a member of the American Craft Council and the World Craft Council.

Brochure: A poster-size brochure is available for $2.00 that pictures several models of fountains and aquariums.
Commissions: Yes.
Studio Hours: By appointment.
Telephone: (802) 453-3778.

This stoneware hanging aquarium is suitable for either salt or fresh water. They are available in either hanging or standing styles and have a textured exterior with a smooth glazed interior for easy cleaning. Equipped with an under gravel filter, airline hose, pump, operating instructions and a concealed light to illuminate its interior. Shown here is the seven-gallon size; $560. Also available in one-gallon ($170), three-gallon ($280) and fifteen-gallon ($1500).

The sculptural waterfall fountain is Bob's favorite design. They have self-contained reservoirs and need no special plumbing. Made of a stoneware clay body, they come equipped with pump and operating instructions. "These durable fountains can be used indoors and outdoors for year-round enjoyment. Shown here are 28- and 48-inch sizes; $450 and $630. Also available in a 68-inch size for $930.

STEVE ABRAMS

Willy Hill Pottery
RFD 2
Groton, Vermont 05046

After five years of working in the paint-manufacturing business and in the entertainment field, Steve Abrams decided to look for a career that would involve working with his hands. He found it when he took a six-week beginner course in pottery at the Leverett Craft Center in Massachusetts. He stayed on after that course and for the next five years developed his potting skills with the aid of an informal apprenticeship to resident potter Armand Cottrell.

Today, twelve years after that first course, Steve produces a line of stoneware that features a combination of functional shapes, flowing forms and a jewel-like glaze that provides each piece with a simple elegance. "It is an exciting glaze that relates beautifully with the clay," he notes. The glaze is basically blue with brown trim "but it contains a multitude of colors so that each piece is one of a kind yet harmonizes well as part of a collection."

"I like the plasticity of clay," he says. "It's very gratifying to take a ball of clay and form it into a vessel. Throwing on the wheel is my favorite part."

In 1976 Steve moved to Vermont with his wife Jackie, a basketmaker. "We have two wonderful girls who enjoy playing with clay and using their daddy's dishes." Steve, thirty-nine, is a member of Craft Professionals of Vermont, League of New Hampshire Craftsmen and Vermont Handcrafters.

Brochure: Yes.
Commissions: Limited.
Studio Hours: By appointment.
Telephone: (802) 439-6265.

Wheel-thrown, high-fired stoneware is oven proof, lead free, dishwasher and microwave-oven safe. "Their hard, glossy surface makes each pot extremely durable, scratch proof and easy to clean." Left: Casserole can be used for baking or as a covered snack bowl. 1½-quart capacity; $34. Center front: Baking/serving dish is paddled to a square shape and "nice for nuts and fruits." Diameter 8½ inches; $34. Center rear: Vase is ideal for arrangements of fresh and dried flowers. 8 inches tall; $22. Pitcher, can also be used as a vase, 8½ inches tall; $25. Right: All-purpose bowl, 4½ inches high and 9½ inches wide; $20. All prices plus shipping.

ROGER ROBERGE

PO Box 31
Topsham, Vermont 05076

"Just about all of my adult life has been spent studying and making pottery," says Roger Roberge, "first in Boston, then in Kyoto, Japan, and now in an old schoolhouse in the hills of east-central Vermont."

Inspired by the "common appeal of folk crafts from throughout the world," the forty-year-old potter aims to make his work "compatible with everyday life and nature."

"Usefulness for the hand, delight for the eye and thoughtfulness for the mind are features I try to combine in the work I make," Roger told me, adding, "My pieces are there for you to look at whenever you want, but are not meant to draw your attention to it. That is the difference between that and the New York style. The forms and designs are reflections of the surroundings of northern New England, filtered through the universal motifs of East and West."

He throws much of his functional stoneware on the wheel, while molding other pieces by hand from slabs of clay. They are all high-fired and are "with care, meant to last a very long time."

Roger is a member of Craft Professionals of Vermont, the American Craft Council, the League of New Hampshire Craftsmen and the Potters Guild of New Hampshire, of which he is Vice-President.

Brochure: In work.
Commissions: Yes.
Studio Hours: By appointment.
Telephone: (802) 439-5734.

Jar with cover and handles is made from stoneware with impressed lattice design on shoulder. Blue glaze, 4 inches high; $40.

White porcelain lamp has a blue and brown underglaze design. The shade is hand painted. Total height 17 inches. Lamp $40; shade $34.

Fiber

DAHLIA POPOVITS-RECHEL

North Road
Ashford, Connecticut 06278

Dahlia Popovits-Rechel is a clothing designer and weaver whose stated intent is to make functional and beautiful clothing. "I can see a grouping of yarns and I'll know what to do," she says, adding that she "works for the purity of creating the fiber."

Dahlia, who studied painting in college, remembers that her painting had started to strongly resemble weaving, what with their crossings of vertical and horizontal stripings. Thus inspired, she decided to go for the real thing. She originally worked in primarily off-loom techniques. "I enjoyed the experience of using my fingers and hands rather than tools like a shuttle," she told me. For the last two years Dahlia has been weaving on loom.

"What's important to me is the construction of the fiber, how it comes together and the movement of the fabric: Is it stiff, loose, tight?" She usually doesn't design her clothing until she sees the completed fabric, which, she notes, is an important element in the garment's design. "My work is for people who want a different texture on their body, who appreciate long-lasting clothes and who enjoy expressing themselves."

Dahlia, thirty-two, lives and works in a "wonderful 250-year-old farmhouse high on a hill surrounded by alfalfa and clover." She is a member of the American Craft Council.

Brochure: Yes.
Commissions: Yes.
Studio Hours: None.
Telephone: (203) 429-3822.

Dolman tunic is woven in various textures of cotton, silk and rayon boucles. It sports clean, straight and simple lines, bateau neck, dramatic dolman sleeves and can be worn with or without a belt. A seasonless garment designed in eloquent shades of peach, blue, ivory or black. S, M, L; $130.

Diane Graham Terry

174 Lenox Avenue
Bridgeport, Connecticut 06605

Diane Terry has been weaving functional pieces since 1979. Her fiber of choice is increasingly silk. "Besides the obvious luxury of silk, there is the comfort and breathability associated only with natural fibers," she explains. She also cites the "unusual hand" afforded by the fabric and the way in which it receives dye. Most important to her in her choice of silk is the drape of the finished garment that results when using the fiber. "No other fiber I have ever worked with could contribute as much to my designs," she told me.

Diane, twenty-eight, emphasizes that her clothing is "functional first, and beautiful second." "I will never make a piece that could be termed 'wearable art,'" she says, "since I am concerned with making comfortable and practical clothing that is classic and distinctive."

Most of her pieces are of a plain weave with more complex weaves used as decorative accents. "I think that juxtaposing two weaves in one piece helps draw attention to the complex weave." She often chooses fine yarns for use in her clothing rather than the heavier yarns that tend to make a stiffer fabric. Her garments also feature "loom-shaped" rather than tailored designs for the simplicity and classic styling that results.

Diane holds a degree in art education from Rhode Island College with a studio concentration in fiber. She is a member of the Connecticut Guild of Craftsmen, Handweavers Guild of Connecticut and the Brookfield Craft Center. Her work has been shown in several one-woman and group shows.

Brochure: No.
Commissions: No.
Studio Hours: None.
Telephone: (203) 334-8014.

Pure silk shirt with hand-dyed color features a finger-weave bodice with a charming arrangement of techniques and color. Three of these colors are used: lavender, blue, blue-green, gold, silver, coral, light green. Please specify five acceptable colors. S, L; $110.

Pine brushed silk scarf with hand-dyed color. Finger-weave border is woven with a variety of techniques and three of the aforementioned colors. Please specify five acceptable colors. Handstitched hem. Width 10 inches, length 40 inches, $40.

115 · FIBER

Patri Feher

WiseEye PhotoGraphics
27 Churchill Street
Fairfield, Connecticut 06430

Patri Feher utilizes a primitive photographic process called cyanotype, which she applies on fabric and rag paper to create stationery items, wall hangings, window transparencies and scarves in a variety of designs.

Cyanotype requires the application of a two-chemical solution, which is brushed on the material to be exposed making it light-sensitive. Patri then takes either found objects such as leaves or feathers or specially cut-out paper stencils and arranges them on the sensitized surface, covering them with a sheet of clear glass. This assembly is then brought out into strong sunlight for five to fifteen minutes. When the exposure is complete, the material is rinsed in water, which leaves a bright blue image in the exposed area and a white surface in the area shadowed by the objects.

Because the method is uncomplicated, the design can easily be manipulated and the image altered in a variety of ways to produce unique and beautiful utilitarian art.

When asked why she chose this rarely used process, Patri, thirty-one, talks about the "useless distinction" between craft and art and her intense curiosity about practical applications of decorative arts. She is emphatic. "Textures drive me crazy, color brutalizes my senses, form makes me drool and I really like to wear frumpy clothes and get all messy and wet. My hands are always dirty too and my true color is blue."

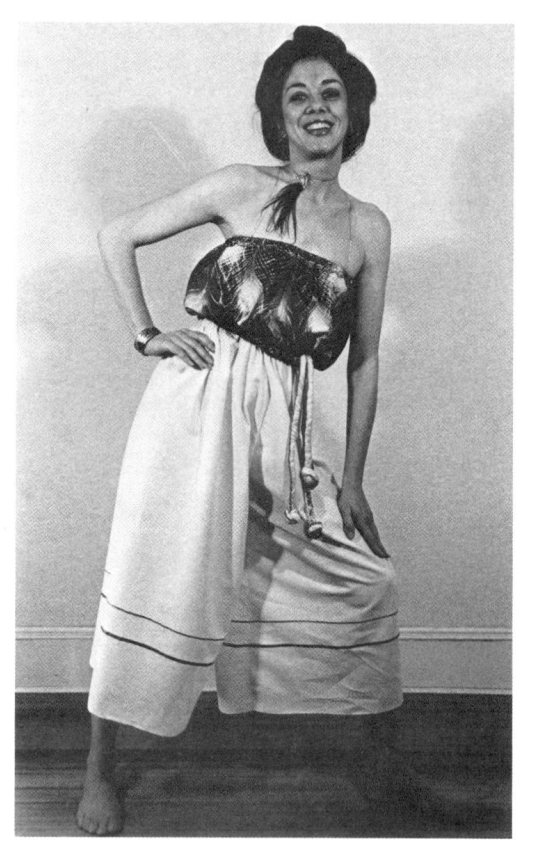

"Moxie," a blouson-printed camisole with attached extra-wide culotte pants tied with sausage belt. Natural and bleached cotton; $65; pima or sateen cotton; $70.

Brochure: Catalog describing wearable art, mailables and unusual gifts available for $1.00. Sample swatches and illustrations sent with catalog on request.
Commissions: Yes, including personalized cards, piece work for sewers, retailers, fashion designers and craftspeople.
Studio Hours: By appointment.
Telephone: (203) 259-2541.

Handcrafted notes and envelopes of translucent rice papers or rich, textured rag bond. Print area is 7 by 14 inches, folds to 5-by-7-inches; $3 each, $26 for one dozen.

Judy Robbins

1324 Neipsic Road
Glastonbury, Connecticut 06033

"I love quilts," declares Judy Robbins, who's been designing and making them since 1981. "But I don't have any romantic notions about them. It seems perfectly logical to me to see these graphic arrangements of fabric as primarily decorative. The fact that they can also keep a body warm seems like a curious bonus."

Judy usually does the quilting of her one-of-a-kind quilts by hand. "This quiet, mechanical work often lulls me into a meditative consciousness," she says. It is in this state of mind that she finds that new design ideas and feelings can be best explored on an intuitive level.

"Tapping into the rich, infinite world of design possibilities, with its limitless color combinations and kaleidoscopically shifting patterns is always exciting to me," the thirty-seven-year-old quiltmaker says. "While I am working, I often have a feeling of anticipation, as though something wonderful and unexpected is just about to happen. And sometimes it does."

Judy works by commission quite often, tailoring her work to her client's needs and desires. She is a member of several craft organizations, and is co-founder of the Greater Hartford Quilt Guild. She has participated in many shows and has had her work featured in quilting magazines. She teaches and lectures extensively and is co-author of *Not Just Another Quilt* (Van Nostrand Reinhold, 1982).

Brochure: No.
Commissions: Yes.
Studio Hours: None.
Telephone: (203) 633-0138.

"South for the Winter" wall quilt is inspired by the autumn migration of Canada geese. The traditional quilt pattern, "wild goose chase," is freely adapted here. Black-and-white geese fly in a V-formation against the clear blues of the October New England sky. Hand quilting defines imaginary patterns of wind current. 56 by 74 inches; $600.

"Ancient Mariner" wall quilt is machine pieced and hand quilted. Made of cotton fabrics in a monochromatic color scheme, the traditional pieced pattern is known as "mariner's compass." A verse from the poem Ancient Mariner is rendered in machine calligraphy in the border. 26-by-26 inches; $175.

Barbara Lee

Fiber Artistry
30 West Elderkin Avenue
Groton, Connecticut 06340

"Anything that one can possibly do with a sewing machine or with a needle by hand" is represented in Barbara Lee's eclectic collection of fiber art, which she calls "embroidery-quilted appliqué with embellishments."

Her collection of both one-of-a-kind and production pieces ranges from functional soft sculpture and wall hangings to sophisticated wearable art. In addition to using a variety of fabrication methods, Barbara will use any and all fabrics to achieve the effects that she envisions, intermingling such opposites as velvets with grocery string, lamé with suede or corduroy and burlap with silk, all with striking results.

After consecutive careers as a dance-school proprietor and a legal assistant, Barbara, now fifty-one, decided in 1979 to give in to her creative urges and became a full-time fiber artist after nearly thirty years as part-time.

She states that she has three goals: "To design and create as many pieces of fiber art to adorn the body and home as my lifetime permits, leaving a legacy of a dedicated master craftswoman; to publish a book on the unusual techniques that I've developed; and to educate the public that pillows do not have to be round, square or rectangular."

Barbara's work has been exhibited in more than twenty shows since 1978, including Sotheby–Parke Bernet in New York City. She is a member of the Mystic Art Association, the Society of Connecticut Craftsmen, the American Craft Council and the National Standards Council of American Embroiderers.

Brochure: Yes.
Commissions: Yes.
Studio Hours: None.
Telephone: (203) 445-6334.

All designs copyright Barbara Lee.

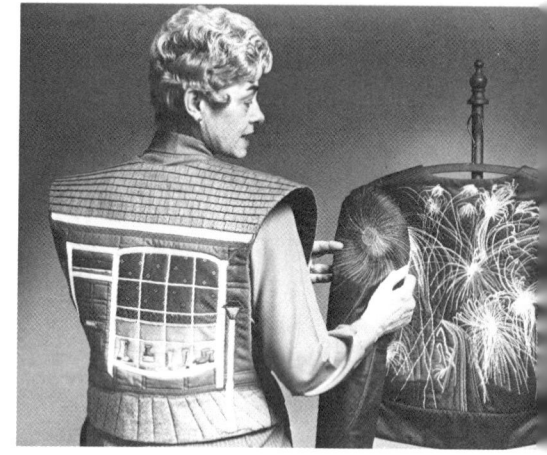

Barbara models her wearable art vest, "Boots," as she points out the stitchery detail in her "fireworks" wearable art jacket of multi-colored embroidery stitched firework design on black-polished cotton. Red silklike polyester lining. "Wearable art becomes a living, moving exhibit not constrained within the walls of a museum, to be viewed by those not regularly exposed to the fine arts." Free-machine-embroidered firework design may vary. All measurements required for accurate fit; $975 postpaid.

Soft-sculpture "stuffed shirt" pillows of embroidery-quilted appliqué. "An artistic touch to identify his favorite chair. For a great conversation piece, hang a grouping on the wall in his office or create a headboard for a bed/sofa for a terrific accent in a 'bachelor pad.'" Cotton/poly fabrics, corduroy "vest," gold/silver metal-button tie tack and cuff links. Solids or striped autumn colors with a solid tie. Choice of colors. Shirt stripes width will vary. Width 14 inches, height 17 inches. Without vest, $64 postpaid; with vest, $75 postpaid.

Cynthia H. Neely

PO Box 221
Guilford, Connecticut 06437

"I think there's a similarity between scientists and artists," says Cynthia Neely, a thirty-year-old fiber artist. "Both are looking for different ways to view things." Cynthia's work, mainly one-of-a-kind wall pieces and rugs, reflects her view of the natural world by incorporating designs and patterns that she sees in nature.

She recognizes that there is an "inherent mathematical structure" in the natural world and strives to reflect its underpinnings in her work, which attractively meshes art, math and science in one package. "Through my weaving, I attempt to express the artistry and simplicity of abstract structure—the logarithmic spiral of a sunflower, a pine cone or a moth's path to light," she told me.

The patterns, colors (often gradated) and textures in her work are intended, according to the artist, to embody "an essence of the internal structure of all things and explore naturally occurring formulas and configurations."

"My work describes my relationship with art and nature and is a sincere expression of the point of view from which I perceive the world," she emphasizes. What makes her viewpoint so appealing to the viewer is that she has created colorful and pleasing works of art in the process.

"Carmichael's Gold" is the first in a series of tapestries inspired by the Canadian Group of Seven paintings. Colors range from purples and blues made from lichens and blueberries, to oranges and golds from Saint-Johns-wort and Solomon's seal. 30 by 36 inches; $2000.

Brochure: No.
Commissions: All work is one of a kind and commissioned.
Studio Hours: None.
Telephone: (203) 453-5947.

"Arc" tapestry exhibits a gradation of colors from cool greens, blues and greys to warm tans, orange-reds and purple. "The intersecting lines that seem to recede into space are designed to give the impression of depth and light." Woven in a half-tapestry laid-in technique of wool and linen, it measures 65 by 55 inches; $2500. Work similar in size and technique would be comparably priced.

CAMILLE FORMAN

1010 Warrenville Road
Mansfield Center, Connecticut 06250

"One of my earliest memories is of a green silk dress that was given to me when I was four years old," says Camille Forman. "The excitement of its color and texture still remains with me." She remembers that while she was growing up, her mother and grandmother were "always sewing, knitting, crocheting, spinning, making clothes and then making clothes over." She began to embroider cross-stitches when she was seven and later started making and then designing her own clothes.

With all that work being done by Camille and her relatives, fabric scraps began to pile up. So Camille started to make hooked rugs, then quilts and other "pieced items" such as vests, kimonos and soft sculpture. Recently she's concentrated on creating brightly colored wall hangings and quilts.

Camille cites as sources of inspiration such artists as Paul Klee, Sonia Delaunay and Gustav Klimt and "forms from ancient Japanese kimonos, African kente cloth and ecclesiastical motifs in medieval art."

"I need to experience art and architecture first hand," Camille told me. "Trips to museums and walking in the woods are both essential. Out in the country where we live the changing seasons provide stimulating contrasts of color and texture."

Camille, forty-nine, is a member of the Society of Connecticut Craftsmen. She exhibits her one-of-a-kind pieces at juried and invitational exhibitions throughout Connecticut.

Brochure: In work, as of this writing.
Commissions: Yes.
Studio Hours: By appointment.
Telephone: (203) 486-2526.

"Celebration" wall hanging or quilt is made of predominately iridescent Thai silk in intense reds, blues and purples merging into lavender, pinks and off-whites. Small insets of multicolored silk swatches are machine-appliquéd, then machine-pieced. Dimensions 88 by 83 inches.

"Winter Landscape" wall hanging in muted colors of brown-mottled velveteen, beige, off-white cotton jersey. "Weed stalks" are gray-printed wool and acetate beige-gold, highlighted with red-and-blue Indian silk. Machine-appliquéd and pieced. Dimensions 27 by 19 inches. Prices based on choice of fabrics and complexity of design. Large works range from $15-to-$25 per square foot. Smaller works begin at $300.

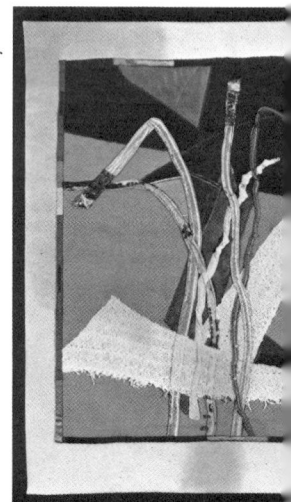

NORMA MINKOWITZ

25 Broadview Road
Westport, Connecticut 06880

Norma Minkowitz's artwork over the past ten years has encompassed both crocheted sculpture and wearables. In her miniature sculptures, she works mostly in neutral tones, using a single stitch and very fine threads to build intricately worked figures and shapes that create a delicacy of form and image. Much of her work is characterized by recurring images and forms that enable the forty-five-year-old artist to explore themes she describes as "containment, repetition, inside coming out, small-to-large and continuous motion."

Her one-of-a-kind wearable art relies more on linear expression. "The direction and movements in the forms and textures of my wearables are related to my past involvement with fine pen-and-ink drawings," she told me, "and designed to reflect the motion of the human body."

"Exploring the shoe for its sculptural possibilities is a new direction for me," she explains, "and seems to be a connecting point between the sculptures and wearables. Using an epoxy technique to stiffen her crochet, Norma creates "skinlike shells of shoes in combined forms and textures," which become for the artist "a canvas on which I could further develop my thoughts and images."

Norma's work has been featured in nearly sixty one-woman and group exhibits since 1972 and is in the permanent collections of the Metropolitan Museum of Art and the Smithsonian's Renwick Gallery, among others. She teaches at Brookfield Craft Center and is a member of Artist Craftsmen of New York, Society of Connecticut Craftsmen, American Craft Council and New York State Craftsmen. She is a graduate of Cooper Union Art School in New York.

Brochure: No.
Commissions: Yes. All work is one of a kind.
Studio Hours: None.
Telephone: (203) 227-4497.

"Jacket" is crocheted and knitted of very fine threads. 30 by 16 inches; $900.

"Looking for the Right Mate" crochet sculpture utilizes a stiffening procedure of epoxy. "I am exploring the shoe for its sculptural possibilities as well as using it for a vehicle to express personal thoughts and images." Height 4 3/4 inches, length 8 1/2 inches, width 3 1/2 inches. Price range for similar sculptures — $900 to $1600.

Elinor Klivans

Fiber Works
PO Box 883
Camden, Maine 04843

Elinor Klivan's woven work consists largely of functional pieces that often exhibit pronounced and unusual textures coupled with a wide array of colors.

"I enjoy experimenting with many yarn textures and combining these textures to achieve unique effects," notes Elinor, who will combine as many as twenty yarns into one strand in order to get the desired textures.

She often dyes her yarns utilizing a pre-planned color chart, which she created in concert with other weavers, that allows her to vary color shades and hues incrementally through some 500 gradations. "Each yarn takes color differently," says the thirty-nine-year-old weaver. "Thicker yarns take color lighter than thinner yarns." Some of her work, particularly her shawls, may have up to twenty-five different, flowing colors.

"Every time you use a different yarn, or stitch, or color, you're going to get something different. All of these factors together comes out very pretty." Using three large floor looms and several smaller looms, Elinor weaves a line of items that includes shawls, rugs, pillows and bell pulls.

A weaver since 1972, Elinor says that she enjoys teaching others "the excitement and possibilities of weaving." Recently as artist-in-residence at her local elementary school, she taught 600 children over a 10-week period how to weave on the loom.

Brochure: No.
Commissions: Yes, "especially rag or wool rugs."
Studio Hours: Call for appointment.
Telephone: (207) 236-9630.

Woolen bell pulls with handmade ceramic bells. Small size is about 8 inches by 32 inches including fringe, $40. Larger size is about 16 inches by 34 inches with fringe; $75.

Textured wool pillows shown here in creasm and tweeds. Available in any color combinations and with or without fringe. Size 12 by 12 inches, $30; 14 by 14 inches; $35.

MONICA M. BARRY

PO Box 1051
Caribou, Maine 04736

Monica Barry thinks of her weaving as a link to another era, a time when clothing and household articles were created by hand. "I often think about the past as I work at my loom," she told me. "I think of the incredible quantity of handwoven fabric turned out by a single weaver." She remembers as a child admiring a large number of woolen blankets that had been woven by her great-grandmother. "Years later, I too am weaving wool blankets and I definitely have a greater appreciation for that dear lady's time."

The blankets and throws that Monica weaves share a few characteristics with those of her ancestor. She uses only natural fibers, preferring wool for its warmth and feel. "One of the most pleasurable features of my work is that it feels soft to the touch. You don't want something to feel like cardboard." Her work is also center-seamed with a Guatemalan blanket-joining stitch. Due to the size of her looms and the extent of her reach, her blankets are woven in panels and sewn together by hand.

Monica makes basically two types of blankets. The first is made of a plain-weave fabric with color variations carried by stripes, plaids, check patterns or border designs. She also specializes in blankets woven with huck-lace figures, an open weave rarely used nowadays that creates distinctive decorative patterns.

Monica, twenty-four, received her degree in textile design from the University of Vermont. She is a member of the Aroostook County Weavers Guild.

Brochure: Yes.
Commissions: Yes.
Studio Hours: By appointment.
Telephone: (207) 328-9372.

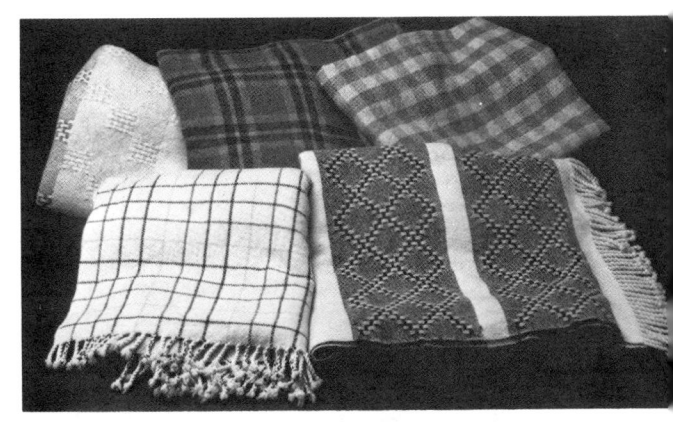

All-woolen blankets and throws in an assortment of designs, colors and sizes. Monica specializes in various plaids and huck-lace weaves. The two blankets on the top right and the one on the bottom left are examples of her plaid designs. At top left and bottom right, and in the other photo, are examples of huck-lace blankets. All designs are available in the following sizes. Throws: 36–by–64 inches; $90; 52–by–70 inches; $140. Blankets: 70–by–90 inches; $250; 100–by–90 inches; $360.

CAROL SHUTT

Carol Shutt, Quiltmaker
PO Box 65
North Sullivan, Maine 04664

"People often shake their heads at quiltmakers," says Carol Shutt, "and wonder why they start with a big piece of fabric, cut it up into small pieces, and then sew it back together into a big piece again."

Acknowledging that that is "certainly one way of seeing my craft," Carol, thirty, views the process in a much different light. "When I make a quilt it often feels like the unfolding of a flower's petals from beginning bud to full bloom." Each step of this process excites her. "I am continually seeing new colors and shapes relate and interact as I place them together in various patterns."

Carol first became interested in quilts when she moved to coastal Maine in 1979. Noticing old family quilts on clotheslines, in shops and in people's homes, she began to get involved by restoring old, tattered quilts that she found. She soon started making her own quilts of traditional designs. Now she often reinterprets those old patterns in "new and exciting ways," using her growing collection of fabrics as a palette of textured and patterned colors. "For me, quilting is a dynamic process that is always changing and growing, which makes me do the same."

Carol is a member of the board of directors of Directions, a Maine professional craft group. She is also president of Eastern Maine Craft Cooperative and a member of Pinetree Quilter's Guild. She received her degree in fine arts from Syracuse University and has had exhibitions in Pennsylvania and Maine.

Brochure: No.
Commissions: Custom work and commissions welcomed.
Studio Hours: None.
Telephone: (207) 422-9511.

Vest is made from 100-percent cottons and cotton blends with polyester fiber fill. Machine pieced and machine quilted. "Rich, deep colors" include burgundy, teal, forest green, deep rust, navy, plum, olive and grey-blue. Fabrics used include solids, subtle prints and bits of "exotic" cottons. Send measurements for correct fit; $110.

Jo Diggs

*PO Box 6685 Woodfords Station
Portland, Maine 04101*

Jo Diggs specializes in creating hand-stitched, multilayered appliqué clothing and wall pieces. Working out of her home studio, "a crowded one-woman affair with tons of fabric stacked along the walls," she produces mostly one-of-a-kind apparel and wall hangings along with a limited-edition line of clothing that she sells through stores and galleries. In addition to her established work, she has recently started work on the first in a planned series of large wall quilts.

"My interest in needlework and fabric approaches addiction," she told me. "I can remember seeing beautiful stitching when I was a very little girl and vowing that I would learn to sew like that." Jo, forty-six, learned her lessons well indeed and began sewing professionally nearly twenty years ago.

Initially inspired by molas and reverse appliqué, Jo's current work is thematically characterized by landscape designs and flower forms. "Now that I live in Maine my landscapes look Eastern" she says, "but when I lived in Mexico they were hot and Southwestern."

Jo's formal training was in art history at Wellesley College and art education at Harvard Graduate School of Education. Her work has been exhibited in numerous shows and has been featured in publications and television programs. She teaches her craft in workshops across the U.S. and in Canada and is active in several craft organizations.

Brochure: Yes.
Commissions: Superbly detailed landcape wall pieces on commission, in addition to clothing.
Studio Hours: By appointment.
Telephone: (207) 773-3405.

Quilted kimono coat is one of a kind featuring handstitched appliqué and handstitched quilting on the entire coat. Materials used are primarily cotton; silk and wool are also available. Swatches and combinations will be sent on request. The fully lined coat can show a landscape design rather than flowers and other coat patterns are also available. Size determined by measurements; $750.

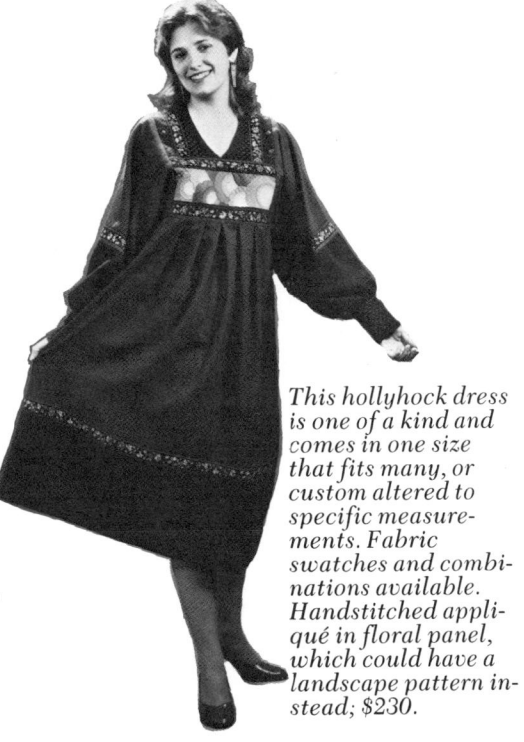

This hollyhock dress is one of a kind and comes in one size that fits many, or custom altered to specific measurements. Fabric swatches and combinations available. Handstitched appliqué in floral panel, which could have a landscape pattern instead; $230.

125 · FIBER

BOBBYE TURSHINSKY HERTZBACH

66 Overlook Drive
Amherst, Massachusetts 01002

There are primarily two things that give Bobbye Turshinsky Hertzbach great pleasure in her hand-woven clothing: the use of color in her garments and the joy she gets when she sees people wearing her creations.

"Working with color makes me feel good!" she exclaims. "Early on it was very clear to me that I was not interested in using thin yarns and complex patterns. I prefer to let the texture and color speak for themselves."

With these elements carrying the design of her garments, Bobbye produces a line of apparel that includes tunics, shawls, jackets, vests, ponchos and accessories. She designs her garments for the person who likes a "classic yet updated look." "I don't do things that are really far out," she says. She generally uses yarns made from natural fibers, although occasionally she'll come across a partially synthetic, highly textured yarn that she finds irresistible.

Weaving was an avocation for ten years until Bobbye decided in 1981 to become a full-time professional. "I look forward to having my wearables featured in galleries and participating in major craft fairs throughout the country." She is a member of Pioneer Weavers Guild, Amherst Weavers and Leverett Craftsmen and Artists, Inc.

Brochure: Yes. Thirteen styles plus accessories are illustrated.
Commissions: Yes.
Studio Hours: By appointment.
Telephone: (413) 253-9568.

The pullover poncho has a cowl neck/hood that protects its wearer from the wind when worn as a hood and drapes elegantly when worn as a cowl-neck collar. It is woven from a combination of wool and mohair yarns with a contrasting band on the body and multiple bands on the hood and is available in a wide spectrum of fashion colors. Either standard size or by measurements; $300.

JEANNE G. COSTELLO

J. G. Silks
50 Richfield Road
Arlington, Massachusetts 02174

Jeanne Costello's formal education in the arts took place in her birthplace, Lyon, France, at Les Atelier de Trois Soleils, where she studied "all types of media from jewelry to painting and pottery." After graduation in 1969, she spent a couple of years working as a silversmith in the south of France while searching for an artistic medium that would allow her to stretch her creative abilities.

She found it in 1972, when her "love for color and design" was the impetus to teach herself to paint on silk. She's been doing that ever since.

"I can't paint on anything else other than silk," she told me. "The texture, softness and touch of silk inspire me."

Scarfs and wall hangings are created by the artist spontaneously on the silk without any previous sketching. The aniline dyes imported from France are applied directly to the white silk with a bristle brush. The colors are separated by a resist line that prevents them from running together. Each piece is steamed after drying, making them color fast. They can be washed by hand or dry cleaned. The two scarves here are each 9 inches wide and 50 inches long; $36 each. The wall hanging is 4½ feet high by 3½ feet wide; $375.

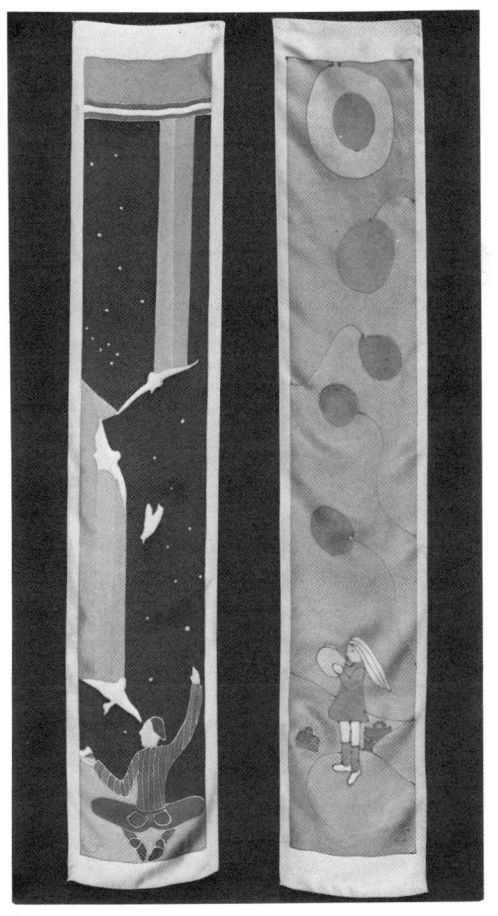

Jeanne, thirty-three, creates her one-of-a-kind wall hangings and scarves without the aid of prior sketching.

In addition to the inspiration that "everyday life, music, art, dance" give her, she says that she has received much inspiration from the cities in which she has lived—Rome, Paris, San Francisco and New York City. Her work has been shown in some half-dozen one-woman shows and in many group shows throughout the Northeast and in Europe.

Brochure: No.
Commissions: Yes.
Studio Hours: None.
Telephone: (617) 547-9270.

127 · FIBER

SALLY SNOW-EKLUND

76 Myricks Street
Assonet, Massachusetts 02702

Although she also makes traditional quilts and restores antique quilts, it is producing her line of quilted clothing that Sally Snow-Eklund most enjoys. Working in apparel gives her the opportunity to use traditional quilting techniques in a contemporary way—to create limited-edition clothing as wearable art.

"I like to make clothing that makes you feel good," says the forty-five-year-old quilter, "clothing that has subtleties of color and design that are unique without being outrageous, that are noticeable and comfortable at the same time." In her clothes, Sally makes regular use of "natural things" like floral designs, natural fibers and logical colors. She prefers to use silks rather than the more traditional cottons for their "luster and luxury" and because the material shows the shadows of the quilting particularly well.

She teaches her craft extensively and enjoys spreading a knowledge of her craft to her students. "I show my students new ways of using old techniques. Quilting opens their eyes and gives respect for craftsmanship and design. Classes offer group support when involved with a long project like a traditional quilt. And women learn that their grandmothers really did know geometry, so they don't have to be afraid of things like mathematics that are considered male domains."

Sally has been practicing her craft for twenty years. She is past president of Plymouth County Cranberry Quilters and is a member of the New England Quilter's Guild. She sells her work through galleries, shops and at shows.

Brochure: Yes.
Commissions: Special wearable art, quilts and restorations on commission.
Studio Hours: By appointment.
Telephone: (617) 822-3581.

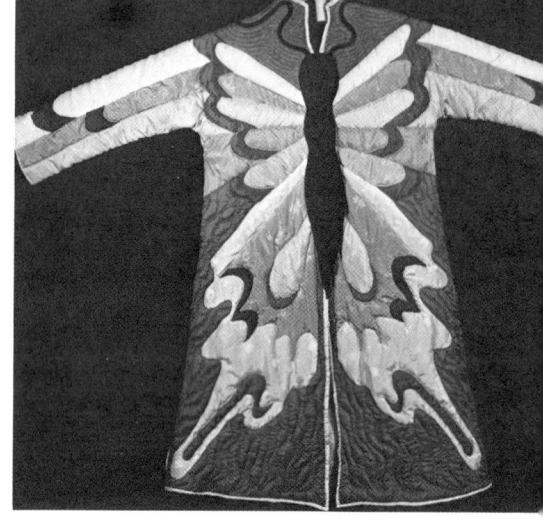

Butterfly coat is of appliquéd and hand-quilted silks with wool batting. Pink, mauve and purple butterfly on peacock ground. "Spectacular and luxurious but also warm and comfortable to wear." $1000.

Sally wearing her Amish blouse and dress with screen-printed quilt squares, which are produced with Linda Larsen of North Darmouth, Massachusetts. Cotton fabric and polyester batting. "Colors are selected to flow and should be ordered in ranges such as blue/violet, rose/maroon, peach/brown, etc." Her line of clothing includes strip-pieced cotton vests, stipple-quilted silk vests, strip-pieced velveteen jackets, several types of dresses with pieced or quilted embellishments and other pieces. Prices range from $30 to $300 plus shipping.

DORIS R. OPPENHEIMER

Functional Fibers
PO Box 651
Belmont, Massachusetts 02178

Functional Fibers is not only the name of Doris Oppenheimer's company; it is also a "personal goal" for much of her work, which comprises a variety of textiles for private homes and office spaces. "My work is a product of spontaneity, sensitivity and hard work, all of which are strong characteristics of my personality," says the twenty-four-year-old weaver.

Doris does a great deal of commissions but also produces a line of rugs, place mats and wall hangings that she mainly sells direct and through a craft cooperative, the Christmas Store, in Cambridge. "I feel the need to make my work superior in quality and design to anything commercially available," she says. "I enjoy working with clients on pieces that have a specific space and function. It is a wonderful feeling to see a finished piece enhance an environment, whether it is a functional or nonfunctional textile." She prefers to do one-of-a-kind pieces, working with her client on size, color, function and price range to produce a fully personalized piece.

"Designing and weaving cloth is a laborious personal process for me," she says. "I am inspired by the patterns and color I see in my environment. In some of my work you will detect the natural colors and shapes of the New England seashore. In other pieces you will sense my attraction to the modern cityscape."

Doris has been weaving since graduation in 1980 from Rhode Island School of Design with a fine-arts degree in textile design. She is a member of The Weavers Guild of Boston and Print and Dye Works. Recently she opened her studio in the Kendall Center for the Arts, a former Belmont grammar school that has been rehabbed into a center for some forty artists.

Brochure: No.
Commission: Yes.
Studio Hours: Wednesday from 10 to 2.
Telephone: (617) 484-6333.

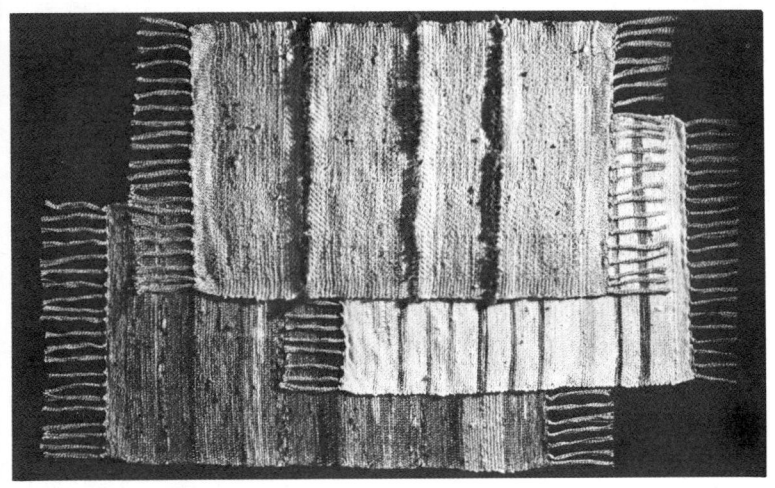

These one-of-a-kind rugs are made from a variety of fibers including 100-percent hand-dyed cotton rags, silk and strips of beaver fur. They can be made in any size and any color. Doris does much of the dying herself and such work can be commissioned at about $12 per square foot.

Three-dimensional wall hanging is of a double-weave construction and made of hand-dyed linen, cotton and silk. It is 24-by-40 inches; $250.

ANNA DUNWELL

Anna Dunwell Tapestries
PO Box 390 Back Bay Annex
Boston, Massachusetts 02117

Anna Dunwell specializes in producing traditional summer-and-winter weaves. This durable weave, she says, "marked the pinnacle of America's traditional weaves before the appearance of the Jacquard loom and mass-produced textiles." The weave achieves its noted durability from the pattern threads being very closely interwoven with the plain weave background. The resulting textile is fully reversible, light with dark patterning on one side and dark with light patterning on the other.

While continuing this American textile tradition, Anna also adds to it, modifying and strengthening historic designs and using a variety of color combinations in addition to the traditional red and blue. The design she uses, Lovers Knot, Stars and Roses, "spoke to the ideals of America between 1781 and 1825." Anna has fashioned a large line of items from the weave, which is woven from alternating rows of wool and cotton.

She says that she is inspired by the "possibilities of creating small areas of permanence for time's scrutiny" through her work and is comfortable weaving either her summer-and-winter pieces or a large-scale commission in another style. "There is no difference. It is all weaving," says the forty-year-old textile artist.

After earning her undergraduate art degree from New York's Hunter College, Anna did further work in weaving and design at San Francisco State and Rhode Island School of Design before receiving her masters in fine arts from Boston University's Program in Artisanry.

Brochure: Yes.
Commissions: "I do custom work and architectural commissions."
Studio Hours: None.
Telephone: (617) 247-2583.

Anna's coverlets, come in red, black, plum, dark blue, pewter grey, russet brown, teal green, aster pink and cornflower blue. All coverlets are in the Lover's Knot, Stars and Roses pattern and have a 4-inch cotton fringe. All work is in 70-percent wool and 30-percent cotton and reversible. Full bed coverlets, 85-by-135 inches; $300; twin size, 80-by-90 inches; $175; crib blankets and throws, 40-by-60 inches; $120.

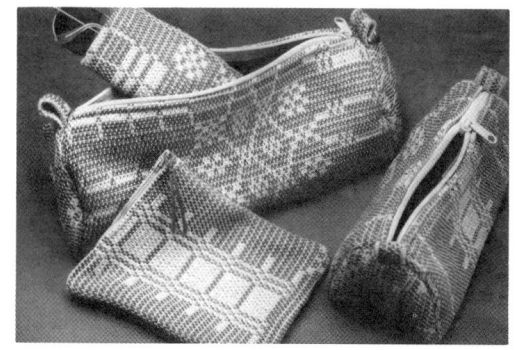

Travel kits are zippered and lined with plastic. Small size is 4 by 9 inches; $12; large size is 6 by 13 inches; $15. Eyeglass case is lined with smooth fabric, 3½-by-7½ inches; $5. Small unlined pouch (center front) is ideal for small items, 6-by-5 inches; $8. Colors same as coverlets.

Lee Farrington

11 Stillman Street
Boston, Massachusetts 02113

Lee Farrington constructs her one-of-a-kind collages by machine stitching pieces of fabric onto quilt batting or heavy duck fabric. Her work can be displayed either by inserting a curtain rod through the sleeve sewn onto the back of the piece or by mounting on linen and framing.

The thirty-three-year-old artist first began to make fabric collages in 1975 and had her first one-woman show three years later at Boston's City Hall. Her early collages were more figurative than her current abstract work. The imagery in her pieces evolves as she works with the shapes and colors of the fabric pieces. Lately she has been experimenting with placing shapes underneath sheer fabric for a different effect in her pieces.

"Each collage is carefully designed before the sewing process begins," Lee explains, "as I find that I continually shift fabrics until the whole thing feels complete. Sometimes I begin by making rough sketches of my idea and sometimes I just plunge in, deriving ideas solely from the fabrics."

Lee graduated in 1981 from Goddard College in Vermont. She has had five one-woman shows and has been included in numerous group exhibits. She teaches her craft under the auspices of several different organizations and is a member of the American Craft Council.

Brochure: No.
Commissions: "Almost no commissions by choice," but it can't hurt to inquire.
Studio Hours: By appointment.
Telephone: (617) 367-2460.

Fabric collages are either abstract or figurative designs. A wide assortment of antique and contemporary fabrics are used, including wool, satin, velvet, cotton and linen. Sizes range from 20-by-20 inches up to 70-by-70 inches and prices from $200 to $2,000. To order, give Lee a brief description of what you have in mind and she'll mail you slides of appropriate past collages to consider. "Rooms II", 62-by-55 inches; $2,000. "Spaces of Light," 50-by-40 inches; $700.

131 · FIBER

ROCHELLE NEWMAN

PO Box 162
Bradford, Massachusetts 01830

The Native American Indian has always had a deep understanding and respect for the natural order of things. It is this universal order, "this relationship and connection," that Rochelle Newman calls "the bones to the body of my work." Her tapestries, which are visually related to American Indian forms, enable Rochelle to "give structure to my understanding of the universe." "I seek simplicity, clarity, directness, contrast, symmetry and a reduction of elements to basic units after which there are none."

Creating her tapestries through both "passion and patience," Rochelle utilizes simple elements such as squares, lines, slits and tails to create complex forms that she describes as representative of a "sense of order that cannot be broken."

With color providing a feeling of warmth and vibrancy, the surface and structure of her tapestries are "forever locked in a yin-yang embrace, a harmony of opposition. The truth lines in their marriage," declares the forty-four-year-old fiber artist.

Rochelle leads "two full-time lives," teaching art full time at Northern Essex Community College in Haverhill, Massachusetts, and working at fiber in the evenings. Her work has been featured in more than thirty shows throughout New England and in New York state.

She is presently coauthoring a book on the relationship of art, math and nature and is a member of American Craft Council, Massachusetts Association of Craftsmen and "Boston Seven," an exhibiting group of seven women fiber artists.

Brochure: No.
Commissions: All one-of-a-kind work.
Studio Hours: By appointment.
Telephone: (617) 372-3129.

Left, "Guardian Spirit" is a woolen weft over a cotton warp. "The interest is in the tension between the three-dimensional form and the flat pattern." Width 40 inches by length 70 inches; $1500.

Right, "Mesa Verde" is done in same technique and materials. "American Indian culture forms and philosophy influence my work. The desire is to find the underlying unity of things." Width 33 by length 52 inches; $900.

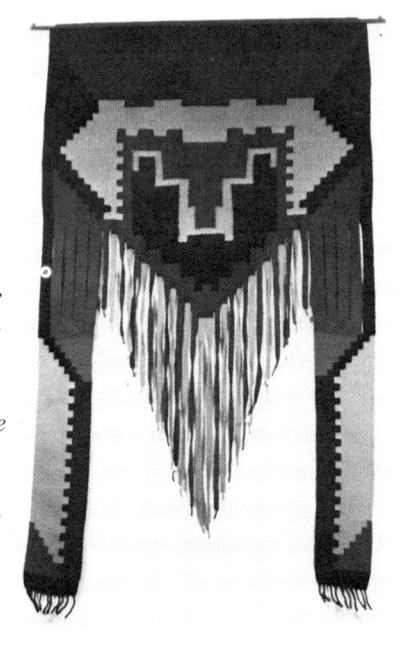

NANCY RIAL

*49 Kirkland Street
Cambridge, Massachusetts 02138*

Nancy Rial's one-of-a-kind work is made from 100-percent cotton velveteen, which she likes for the potential of its napped surface. "The napped fabric gives me an opportunity to explore lighting effects on color saturation," she explains. "Although the nap direction has to be carefully arranged even in my multicolored works, it is the monochromatic pieces that offer the most exciting design possibilities." This use of only one color gives those pieces a subtlety of design and color uncommon to other fabrics. "Because the nap changes shades in relationship to the viewers, my hangings have a sense of movement as one passes by," she says. "Light areas become dark; dark areas lighten."

Nancy cannot remember when she did not sew, knit or embroider. One of her earliest memories is of her great-grandmother fabricating quilt triangles by hand. Between college fine-art degrees, she took an independent tour of Finland, where she rediscovered fiber. She found that the Finns used fabrics on a large scale, with simple uncomplicated designs and clear colors. Inspired by that trip, she did some weaving for a while and then started using her sewing machine as her creative outlet. She finds that machine piecing and quilting is a stronger method of construction because of the thick materials that she uses in her work.

Nancy is a member of Quilters Connection and the American Craft Council. In addition to direct sales, she distributes her work through private art consultants and the Society of Arts & Crafts in Boston.

Brochure: No.
Commissions: Yes.
Studio Hours: By appointment.
Telephone: (617) 492-2433.

This commissioned piece hangs in a two-story stairway. The background stripe effect is actually one shade of green, cut and sewn together with nap direction running opposite to its neighbor's. "The horizontal lines are of a lighter green, creating a highlight effect while the diagonal lines provide color and a place to slice into the background, making the green-stripe background into a harlequin pattern." This is 4 feet by 8 feet. Similar work will run about $25 per square foot.

"Stripe" is in a monochromatic color scheme. In this case it is a soft sea green, accented by a blue/green stripe. It has a changing background due to the varying directions of the cotton velveteen nap. 25-by-26 inches; $150.

ANNA V. A. POLESNY

Anava Textiles
17 Stanford Street
Holyoke, Massachusetts 01040

As a European child growing up in Pakistan, Anna Polesny was dazzled by the exotic garments worn in the homes and displayed in the bazaars. "Our house boy could invariably spot the look in my eyes when I desperately wanted him to take me to the city to touch and feel the sumptuous fabrics, smell the spicy aromas and devour the colors, sounds and sights," she remembers.

As an adolescent and young adult in America, Anna "strayed to practical matters": mathematics, art history, psychology and education. But during her spare time and summers she always found herself working with fabrics, studying crafts, visiting museums, galleries and fairs and developing ideas regarding fabric.

"Finally, in my late twenties, I found myself again in the Middle East, watching the weavers in Damascus, the rugmakers in Cairo, the dyers in Beirut, and once more experiencing the souks with their brilliant colors, heavy smells, lusty cries and endless stalls of exotic fabrics." She realized then what her artistic direction was to be and committed herself to fiber.

Through her silk garments and accessories, the thirty-eight-year-old artist explores the "possibilities of the art of batik and the fabric that is made using this technique." Using successive overdyes, she brings to the fabric an increased subtlety of expression. The construction of the garment is simple, with each piece designed to display the flow, natural sheen and drape of the batiked silk. "Without reference to pictorial design, I try to create an otherworldly quality with the interplay of scattered forms and luminous color."

Anna has exhibited her garments nationally and internationally in many museums and galleries. She received her masters in fine arts from Rochester Institute of Technology and has done additional postgraduate work at Columbia University, Hunter College and Instituto Allende in Mexico. She is a member of the American Craft Council, the World Craft Council and the National Council on Apprenticeship and Celebrations, an Amherst, Massachusetts, artist's collective.

Brochure: No.
Commissions: Yes.
Studio Hours: By appointment.
Telephone: (413) 534-7518.

The silk twill harem outfit consists of two pieces: a bodice with a long sash that wraps around the waist and ties in the back and a pair of flowing harem pants. The hand-batiked fabric is of pale pink, light blue and fuscia lines-and-dot patterns on a deep purple background. "The garment conforms to and flatters most body types because of the drape of the fabric and the tied-bodice construction. Although very comfortable, the piece is glamorous and flattering and would be appropriate for dressy occasions." Available in S, M, L; $295.

Katharine Pincus

Under Mountain Road
Lenox, Massachusetts 01240

After abandoning a career in music more than twenty years ago, Katharine Pincus indulged her long-held love for yarns, fabrics and textures and turned to weaving to fill the creative void.

Today, she uses mostly natural fibers—cotton, silk, wool and linen—and occasionally rayon to produce all kinds of fabrics including rugs, draperies, wall hangings, window shades, table linens, clothing accessories and clothing yardage.

"Basically my work appeals most to people who have a love of beautiful fabrics, and to other creative people," she says. Mostly selling to small shops, Katharine's accounts include fashion designer Mary McFadden, for whom she weaves several fabrics of her own design each season, and Henri Bendel in New York City, who purchases scarves and stoles.

Since her initial five lessons on how to dress the loom, she has been completely self-taught. "For me it is a pleasure to be creating something functionally beautiful and I have a special love for blending colors." Katharine, fifty, has been weaving professionally since 1960 and is a member of Handweavers Guild of America.

Brochure: No.
Commissions: Nearly three-quarters of her work is commissioned. In addition to the items mentioned above, she has produced yard goods for men's sports jackets and for women's suits, coats, evening wear and dresses.
Studio Hours: Daily, by appointment.
Telephone: (413) 637-1289.

Three samples of woven stoles. The check-type weave on left contrasts large, fuzzy mohair with a very fine wool worsted and is available in various colorings. The white honeycomb weave in center incorporates various textures in a monotone. The soft, loose mohair at right has accents of contrasting colors and/or texture in the wool. All these weaves are also available in blanket throws. Stoles are 24 by 100 inches; $110 each.

ANDREA ZAX

Fiberworks
22 Lovell Street
Somerville, Massachusetts 02144

Andrea Zax has striven to perfect her sewing technique ever since she's had the co-ordination to use a needle, thread and scissors. Beginning with sewing clothes for her dolls and later progressing to making the dolls and sewing clothes for herself, she's continued to stretch her creative muscles long after perfecting her technique.

Studying art and fiber during high school and college gave Andrea the necessary tools to express her visions in soft sculpture. College was additionally a place where she "unlearned all the rules and constricting attitudes forced on me throughout public school." "I learned how to think," she says of her college days, "and tap into my creative spirit more."

Andrea likes to make people smile. "My work is often humorous," she notes. "I believe very strongly in one's sense of humor. Silliness is a key to survival in this cruel world."

Andrea, twenty-six, is influenced in her work by everything that happens around her—the jobs she's had, her love for dancing, movies and art—it all becomes inspiration for her silly stuffed-fabric cartoons and other works. "At this point my work and my sanity are very closely related," she says. "I need to work. I'm a project-oriented person and like to have a couple of pieces going on at a time."

Andrea's fabric artistry takes the shape of everything from six-foot palm trees to human-sized insect costumes or promotional cushions adorned with silk-screened logos. She graduated in 1978 from Massachusetts College of Art in Boston.

Brochure: Yes.
Commissions: Yes.
Studio Hours: By appointment.
Telephone: (617) 623-3942.

These bags may look like paper but they're not. Lunch-size fabric bags are available by the dozen in assorted colors and patterns. Also available are wine-bottle size bags at the same price. By the dozen, $50 plus shipping. Individual bags, $6 each plus shipping.

This street light is made from satin that is quilted and stuffed. It is a working lamp with a globe bulb that works well as a floor lamp and gives off a good amount of light. "It is graceful and quiet but at the same time extremely unusual and exotic. A must for any living room or den!" The black lamp is 5 feet–6 inches tall; $300 plus delivery.

JIM FLYNN

Laughing Sun Design
PO Box 239
White Horse Beach, Massachusetts 02381

Jim Flynn weaves limited-edition and one-of-a-kind tapestries that are intended to be a contemporary interpretation of several ancient art forms. "Celtic art has been a great influence on my work as have the religious symbols of Hopi and Mayan-Toltec cultures," he told me. Jim has also utilized cave paintings as a source of inspiration for his work.

He works in natural fibers, mostly jute, cotton and wool, "for the tactile and visual texture they impart." After washing the cord, the thirty-four-year-old artist hand-dyes them using direct dye to get a rich, vibrant color. He then weaves each tapestry using an off-loom, handweaving technique.

Much of Jim's work is by commission for an original piece or a custom order of a limited-edition design in the colors of the customer's choice. Jim has been a tapestry artist for eight years. He is a member of the American Craft Council.

Brochure: Yes.
Commissions: "I enjoy the challenge of working with a customer to create a tapestry that will blend with and enhance the decor of the room in which it is hung."
Studio Hours: None.
Telephone: (617) 224-6636.

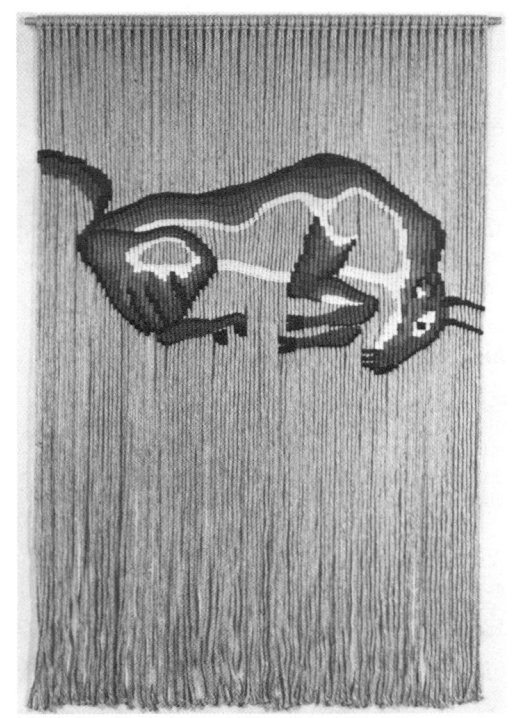

"Bull." The piece is done on natural jute using hand-dyed jute for the design. "The inspiration came from the cave paintings of Altamira, Spain." "Each copy varies enough to give it a unique feeling. This is one of my favorite designs because the bull actually seems to be in motion." 4 by 5½ feet; $350.

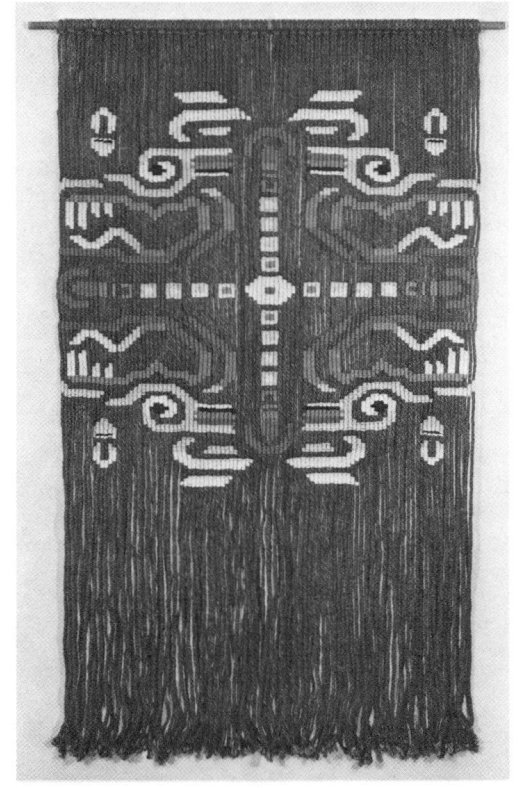

"Four Serpents." Done with hand-dyed jute. The design shares elements used in a Mayan-Toltec carving depicting a priest's headdress. Limited edition piece is 4-by-5½ feet; $450.

ANNA CARLSON

Log Cabin Creations
Brown Hill Road
Bow, New Hampshire 03301

"I am not an artist who does art for myself," says Anna Carlson. She delights in the "bond" that she feels with the people who possess and use her creations. "I often imagine the fate of my products," she says, "especially those that I know have traveled to other continents."

Anna has several favorite designs that she does repeatedly but with differing color patterns, each unique. Her smaller works, such as totes and pillows, are made in sets of four or six and are all conceived as one design with about twenty basic color ideas and "infinite variations" in the color details. She emphasizes that her products are designed to be used. They are machine stitched for durability and are machine washable. Her quilts are one of a kind and made to order. They are all variations of a "log-cabin" design, but each has unique deviations that make them nontraditional.

Anna, thirty-five, graduated from Boston University with a major in piano and music composition. She learned through composing and performing music that "ideas like color and rhythm are shared in common by all the arts." She is a member of the League of New Hampshire Craftsmen.

Brochure: Yes.
Commissions: Yes.
Studio Hours: None.
Telephone:
(603) 774-4717.

This queen-size quilt is done in brown, rust and cream. "The interlocking idea is an original design and is the distinguishing feature of my work." To make the interlocking design three colors are necessary. All quilts are custom designed in "infinite color arrangements." A special favorite is blue, burgundy and cream. Other variations of the interlocking theme are available, all giving similar illusions as seen here. Available from crib or wall-hanging size to king size; $60 to $400.

Tote bag is made of double-quilted calico. A large pocket on the front and a smaller pocket on the back are made in patchwork. "They are constructed for durability as well as charm." Available in blue, navy, brown and maroon. Two-pocket 16-inch tote, $27. One pocket 14-inch tote, $20.

TAFI BROWN

The American Wing
East Alstead, New Hampshire 03602

"My pleasure," explains Tafi Brown, "is to make fiber pieces for people of things or experiences that are important to them at a specific time in their lives." Her chosen medium for this is a synthesis of an early form of photography called cyanotype with the art of quiltmaking.

Originally trained as a potter, Tafi discovered cyanotype, a blueprint process developed in 1840 by the British scientist Sir John Herschel, during a workshop that she attended in 1975. She decided that this would be an interesting and permanent way to document the building of a family house. So she took some of the slides that she had taken of the construction process and printed them on a quilt using cyanotype.

"I noticed that the images changed from colored pictures—slides—to rather abstract shapes in blue and white." By piecing together images that were sometimes reversed, sometimes upside down, she found that she could create an endless variety of patterns on the quilt. That first quilt led to experiments with succeeding quilts, each with its own distinct graphic image. It has become, she says, "an almost obsessive interest in graphic organization, in surface patterns and designing."

Using her own photographs, Tafi makes a negative the exact size of the desired image. After coating the fabric with light-sensitive chemicals, she makes a contact print by placing the negative on the fabric, clamping a piece of glass over both and exposing the "sandwich" in the bright spring or summer sunshine for about six to eight minutes. After washing and fixing the print, what remains is a permanent blue-and-white image that will last as long as the fabric on which they're printed.

Besides her quilts, Tafi, thirty-eight, also creates banners and pillows using the cyanotype process. She earned her undergraduate and graduate art degrees from Pratt Institute in Brooklyn, New York, and received a Fulbright-Hays Grant for study of art history and architecture in Belgium and the Netherlands. She has participated in numerous national and regional shows and has won several awards for excellence. She is a member of the League of New Hampshire Craftsmen and the American Craft Council.

Brochure: Yes.
Commissions: Yes.
Studio Hours: None.
Telephone: (603) 835-6952.

"The Bley's Place" is a cyanotype machine-pieced, hand-quilted work of 100-percent cotton and dacron batting. "This is one of the older residences in Alstead." This one-of-a-kind quilt is representative of the type of work that Tafi does on commission. Her quilts are usually used as wall pieces. This one is solid blue and blue print fabric. Width 40½ inches by 51 inches long; $800.

Kim Wintje

RFD 1, PO Box 67
Farmington, New Hampshire 03835

Kim Wintje is a fabric artist who specializes in whimsy. "With my work, I want people to be relaxed and comfortable," she told me, "to bring on a smile, and to place in each visualized fantasy a heart that reaches out to unite with others in a universal language."

To Kim, twenty-nine, turning common cloth into a fantasy sculpture is her own fantasy fulfilled. Using pieces of white cotton fabric, she sews it, stuffs it and turns it into a three-dimensional visualization of what had been in her mind.

"My work must be subtle and humor must be evident," she explains. Whether it's a winged unicorn, a "personified moon" or angels with tennis shoes, Kim revels in the process of making "the extreme out of the basic."

She received her formal training at Alfred University in New York State and became involved with fabric upon her graduation seven years ago. A member of the League of New Hampshire Craftsmen and the American Craft Council, she has had a one-woman show at New Hampshire College and has participated in many group shows and exhibitions.

Brochure: No.
Commissions: Yes.
Studio Hours: None.
Telephone: (603) 859-7921.

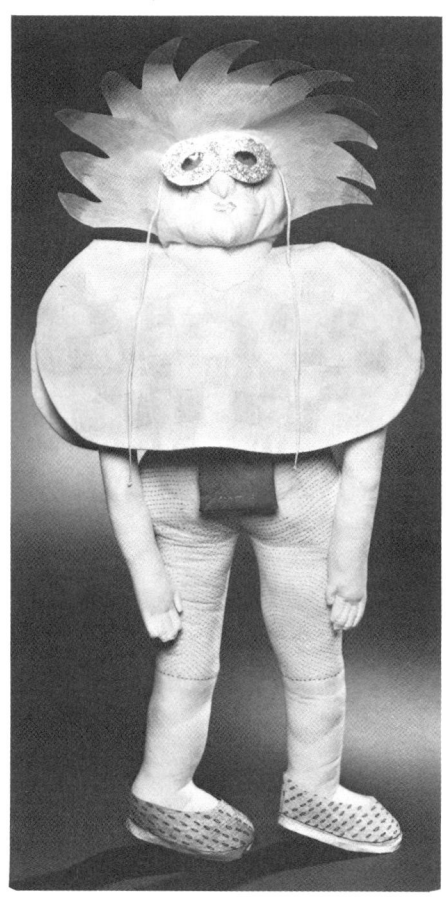

This soft sculpture doll, "You Can't Have Your Cake and Eat It Too," is intended to be hung against the wall. "It invites the viewer's participation in viewing the pop-out cake located in the stomach box. I see this piece as a type of modern ritual doll." It is made of white ecology cloth stuffed with polyester fill. Details are handstitched with embroidery floss. Grey and yellow shoes and gradated yellow/red headdress are painted paper covered by lacquer spray; mask is made of paper covered by silver glitter; the internal box structure is orange plastic. "This represents my most decadent in a series of one-of-a-kind dolls containing internal box structures. The series also includes 'Open the Door to My Heart,' in which the box is located in the chest area and contains a suspended heart." Pictured doll is 24 inches high by 10 inches wide by 5 inches deep; $250.

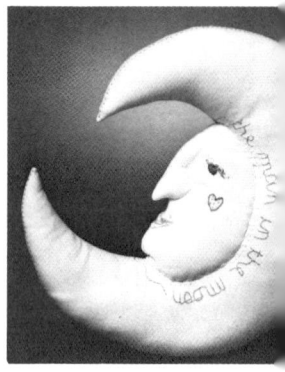

"Personified Moon" of white ecology cloth with polyester fiber fill. Details are handstitched with different colored embroidery floss. Comes with an attached thread to hang it from the ceiling. Like other work, it is Scotchgarded to protect the fabric. "It makes not only an ideal baby amusement, but an adult delight as well." This production piece measures 10 inches in length by 6 inches in width by 3 inches in depth; $25.

140 · FIBER

Judith Kohn

*35 Lamson Drive
Merrimack, New Hampshire 03054*

Judith Kohn was an exchange student abroad when she first learned to weave in 1971 under a master craftsman in Istanbul. The traditional Turkish rug-weaving techniques learned there are the basis for her present contemporary fiber work.

Weaving in the classic Gobelin flat-tapestry tradition, Judith makes frequent use of a technique called hatching, which allows two areas of color to be blended. To produce additional gradations of color, she combines up to four strands of related or different hues, then weaves the combined threads as one weft.

For more textured work, she wraps warp threads, allows areas to remain unwoven and combines crochet with woven areas. An off-loom technique such as soumak or crochet "guides the design" of the finished piece.

She credits the two years that she spent in Morocco as crucial to the development of her style. "Under the intense Moroccan sun, areas of light and shadows were very distinct and colors and shapes were often transformed by the shifting light." This contrast between light and dark figures as a theme in much of her fiber work.

Judith, thirty-six, is an instructor at the Craftworkers Guild in Bedford, New Hampshire, and has participated in many exhibitions and shows. In 1979 she won an award for excellence from the Handweavers Guild of America. She is a member of the American Craft Council, New Hampshire Weavers Guild, New Hampshire League of Craftsmen and A Common Thread: Fiber Artists.

Brochure: No.
Commissions: Yes.
Studio Hours: By appointment.
Telephone: (603) 882-3513.

"Broken Rainbow" is a 100-percent wool tapestry using interlocking technique. Grey background, with the motif woven with shades and hues of yellow, blue, green and purple. Width 30 inches by length 50 inches; $500.

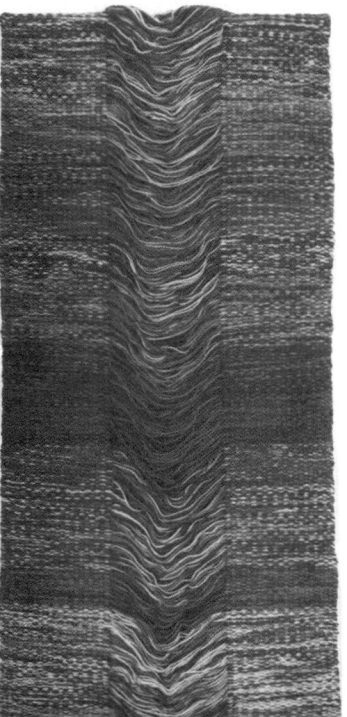

"Dawning" wool tapestry uses combined colors in the weft. "Center portion is unwoven to provide sculptural effect and visual focus." Shades and hues of red, yellow, brown. Width 22 inches by length 48 inches; $400.

These pieces are representative of one-of-a-kind tapestries. Approximate price per square foot for commissioned pieces is $50 to $65. All her yarn is mothproofed and treated with a fire retardant.

PENELOPE B. DROOKER

RFD 1, PO Box 2180
Sanbornville, New Hampshire 03872

Although she produces a wide range of household items from hand towels to blankets, Penelope Drooker primarily creates translucent woven hangings, often embellished with embroidered details, which can be used as window screens, room dividers or wall hangings. These pieces achieve a chameleonlike change of appearance in color, opacity and texture, depending on whether light is shining on them or through them.

"In all my work, I strive to design items that, while eminently suited to the medium of handweaving, also include techniques or design details not reproducible by machine." Intrigued by geometric shapes, Penelope's designs are derived from such sources as weave structures or traditional quilt patterns. She frequently gains new inspiration from museum research into areas like pre-Columbian South American Indian work or Victorian needlework embellishments and techniques. "I particularly enjoy combining traditional techniques in original ways," she notes, "and investigating little-known fiber structure in order to put them to new uses."

Her interest in innovative ways of combining weaving and embroidery culminated in a research project that earned Penelope the Handweavers Guild of America Certificate of Excellence and her authorship of a book, *Embroidering with the Loom: Creative Combinations of Weaving and Stitchery* (Van Nostrand Reinhold, 1979). A second book on hammock-making techniques emerged from her experiences in an advanced weaving education course at Keene State College in New Hampshire.

Penelope, thirty-nine, teaches weaving and embroidery through the League of New Hampshire Craftsmen and travels nationwide to present workshops and lectures in advanced techniques. She has been weaving full time since 1975 and is a Master Weaver of the New Hampshire Weaver's Guild.

Brochure: No.
Commissions: Yes.
Studio Hours: None.
Telephone: (603) 522-3144.

A detail of "Interlacement," a translucent hanging of linen and cotton in natural white tones. Shown here frontlighted. Overall size is 41 inches wide by 71 inches long; $500. A similar design in any size would be $25 per square foot.

"Bird and Tree" translucent hanging of natural white linen and cotton. Shown here backlighted; 18 inches wide by 63 inches long; similar design and size, $300.

These hangings are handwoven using a technique called "inlay." As in woven tapestry, each pattern thread is placed individually and not controlled by the loom. Unlike tapestry, this placement results in a translucent fabric with gradations in opacity. Details are inserted by embroidery.

Lois D. Hurd

PO Box 544
Coventry, Rhode Island 02816

In 1971 Lois Hurd left her art-teaching job to raise a family. Finding that her craft of pottery did not mesh well with family life, she "resurrected" her needlework supplies and began producing and selling some embroidered and quilted articles.

After getting involved in 1975 with the Liturgical Artisans Guild in Coventry, Rhode Island, she found that there was a demand by different religious denominations for handmade church textiles used in vestments.

"Each church has its own character," she told me. "These include architecture, lighting, size, color, scheme, location and 'parish personality.'" Lois establishes design guidelines for her custom-made garments through correspondence or meetings with clergy or parish representatives. "I feel that good use or color and proportion within the limits of the liturgical spectrum provide my designs with genuine strength," she says.

Lois, thirty-seven, creates garments either for regular church use or special occasions. In 1980 she designed and directed the construction of a cope and mitre for the consecration of the new Anglican bishop of the Rhode Island diocese.

Lois recently received her graduate degree in textiles from the University of Rhode Island, where her major research dealt with the use of Christian symbolism for historic and contemporary liturgical vestments.

Brochure: In work.
Commissions: Yes.
Studio Hours: None.
Telephone: (401) 397-5057.

White celebration chasuble and stole are made of poly-cotton. Hand appliquéd orphreys bear symbols of fish and crosses and are embellished with embroidery. Stole is 108 inches long, chasuble 50 inches long and 60 inches wide; $600.

Blue chasuble and stole are used for Advent season and made of poly-cotton and antique satin fabric. The iris and leaves are worked in crewel embroidery and are symbols of the Virgin Mary. Chasuble is 50 inches long and 57 inches wide; stole is 108 inches long; $575.

NANCY ROWE

PO Box 297
Kingston, Rhode Island 02881

During her ten-year career as a carpenter, Nancy Rowe always enjoyed filling out the occupation space on forms with the title "homemaker." Two years ago, she turned to quilting.

"The use of color to create depth, the use of pattern as texture and the blurring of distinction between two- and three-dimensional shapes are all important to me," Nancy points out. "The quilted line offers a subtle texture that changes with lighting conditions. The feel of the fabric, its softness and flexibility make the pieces approachable and offers the possibility of function."

The home is still central to her work and is the reason that she chooses to work within a craft tradition rather than a fine arts tradition. "I am oriented to the home, not the museum," says the thirty-five-year-old craftsperson. "I like to think my work will share space with giggles, popcorn and dog mats, not with tape-recorded explanations and echoing footsteps."

"I feel comfortable acting as a mirror, reflecting the world around me within an essentially feminine tradition. I also enjoy seeing how my perceptions distort and alter that tradition without casting it aside."

Nancy creates only one-of-a-kind quilts. She is a member of the American Craft Council.

Brochure: No.
Commissions: Nancy will do appliquéd family-history quilts, appliquéd pictures commemorating special occasions, crib and storybook quilts.
Studio Hours: None.
Telephone: (207) 778-6658.

"Artichoke" wall hanging is made from cotton fabric in six shades of green. Reverse appliqué quilted and pieced. One of a kind, 48-by-48 inches; $425.

"Crazy Ice Rays" wall hanging, also of cotton fabric, has a purple background with the interior a variety of solids and prints in all colors, pieced and quilted without batting. One of a kind, 39 inches wide by 74 inches long; $450. It can be hung either on a wall or as a window panel.

144 · FIBER

EVE S. PEARCE

Weaving on the Wind
RD 1, Carpenter Hill
Bennington, Vermont 05201

Eve Pearce remembers that she used to take great delight in her grandmother's collection of Chinese silks, European linens and ancient rugs. "We used to sew together for hours," she recalls. As Eve got older she became absorbed in geometry and "other activities that played with form and required construction."

Coming to Vermont because "the land and the mountains gave me a sense of myself in the proper proportion to time and space," she started to weave during the winter months, "when the farm asked for less care."

"In making tapestries, I can recreate the images with which this place so fills me," she says. "In tapestry, the weaver builds the image. The image and the cloth are constructed simultaneously; they are one."

"Each of us has our own way of seeing the world," the forty-year-old weaver says, noting that her tapestry making has allowed her "to see and consolidate" her own perspective. She welcomes commissions where she can "express a moment of someone else's vision."

Eve works and lives with her three children on her farm overlooking a valley in southern Vermont. "The longer I weave," she told me, "the more I feel myself drawing together life's threads, interlocking them, constructing with them fabrics whose textures one can know first hand and whose images reveal our patterns, our journeys."

Brochure: Yes.
Commissions: Yes.
Studio Hours: By appointment.
Telephone: (802) 823-5580.

"The Mountain Beyond" is on all-wool tapestry in two parts: the upper, "Annapurna III, IV and II Seen from Pokhara, Nepal" and the lower, "Mount Graylock, North Adams and the Dome." Predominantly blues, purples, whites and greens. "Once on a day full of cumulus clouds, I approached a familiar overlook and, for a moment, was sure I saw above it the high peaks of the Himalayas as they rise above the foothills, above the clouds in November." Each part measures 28 inches deep by 70 inches wide; $2500.

"Shenandoah on the Porch" tapestry in all wool. "A small person on a big Victorian porch" in blues, whites, apricot, greens and black; 24 inches wide by 30 inches long; not for sale.

DIANNE SHAPIRO

Soft Sculpture
19 Cedar Street
Brattleboro, Vermont 05301

If you've often yearned to decorate your den with an animal trophy but couldn't handle the idea of killing some poor moose or rhino, look no further. Dianne Shapiro has the perfect solution.

While growing up on a working farm in Tennessee, Dianne learned taxidermy, the art of preparing, stuffing and mounting animal skins. After receiving a degree in zoology she served in the Peace Corps in Ethiopia where she studied the exotic local fauna. It shouldn't come as a great surprise that with this background Dianne has chosen to stuff animal heads for a living. Luckily for the fauna, her animal heads are silly, endearing creations made of fabric and stuffed with polyfill. Dianne calls them "humane trophy heads."

Dianne, now thirty-eight, stuffed her first moose in 1971. Still her favorite, the droopy antlered, wild-eyed moose was inspired by a drawing by cartoonist Skip Morrow. This soon led to the creation of a whole menagerie of beasts—elephants, sabertoothed cats, rhinos, giraffes, musk oxen, sheep and polar bears—all ready to hang on your wall and guaranteed to raise a smile from both ardent conservationists and avid big-game hunters.

Dianne's work is featured in craft shops, specialty stores and galleries around the country. She is a member of the League of New Hampshire Craftsmen.

Brochure: A full-color flyer is available showing her complete line of trophy heads as well as her family of soft-sculpture "pillow people."
Commissions: No.
Studio Hours: None.
Telephone: (802) 254-4439.

Two young owls in acrylic furs make a cuddly companion or a charming sofa pillow. The eyes are safety locked. 17 inches by 17 inches by 5 inches; $35 plus $1.50 shipping.

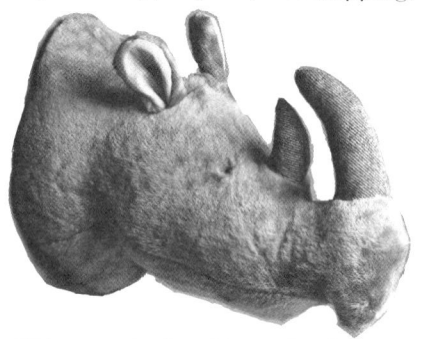

Rhino trophy head is made of grey acrylic fur, wool horns and little red safety-locked eyes. Hang in den, family room or living room. Length 24 inches; $60 plus $3 shipping.

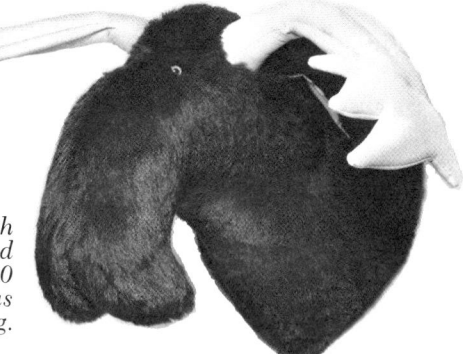

Moose head of dark-brown acrylic fur with tan cotton antlers and goofy safety locked eyes. Ready to hang. Length 19 inches and 30 inches from antler tip to antler tip; $75 plus $3 shipping.

HELEN M. GORDON

Patchwork Puffery
RD 2, PO Box 238-6
Bristol, Vermont 05443

"The best part of making a new quilt," says Helen Gordon, "is picking out the fabrics and the colors. I like to put all the bolts and pieces up on my work table and shuffle them all around and play with them. Then I rummage through my scrap boxes to see if I missed anything. It's like ice cream in an ice cream parlor!"

Helen has created a line of quilts with five variations of designs using the basic "grandmother's fan" square as a basis. "I try to design my quilts so they reflect movement," Helen says. "I want the quilt to flow through the design and through the colors." She describes her fan quilts as "soft, gentle ribbons of colors that flow continuously from light to dark."

Helen, thirty-three, is a member of Vermont Handcrafters and has been quilting for four years. "Quiltmaking is my art, my trade, my livelihood, my joy in life," she says.

Brochure: In work.
Commissions: Yes. "I especially love designing quilts with people."
Studio Hours: By appointment.
Telephone: (802) 453-3570.

"Mohawk Trail" quilt is 100-percent cotton with poly-fill batting. The fans are machine appliquéd onto the background. "This is a scrap quilt where fabrics are selected at random for the variegated look." The background is black. Queen-size quilt, 84 by 96 inches; $360.

"Wandering Fans" quilt, of the same technique and materials, projects a ribbonlike effect. The background is soft white and the fans are shaded light rose to dark maroon. This double-sized quilt is 82 by 93 inches and sells for $340. "Of course quilts can be made to order in any size or color."

Alice Blistein

24½ Brookes Avenue
Burlington, Vermont 05401

Alice Blistein remembers that she was inspired to weave prayer shawls the year her father was president of their congregation. While taking a weaving class that year, Alice learned from a synagogue elder how to tie tzizit, the traditional macrame that transforms a piece of rectangular cloth into a prayer shawl called a tallith. Today, she makes beautiful and unique tallithim of varying patterns and colors. Working with fine wool and a rainbow of color, she enjoys both weaving the shawls in the more traditional black-and-white or blue-and-white motifs or using a spectrum of colors to create striking contemporary versions of the ancient religious garment.

Her inspiration ranges "from the sublime to the mundane: From flowing with creative rhythm, to knowing I have deadlines and commitments, to feeling deeply in tune with the person and occasion I am making the piece for, to knowing that payment for the piece will pay bills. I have not regretted taking this leap of faith out of the world of the nine-to-five paycheck. It's hard and risky and profoundly satisfying."

Alice, thirty-seven, has been weaving for twelve years. She is a member of Vermont Handcrafters, Frog Hollow State Craft Center and Twist of Wool Guild. In addition to her weaving activities she teaches macrobiotic cooking and studies yoga.

Brochure: In work.
Commissions: Yes.
Studio Hours: By appointment.
Telephone: (802) 864-4025.

These tallithim are woven with fine white wool. "The pieces feel light and elegant and each one has its own individuality. I try to get a sense of the person I'm weaving for and design the striping and decoration with that specific person in mind." Tallithim are either 20 inches wide by 80 inches long or 30 inches wide by 80 inches long and are $100 and $150 respectively.

Sara Goodman

Pike Hill Road
Corinth, Vermont 05039

Sara Goodman was sixteen when a friend of her older brother brought back a sizable collection of Ikat fabrics that he had collected while spending a year in Bali. Sara loved the cloth and later, as she began to teach herself to weave, the images on the material remained with her. Always concerned that her work be functional as well as attractive and well made, she first studied Colonial overshot and Scandinavian Krokbragd rug patterns before beginning in 1982 to use the Ikat resist-dyeing technique on raw silk.

She uses only primary colors in her dye work and finds that being able to explore color through the use of chemical dyes is "the most exciting part of the process."

Fascinated by "the relationship between clothing and the structure of daily life in traditional Japanese society," she uses such forms as kimonos and hippari jackets for her clothing designs.

Each piece is dyed with different color combinations, with no two being exactly alike. Sometimes she uses sharply contrasting colors and other times different intensities of the same color for a more subtle effect. Always there are the distinctive resist sections in between two colors where the dyes bleed in the white section and create a halo effect.

Sara, twenty-six, says that living five miles down a dirt road on seventy acres in a very rural part of Vermont is an important factor in her work. "My studio is a cathedral of light, encased by sliding glass doors and skylights," she told me. "As I work, I am open to the sky and the changes in the weather. My aim is to make fabric that captures the movement and color of sunsets, clouds and the Northern Lights."

Sara is a member of the Society of Arts and Crafts in Boston, Connecticut's Brookfield Craft Center and the Artisan's Hand Co-op in Montpelier, Vermont.

Brochure: "Not yet."
Commissions: Yes.
Studio Hours: By appointment.
Telephone: (802) 439-5746.

Woman's kimono in rose and green with contrasting obi sash in blue and gold. The woman's style has longer sleeves with the traditional underarm slits. The man's style is larger, with shorter sleeves and no slits. All pieces are finely woven out of tussah silk at a density of sixteen threads per inch. Many different color combinations are available. Kimono for either men or women is $400 without obi; obi sold separately for $40.

Boat neck shirt made with compound ikat-resists in both weft and warp threads. Man's shirt is in yellow and red, woman's in rust and purple; $100 each.

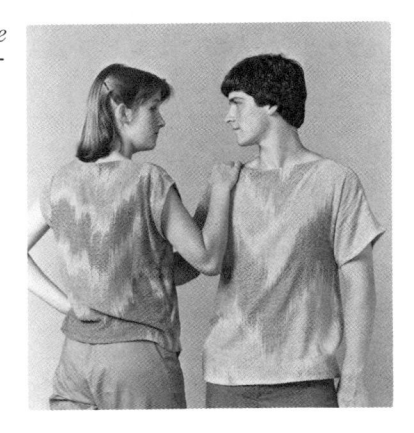

JENNIFER DICKERMAN & BARBARA HEILMAN

RR 1, PO Box 140
Hinesburg, Vermont 05461

Jennifer Dickerman and Barbara Heilman's machine-appliquéd quilts and wall hangings are fabric depictions of the people, places, animals, activities and homesteads of their customers. They encourage purchasers of their work to include any unique or personal details so that each piece is truly an heirloom.

"Our work is ideal for us," they told me, "allowing time and flexibility for being with our families and at the same time providing us with a chance for creativity and some added income."

The neighbors, both forty-two, started working together nine years ago when their youngest children started school. Their first workplace was a small room in a barn. After three years, they moved into a dining room and later to a "full-fledged workroom" in one of their homes where they now work. "We have gradually increased our production, learning mostly from experience but also by taking an occasional course in art or sewing."

Both craftspeople are members of Frog Hollow Craft Center and Vermont Handcrafters.

Brochure: No.
Commissions: All work is special ordered.
Studio Hours: None.
Telephone: (802) 425-2255.

A detail of a custom-made king-size "picture quilt." Machine appliquéd in multicolored cotton fabrics. Prices vary according to size and complexity of design. This quilt is approximately $1200.

Custom-made wall hanging of your house and surroundings can also be commissioned. Machine appliquéd in multicolored cotton fabrics; 27 by 36 inches. Prices vary; hanging shown is $325.

150 · FIBER

Alison Taylor-Parsons

PO Box 130
Hinesburg, Vermont 05461

It was the satisfaction of seeing her artwork worn or used in some way that triggered Alison Taylor-Parson's interest in crafts. Striving for a "variety of subject and style," she has been using batik since 1976 to create a line of items that includes wall hangings, T-shirts, lampshades and puppets.

"Batik is a dyer's art," she notes. "I am intrigued with the resist process as well as with its results. The excitement of watching the fabric's color transformation is heightened by the unpredictable nature of both dye and wax. The process forces me to make decisions, continually testing my ability to compose shape and color." It becomes, she says, a cross between painting and printmaking, which offers her comfortable balance between her fine-arts background and the influence of craftwork.

"Shades of nature seem to provide a common ground among people," she points out, "and I enjoy the response provoked by familiar scenes. I look forward to continually rediscovering batik's unusual properties and endless possibilities. It has become my ultimate means of expression."

Alison, twenty-five, is a member of the Vermont State Handcraft Center at Frog Hollow and Vermont Handcrafters.

Brochure: No.
Commission: Yes.
Studio Hours: None.
Telephone: (802) 425-3246.

"Mayan Woman" batik in tones of red and brown. This custom batik is done using procion dyes on cotton. Width 15 inches by length 19 inches; $150.

Tiger puppet is 100-percent cotton batik on white, orange and brown. Pigs, sheep and other animal friends are also available. Height 8 inches; $8.50.

Batik lampshades are of cotton laminated to a handmade, hand-packed shade. Production size shades are 7 inches top diameter by 14 inches long by 10 inches bottom diameter and 6 by 13 by 10 inches. Both sizes are $40.

FIBER

SARAH MUNRO-DORSEY

PO Box 261
Plainfield, Vermont 05667

"I like working in my house with good music, tea and friends dropping by," notes Sarah Munro-Dorsey. Although she has been working with fabric dyes since the mid-Seventies, it wasn't until her daughter Jasmine started day care in 1981 that Sarah was able to concentrate on establishing her business.

With an initial investment of $100 in materials, she is determined to build her business to the point where she will some day be able to buy some land and build a house for herself and her daughter. She is cautious, however, about pushing too hard. "It's important to avoid frustration, too hectic a schedule and too high expectations," she told me. "I'm not Superwoman, no matter how hard I try."

Her colorful one-of-a-kind wall hangings and scarves are hand painted, using a direct dye application. Her favorite images are, she notes, a '54 Chevy truck, a hovering kingfisher and other birds, dragonflies, real and imaginary flowers, all of which recur in fanciful landscapes featuring mountain and water scenes.

Her small cotton hangings and some of her silk hangings use wax as a resist before they are dipped in a vat of dye to achieve a batiklike crackle effect. On her silk pieces, she uses a Gutta resist, which is applied with a squeeze bottle.

Sarah, twenty-seven, studied at Goddard College in Plainfield and at the School of the Museum of Fine Arts in Boston. She is a member of the State Craft Center at Frog Hollow, the Artist Resource Association and Vermont Handcrafters.

Brochure: Should be ready by publication.
Commissions: Yes.
Studio Hours: Open one day a week during summer, by appointment.
Telephone: (802) 454-7175.

"Cattails" silk scarf has bright-yellow foreground with olive cattails. Blue-greens-to-purple-to-crimson create the large land mass. Light olive mountains surround an inner blue sky from a purple-blue outer sky. 22 inches square; $60.

Silk scarves from left to right: "Musical Jukebox" in warm yellow, orange and reddish tones in the center, surrounded by blues, purples and olive shades. "Waterfall" is in blue-green tones, purple pansies, olive green with specks of crimson blending into a lime green grassy foreground under a turquoise sky. "Chevy Truck"; a burgundy-brown 1954 Chevy truck emerges from olive-green cattails; purple mountains and a turquoise cloudy sky. "Hovering Kingfisher" in deep purple blues fading into navy then into turquoise sky. Each scarf is of 100-percent silk crepe, 9 inches by 40 inches and $44.

Karen Gutkowski

PO Box 395
Putney, Vermont 05346

"All facets of my life have influenced what I am now producing at the loom," observes native New Englander Karen Gutkowski. When she first became interested in rug weaving in 1974, she had the opportunity to work for Peter Collingwood, a rug weaver and author who has a workshop in England. During the six months that Karen spent there she learned the "technical expertise and discipline of rug weaving." From there she studied painting with Nyoto Nawagawa, acquired skills in conserving antique and oriental textiles and studied Tibetan Buddhism at Manjushri Institute of Buddhist Studies in England.

"The weft-faced techniques I use become canvases on which to play with pattern and color," she told me. "Color has always been important in my work and the emotional, intuitive response generated by its use."

Her design series developed from simple rhythmic geometric patterns that, notes the thirty-one-year-old weaver, "when translated to black and white resemble motifs that have common threads in textiles from ancient or 'primitive' cultures. Although the motifs seem inherent in the warp-and-weft structure of the fabric, they also appear to have a somewhat universal familiarity."

"Combining color and pattern, my objective is to create an illusion of depth and space, not only within the surface of the rug but reciprocally in the mind of the observer." Karen belongs to the American Craft Council and Putney Artisans.

Brochure: No.
Commissions: Yes.
Studio Hours: By appointment.
Telephone: (802) 387-5365.

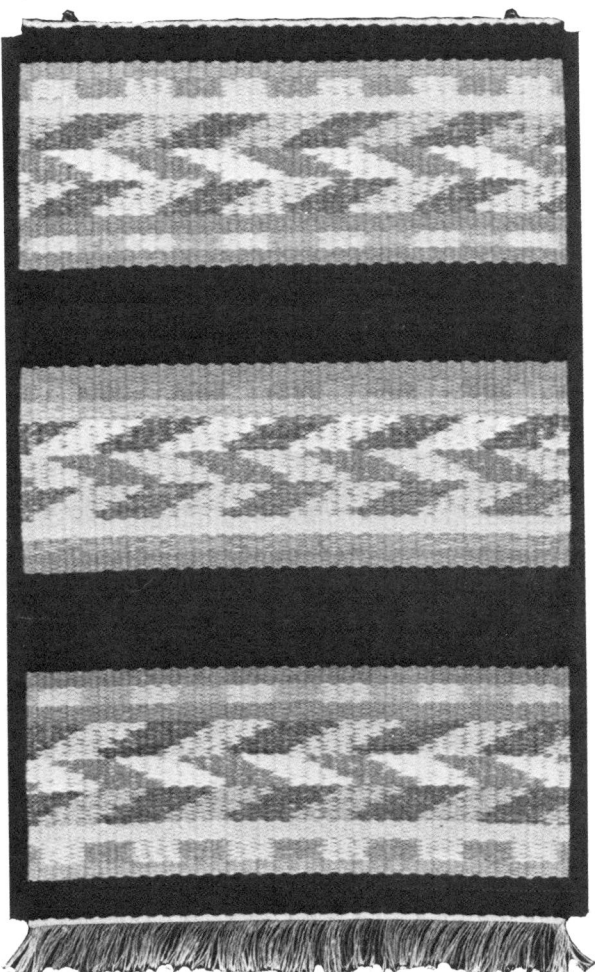

From Karen's "Landscape Series" of limited-edition designs, this piece will be reproduced in a one-of-a-kind combination of pastel patterning on a slate-blue background. This, like Karen's other work, is woven using the shaft-switching technique to develop the pattern. They are 100-percent wool on a linen warp and are suitable as rugs or as wall pieces. These and her other designs are in standard sizes of 4-by-6 feet; $880; 3-by-5 feet; $550; and 2-by-3 feet; $250. Specially commissioned pieces are $45 per square foot.

Tamar and Paul Maynard

Atelier Shadur-Maynard
PO Box 429
Putney, Vermont 05346

Tamar and Paul Maynard design and weave tapestries in the Renaissance tradition of Aubusson, France. One distinguishing feature of the Aubusson method is the use of a large floor loom across which the warp is stretched horizontally. Another is the pre-spinning by hand of five fine threads to produce a single weft thread, a technique that permits a very fine integration of colors.

According to Paul, Aubusson is "the technique par excellence for transposing the work of abstract painters into tapestry." While learning their craft in the late Seventies at Jerusalem Tapestries, a center for tapestry experimentation, they wove traditional designs as well as the "cartoons" of several renowned artists. Since their return to New England in 1980, they have woven both their own original designs and those of other artists in their one-of-a-kind tapestries. Their styles have included motifs from the ancient Near East, stylizations of native flora and fauna, narrative and abstract tapestries.

"Tapestry has as much to give the contemporary environment as it did to those of the Middle Ages and the Renaissance," they told me. "Environments of steel and concrete, glass and firebrick cry out for a touch of human warmth and elegance that only tapestry can give."

Having had the experience both of working with other artists and designing their own tapestries, Tamar and Paul, both thirty-two, feel that they are in "a unique position to design and weave tapestries that meet precise architectural criteria." They are members of the American Tapestry Alliance and Putney Artisans.

Brochure: Yes.
Commissions: Most of their work is custom-made. "We specialize in narrative tapestries on Biblical themes and in abstract tapestries meeting precise environmental specifications."
Studio Hours: Monday through Saturday, 9 A.M. to 6 P.M.
Telephone: (802) 387-4770.

"In the Outfield" was designed by Gerald Garston in collaboration with Tamar and Paul. It features a modified millefleur background. Size is 4-by-6 feet. Similar work usually runs $2,000 per square yard for design, cartoon preparation and weaving.

Designed by Y. Shadur, this tapestry represents Isaiah 52:7 — "How beautiful upon the mountains are feet of him that bringeth good tidings," here symbolized by the deer. The dove represents salvation. The city is Jerusalem. 24½ by 18½ inches; $900.

Jean Carlson Masseau

PO Box 90-60
Richmond, Vermont 05477

Jean Masseau started using fabric as a medium for her art while an illustration major at Rhode Island School of Design. Fabric soon became her medium of choice. "It combines the use of drawing, painting, sculpture and graphic design with the play of light and shadows on the final construction," she told me. "It is especially satisfying to me when a piece can be photographed and used as illustration."

Three-quarters of her business involves her production pieces, which she created to provide continuity and introduce her work to growing numbers of people. "My line of quilts and pillows are practical and functional, yet still incorporate painting, quilting and trapunto as an art form." The original designs are painted on the fabric with dyes and quilted. She sells them through shops and galleries as decorative art objects and conversation pieces.

In her one-of-a-kind work, she will usually explore an idea by working in a series, experimenting with an aspect of the design until it leads to a new discovery. "It allows me to do research through drawing, painting, photography and reading, which fuels inspiration for new pieces."

Jean's art training was in illustration, weaving, printmaking and photography at the Rhode Island School of Design. She taught high-school art in Vermont for five years before becoming self-employed as a fiber artist and illustrator. She belongs to some half-dozen craft and art ogranizations and has recently organized a traveling exhibition entitled "Pieces of the Puzzle; Works on Paper and Fabric" for the Vermont Council on the Arts. Her work has been shown in numerous solo group exhibitions in New York and New England.

Brochure: No.
Commissions: Yes. Inquiries welcome on soft sculpture wall hangings.
Studio Hours: None.
Telephone: (802) 482-2407.

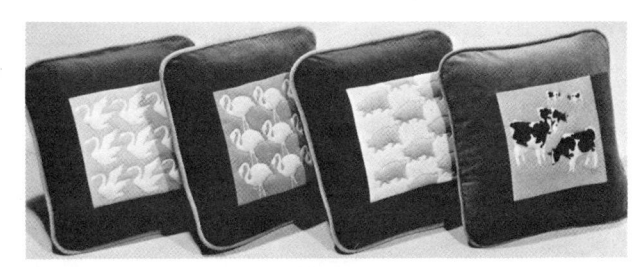

Popular designs from Jean's production line of pillows are, left to right: Swan pillow has white swans on a light blue background with medium-blue border and light-blue piping. Flamingo pillow shows light-pink flamingoes on a medium-rose background with medium-purple border and pink piping. Piglet pillow has peach piglets on a beige background with a cinnamon border and peach piping. Cow pillow shows black-and-white holstein cows in relief on grass and moss-green background. All pillows are 100-percent cotton velveteen with hand-silkscreened designs. The dyes are permanent, washable and color fast. There is a flap opening in the back. Each pillow is 12 by 12. Swan, flamingo and piglet are $34.50 each. Cow is $38. Add $1 for shipping.

"Pasture Puzzle Triptych" is a hand-appliquéd wall hanging that depicts cows grazing on rolling hillsides. Done in cotton velveteen and satin leather, it is quilted with trapunto relief techniques. Colors are green landscape, green-blue and mountains, and blue sky. The piece is 15 inches high by 45 inches long by 3 inches thick; $490.

LINDA CLIFFORD

Wobbly Land Patchwork
109 Temple Street
Rutland, Vermont 05701

Linda Clifford was once a buyer for the country's second-largest retail record store chain. Even though she loved the music, she felt that she was about to burn out on the job. "The pace of the record business began to wear on me," she remembers. "I left my job and moved to Vermont."

She began to make pillows and wall hangings "for gifts and to fill time in the evenings." Her husband, the sales manager for Killington Ski Area, thought that there might be a market for Linda's wares and convinced her to try selling them. He was right. Linda met with success first at local craft shows and then at professional-level craft shows.

"I like the idea of running my own business," she told me. "I was afraid when I left my regular job to make quilts fulltime that I would lose my discipline. Was I wrong! I work harder than ever eight hours a day seven days most of the time."

Most of her work is traditional in design, although she does some original contemporary motifs. "I like working with color and fabric patterns," she says. "Even though I might make the same designs over and over, the use of new fabrics and colors makes every piece different."

Linda, thirty-three, told me that her maiden name was Batts. Her family can trace themselves back to two Batts brothers who came over on the *Mayflower*. They were, it turns out, mattress makers. "Interesting coincidence that I should wind up making bedding also."

Brochure: No.
Commissions: Yes.
Studio Hours: By appointment.
Telephone: (802) 775-4107.

This "log cabin" quilt is of 100-percent cotton calico with dacron batting. Standard color schemes include antique blue, French blue, burgundy rose, sea green, "autumn," "Vermont," and "Desert." Other colors and patterns can be requested and matching dust ruffles, pillow shams and drapery fabric are available. Pictured quilt in twin size, $200; full/queen, $285; king, $300.

JUDY DODDS

Judy Dodds/Patch-It
PO Box 14
Waitsfield, Vermont 05673

Judy Dodds' love of the Vermont landscape that surrounds her is equalled by her appreciation of the artistry of ancient Japanese prints. Perceiving a "mystical connection" between the landscapes of Japan and those of Vermont, she creates large fabric works that are clearly influenced by both.

Her one-of-a-kind pieces have recently taken the form of large, transparent wall hangings, often in a three-panel, triptych style. She also fashions soft sculpture apparel and a line of Kabuki quilts, which are reminiscent of the fabric combinations seen in the kimonos worn by actors in Japanese Kabuki Theatre.

"I like to use the colors and textures of fabrics the way a painter uses paint and canvas to create spatial relationship and changes in mold," she notes. "The fact that the work is sewn, whether by hand or sewing machine, is not important to me. My hands and the machine are simply tools to achieve the desired effect." Depth, dimension, emotion and humor are important to her and she incorporates them in her work with a high degree of versatility.

Judy, fifty-five, has been a fabric artist for twelve years. She studied art at Tulane University and later was a curator at the Louisiana State Museum and at the Boston Children's Museum. She has exhibited widely in the United States and is part owner of a craft shop in Waitsfield, Vermont, where she lives with her husband in a 150-year-old farmhouse.

Brochure: Yes. Please send 50 cents for handling.
Commissions: Yes: murals, banners, room dividers and wall hangings.
Studio Hours: By appointment.
Telephone: (802) 496-2027.

This transparent stitchery banner or room divider is called "Apocalyptic Vision #2/Fantasy Island" and can be viewed from both sides. Done in silks, cottons and polyester sheers. "The second in my series of political statements done in the mystical Japanese style." 58 by 90 inches; $1200.

"Kabuki" quilt in a three-panel screen with a solid maple frame. Done in cottons, polished cottons, printed poly-cottons with an appliqué center. Fabrics can be matched to client's wallpaper, carpeting, etc. Matching comforter, shams and pillows available. Total size of screen is 60 inches wide by 66 inches high; $550. All work is copyrighted and trademarked by Judy Dodds.

Carol Schnabel

RFD 4, PO Box 296 B
West Brattleboro, Vermont 05301

For as long as Carol Schnabel can remember she has been involved with both fiber and the visual arts. She started sewing her own clothing at age twelve, which led to later experiments with patchwork, a process that she has now translated to woven strips of fabric. Noting that she is most concerned with color and texture, Carol primarily designs handwoven clothing from natural fibers. Each article is one of a kind.

"The joy of handweaving to me is the union of the repetitive rhythmic motions," she says, "with the continual exploration of new color combinations." Living in a rural environment, she is influenced by "the seasons and the time of day" and inspired by the landscape around her. She often conceives of new designs on her daily walks.

Carol, twenty-eight, sells her work in stores throughout the country and occasionally at craft fairs. In addition to her weaving and her interest in outdoor activities, she is also involved in folk music and contra dancing. She has been weaving professionally for five years and is a member of the Vermont State Craft Centers, the League of New Hampshire Craftsmen and the Handweavers Guild of America.

Brochure: Yes.
Commissions: Yes.
Studio Hours: None.
Telephone: (802) 257-1894.

Handwoven drawstring skirt of all cotton with a basket-weave border and a cotton calico yoke. "This skirt blends gently from light to dark to create beautiful movement across the body." Each is one of a kind. Custom-color families available and one size fits all. Machine washable, tumble dry; $95.

The Bolero vest is handwoven of all cotton and fully lined with calico, which makes it reversible. Lace-weave vest yoke is made of woven strips of calico, forming a graceful line. The body of the vest is beige and the yoke can be made to order in color families specified by the client. "Lovely to wear with the skirt!" Hand wash only. Women's sizes S, M; $110.

DEBORAH BROWN AND DREW KOVACH

DJB Designs
PO Box 573, West Main Street
Wilmington, Vermont 05363

Deborah Brown and Drew Kovach design fabrics and clothing that are versatile and elegant, with just "a touch of country." Using natural fibers with an occasional rayon or metallic fiber for luster, they weave unusual colors and textures into their fabrics, which they then tailor into fashionable and practical designs meant to be worn for many years.

"A delight in color is evident in all our work," says Deborah. "Making a warp is like mixing colors on a palette, only with paint the color mix is complete; in weaving each color retains its identity, interacting with the others to create new and exciting effect."

Custom-ordered clothing and fabric is a "challenge" that the weavers find especially appealing. "To create a piece of clothing with a particular person in mind —considering their style, coloring, preferences and even character—is very satisfying."

As their studio and retail store is open to the public year round, their workday often includes "as much demonstration and discussion as it does production," something that they greatly enjoy. Both Deborah, thirty-four, and Drew, thirty-one, have been weaving and designing clothing for twelve years. They are members of the American Craft Council and the State Craft Centers of Frog Hollow and Windsor.

Brochure: "Not yet."
Commissions: "We do custom clothing and custom fabric."
Studio Hours: Six days a week from 10 A.M. to 5:30 P.M. Closed Wednesday.
Telephone: (802) 464-3146.

Vest for men, women and children, right, is tailored in a medium-weight cotton/wool blend. Sewn to last with 100-percent cotton lining and topstitching. Hand washable. Men's sizes 36 to 44, $59; women 6 to 14, $54; children 2 to 12, $32. Shown is a man's vest in blue with brown and rust accents.
Necktie is silk and cotton blend with vertical stripes. Comes in a medium width with either a square-cut or pointed tip. Silk lined and hand washable; $25.
The tunic is available in silk/cotton blends or wool/cotton blends. It's faced with 100-percent silk and is hand washable. Shown here is natural wild silk with ocher and lavender accents. Can be ordered in colors and accents of your choice. S, M, L; $54.

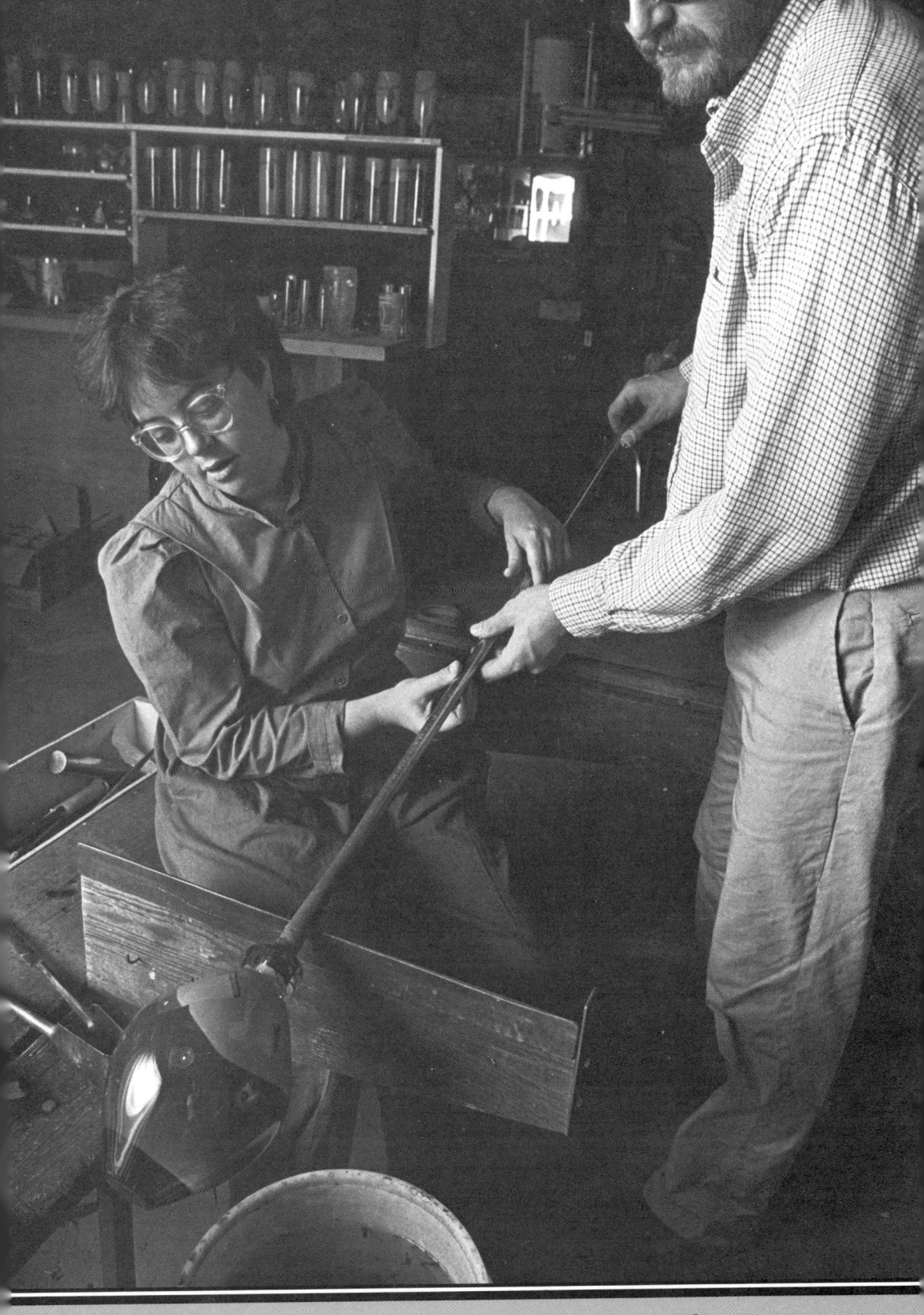

Glass

STEPHEN FELLERMAN

*Bull's Bridge Glass Works
Route 7
Kent, Connecticut 06757*

"There is a great challenge in going into the studio every morning and doing a high level, quality piece with freshness," says Stephen Fellerman. "I try to make sure that each piece has something special going for it. It's a combination of repetition and spontaneity that makes for a successful piece," he observes.

Steve's work has its design foundations in Art Nouveau, which he adapts into more contemporary forms. "Glass has a great tradition of being collected and bought. I try to be original but I use some of the traditional things that a broader base of collectors can relate to."

All of his work is completed in the molten stage, with all the decorating and draping done with hot glass. He often uses minerals on the surface of his work to create lusters. "My work is designed to catch the eye and give the beholder a sense of magic in that the luster of the glass is ever-changing."

Steve likes to push the shapes of his pieces to the extreme, as exemplified by the form of his lamp base, which is very long, very narrow and wide at the base. "It's a lot of glass to maneuver," he notes. "It's a lot easier to do a baggy shape like a potato."

Steve, thirty-one, has been making glass for more than ten years and sells his work through galleries and to private collectors directly through his studio. He graduated from Pratt Institute in 1972 and pursued advanced training at the Sausalito Art Center in California. He has won numerous prizes and awards of distinction at major exhibitions and is a member of the American Craft Council and Glass Art Society.

Brochure: Yes.
Commissions: Yes.
Studio Hours: Open to the public from 11 A.M. to 5 P.M. daily. (For blowing demonstrations, it's best to call first.)
Telephone: (203) 927-3448.

Copper ruby sea form is cased glass with hot-tooled decoration. Shape and luster are achieved while piece is still molten at 2000°F. 18 by 6 inches; $250.

This cream optic table lamp is made of cased glass with hot-tooled optic decoration. Approximately 30 inches high; $400.

R. Bruce Laughlin

310 Hackmatack Street
Manchester, Connecticut 06040

"It would be fun to say that I came to crafts through beachcombing and dump-picking," says Bruce Laughlin. "However, that is not the case. I have a background of a four-year commercial art schooling, twenty years as a graphic designer/art director in New York City and many craft workshops in fused glass, flat glass, painting on glass, glassblowing and blacksmithing."

Bruce first studied fused glass in the early Seventies with Maurice Heaton, who had developed the basic fused-glass techniques more than thirty years before. Bruce uses commercial glass or stained glass, which can be laminated or fused under heat and hand colored with selected enameling colors.

Bruce uses nature and organic forms as the design inspiration for his work. According to the forty-seven-year-old designer, his interest in nature motifs developed from his youth on the coast of Maine and later from the time he spent working on estates or with commercial flower growers.

He is a member of the Society of Connecticut Craftsmen, Brookfield Crafts Center, Society of Arts and Crafts in Boston and the Ridgefield Guild of Artists.

Brochure: No.
Commissions: Yes.
Studio Hours: By appointment on
   Fridays, Saturdays and Sundays.
Telephone: (203) 646-0898.

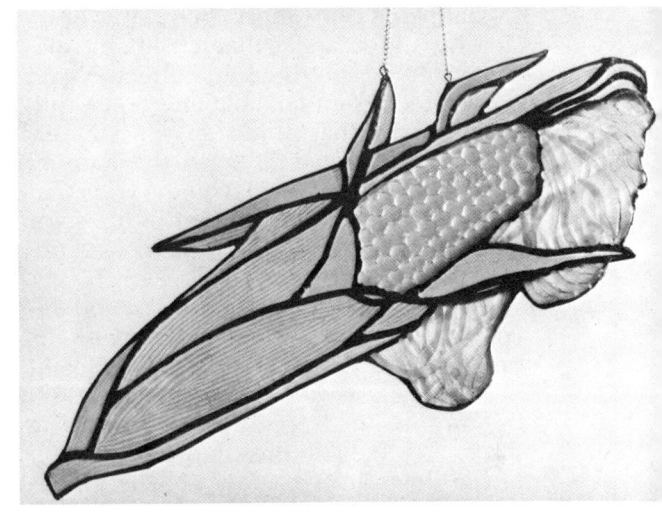

Corn on the cob designed in fused/leaded glass, which is cut from flat glass and hand colored with enameling powders. Colors are fired and elements fused together in an enameling kiln. Final assembly is with copper-foil technique. Kernels and corn silk are created with glass-fusing techniques. Indian corn also is available, 8 inches high by 14 inches long; $325 plus shipping.

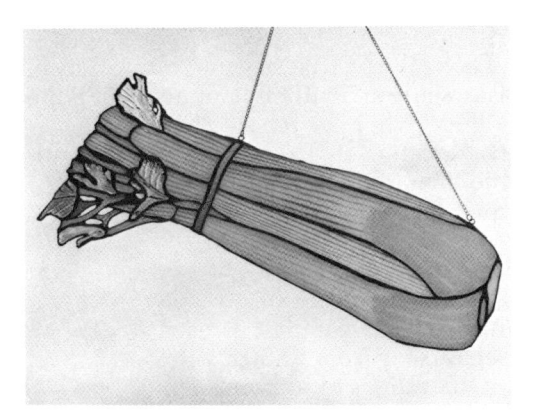

Celery of fused/leaded glass. Translucent white glass for stalk, band is red clear glass and the leaves are shades of green clear glass. Leaves are created with fusing techniques. 7 inches high by 14 inches long; $325 plus shipping. Also available are asparagus and iris pieces.

DAVID R. BOUTIN

Rainbow Glassworks
Banner Road
Moodus, Connecticut 06469

"What people like most about my work," says Dave Boutin, "is that it contains relatively simple motifs. Both collectors and non-collectors understand and relate to it well." Noting that his designs have undergone a "drastic change" since the opening of his studio in 1978, Dave now feels that his work has "the combination of color and form, coupled with a touch of excitement, that I have been striving for."

Through the use of pastel colors and uncomplicated decorations in most of his pieces, Dave has created attractively embellished glass work that also allows him to emphasize his love for "exciting forms." "I feel that the simple decoration of the flower at the crown of the pieces doesn't detract from the form," he explains, noting that it is in his perfume shapes that he feels he best displays his "interest in shaping."

"As many artists will tell you, we always are striving for that perfect piece—more unique, more stunning, more pleasing to the eye and functional yet a little out of the ordinary," he says, adding, "as always, my next piece is my best."

Dave, thirty, first became interested in glass while at Southern Connecticut State College, where he received his masters in art education in 1976. His work is available in more than 100 galleries and shops around the country.

Brochure: No.
Commissions: No.
Studio Hours: Sunday, Tuesday,
    Thursday from 10:30 A.M. to 5 P.M.
    Other times by appointment.
Telephone: (203) 347-7059.

Two perfume bottles, center and right, embellished in copper blue, opal white and silver. The opal and copper blue are pulled through the silver field, which causes a flower pattern to form at the crown. The bottles are about 4 and 5 inches high respectively to their stoppers and are about 3 inches in diameter at the shoulder; $60 for either size. The vase at rear is blown with opal-white and amethyst threads pulled through the field of silver to form a flower. It stands about 8 inches high and is 7 inches in diameter; $90.

ROGER GANDELMAN

Rainbow Glassworks
Down on the Farm
Moodus, Connecticut 06469

Before Roger Gandelman became a glassblower in 1977, he was a touring solo blues artist. One day, while looking for a wedding present in a craft shop, he noticed a vessel that he thought was ceramic. It turned out to be blown glass and Roger spent the next hour talking to the shop owner about the medium. He decided that he wanted to try to do that himself. So it was goodbye, blues; hello, glass.

"The skills are the same for both music and glassblowing: coordination, timing and judgment; getting your hands to do what you're thinking in your mind. It takes discipline," he says.

Roger, thirty-one, describes his glass as "pretty." "The colors are pretty and not shocking. They'll look good in someone's home." He leans toward floral decoration because, "simply, flowers are beautiful. They also allow me a tremendous amount of freedom when choosing my colors." Roger strives to "blend the colors the way nature blends the rich colors of spring and fall."

His present work reflects his interest in "exploring the optic qualities that the lenslike walls of a thick vessel take on, enhancing the multilayered decoration within its center."

"I try to get the beauty that I see in flowers in my work. There are no gimmicks," he told me. "I'm not making my glass thinking about getting it into galleries or shows. I'm making it thinking about whether it looks good to me and what will look good to others."

Roger, thirty-one, sells his work through fifty galleries across the country.

Brochure: No.
Commissions: No.
Studio Hours: Monday through Saturday, 11 A.M. to 4 P.M.
Telephone: (203) 873-9518.

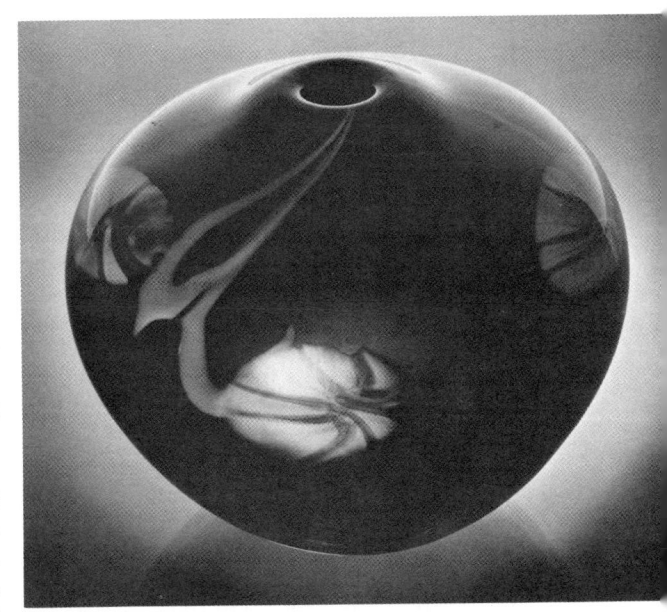

Black amethyst vase is decorated with orchid-colored vines and blue-grey morning glories. 4 inches tall and 6 inches wide; $110.

Floral perfume bottle exhibits green vines with pink-and-white flowers. Height 5 inches, width 1½ inches; $90.

BEBE HOLLAND DRING

*Le Jardin de Verre
197 Connecticut Avenue
New London, Connecticut 06320*

Bebe Dring likes to say that she "has been looking at life through rose-colored glasses for the past ten years," adding that "actually you would have to include almost every other shade of color that you can imagine and several combinations of those to really see the world as I do."

Referring to the fifteen years that she worked as a hospital electroencephalograph technologist, Bebe explains that "there is great satisfaction in caring about people and doing a necessary job, but there is pure joy in bringing fantasy and expression through light and glass to the eyes of those that see my glass designs."

Bebe's designs are an outgrowth of fifteen years of painting and the "desire to put ideas of expression into the brilliance of glass." She is currently working in contemporary designs that "reflect the moods of our modern architectural structures." Most of her pieces are autonomous and "designed to blend with simple lines."

Bebe, forty, is challenged by trying to impart three-dimensional perspective to the inherently flat surface of glass through the use of line, light and color. "Most importantly," she told me, "each work is a specific and unique design that will reflect the style that I have worked to achieve."

Bebe's art studies started, she says, with the teaching of her mother, who was a painter. She attended New Jersey's Montclair State College, The New School of Social Research, L'Ecole de Beaux Art in Montreal and the Albert Einstein Institute of Technology in New York City. Her work has twice been recognized in the Glassmaster's Guild Annual Competition and has won an Olympic Arts Award and a grant from the Connecticut Commission on the Arts. She is a member of the Stained Glass Association of America.

"Urban Renewal #20" is part of a series depicting a variety of urban images. This panel represents city life in industry, fine art, music, dance, sports and business. Made of imported and domestic glass, it is 3 feet by 5 feet and is one of a kind. Framed, $8,000. Other pieces range from less than $1,000 on up, depending on complexity.

Brochure: No.
Commissions: Yes.
Studio Hours: By appointment.
Telephone: (203) 442-5579.

ROSEMARY MILLER, LESLIE POTTER, VICKY HARRISON

MPH Stained Glass
2 Bailey Drive
North Branford, Connecticut 06471

The partners at MPH, Rosemary Miller, Leslie Potter and Vicky Harrison, have been working in stained glass for about twelve years, creating mostly small pieces intended to be displayed in a window. "New England stained glass collectors often have small window panes," they note, "and display their collection by hanging one piece on each pane."

They have accumulated a repertoire of more than 400 designs over the years and specialize in many motifs including music, sports, animals, holidays and religious symbols, professions, hobbies, birds, fruit and flowers. "We derive great satisfaction in providing that particular design someone wants, usually in intricate detail—whether it is a special flower, a special interest or life's work, a memory or whatever."

All their work is crafted in the lead-came method. The glass is cut, then wrapped with lead-alloy came and soldered together. Glass texture and color are individually selected for each piece as it is being created.

The trio all belong to the Connecticut Guild of Craftsmen, where Rosemary was formerly a member of the board.

Brochure: An illustrated catalog of more than 400 designs is available for $1.
Commissions: Special requests are welcomed.
Studio Hours: By appointment.
Telephone: (203) 488-8171.

This car is a realistic replica of a classic Packard. "Great care has been taken to feature its unique details." Height 4 inches, length 8½ inches; $40 plus shipping.

This colorful fruit arrangement features a rich-red apple, amber pear, bright-yellow banana, textured-red strawberries, raised purple grapes and shades of green leaves set in a bowl fashioned from opalescent glass. Height 3½ inches, length 4¼ inches; $15.25 plus shipping.

ELEANOR DOLE TAMSKY

City Lights Glass
PO Box 48
Stonington, Connecticut 06378

Eleanor Dole Tamsky is fascinated by the linear properties of the leaded stained-glass window. "The lead line is the basis of my work," she explains, "for within it lies the strength of my designs as well as the physical strength of the window."

Working mostly with framed autonomous panels of varying shapes and sizes, Eleanor uses techniques such as sandblasting and etching to control light diffusion, add surface texture and to draw directly on the glass. Her panels are finished either in a variety of hardwoods or zinc came, which create an aesthetic border while providing the structural integrity that allows the panels to be hung freely.

"I feel that working through the medium of framed autonomous panels frees me from the physical and aesthetic boundaries imposed by permanent installation," which, she says, allows her to develop her full potential as an artist and craftsman and also provides an important link to her commission work.

"When working on a commission I have to incorporate the client's desires and architectural boundaries into the finished piece," she told me. "My interaction with the client and studying the proposed location of the piece are very important to me. I find it very challenging to use the knowledge that I have gained from my own work to translate clients' ideas into a finished product that will serve their needs and become an integral part of their environment."

Eleanor, twenty-three, has been working professionally in stained glass for four years. She is a member of the American Craft Council.

Brochure: No.
Commissions: Yes; three-quarters of her work is made to order.
Studio Hours: None.
Telephone: (203) 535-1580.

This panel consists mainly of black, white and grey antique glass with accents of purple, green and blue. It is constructed in the copper-foil technique. The appliqué lead lines are fastened through the glass to assure permanence. Framed in ebony and 27½ inches wide by 38½ inches long; $700.

The lamp is made of purple, gold and green antique glass. Each piece was individually stenciled and acid etched to create the design. The etched sections diffuse the light, creating soft pastel shades. The untreated areas emit brilliant light and color. Overall height 22 inches with solid-brass base. The shade, is 10 inches high by 13 inches in diameter; $600.

FRED TENENBAUM

Northern Lights Glass Studio
RFD 2, Box 5160
Canaan, Maine 04924

Fred Tenenbaum's emergence as a stained glass artist occurred only after he had traveled a path of personal growth that had encompassed earlier incarnations as an oil painter and watercolorist, a carpenter and a family therapist.

After graduation from Pratt Institute in New York City, where he had studied art design and technique, Fred discovered that he had a talent for construction and turned to carpentry. This skill served him well when he and wife Eve moved to rural Maine in 1970. Using the plans that Eve had drawn up, Fred built their house and later began work as a family therapist at a residential mental-health community center. While there he started working with stained glass as a hobby and discovered that it was the perfect outlet for his talents and goals. "My background in art and construction seemed to magically meld," explains the forty-one-year-old artist, "and there grew an intense love affair with glass."

From the beginning, he avoided abstract designs, opting for more realistic themes involving flowers, women and animals. "Abstract line and form is subjectively interpretive," he notes, explaining that "probably due to my intense involvement with the human psyche and unconscious, I want to create something that is universally recognizable."

"My favorite art period is Nouveau," he told me. "I've been influenced by Mucha, Tiffany and, later, Parrish." Recently he has added sandblast etching to his repertoire of techniques, which has enabled him to better explore the creative potential of his designs.

"My goals, personally and professionally, are basically the same," says the forty-one-year-old artist. "To be and create to the best of my ability, to put the same energy and fervor into the smallest that I put into the largest."

Fred has been working professionally in stained glass since 1973 and has received several awards at Northeastern exhibitions and shows.

Brochure: No.
Commissions: Yes.
Studio Hours: By appointment.
Telephone: (207) 474-6161.

The elegant lampshade has a Victorian pattern that was sandblast-etched into mouthblown or "antique" glass. Pictured is a smoked grey shade with wine-red corner pieces and a pewter-finished fixture. Fixture can be antiqued brass, polished brass or pewter finish. It is completely wired with a 36-inch chain — 19½ by 19½ by 19½ inches; $595.

"K.J.'s Lady," this Art Nouveau style panel can be reproduced in a choice of colors and backgrounds. It is made of hand-cast and rolled glass in the copper-foil method and requires no unsightly reinforcement bars. The size can be expanded to meet your requirements. Comes with a zinc frame, 30 inches square, or in a choice of wooden frames; $1040.

169 · GLASS

JANET REDFIELD

*Cape Rosier Road
Harborside, Maine 04642*

Janet Redfield is quite a different person from the "miniskirted, New York City, career-girl ad writer of the early Seventies" that she once was. "The former suburban school girl has changed," she told me, "blossomed forth to raise prizewinning vegetable gardens, clucking chickens, gobbling turkeys, grunting pigs and the world's handsomest baby with my chairmaker husband here on a Maine coast salt marsh."

She credits this lifestyle change to discovering the joy of working in stained glass, which she calls "the key to the door that let me into my real life." Janet, thirty-five, has been working in glass professionally for nine years. She primarily executes one-of-a-kind commissions as well as a line of limited-edition designs. Included among her pieces are doors, windows, folding screens, terrariums, hanging lampshades, mirrors, planters and hanging panels. Most of her work is done with hand-blown German and French glass and tends toward flowing designs with stylized natural forms. "I like to make fairly simple lines in my work and not chop it up a lot," she says.

Janet is a member of Directions, a statewide professional crafts group. Her work can be seen in selected galleries and has been exhibited throughout Maine.

Brochure: No.
Commissions: "I would be delighted to create a stained glass piece for you that no one else in the world will have."
Studio Hours: 10 A.M. to 4 P.M. "almost daily."
Telephone: (207) 326-4778.

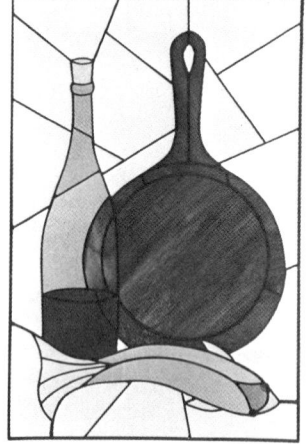

Kitchen still life and eggs panels are made of antique and opalescent stained glass with clear glass background and leaded in copper-foil technique. Still life has green fish, blue or brown pan, red wind. Ready for hanging. Eggs panel features blue or green bowl and white eggs. Both panels are 16 inches wide by 24 inches deep. Each can be brass framed, $150, or wood framed, $175. They are part of a series that includes panels featuring lemons, onions, mushrooms and radishes.

Climbing rose door is stained glass in a walnut frame. Both interior and exterior doors can be made to order in hardwood. Prices start at $2,000. All prices do not include shipping.

NANCY GUTKIN O'NEIL

Quaking Aspen Stained Glass
RFD 1, Box 191
Kezar Falls, Maine 04047

Nancy Gutkin O'Neil's stained-glass panels are a direct outgrowth of her college training in painting and drawing coupled with her interest in "line, color and light." "My stained-glass panels are basically big line drawings colored in with glass instead of pigments," she explains, noting that the challenge is to keep the "freshness and fluidity of the originally drawn design" in the finished piece.

When designing a piece she will often use "the natural world" as her starting point, from floral motifs to exotic life forms such as giant tube worms and large abstractions based on aerial views of Mother Earth. "I often look at things from unexpected perspectives," she says, "taking them out of their natural environments, combining them with grids or other design devices."

Nancy uses mostly imported, mouth-blown glass in her work, favoring glass that is embellished by unusual swirls, bubbles and other markings in order to further enhance her designs. Often using beautifully textured clear glass in conjunction with tints and intense colors, she creates pieces that range from the decorative to the surreal.

"Stained glass can introduce color and light into an environment in a way that nothing else can," she told me. "It can be subtle and unexpected, glowing quietly, or strong and dramatic, filling the room with colored light and colored reflections."

Nancy, thirty-three, has been an independent stained-glass artist since 1975. Her work appears regularly in galleries in the greater New York area and New England. She has executed architectural commissions in both public spaces and private homes throughout the Northeast.

Brochure: A full-color flyer illustrating six of her panels is available.
Commissions: All work is by commission.
Studio Hours: By appointment.
Telephone: (207) 625-8603.

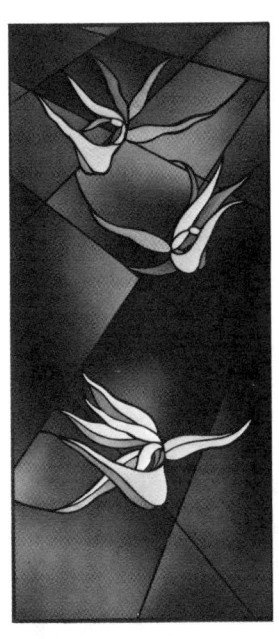

"Orchids in Space" is a one-of-a-kind window of dark-blue glass gradating to plum to red to pale coral in the background. Flowers are shaded white and grey. French and German blown glass used with copper-foil technique. Width 18 inches, length 40 inches; approximately $850 to $950.

"Orchid Chorus Line" mirror is inlaid and used iodized glass throughout. Second dancer from right has engraved black fishnet stockings. Width 36 inches, height 26 inches; approximately $750 to $850.

MARY GROVER AND JIM MILLER

Asylum Glass Studio
Grove Street
Newport, Maine 04953

Since Asylum Glass Studio was established in 1974, it has grown from a small stained-glass business to a professional studio "capable of providing any type of stained-glass piece from light fixtures to architectural installations," according to its founder, Mary Grover.

Mary's work consists chiefly of images that are derived from nature. "Wild flowers and birds are my consuming interest," she says, noting that there's a "large variety to draw upon abounding in the Maine woods." Often sandblasting and painting the glass to highlight patterns and subject matter, she likes to "isolate and magnify" her subjects, bringing them to the point of abstraction.

"I'm intrigued with the complexities of glass and light as a medium," says her associate Jim Miller, thirty-one, who's been working at the studio since 1979. "I find in these common elements a powerful and emotional appeal." He favors abstract designs "to provide the least interference with the natural beauty of the glass."

Jim received a bachelors degree in art education and a masters in instructional media from the University of Maine. He was a finalist in the 1980 Glassmasters Competition in New York City and is a member of the American Craft Council.

Mary, thirty-one, earned her bachelors degree in special education at Southern Connecticut State College. Her work has been featured in several one-women shows in New England. She is a member of Chosen Works Crafts Cooperative in Bangor, Maine, and the American Craft Council.

Brochure: Yes.
Commissions: "We can handle virtually any stained-glass application for the homeowner, builder or architect."
Studio Hours: By appointment.
Telephone: (207) 368-5340.

Harrier window is brown antique and streaky glass. This is one in a series of ten windows of hawks and owls. Brass framed, 22 inches in diameter; $275.

ROGER R. RICHMOND

Sho-Shin Studio
5 Exchange Street
Portland, Maine 04101

Roger Richmond sees many similarities between his intricately worked stained glass portraits and his original profession of architecture, most notably in the areas of design and construction. "Within the design of a piece lies the spirit of the finished expression," he says. "Within the execution of the piece lives the pleasure of seeing the concept come to life."

"In glass work as in a fine building," he continues, "light is the key. Glass honors the light through its color, texture and transparency. The personality of a glass portrait is continually changed by the nature and quality of the light that passes through it. It has mood and is never static because it is always reflecting the aliveness of its subject matter."

Roger, thirty-seven, is plainly intrigued with the versatility and impact of the medium. He suggests that his pieces "may be located more inside a space instead of being traditionally exhibited in front of a window or even as a window. Expressed in this way, a glass portrait begins to create its own place within the larger room, which gives it its living quality of presence."

"All at once," he concludes, "glass becomes the perfect material to capture the aliveness and drama of the human form."

Roger's work won the grand prize in the 1981 National Art Glass Competition of the Glass Master's Guild in New York City. His work has been exhibited in New York and in Maine.

Brochure: No.
Commissions: All work is by commission.
Studio Hours: Usually 10 A.M. to 4 P.M. Call first.
Telephone: (207) 773-8837.

Portrait of Teco Slagboom, a pastel artist living on Monhegan Island, Maine. The piece was designed, as is any Richmond portrait, to reveal the character and personality of the individual through the modeling of light expressed in glass. The work is basically monochromatic so that glass color will not dominate the subject matter. Solid oak frame with an inset oak mat — 34 inches wide by 72 inches long; $8000 to $10,000.

This portrait of Albert Einstein, like all Roger's portrait commissions, was designed to be experienced in a wide variety of light conditions. "Different and distinct sides of the subject's personality emerge depending upon when the piece is viewed. Transmitted light during the day is quite different from the light reflected off the piece at night." The dominant colors are blues, greens and whites. Width 28 inches by depth 50 inches. The average price for a portrait of this complexity ranges from $2500 to $4500.

CHRIS AND JOYCE HEILMAN

Heilman-Roessler Studio Glass
112 Mason Street
Westbrook, Maine 04092

Joyce Roessler-Heilman and Chris Heilman started their hot-glass studio five years ago in Bremen, Ohio. In 1982 they moved lock, stock and furnace to southern Maine, where they continue to create their highly decorated glass vessels.

During the intimately collaborative process, Joyce lampworks colored glass onto the surface of the vase, in effect drawing the imagery, while Chris does the handling and blowing of the piece. All throughout the process, they're continuously exchanging design ideas and suggestions between them.

"Our new work has evolved into layering of cased, lampworked imagery," Chris told me, "creating a repetitive decorative style." Influenced by Oriental prints as well as the landscape around them, they produce stylized interpretations of nature that are enhanced by the thickness of the many glass layers contained within each piece.

Chris draws the glass from the furnace and turns it over to Joyce who then takes fine pieces of multicolored glass cane to the draw, applying the intricate decorations. As the glass must be quickly and repeatedly returned to the furnace, she has only a few minutes to work on the design before Chris must again take over the process. "The sense of timing becomes a real critical thing," he notes. When the piece is finally completed after four to six hours of work, the layers of decoration separated by the casings of crystal glass create a multidimensional image of striking impact.

Chris and Joyce's work is represented by craft and art galleries throughout the country and has been included in more than a dozen invitational exhibitions. They are members of United Maine Craftsmen, American Craft Council and Directions, the Maine craft group.

Brochure: Yes.
Commissions: Yes.
Studio Hours: By appointment, serious collectors only.
Telephone: (207) 854-1597.

"Autumn Landscape" is blown freehand, giving it a soft natural form. Brilliant reds, oranges, yellows and greens comprise the foliage. The bottom of the vase is mossy greens and brown ferns. The imagery is torchworked or lampworked with colored glass rods and cased between layers of crystal. Colors may vary according to availability. Height 7¾ inches, diameter 5¼ inches; $500.

Andrew Magdanz and Susan Shapiro

Avon Place Glass
167 Pemberton Street
Cambridge, Massachusetts 02140

Each of the partners in Avon Place Glass discovered their affinity for glassblowing somewhat by accident. While an undergraduate student at the University of Wisconsin, Andrew Magdanz became attracted to the medium while helping to build some equipment for a glass studio. A couple of years later at the University of Massachusetts in Amherst, ceramics-major Susan Shapiro used to watch the student and faculty glassblowers at work through the window separating the clay from the glass studio. She was similarly entranced.

The future partners' paths crossed at Pilchuck Center for Glass Studies, where Andy was a teaching assistant. They stuck together through graduation from the California College of Arts and Crafts, Andy earning his masters degree and Susan her bachelors in fine arts. After graduation, they decided to open a studio and in 1978 they fired up the Avon Place Glass furnace and began producing glass.

Their work involves multiple overlays of strikingly intense colors and crisp graphic patterns of glass within glass shaped by hand into an elegant and graceful object.

They make the same general design over and over. Nevertheless, each piece is an "independent thought and an independent object." "When we find some new variation, we incorporate it in successive pieces," Susan told me. "The change is a subtle one. The work builds upon itself and evolves into many similar but varied pieces."

"We are both into a lot of things that influence our work," she adds, "architecture, fashion, nature, anything." They collect things ranging from old toys to postcards. "We're fascinated by the way things are put together. For example, by collecting Art Deco objects, we get a sense of form and color relations that we can then transfer back to our own glass, interpreting them in our own way." In addition to their collaborative work, each partner does their own one-of-a-kind pieces, which often involve sandblasting, enameling and grinding.

Both glassblowers are members of the American Craft Council and the Glass Art Society, of which Andy is a board member. Their work has been shown in many leading exhibitions and has been selected for review and publication in numerous magazines.

Brochure: A full-color postcard will be sent on request.
Commissions: Yes.
Studio Hours: By appointment.
Telephone: (617) 576-2089.

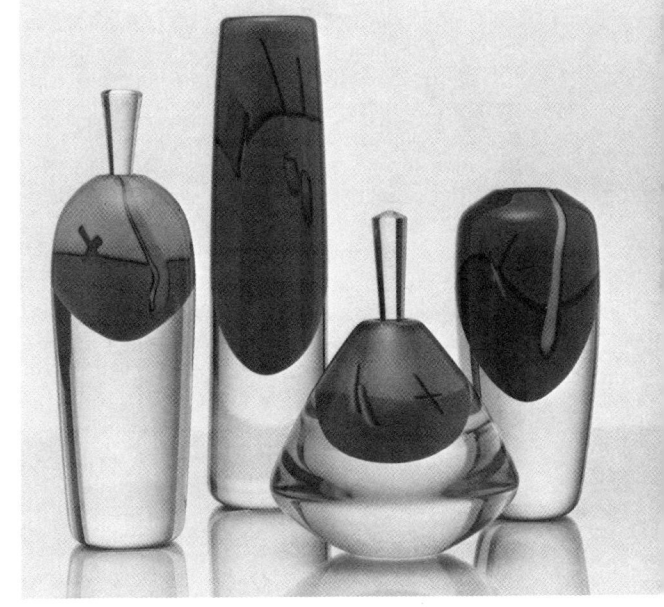

Grouping of blown-glass objects, from left to right: tall perfume-bottle bud vase, low perfume bottle and miniature vase. Designs are available in wide range of colors including violet/purple, purple/red, red/black, grey/pink, mauve/violet, white/black and more. "The large vases are designed to be decorative objects for the home, either alone or with a splash of color derived from flowers." The perfume bottles have individually ground stoppers that form an airtight fit.

CHARLES M. CORRELL

*Correll Glass Studio
85 Sargeant Street
Holyoke, Massachusetts 01040*

Charles Correll began his apprenticeship in glass in 1971 at the Jamestown Glasshouse in the Colonial National Historical Park in Virginia. "I fell in love with it immediately," he told me. "We cranked out pieces all day long and were able to practice a great deal and watch experienced glassblowers at work, which is usually not the case at most schools."

While there Charles learned how to work fast while controlling the molten glass. "If you can't control the medium, you can't make art," he maintains. "Art is the expression of the artist and not the medium." He continued his training in production work over the next few years and opened his own studio in 1977.

Today he makes primarily functional and "understated" pieces that emphasize three-dimensional form rather than heavily decorated surface. "Glass is best expressed by its smoothness of form," he notes. "There's equal attention paid to detail in the emphasis of form as there is in ultradecorated work." He works quickly in order to achieve just the right clarity of line and simplicity of form. "Glassblowing is a dance and the rhythm of the dance must be accurately pursued and controlled," says the thirty-three-year-old artist. "It's similar to music in that it's very time conscious. The glass is always cooling when it's not in the furnace. Timing and a sense of where the heat is is critical. If you're late, you can destroy it."

Rhythm and good hand-eye coordination are the two main components to controlling the glass, says Charles, who adds, "You're in a unique time sense with the making of glass. It's almost a different world. You can't stand back and look at your work in progress. It's immediate and time sensitive and the finished piece is the static representation of your movements and efforts."

Charles' work is on display in shops and galleries in thirty-six states. He has exhibited in numerous shows and fairs nationwide and is a member of the American Craft Council.

Brochure: Full-color sheets showing the entire line are sent on request.
Commissions: Yes.
Studio Hours: By appointment.
Telephone: (413) 534-4994.

Red strike goblets and decanter. They are cased over white glass. Decanter is 11 inches high, $110; goblets are 8½ inches high, $42 each.

Amber-strike compote dish with added shaped stem and foot. Height 6 inches, width 4½ inches; $60.

176 · GLASS

TOLAND PETER SAND

Toland Sand Art Glass
RFD 2, Box 422
Tilton, New Hampshire 03276

Toland Sand started working full time in glass in 1977, the year that he bought an account list and some supplies from a person who had made small window "suncatchers." Being an experimental and resourceful type, Toland soon began to acquire new techniques and expand his repertoire. Today he creates one-of-a-kind, flowing, abstract glass windows, panels and folding screens that incorporate many facets of glasswork.

Using mouth-blown rondelles and antique glass in his constructions, Toland employs sandblasting, beveling, slumping and gold-leaf techniques in order to achieve his artistic goals. "I want to be familiar with all techniques," the thirty-three-year-old artist told me. "Then I can choose the best one to construct what I have in mind. Anything else is being less than a professional."

The glass that Toland uses is carefully chosen not only for its hue but also for its unique patterns of bubbles and its subtle lines. Some of his windows and screens are made exclusively from different forms of clear glass with a clear crystal-blown rondelle accent. The effect is spectacular for any location that needs screening while still allowing all available light to be admitted.

His plans include getting into large glass sculpture forms. "I want to receive as many large commissions as I can," he says, noting that he is presently working on a three-piece movable stained-glass sculpture that utilizes an aluminum superstructure that will allow it to be manipulated into various configurations for entirely different effects. That's a long way from window suncatchers.

Toland works in a studio adjacent to his home where he is helped by wife Bobbi, who does the copperfoiling and paperwork for the business. He has done windows for homes from New England to Hawaii and points in between and has been exhibited in invitational shows in New York City, Boston, Cape Cod, San Francisco and Washington, D.C. He is a member of the League of New Hampshire Craftsmen.

Brochure: Yes.
Commissions: Yes.
Studio Hours: By appointment.
Telephone: (603) 286-4589.

Circular autonomous panel in textured clear glasses designed to be hung in window. Blown rondell, optical lenses, sandblasted mirror, bent traverse-mounted bevels and framed oak. "It's especially rewarding to work without color." Diameter of piece is 28 inches; $750.

Rectangular autonomous panel is done in purples, lavenders and clears. Also for window hanging, it incorporates blown silvered rondell, sandblasted and flashed glass, sandblasted colored mirror, plated mirror and is framed in oak. Width 16 inches, length 40 inches; $675.

177 · GLASS

CATHLEEN SCANLAN

259 Water Street
Warren, Rhode Island 02885

During her senior year as a sculpture major at Rhode Island School of Design in 1978, Cathleen Scanlan noticed the sandblasting machine used by the glassblowers to etch designs onto their work. She was intrigued and soon became fascinated with the possibilities of using this technique in conjunction with glass panels.

"Traditionally, stained glass relies upon the use of color, lead lines and paints to draw the image," explains the twenty-nine-year-old glassworker. "Etching glass offers the possibility of drawing on the glass itself. The lead line could be totally eliminated if necessary." After reading everything she could find on stained-glass construction, she found a workspace, bought a sandblaster and began doing her own work. She's been specializing in etched glass ever since.

Working within the limits of the one-eighth inch thickness of the glass, Cathleen etches up to six different levels into the glass. The effects, ranging from a light frosting to a deep etch, impart a pronounced three-dimensional quality to her pieces. She has expanded her repertoire to include the use of colored antique glass, which she likes for its characteristic "seeds" (small bubbles) and striations that make the glass "sparkle with illuminated color."

"I need to establish a striking presence through my work," Cathleen says, "whether it be through the etched-glass animals series, or through the larger stained-glass panels." She distributes her work through shops and galleries, direct sales and through the crafts cooperative, The Christmas Store, in Cambridge, Massachusetts.

Brochure: Yes.
Commissions: Yes.
Studio Hours: None.
Telephone: (401) 247-0159.

Etched-glass-rabbits window panel has a background of clear glass. The rabbits have been etched by sandblasting the details into the glass. Dimensions with ash frame 18 inches wide by 24 inches long; $675.

Unicorn etched on a clear glass rondel with leaded border. Diameter 9 inches; $32.

MATTHEW BUECHNER

Thames Street Glass House
688 Thames Street
Newport, Rhode Island 02840

When asked to characterize his work and the technique used to create it, Matthew Buechner's response is succinct and evocative: "It's open and free; it's loose. You spin the glass around and throw it out."

Matthew's line of production pieces, which often are embellished by swirling forms and graceful, subtle changes of color, includes vases, perfume bottles, paperweights, goblets, mugs and Christmas tree ornaments. "A factory can manufacture a more practical and perhaps more functional object at a lower price," he says, "but it can't reproduce the essence of craft. When someone buys a craft, he is buying a small part of the craftsman, some of his or her time in making the object, his skill and his sense of design and color."

Matthew's introduction to glassblowing was in 1975 when he spent a summer as an apprentice in Caton, New York. After additional studies in glassblowing at Hartwick College in Oneonta, New York, he served as a bit gatherer/apprentice for a year at Glashutte Eisch in Frauenau, West Germany. He returned to this country in 1979 to cofound a glass studio in Corning, New York, with his brother and sister-in-law. In 1981, he and his partner Adrian Chapman moved to Newport and opened their present studio.

"A craftsman can be in charge of his own life, do what he wants to do and earn a living from his hard work, design sense and skill," says the twenty-five-year-old glassblower. "Through his craft he might even experience a small sense of immortality—that the work will live on long after him. This is why I like glassblowing and will probably spend my life involved in it."

Matthew's work has been exhibited in invitational shows in West Germany, Japan and the United States. It is sold in galleries and shops across the country.

Brochure: Yes.
Commissions: No.

Studio Hours: Open year round Monday through Saturday from 10 A.M. to 6 P.M.; Open Sundays during the summer from 12 to 5 P.M., or by appointment.
Telephone: (401) 846-0576.

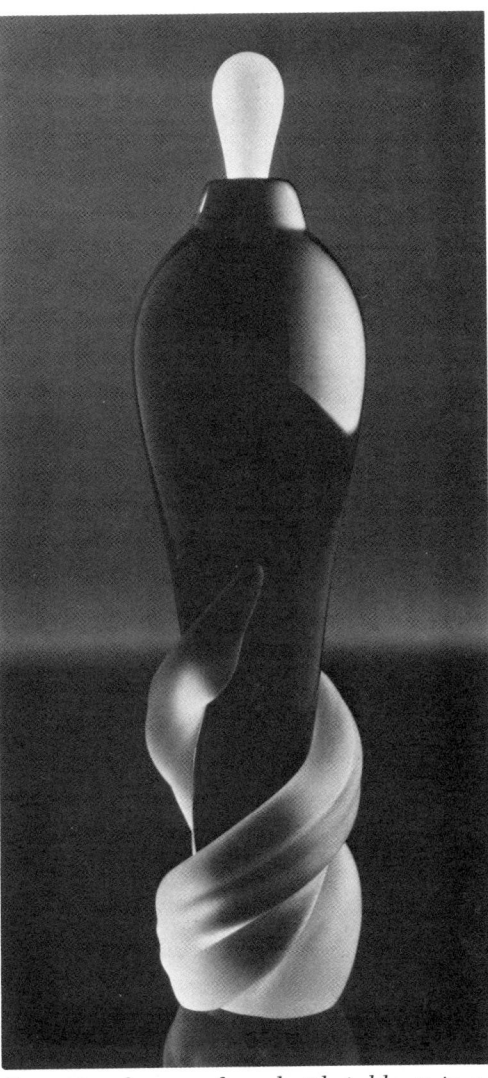

Emerging-form perfume bottle is blown in a variety of opaque and transparent colors with colorless bits applied to the base. After the bottle is annealed, the base is sandblasted and the stopper is fit and sandblasted. You twist the stopper gently into the bottle to form a seal. About 6½-inches high with stopper; $90 postpaid.

EDWARD J. MCILVANE

235 Promenade Street
Providence, Rhode Island 02908

While Ed McIlvane's work in glass is usually executed in "time-tested techniques," he points out that it is unusual in a couple of ways: "First of all, its source of inspiration is really the history of modern art, architecture and design rather than the history of stained glass exclusively. Secondly, I often use handblown or cast-glass elements which I make and color myself, giving my work qualities which are unique and impossible to duplicate. In this way, I hope to make my work particularly personal."

Initially attracted to stained glass in 1969 because it "seemed to offer a way of life which integrated both intellectual and manual skills," Ed began seven years of "traditional and thorough training as an apprentice and journeyman-craftsman" in a succession of metropolitan New York area studios that specialized in liturgical stained glass and restoration. After completing this training and desirous of improving his design skills, he entered the glass program at Rhode Island School of Design, where he received his masters degree in 1978. He credits his experience at the school as having a "profound impact —both technically and stylistically" on his work.

"Because stained glass is influenced by the ever-changing light conditions," says the thirty-five-year-old artist, "and because of its unique light-and color-transmitting qualities, I believe this medium offers the greatest potential for bringing us close to nature and beautifying our architectural environment. In the future, I hope to continue investigating the creative possibilities of glassblowing and stained glass both for private residences and public buildings."

Ed has taught at workshops and schools throughout the country and is presently an Instructor in the Stained Glass Program at Rhode Island School of Design. He has executed numerous public and private commissions and is the recipient of fellowships from the National Endowment for the Arts and the Rhode Island State Council on the Arts.

Brochure: No.
Commissions: All work is by commission only.
Studio Hours: By appointment.
Telephone: (401) 274-6909.

"Primary Tryptych" is an interior wall or divider in semiopaque glass and primary colors. Based on a DeStijl painting, it incorporates blown-glass rondelles, handblown antique glass and leaded glass techniques. "The rondelles function as a counterpoint to the background and center composition of random squares and rectangles, adding an element of softness to the rigid structure of the background." It is 4 feet wide by 5 feet high; $3000.

Oak door frame by Spencer Morris with an insert of leaded glass with handblown rondelles and sheet glass made especially for this project. "While using traditional techniques for the construction, the design of this door is quite unusual, creating an impression of free-floating elements." The opening in the frame is trapezoidal, enhancing the unusual effect of this piece, which was done in collaboration with James Harmon. Door measures 3½ feet wide by 7 feet high; $3000.

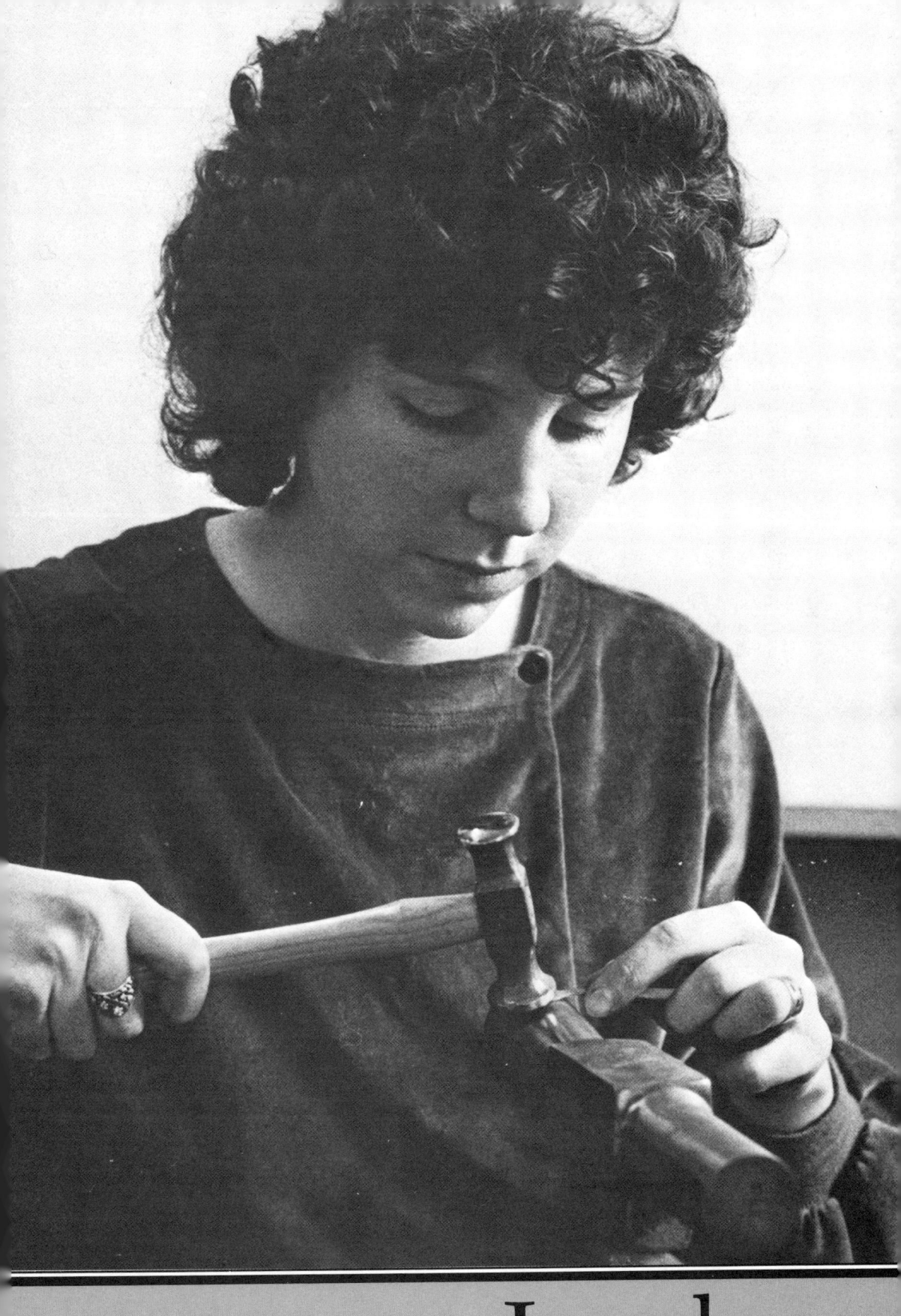

Jewelry

NANCY K. YOLEN

1022 Chapel Street
New Haven, Connecticut 06510

Jewelry had always been one of Nancy Yolen's personal loves. "Shining metals and brilliant gems, detail and flowing lines attracted me," she recalls. In 1976, dissatisfied with her years of experience in sales, banking, hospital and office work, she searched for a more satisfying outlet for her creativity, saw that some friends had started successful crafts businesses and decided that perhaps jewelry making could at once be creatively satisfying and capable of supporting her. She was right.

After taking a few beginner courses in construction and design, she apprenticed to a master metalsmith for a couple of years and generally learned everything she could about her craft. Today, she is the resident jeweler at a boutique in New Haven, where she produces and displays her work.

"I've come to think of jewelry not just as ornamentation," says the twenty-eight-year-old artist, "but as sculpture—to enhance as well as be appreciated for itself." In her recent series of jewelry, she has chosen to "fantasize about the possible forms of future civilizations, drawing from present-day, high-tech engineering as well as ancient civilizations, which I believe will transcend time and space." Within her pieces lie representations of "interplanetary voyagers," "high-tension energy sources" and "views of the galaxy," all constructed of silver, gold, gemstones, titanium and acrylic.

Nancy is vice-president of the Society of Connecticut Craftsmen, a member of the American Craft Council and the Society of North American Goldsmiths. She sells her work through shops and galleries, special exhibitions and at major juried craft fairs, as well as out of her own shop.

Brochure: Yes.
Commissions: Yes.
Studio Hours: Monday through Saturday, 10 A.M. to 5:30 P.M.
Telephone: (203) 562-4770.

"High Tension VII" pendant is a one-of-a-kind pendant made of sterling and fine silver, a sky-blue drusy chrysocolla, and a naturally formed quartz crystal. Pierced, formed, folded and constructed design; cymbal forms are movable. Sterling chain is 18 inches long; pendant is 3½ inches high by 1 inch wide by ¼ inch deep; $510.

STEVE AND JUDY BROWN

Brown Goldsmiths
One Mechanic Street
Freeport, Maine 04032

Steve and Judy Brown began creating sterling-silver jewelry in 1967, while they were attending the University of Maine. Their designs proved attractive to their friends, who bought enough work to provide the Browns with both encouragement and the funds to invest in new tools and materials. They soon began to sell their work to fine craft outlets throughout the East and their budding business prospered. For the last ten years, Judy and Steve have marketed their jewelry through their own studio and store in Freeport's old Masonic Hall.

"Since our beginnings, we've felt a dedication to jewelry that functions as it decorates its wearer," Judy told me. "Comfort, ease of clasping and a lack of cumbersomeness are qualities that we expect from our creations."

Several years ago, the Browns began formal studies of gemstones, which Judy calls a natural outgrowth of their "love affair with diamonds and precious stones." They have a large collection of unmounted diamonds and precious gemstones in their studio, which, according to Judy, serves to "seduce and inspire" them. Both jewelers are certified gemologists with the American Gem Society.

The Browns emphasize that they love working with their clients to design jewelry that makes a "very personal statement" about their customers' varying styles. "The shared ideas and interaction are a vital part of the designing process," says Judy.

The Browns are members of the American Gem Society, Jewelers of America and United Maine Craftsmen.

Brochure: No.
Commissions: Their production work is sold only in their own studio. Most of their work is specially commissioned.
Studio Hours: Monday through Saturday, 10 A.M. to 5 P.M. Open Thursday evenings during the summer.
Telephone: (207) 865-6263.

RememberRing™ is available with one, three five full-cut diamonds in white, yellow or rose 14-karat gold. "The simplicity and durability of this design has universal appeal." Single diamond ring has 3/100 carat diamond, $235. Three-diamond ring has 9/100 carat total weight, $325. Five-diamond ring has 15/100 carat total weight; $375.

Each flower and leaf on this gold wedding ring is carefully cut by hand and the tiny pieces of different colored golds (yellow, rose, green or white) are individually assembled. "The hours of work produce a rich and subtle contrast of golds and flower." From $1,000.

Commissioned belt buckle in 14-karat yellow gold and sterling silver. The doubleheaded eagle was hand carved and cast in gold by the lost-wax method. The eagle holds in its talons an oval ruby scepter and an orb of golden tourmaline and is on a sterling background framed in gold. "This one-of-a-kind project, which took several months, is an indication of the scope of our work."

183 · JEWELRY

MARIAN AND WILLIAM FRETZ

Fretz Gallery
Box 500B, Maine Street
Kennebunkport, Maine 04046

William and Marian Fretz design and produce cleanly sculptured jewelry in 18- and 14-karat golds and in sterling silver. According to William, their work "falls into two categories: very controlled and tailored pieces with inspiration from classical periods and a very free-form style."

"Our work is strongly influenced by contemporary design," adds Marian, "although our use of varying techniques adds a realm of individuality to each designed piece." Many of their pieces are first sculpted in wax and then cast into precious metal. After casting, they'll often use such techniques as forging, fabricating, holloware and granulation of gold particles to finish the piece.

"Foremost in my mind when designing a piece of jewelry is how it is going to look when it adorns the wearer," Marian says. "Jewelry should enhance and complement the body."

The Fretz's studio workshop and gallery are attached to their home, which, says the couple, makes their work "an integral part" of their home life. It is, they say, a "simple complexity," which also includes their two young sons and "an assortment of four cats and one furry dog."

Several months during the winter are spent making new show pieces and organizing their annual July "Summer Show" held in their gallery and featuring both their work and that of "other creative and talented craftspeople and friends in New England."

Marian, thirty-five, graduated from the University of Maine with a degree in marketing. Although principally self taught, she received her basic training from her husband. William, also thirty-five, graduated from the Rochester Institute of Technology with a degree in metalsmithing. Both Marian and William have taught their craft at several professional art schools. Their work has been exhibited at the World Silver Show in Mexico City and at other invitationals. They are members of the American Craft Council, Maine Retail Jeweler's Association and the Kennebunk-Kennebunkport Chamber of Commerce.

Brochure: No.
Commissions: Yes.
Studio Hours: Open year round Tuesday through Saturday, 9 A.M. to 4 P.M.
Telephone: (207) 967-4757.

Combination cast and fabricated high-prong ring of 14-karat gold, set with either a green or pink Maine tourmaline that was mined and faceted in Maine; $850.

Pendant of 18-karat gold is a cast, abstract sculptural piece set with either a green or pink Maine tourmaline and a .25-carat diamond; $1550.

184 · JEWELRY

Peter Aylen

Aylen & Son Custom Jewelry
PO Box 392, Main Street
Southwest Harbor, Maine 04679

"Designer-crafted jewelry from competent hands is alive with an identity all its own," notes Peter Aylen, who has been creating custom jewelry for the past fifteen years. "Born of inspiration and vision from the roots of soul, it screams with joy, frustration, fury or any of a thousand emotions. Or when the magic is right, a piece can soothe with love's caress or excite with the erotic emotions of springtime lovers."

To Peter, forty, the creation of each piece of jewelry is exciting, every job fires him up anew; he finds beauty in simplicity, poetry in complexity. The language of his art is drawn from "the carefree flamboyance of nature at one extreme and the rigid discipline of the Victorian era at the other," he says. This "universal language," when coupled with the versatility of the rare metals and minerals used in his work, creates a repertoire, "limited only by the scope of the practitioner's imagination."

"The unique requirements of each person necessitates a certain amount of sharing and understanding between us," he says. "I like to meet with people, discuss their likes and feelings about what they would like the piece to say. This personal contact allows me to guarantee satisfaction."

Peter also specializes in restyling or remaking old pieces into new. He'll take "valued materials and sentiments—a broken chain, one earring, grandma's diamonds, a worn wedding band," and refashion them into "new statements of love (or whatever)." "It's magic, wonderful and satisfying," he exults. "Come see me. Let's talk."

Peter is a member of Directions, the professional craft group of Maine.

Brochure: No.
Commissions: All work is custom made and one of a kind.
Studio Hours: Monday through Saturday, 9 A.M. to 5 P.M.
Telephone: (207) 244-7369.

Necklace in 14-karat gold with Priday Plume agate. A one-of-a-kind casting with handmade chain featuring apricot-hued freshwater pearls. "This necklace is at its best when worn on bare skin or over a grey or black turtleneck. A strong central statement for semiformal wear in most any environment." The stone, cut forty years ago by Fred S. Young of Portland, Oregon, is 20mm by 18mm. Chain length is 18 inches; $2550.

ANDREW GRAD

Box 1667 GMF
Boston, Massachusetts 02205

Change and contrast are central to Andrew Grad's recent arrival as an innovative ceramic jeweler. Twelve years ago he had entered college bound for a career in biochemistry. His career plans changed, however. Prior to creating his line of jewelry, he had been working part-time "doing heavy lifting for UPS," while pursuing ceramic sculpture and casting about for a practical way to set up a craft business.

He became involved with jewelry quite by accident. Nearly two years ago, while comparing glaze and clay tests for a potential line of ceramic tabletop tiles, a friend noticed them and asked Andy if she could have a few pieces to wear as pendants. Andy started to see some possibilities. "The process seemed a natural for jewelry," he says, "It's affordable to the wearer and doesn't require a large amount of labor time for each piece." After ten more months of testing, he introduced a series of ceramic jewelry, each piece handpainted in a variety of designs with sleek, intense color combinations.

Using a white clay that has the consistency of whipped cream, Andy first forms the shapes, then in effect draws on the surface by forcing colored slips through a narrow aperture, something like a baker decorating a cake surface. Each piece is fired twice: once after the slip application and again after an overall clear transparent glaze is applied. The result is a line of contemporary and affordable jewelry.

Five nights a week, Andy, thirty, exchanges the artist's delicate touch and hand-eye coordination for the exaggerated motions of a weightlifter. He enjoys the contrast between those two activities and is intrigued by contrast in his work. "Contrast is integral to my jewelry," he notes, "among color, in movement, in texture and in form."

Brochure: Should be ready by fall, 1983.
Commissions: Yes.
Studio Hours: By appointment.
Telephone: (617) 268-6394.

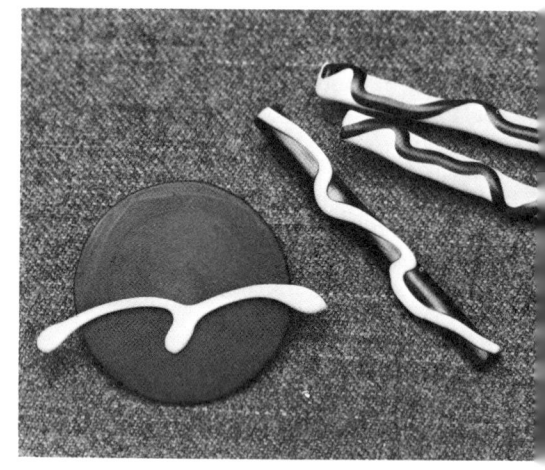

Stick earrings are available in white on black or black, yellow, blue or green on white. Two sizes: 1 inch, $6.50; 2 inches, $7.50, postpaid. "Bird in Flight" earrings and pins (lower left). The white porcelain bird is drawn and attached to the deep-blue disk, then fired. Approximately 2 inches from wingtip to wingtip. Earrings $9.50; pins $4.50 postpaid. Larger or smaller earrings as well as other shapes and designs can be custom made. Gold-filled screwbacks can be ordered for earrings larger than ½ inches in diameter at a $2 additional charge.

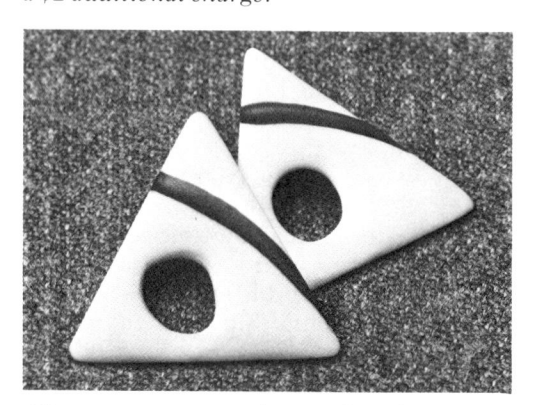

All earrings are porcelain with 14-karat gold-filled posts and nuts. With liquid porcelain Andy draws the designs on each earring freehand. Black-colored porcelain slip is shown here on top of white uncolored porcelain triangles. Stripes are available in black, pink, maroon, yellow, blue and green. Triangle has 1-inch sides; $9.50 postpaid.

Shirley Drevich

476 Franklin Street
Cambridge, Massachusetts 02139

It would be accurate to call Shirley Drevich a space-age jeweler. Her material of choice, epoxy resin, is the stuff used to coat spaceships and her abstract designs evoke the spirit of the Eighties. Using geometric frames of silver to contain her colorful, high-tech designs, she produces a series of men's and women's jewelry that could win NASA's seal of approval.

Each piece acts as a miniature canvas for Shirley to juxtapose varying combinations of colors in her ongoing exploration of "the freshness in what is modern." She calls her pieces "bridge jewelry," because they fill a gap somewhere between precious jewelry and throwaway fashion.

Shirley first blends colorful pigments into the clear epoxy base to create her palette of colors. The resin is then solidified, cut into forms such as lines or dots and carefully inlaid into shallow wells of silver. More resin is then poured into the shapes and the pieces are cured to form a durable surface of color, comparable to the hardness of ivory or ebony. Finally, she sands the pieces, producing a flat, abstract pattern that is comfortable to wear and a striking use of color, line and form.

Shirley, thirty, sells her jewelry through numerous shops nationwide. Her work has been featured in invitational and juried exhibits across the country. She graduated from Tulane University with a bachelor's in fine arts and did postgraduate work in Boston College's Program in Artisanry. She is a member of the American Craft Council and Society of North American Goldsmiths.

Brochure: Yes.
Commissions: Yes.
Studio Hours: By appointment.
Telephone: (617) 547-8539.

These earrings are inlaid with metal against a colored background with a metal frame. Available in either sterling silver or gold plate and either pierced or clip-on styles. Background colors are black, dusty pink, deep grey or red. Length 1 1/4 inches, width 7/8 inch, depth 1/8 inch. In silver, $90; gold plate, $75. Add $5 for clip-on.

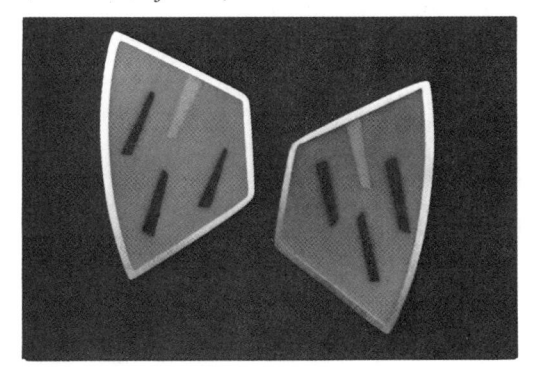

Cufflinks are inlaid with contrasting strips of color into sterling silver. The colors available are black and white, grey with pink or white and red with white. This shape and pattern also available as earrings. Dimensions are 1/2-by-1/2-by-1/8 inch. Cufflinks in silver, $55; in gold plate, $45. Earrings in silver, $45; in gold plate, $40. Add $5 for clip-on.

Saturn bracelet is constructed from sterling silver and inlaid with epoxy resin. Colorful two-tone combinations available in violet and grey, red and white, or black and white. 4 inches long by 2 inches wide by 3/8 inch thick; $190.

187 · JEWELRY

Laurie M. Wise

L & R Wise, Goldsmiths, Inc.
81 Church Street
Lenox, Massachusetts 01240

"My style is difficult to pin down," explains Laurie Wise. "In fact, I don't really have one. After I've done a piece or two using a particular motif or technique, I get frustrated and feel stagnant. For me the doing of art is constant exploration."

Consequently her pieces sometimes reflect a concern with the juxtaposition of textures, while at other times they may reflect her desire to make a piece of sculpture that will stand on its own. At still others, as with her "An Arrested Fantasy" piece, the twenty-seven-year-old jeweler is involved with recreating the delicacy of line that she achieved in her original sketch and her concern is strictly two-dimensional.

"To be honest, I'm not really all that concerned with concepts," she told me. "My work is much more intuitive and emotional than intellectual."

Laurie first became interested in making jewelry while a design major at Southeastern Massachusetts University, where she had taken several jewelry courses. The summer after she received her bachelors degree in fine arts, she joined with a group of other young craftspeople in opening a small shop. They were quite successful that season and Laurie found that working as a craftsperson provided her with the "intellectual and emotional uplift" that she was looking for in a career. At about that time, she met her future husband, Richard, and began to teach him her craft. In 1977 they decided to "try and make a full-time go of it." Today, they create and sell their jewelry in their Lenox gallery.

Laurie is a member of the Society of North American Goldsmiths and the American Craft Council.

Brochure: Yes.
Commissions: Yes.
Studio Hours: Winter: Monday through Saturday, 9:30 A.M. to 5:30 P.M. During the summer, same hours plus Sunday, 10 A.M. to 2 P.M.
Telephone: (413) 637-1589.

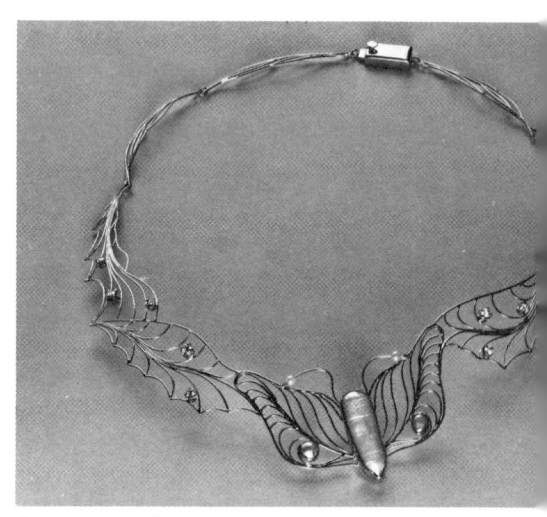

"An Arrested Fantasy" one-of-a-kind necklace forged from 9½ feet of 18-karat yellow-gold wire. Set with three bezel-set pearls, a Chinese freshwater white pearl in center and champagne colored Biwa pearls on the side. Also set with eight full-cut high white diamonds of .45-carat total weight; $5800.

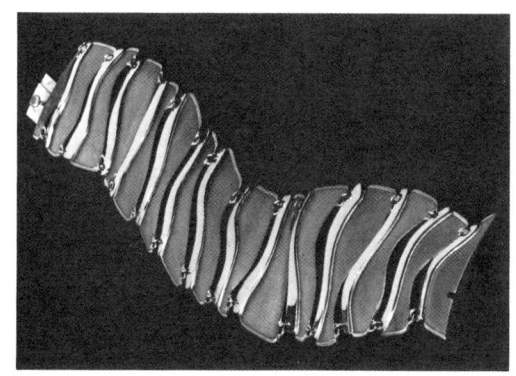

This bracelet has been fabricated of 14-karat gold and sterling silver. It has a khaki patina invented by the artist and is one of a kind; $1600.

LINDA KAYE-MOSES

Plumdinger Studio
95 Chickering Street
Pittsfield, Massachusetts 01201

"People think that my pieces don't look Western," notes Linda Kaye-Moses. "They think that they look Oriental." Indeed, while her pieces do exhibit a variety of styles, they are generally reminiscent of age-old ornament. "I feel that I'm drawing on ancient inspirations—spiritually, aesthetically and ethnically," she told me.

Linda makes both a production line of "earbands" and one-of-a-kind pieces, which she feels are her most exciting pieces. "In this work I am able to go beyond ornament as decoration or statement to ornament as mandala, as empowering object, as instrument for focusing energy. My pieces feel of deep energies and may resemble amulets or symbols of older civilizations."

Formerly a speech therapist, Linda, forty-one, found her way to jewelry making seven years ago. She uses silver, semiprecious stones, handblown glass and occasional details of brass or copper in her work, which is constructed by such techniques as riveting, piercing, chasing, dapping and engraving.

Linda has studied jewelry at the Brookfield Craft Center and the Worcester Craft Center, but is primarily self taught. She is a member of the Society of North American Goldsmiths, the American Craft Council and the Empire State Crafts Alliance. The recipient of a 1982 Massachusetts Arts Lottery Council Grant, her work has been exhibited throughout the Northeast.

Brochure: Yes.
Commissions: Yes.
Studio Hours: None.
Telephone: (413) 442-6535.

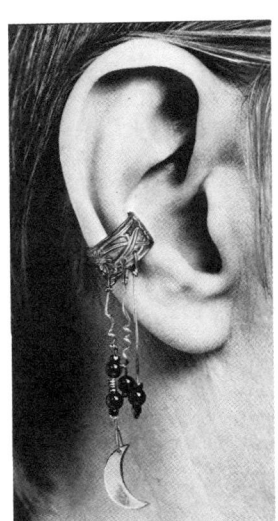

The earband is an updating of an ancient concept combining the old and the modern in a simple, elegant ornament. Worn higher on the ear than earrings, it slides on from the upper curve of the ear and rests in the deep cup. May be worn with other earrings. The flowered band is of sterling silver and the sterling-silver-wire dangles support your choice of a variety of semiprecious beads. $18 each earband.

"Ivory Scent Case Necklace" is sterling silver and incorporates the carved-ivory handle of an antique parasol, a cone-shaped citrine and amethyst beads. The cover removes to allow the insertion of a small piece of scented tissue. As with all Linda's one-of-a-kind pieces, this one has a handmade loop-in-loop chain originally conceived by the jewelers of ancient Mediterranean civilizations. All pieces are sterling silver with occasional brass and copper details and are set with carefully selected and unusual semiprecious stones including amethyst, Mexican opals, rose quartz, gem chrysocolla, malachite, garnet, tourmaline and moonstone. The pieces are oxidized and gently buffed, giving them the look and feel of antiquity. Pictured necklace is $500. Price range $350 to $500.

ELISABETH CARY

Elisabeth Cary Designs
142 Irving Street
Watertown, Massachusetts 02172

As a holder of a masters degree in management, Elisabeth Cary knows that it is smart marketing to find a void and attempt to fill it. In 1982 while at the Rhinebeck Craft Fair, she realized that a market existed for "elegant, yet simple costume jewelry fabricated out of glass." As a user of costume jewelry, she recognized that there wasn't much inexpensively priced, hand-crafted jewelry. "My philosophy is that costume jewelry should be well designed and executed, but reasonably priced so that the purchase decision remains spontaneous and fun."

With this in mind and with the technical and design finesse that she had gained from three years of assisting glass artist Rick Bernstein, Elisabeth set out to create a line of inexpensive but sophisticated glass jewelry. By designing her earrings and necklaces with clean, vivid colorings and strong geometric forms, she has created an elegant line of jewelry with high-tech overtones, and suitable, says the artist, "for the modern woman who believes in making a strong statement about her personal fashion sense."

Her jewelry is crafted from slumped, flat sheets of hand-blown European glass. After first cutting the individual shapes out of the sheets, Elisabeth bevels them to reveal three distinct layers of glass. Other pieces are sandblasted through a template fixed to the surface of the glass, revealing the different colored layers in juxtaposition. All pieces are finally fire polished to create a lustrous, gemlike quality.

Elisabeth, twenty-eight, received her bachelors degree in biology from the University of Massachusetts. She has held positions as a science teacher, organized and led expeditions into remote areas for the National Outdoor Leadership School and has designed and administered market-research studies. She is a member of the American Craft Council.

Brochure: No.
Commissions: Yes.
Studio Hours: None.
Telephone: (617) 899-4206.

Small pattern earrings, lower left, are handblown pink flashed glass over white. Sandblasted checkerboard pattern has a fire-polished finish. Gold-plated pierced earring back. Each side is ¾ inch; $10.

Shard pierced earrings, upper left, are handblown flashed glass in a pale-pink-and-rose color scheme. Geometric shapes are ground and then fire polished. Gold-plated pierced-earring back. About ¾ inch; $18.

Fragment necklace, middle, is handblown flashed glass in an alternating black-and-rose color scheme. Ground and polished with a fire-polished finish. The beads are glass and are arranged in the black/rose color scheme. Pendant size is 2½ inches by 1 inch; $40.

Pattern pierced earrings, upper right, are handblown black flashed glass over white. Features a sandblasted checkerboard pattern with a fire-polished finish. Gold plated pierced-earring back. 1 inch by 1 inch; $15.

David Epstein

RR 1, Box 407
Huntington, Vermont 05462

David Epstein has been a professional jeweler since 1973, the year that he and his wife moved to Vermont. His latest works are composed of laminated matrixes that form colorful and dramatic patterns. "I love to create and I love the work I do," the thirty-three-year-old jeweler told me. "I get a great deal of satisfaction conceiving an idea, transferring it from paper to metal and working with it step-by-step to its conclusion."

When creating a new piece, he will first do a series of drawings before settling on one with just the right shape or design. After deciding on the color combinations and materials that he wants to use, he cuts the semiprecious stones, shells or coral for the piece into the shapes needed to make the desired patterns. The cut pieces are then bonded and the whole matrix of materials is ground to shape. The piece is finished by constructing a silver setting using sterling sheet, wire, tubing and solder.

Basically self taught, David is a resident jeweler at Designer's Circle gallery in Burlington, where he works closely with customers, doing restoration work, taking special orders and designing new pieces in his line. He has exhibited at many juried and invitational shows throughout the East and sells his work through shops and galleries.

Brochure: Yes.
Commissions: Yes.
Studio Hours: By appointment.
Telephone: (802) 482-2174.

Silver post earrings in a geometric style combine crushed-stone inlays of lapus lazuli (royal blue) and chrysocolla (blue-green). About 1¼ by ½ inch; $120.
Prices in gold are available upon request.

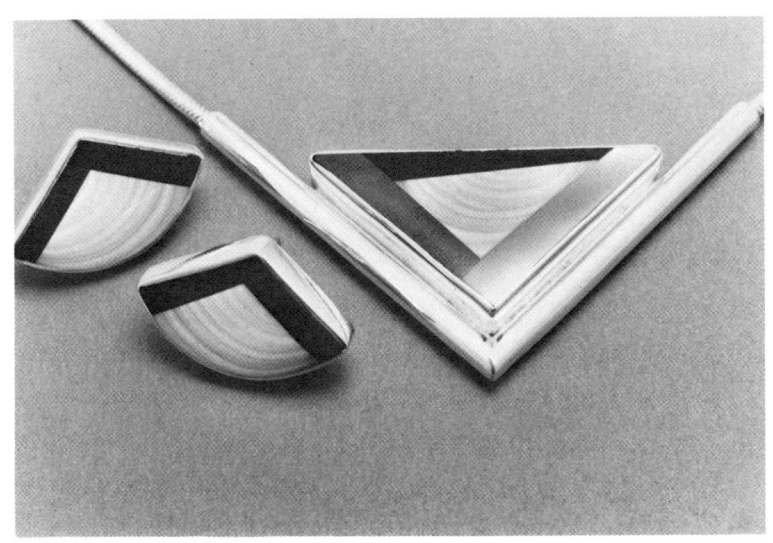

A triangular necklace and matching pierced earrings in silver that combine cameo shell, red jasper and jet. Sterling silver chain is 16 inches; $95.

191 · JEWELRY

Metal

EDWIN R. GROVE

RR 1, Box 527
Brownfield, Maine 04010

There are those who admire iron objects, observes fifty-six-year-old blacksmith Edwin Grove, and those who take it for granted. "Those who like iron seem to appreciate the line, the suggestion of strength yet the delicate, warm and graceful appearance."

Most of Ed's work is made in the traditional manner: in a fire with hammer, anvil and tongs. Working in his large, well-equipped blacksmith shop, which is adjacent to his home, Ed makes a living by teaching his craft, making custom pieces for clients and doing some traditional iron work, including shoeing a few horses each week. Natural forms such as stems, leaves and flowers and the shapes they suggest are often incorporated into his custom work.

His early years were spent on a small farm, where he learned how to make necessary repairs and the proper care of animals. After completing his formal education, he "went to work in the woods." Since woods work also involved some iron work, he often sought out the help of practicing blacksmiths and studied their craft at every opportunity. From these experiences, he developed a life-long appreciation for iron that finally prompted him to become a blacksmith/farrier about eight years ago.

"I am one of the fortunate people in this world who live in an enjoyable outdoor environment and work in a most satisfying way." Ed is a member of New England Blacksmiths, Artist Blacksmith Association of North America, American Farrier's Association, the League of New Hampshire Craftsmen and Directions, the Maine craft organization.

Brochure: No.
Commissions: "I enjoy making pieces for individuals who like owning and using handmade items of iron."
Studio Hours: Because Ed's sometimes away shoeing horses, call first.
Telephone: (207) 935-2262.

This door knocker was made for a family of Scottish heritage who were fond of Great Danes. The knocker portion is a forged Great Dane head and the back plate is cut, carved and forged to resemble a thistle, a plant considered the national emblem of Scotland. Finished as black iron with beeswax and linseed oil, the knocker is attached to back plate in such a way that removal is difficult. Many other combinations of knocker and back plate can be made. Knocker portion is 8 inches long and back plate is 10 inches in length; $350.

Fireplace or wood-stove tools are made entirely in the tradition of blacksmithing. Fire-welded basket handle and shafts with a ring attached to hang the tool. Rack can be made to desired length and tools can be made singly or in sets. Hooks are adjustable and removable, but are secure when in place. Due to the wide variety of materials to which the rack might be attached, fasteners are not provided. Tools are approximately 29 inches in length. Shovel $80; poker $60; rack $15; and hooks $5 each.

194 · METAL

Robert A. Butler

*40 Rugg Road
Allston, Massachusetts 02134*

Robert Butler was first introduced to silversmithing when he spent eight weeks in London working with a master smithy for a senior-class high school project. In that short time he was taught the basics of the craft—fabrication, fitting and handraising—and was quickly captivated by the metal's character and versatility. He returned home to Massachusetts with a tea set, three credits toward graduation and a desire to become a silversmith.

"Silver is sometimes called the queen of metals beause it is clean to work with and it is the most reflective of all materials," he says. These properties, along with the effects of handraising, which causes a flat disk of silver to be shaped into a hollow form, are what attracted him to the art.

"Like clay on the potter's wheel, silver under the hammer becomes pliable and plastic, moving with great speed," he told me. "In my finished pieces I try to show this movement combined with a balance of reflection and light."

Robert, twenty-seven, received his training in a most traditional manner—a four-year apprenticeship to a silversmith in Clerkenwell, a London center for silversmithing since the seventeenth century. He has collected many traditional hand tools and has set up his workshop for the making of one-of-a-kind rather than production pieces. Much of his time is spent in the creation of pieces that are to be given as gifts, something that he enjoys. "Part of the challenge of making an object is to have the finished piece identify with the person giving or receiving it." He likes to meet with and talk to his customers, getting to know their personalities or through them, those of the person who will receive the gift. "What's the point of having a handmade object if it does not reflect something human or personal in its making?" he asks.

Robert has been a silversmith for the past ten years, four as an apprentice and six in his own studio. When not practicing his craft, he is a champion long-distance bicycle racer.

Brochure: No.
Commissions: All work is custom-designed.
Studio Hours: "Normal business hours by appointment."
Telephone: (617) 254-9898.

Sterling-silver coffee pot has a walnut handle and insulator. The handraised offset pear shape is a traditional style enhanced by use of nontraditional lines. 10 inches high and 23 ounces in weight; $1900.

Wheat box of sterling silver is fabricated of three chased or applied wheat heads with grasses. It was made for a September wedding and is 6½ inches high and weighs 5¾ ounces; $780.

195 · METAL

PETER ERICKSON

Erickson Silver Shop
39 Green Street
Gardner, Massachusetts 01440

Drawing upon the traditions of New England's Colonial silversmiths, Peter Erickson uses centuries-old processes to produce a great variety of handwrought sterling-silver flatware and jewelry pieces.

His interest in silversmithing comes from his grandfather, George Erickson, who started Erickson Silver Shop in 1932. From 1971 until his retirement in 1976, his grandfather passed on to Peter the knowledge of more than sixty years as a master craftsman. "His patience and skill were the dominant factors in my development as a silversmith," Peter told me. "I am very proud to be able to carry on his business."

Peter, thirty-one, works only with sterling silver, which is composed of ninety-two-and-one-half-percent silver and seven-and-one-half-percent copper. "The making of handwrought sterling-silver flatware is a long and tedious process," he explains. "A teaspoon, for example, is made from a strip cut four-and-three-eighths-inches long by one-half-inch wide by one-twelfth-inch thick. It is forged out to a pattern by a continuous process of repeated hammering then heating, hammering then heating again. This tempering is what distinguishes hand-wrought silver from commercial, machine-made pieces."

After the forging process, the working end of the spoon is "bowled up" and the handle bent to the proper shape. Polishing, called "finishing," completes the job. "Because the only way to harden sterling silver is by hammering, a hand-forged piece has the extra strength not found in a machine-made utensil."

Peter is a member of the American Craft Council and the Gardner Arts Council.

Brochure: No.
Commissions: Yes.
Studio Hours: Monday through Friday, 8:30 A.M. to 12 noon and 1:00 P.M. to 5:00 P.M.; Saturday from 9:00 A.M. to 12 noon.
Telephone: (617) 632-0702.

Sterling-silver bracelets. The cuff bracelets are 6 inches around and come in three widths: ⅝ inch, $35; ⅞ inch, $38; and 1¼ inch, $40. Octagonal bracelet comes in various sizes; $65.

Handwrought sterling-silver serving implements, from left: tomato server in chino pattern, $100; cake server in chino pattern, $100; pie server in chino pattern, $110; pie/cake server in hume pattern with stainless-steel blade, $90.

Handwrought sterling-silver place setting in chino pattern, from left: Butterspreader, $55; teaspoon, $65; dessert spoon, $85; salad fork, $105; dinner fork, $125; and dinner knife with stainless-steel blade, $95. Pieces may be ordered individually.

JAMES SEAVEY

Halibut Point Pewter
33 Maplewood Avenue
Gloucester, Massachusetts 01930

As a young boy James Seavey used to spend many idle hours watching a pewterer at work in his hometown of Rockport, Massachusetts. He was fascinated by the smithy's two-dimensional metal sheets. This fascination with the nature of form hasn't dimmed after all these years. "I seek to make objects that reflect the tension between geometric purity and organic expressiveness," he told me.

Jim's work also reflects his concern with the quality of everyday life. "The daily rituals of life that require the use of objects are deepened and enhanced when these objects are made with care and insight," he observes.

His line of some thirty functional objects is created primarily through three techniques: scoring and folding, which is the direct working of the sheet into three dimensions; spinning, the creation of forms through rotation and application of the metal; and fabrication, the assembly of cut-and-formed pieces. He will often use more than one technique in his pieces and enhance them through additional techniques such as casting, surface embellishment and silversmithing.

After graduation in 1971 from Rhode Island School of Design with a bachelors degree in fine arts, Jim worked as a designer-craftsman for Old Newbury Crafters, pewterers, and Gorham Silver Co., silversmiths. After an additional stint managing a small factory for a supplier of church metalwares, he started Halibut Point Pewter in 1978.

The thirty-six-year-old pewterer is a member of numerous professional and civic organizations. He has taught his craft at various workshops in New England and has exhibited his work at invitational exhibits throughout the country.

Brochure: Yes.
Commissions: Yes.
Studio Hours: By appointment.
Telephone: (617) 283-7711.

Various-sized goblets are made with a torque motif borrowed from the ancient Greek and Irish goldsmiths who used it for necklace work. In adapting the form to pewter, two ribs are soldered onto a flat bar, then the whole piece is twisted. "I was sure the ribs would fall off on the first one, but my luck and the solder held." Originating the torque technique for his popular letterholder design, Jim next adapted it to these goblet stems. The bases and bodies are spun by forming a sheet of lead-free pewter on a lathe. The goblets may also be ordered with a right-hand twist for left-handed people. From left: 6 inches, 4 ounces; $32; 7 inches, 7 ounces; $36; 7¼ inches, 10 ounces; $40; 8¼ inches, 10 ounces; $40; and 8 inches, 16 ounces; $50.

BARRIE CLIFF

Pewter Crafters of Cape Cod
927 Main Street
Yarmouthport, Massachusetts 02675

Barrie Cliff may be a latecomer to the American crafts scene but since his decision six years ago to become a pewterer, he has clearly made up for lost time.

After twenty-five years on the corporate ladder, Barrie found himself in the mid-Seventies a Senior Vice-President of a Greenwich, Connecticut-based industrial corporation. What with six manufacturing operations reporting to him on matters most pressing, Barrie was starting to feel some unwanted stresses from playing the corporate game. "It was an impossible job," he remembers. "I was working seven days a week, fourteen hours a day all over the country and the world."

Time, he thought, for a change. So in late 1976, when a planned corporate reorganization threatened to drastically change the nature of his job, Barrie said his goodbyes and started to think of a more fulfilling way to make a living.

"I thought about everything from speculative homebuilding to being the maple syrup king of Vermont or maybe a restaurateur," Barrie told me. But before he could settle on a new career, Barrie, his wife, son and daughter decided to take advantage of their new-found freedom and first find a desirable place to live.

Just a few months later in the spring of 1977, the Cliffs found themselves in Yarmouthport rehabilitating an older building that would house Barrie's studio. After some investigation, Barrie decided to become a "craftsman/entrepreneur" working in pewter.

But there was a problem: Barrie had no experience whatsoever in pewter making. He was determined, however, to make it—both figuratively and literally. Without taking one lesson, Barrie taught himself the craft while once again working long work days seven days a week. This time, though, it didn't hurt. "I learned by doing," says the fifty-three-year-old craftsman. "I was lucky to have had a good design ability and hand sense. And I had a good idea of what would sell to the kind of person that I used to be."

The first year's products were simple, traditional items as Barrie learned the basics of pewtersmithing. During the second year, the product line improved as more complex shapes and items were introduced. In the third year Barrie diversified further with the creation of his own contemporary line of pewterware. "My contemporary items reflect a commitment to the elements of classical form," he notes. "That is, well-defined lines, smooth flowing shapes and balance."

Today, Barrie caters to an ever-growing market for his sophisticated pieces, creating scores of different items in both traditional and contemporary designs. He is a member of the American Craft Council and is president of the Society of Cape Cod Craftsmen. He is also active in numerous local civic and arts groups.

Brochure: Please send $1.00 to defray costs for a comprehensive brochure.
Commissions: No.
Studio Hours: Barrie was putting the finishing touches on his new gallery as we talked to him. Hours will be 10 A.M. to 5 P.M. Monday through Saturday.
Telephone: (617) 362-3407.

Wine goblets and decanter made of lead-free pewter. Goblets are 8 inches high, $25 each. Decanter is 9½ inches high, $50.

198 · METAL

Cheryl and Ted White

Stoneham Pewter
RFD 1, Box 656
Brookfield, New Hampshire 03872

Working among the mountains of rural New Hampshire, Ted and Cheryl White create a line of pewter objects that is eminently functional as well as beautiful and eyecatching. "The most important thing," says Ted, forty, "is for people to use our pewter every day and enjoy it. I wouldn't like to see one of our pieces just used as a display piece on a mantel."

Ted and his wife Cheryl, thirty-five, specialize in gravity casting and freehand turning to produce their pieces, although they often apply several other techniques within the context of a single piece. "Pewter is a variable medium," he told me, "fluid at times, rigid at others, which allows for a wide range of design possibilities." All their work is made with an alloy of ninety-two-percent pure tin, which is hardened and strengthened with copper and antimony and is lead free.

Ted is a former Naval nuclear-reactor operator and instructor. He started to work in pewter in 1974 and in 1979 established Stoneham Pewter with Cheryl. "Making our business adhere to a nine-to-five format would be difficult," Cheryl told me, "because of our natures individually and as a working team. We often avoid the studio for a day or more, then work late into the night on other days, following our inspiration as it comes.

"Working for ourselves, we can concentrate on our work as we choose, while striving to satisfy that group of individuals who know pewter, know us or simply enjoy the beauty of fine craftsmanship."

The Whites are members of the League of New Hampshire Craftsmen, Boston's Society of Arts and Crafts and the American Craft Council.

Brochure: Sent upon request.
Commissions: Limited custom work is accepted.
Studio Hours: By appointment.
Telephone: (603) 522-3425.

Candleholder and snuffer. The candleholder is 5¼ inches tall and is extra thick in the base for stability; $64 a pair. The snuffer is available with or without the finial for $25.

Boxes and matchbox are topped by various stones to add an element of color to the highly reflective pewter. The smaller boxes are 2 inches in diameter and suitable for a roll of stamps, small jewelry or pills. The matchbox is 2½ inches tall. Available with onyx, various agates, jasper, malachite, tiger-eye, rose quartz, turquoise, and other stones on special order. Prices range from $40 to $75.

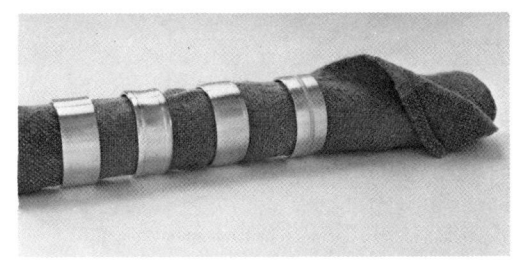

Four styles of napkin rings (from left: #0, #2, #4, and #5), all 2 inches in diameter. The rings are large enough for a handwoven napkin. Please specify style. $9 each. "We finish all pieces in either satin or bright finish as we think best suits the particular piece."

199 · METAL

Nan Winzeler

Nanci Enamels
Putney Hill Road, RFD 1, Box 168
Concord, New Hampshire 03301

"I love the richness of enamel color—the depth that results from the combination of transparent and opaque colors," says enamelist Nan Winzeler. Nan is not referring to the type of enamel that you use to paint your kitchen chairs or your porch. She is talking about the ancient craft of enameling, which dates back as far as the sixth century, many years before the advent of that shiny resinous paint that stole the name of this venerable craft.

Enameling is the process of applying and firing repeated layers of a powdered glass substance mixed with various metal oxides for color, to a metal such as copper, gold or silver. Each piece is fired at a temperature of 1600°F, giving the enamel a translucence and a durability. "I like to think that some of my things may still exist 1,000 years from now," Nan told me.

Nan, fifty-five, produces a line of colorful, whimsical enamel jewelry, decorative boxes, clocks, panels, sculptural toys and miscellaneous objects. Her award-winning, one-of-a-kind panels and sculptural pieces have been in numerous national and regional shows. "I like to do unexpected things—things with surprises, things to make people smile," she says.

Nan is a member of the League of New Hampshire Craftsmen and the American Craft Council. She had a long career as a commercial artist before turning to enameling upon moving to New Hampshire from California sixteen years ago.

Brochure: A full-color brochure illustrating dozens of jewelry designs and a set of color photos of her boxes is available for $1.00 each, refundable with first order.
Commissions: Yes.
Studio Hours: By appointment.
Telephone: (603) 746-3406.

Henry VIII and wife Catherine Howard immortalized in their own pull toys of brightly colored vitreous enamel on copper. When cord is pulled, Catherine loses her head and Henry kicks up his heels and brandishes a headsman's ax. "For the person who has everything or wants it! I could do favorite character/role of Shakespearian actor, opera singer, movie star..." Each is approximately 30 inches high by 17 inches wide; $4500.

Brass boxes, handmade with vitreous enamel lids in a variety of designs. Top three boxes, left to right: Bird nest on white with turquoise eggs; turquoise band on white with rose; line drawing of rooftop and girl on white with multicolor balloons. Bottom row, from left: Red apple, green leaves on black ground; white cat on red/blue-patterned pillow; blue flower; $45 each postpaid.

JACK DOKUS

Box 373
Franklin, New Hampshire 03235

After graduating from the Arts High School in Newark, New Jersey, Jack Dokus entered that state's Kean College, where, as he puts it, he first discovered the "noble metals." Although he had intended to be a fine art painter, all that changed when he took his first jewelry course. It was, he recalls, "love at first sight." "Although the course requirements demanded four pieces, I produced forty!"

Today, at the age of thirty-six, Jack specializes in one-of-a-kind and commission work, ranging from jewelry to bells, boxes and toys. His pieces sometimes transform the commonplace into the extraordinary—an ivory toothpick with a silver-and-bronze fruit handle, for example. Fantasy and humor are also often woven into his work, which sometimes has allegorical or emblematical aspects, invoking mystical visions and medieval magic. "One never knows what will emerge from my enchanted studio next," he says.

"For those who enjoy a special theme or subject, a commission piece will enable me to contribute something very personal to a client's life," he told me. "I enjoy working with people for the purpose of giving shape and substance to their ideas, perhaps creating a family heirloom." He points out that wedding rings are a specialty. "Those who entrust the creation of this very important and significant symbol to me, receive whatever care and attention is necessary to ensure satisfaction."

"The foundations of my work are technical quality and aesthetic validity," he says. "Each piece I create exemplifies these qualities, and radiates the magic of my art. That magic, of course, is love."

Jack is a member of the League of New Hampshire Craftsmen.

Brochure: No.
Commissions: Yes.
Studio Hours: Jack works in the Rainbow's End gallery on Main Street, Meredith, New Hampshire. Shop hours are Monday through Saturday 9:30 A.M. to 5:00 P.M.
Telephone: (603) 279-6221.

"Castle Box for Knight Stand or Round Table" is a cast-silver box and one of a kind. The roof is the box's top; the dragon and the knight chase each other around the castle. "This is an example of one of my humorous concepts and the fun I have dreaming up titles." 2¾ inches by 2⅛ inches; $500.

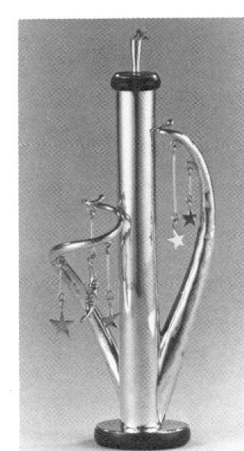

"Burning the Midnight Oil" is an oil lamp of silver and ebony that has been constructed with a cast moon. This one-of-a-kind piece done for shows and exhibitions is 5½ inches high by 3½ inches wide; $350.

201 · METAL

BRIAN CUMMINGS

Extras
Buffalo Road
Rumney, New Hampshire 03266

Most of the products that Brian Cummings designs are based upon a need for that product in some aspect of his own life. This has led to a line of household objects in fine hand-forged ironware, including contemporary-styled lighting devices, cooking utensils and accessories, flatware, fireplace equipment and assorted building hardware.

His involvement in handcrafts began one day when he had discovered a box of antique tools in his grandfather's barn. He soon learned how to use those tools and began collecting others. Finding the price of tools in antique shops somewhat at odds with his budget he decided to obtain a forge and anvil and make his own tools. "Once I began working iron," he says, "I realized it was a medium much better suited to my personality than wood. I never did get back to making those tools that I had originally set out to make."

During the early years of his blacksmithing career, Brian acquired and perfected his basic forging skills through reproducing, with a few refinements, various examples of Colonial ironware such as hardware, cooking utensils and lighting devices. Today, he finds it more rewarding to design his own pieces.

"Although I still use all the traditional forging techniques I work with a variety of materials—high carbon, mild and stainless steel. Recently, in an attempt to add color to my line, I have been experimenting with combining metal with acrylic and acrylic lacquer. The results are products retaining all the charm of hand-forged iron with a more contemporary appeal."

Brian, thirty, is a member of the League of New Hampshire Craftsmen. He graduated from Dartmouth College in 1974 and has been a blacksmith for the past eleven years.

Brochure: Yes.
Commissions: He'll occasionally take special-order work when his schedule permits.
Studio Hours: "By appointment or by chance."
Telephone: (603) 786-9753.

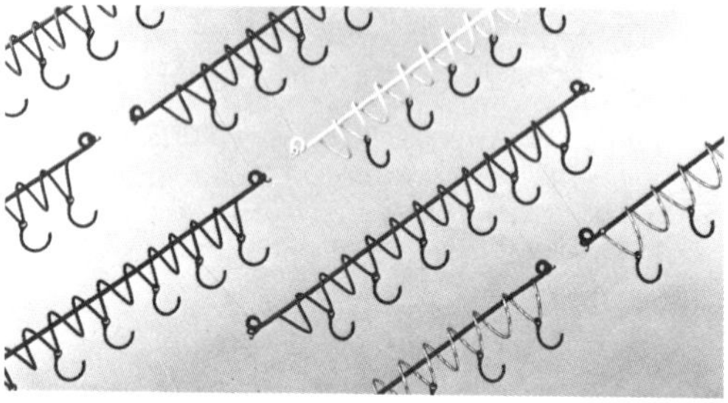

Primarily designed for use with pots and pans, The Rack is equally useful for hanging clothing, towels, plants and the like. The colorful and sophisticated rack can be hung either horizontally or at an angle as shown in the photograph. The distance between hooks can be varied. Forged of mild steel with a lacquer finish of black, red, blue or yellow or with a polished-brass or stainless-steel spiral contrasted against the lacquer hooks and rod. Length is 32 inches with two 36 inch lengths of black nylon cord to suspend it from the ceiling. Custom lengths and colors available at extra cost. Lacquer finish, $50; brass or stainless-steel spiral, $60.

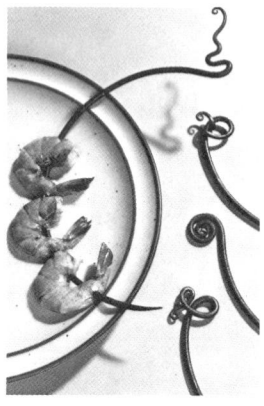

These curved skewers are made from a 15-inch length of steel and fit comfortably on a 10- or 12-inch dinner plate. They can be placed directly on the grill or under the broiler. Sets of four $30, separately $8.

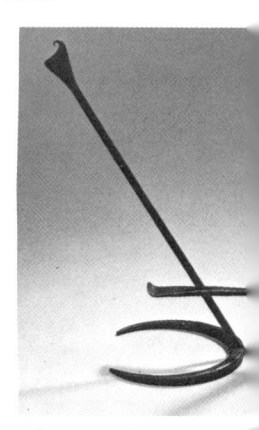

The Cantilever Candle holder is made of mild steel and accommodates a standard-size candle. By slightly tilting the horizontal arm holding the candle it can be adjusted up down. 14 inches high $66.

202 · METAL

Fred and Judi Danforth

*Danforth Pewterers
R.D. 1, Box 292
Lincoln, Vermont 05443*

It was a "blend of ancestral inspiration and artistic challenge" that led Judi and Fred Danforth to pursue pewtering together. Fred, thirty-three, is a direct descendant of Thomas Danforth (1703-1786) of Norwich, Connecticut, his son, Thomas (1731-1782) of Middletown, Connecticut, and *his* six sons, all of whom were well-known, highly skilled Colonial pewtersmiths. Judi, thirty-one, was trained in silversmithing at the Rochester Institute of Technology. After they both apprenticed to a pewtersmith in New Brunswick, Canada, they established Danforth Pewterers in 1975 in Woodstock, Vermont.

"We have striven to provide a complete line of tableware and accessories that is well designed and crafted for either daily or special use," Judi told me. "We hope that our pieces will withstand the test of time as have those of the early Danforths." Unlike Fred's ancestors, who used bronze molds and cast all of their pieces, the present-day Danforths have included in their repertoire of techniques spinning, casting into rubber molds, fabricating flat sheets into various forms and soldering together of parts.

In the spinning process, which provides them with many of their basic forms, they begin by designing and turning a "chuck" on their lathe. Using a tool called a "spinner's finger," they work the pewter over the chuck, creating a shell of unfinished pewter. After sanding and polishing, they solder on cast handles, stems and knobs to complete the piece.

The Danforths are members of Frog Hollow State Craft Center, of which Fred is on the Board of Trustees, Craft Producers Markets, Inc., Vermont Hand Crafters, Inc. and the American Craft Council.

Brochure: Yes.
Commissions: Some custom work is available.
Studio Hours: By appointment.
Telephone: (802) 453-3191.

Pewter place setting, from left: Napkin ring, $8.50; candlestick, 5 inches high, $70/pair; plate, 10-inch diameter, $40; vase, 4 inches high, $32; goblets of 4-ounce and 6-ounce capacity, $28 and $32.

The electric lamp is made of pewter with a solid band of cherry wood through the center. It comes with a hand-pierced lampshade with a brown velvet ribbon and pewter-grey satin cord banding it. Height 20 inches; $225. The pewter berry basket is $80.

203 · METAL

Diane Hildebran

5 Green Hills Drive
Shelburne, Vermont 05482

The artist in Diane Hildebran bubbled to the surface after she had spent many years as a student of literature and history, an English teacher and a newspaper reporter. According to Diane, thirty-six, the common thread in each of these past directions was "an interest in the story of people and life—humankind developing for its humanness."

Consequently, when she became a metalsmith ten years ago, it became for her "an affirmation of the belief that things of value come from and are to be used by people. To create objects with my hands is a personal statement against those pressures of modern life which prevent people from experiencing their humanity."

Diane creates her vessels by forging them with hammer blows on a flat sheet of brass, copper or sterling silver. Although she may occasionally use soldering, the primary form comes from hammer against metal until a hollow vessel has emerged from a flat sheet. "Forging brings me amazing satisfaction as I am able to witness the metal move and grow," she says. "It gives freedom to the form that was hidden within."

Diane, who is self taught, designs her pieces "to celebrate the hidden dimension of the vessel, the space within." She explains that "the curve of the vessel is the visible boundary of this space."

She has always designed her pieces as functional works of art, works of utility as well as beauty. "I like to imagine each piece becoming a part of its owner's lifestyle through frequent use so that whatever beauty is inherent in it is continually experienced by the owner."

Brochure: No.
Commissions: "I am very interested in doing more custom work."
Studio Hours: By appointment.
Telephone: (802) 985-2476.

Copper pitcher with a walnut handle. "Its hammered surface enhances the natural warmth of the metal." Height 14 inches; $500. All work is one of a kind. These items are representative of Diane's work.

This brass bowl was raised from one sheet of metal and has a chased design of grass flowing upward to enclose the space within the vessel. 4-by-4 inches; $300.

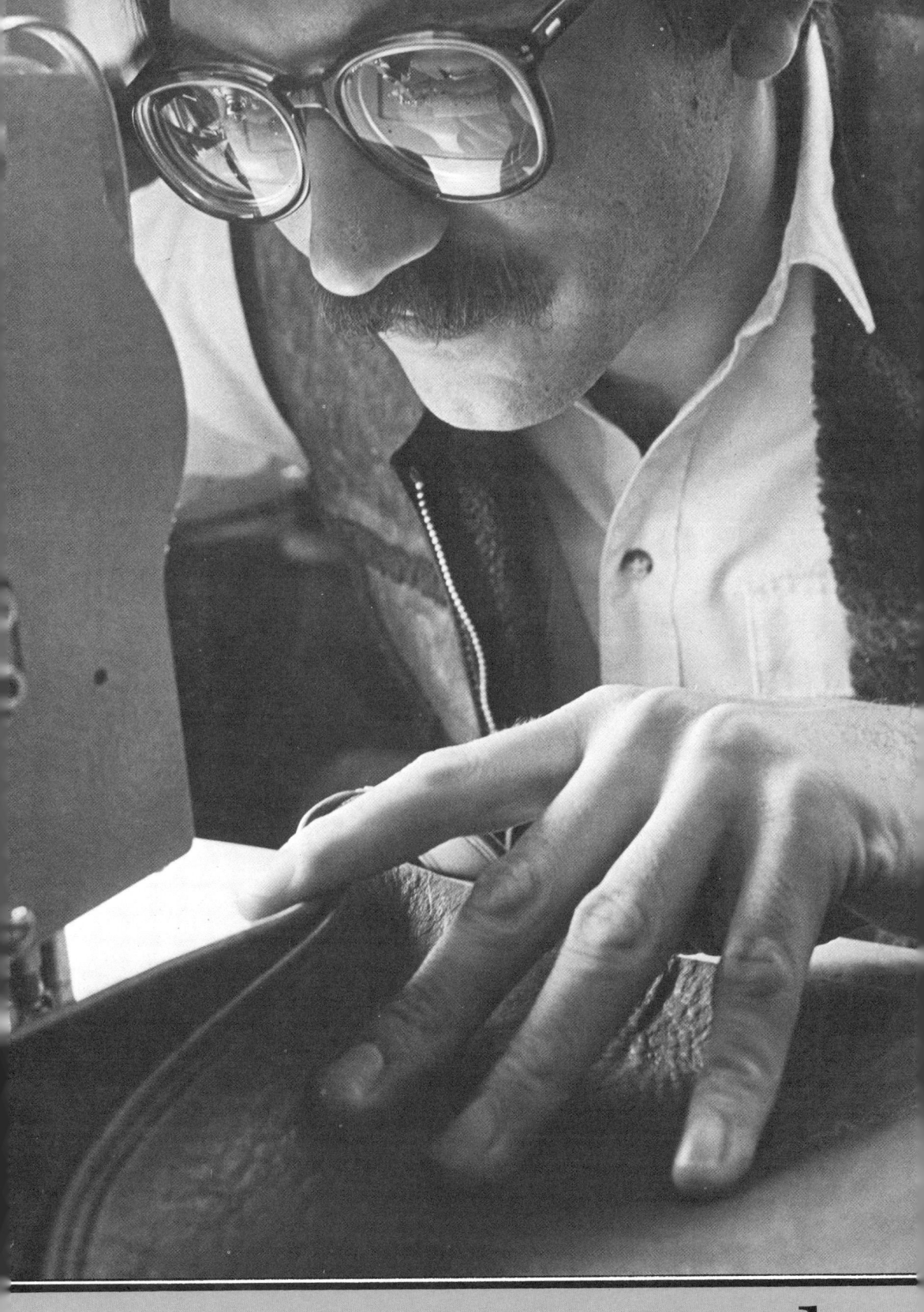

Mixed

JAMES BYRON

Bridgeport Balloon Works
225 Federal Street
Bridgeport, Connecticut 06606

Like father, like son. Sort of. James Byron remembers that as a child he was fascinated by the tales of adventure that his father, an Air Force test pilot, used to spin about his flights into the wild blue yonder. Jim was irrevocably hooked. Only his preferred way to fly isn't by jet propulsion but rather the "most romantic of all means of flight: balloons." When not ballooning, Jim creates and flies extravagantly concocted brightly colored kites.

Jim developed his visual and design sense at the University of Bridgeport, where he received his bachelors degree in graphic design in 1978. While there, he also became interested in textiles and industrial sewing methods as a result of his employment with a fabrics-manufacturing firm. After graduation, his skills and interests in flight, design and industrial sewing converged, the result being the construction of his first hot-air balloon.

The holder of a commercial balloon-pilot's license and an instructor's rating, Jim designs and fabricates his balloon systems starting with the drawing-board calculations of structure and design to sewing the huge envelope and weaving the traditional basket.

Recently he has begun creating and building kite designs using the same techniques and brightly colored material that he uses in his balloons. "Launching these individual creations and allowing the sun's rays to illuminate the often-translucent rip-stop nylon fabric with a stained glass window effect is exhilarating," Jim told me.

Jim, twenty-six, has displayed and flown his hot-air balloons at many festivals. He is a member of the Association of Balloon and Airship Constructors, the Balloon Federation of America and American Kitefliers Association, among others.

Brochure: No.
Commissions: All work is custom-made.
Studio Hours: By appointment.
Telephone: (203) 366-0744.

One of the hot-air balloons designed, built and flown by the artist. It is 52,000 cubic feet with a net lift of 380 pounds making it suitable for two occupants. Constructed of 1.9-ounce urethane-coated rip-stop nylon, nylon webbing and steel cables, it has a woven rattan and willow basket and stands approximately 65 feet tall. Price varies with design and volume; this model is $8500.

Jim in front of his Guatemalan-style kite, which was designed using 6-inch square and smaller pieces of rip-stop nylon sewn with nylon sailmaker's thread and rigged with parachute shroud lines. Diameter is 12 feet; $500.

206 · MIXED

WILLIAM AND MARILYN ROSENQUIST

Lightship Baskets
342 Moose Hill
Guilford, Connecticut 06437

Nantucket baskets were quite possibly the first American basket made by the European settlers, according to Marilyn Rosenquist. "They're certainly among the finest in the world." During the nineteenth century, seamen spent long, lonely months serving aboard the Number One lightship off the Nantucket coast. Out of boredom, they began making baskets, which were used by their wives to bring them provisions.

Two years ago, Marilyn and her husband Bill, both forty-four, had visited Nantucket and became intrigued by the native baskets, admiring their clean and subtle beauty. Over the next one and one half years they taught themselves how to make the baskets and have recently begun to merchandise their line.

They make their baskets in the traditional manner, over their handmade pine molds. The bottoms are hand turned, oiled cherry, their handles and ribs are hand made of oak and the weavers are hand-selected cane from the same tropical source that supplied the old Nantucket sailors.

Until recently, when they both started devoting their full time to making baskets, Bill was a history teacher and a part-time sculptor and Marilyn held a full-time job as a secretary. They are members of the Connecticut Guild of Craftsmen.

Brochure: No.
Commissions: Yes.
Studio Hours: By appointment.
Telephone: (203) 453-4512.

Lightship baskets are made in four sizes and can be nested one inside the other. All have hand-turned cherry wood bottoms, oak staves, select cane weavers and hand-carved oak handles. They are finished with shellac and hand rubbed with an oil finish. Special message can be inscribed on baskets for gift occasions. Egg basket is 5 inches; $150; berry basket is 6½ inches; $160; sewing basket is 8 inches; $180; and market basket is 9½ inches; $200.

A classic Nantucket handbag that has been carefully and authentically crafted. The plaque on the top of the basket is cherry wood with carved ivory whale. All other materials are the same as with other baskets; $400.

Nancy Scribner

N.A. Scribner, Baskets
Indian Hill Road
Norwalk, Connecticut 06850

Nancy Scribner had studied jewelry making in college and was talented enough to be an exhibitor at the 1978 Rhinebeck Craft Fair. It was, however, the end of her jewelry career. "That first show was a strong lesson about displays, buyers and being professional," she remembers. "I also knew that being a production jeweler was not what I wanted."

Shortly after this decision, Nancy was visiting Brookfield Craft Center, where Connecticut basketweaver Kari Lonning was demonstrating and showing her baskets, which Nancy recalls as "big, beautiful, colorful and more than I could afford. I had never seen baskets like hers and was so intrigued that I bought a how-to book, some reed and attempted to teach myself. The results were far from my vision." Luckily, Kari was giving a weeklong course and Nancy signed up. She has been what her husband calls a "basketeer" ever since.

Nancy's work is based on four basic styles: "melon," "hen," round and flat-bottomed styles, all of which she enhances by using colorful patterns and textures. "The utilitarian aspect is not that important to me although my work is technically strong enough to be so." She uses round reed, both in its natural color as well as dyed, as her primary material. "I am very susceptible to poison ivy so I don't gather many 'wild' materials.

"Most people wonder how I can spend so much time in creating a piece," she says. "Time is, after all, what crafts are all about: time and the desire to give of yourself to make something unique, with lasting quality, beauty, thought and with your hands."

Nancy, who's twenty-nine, has been making baskets for four years. Her work has been featured in *House Beautiful* and *Country Living* magazines and has been shown in many basketry exhibitions.

Brochure: A well-done brochure showing seven different styles is available.
Commissions: Nancy will gladly match special colors in her baskets to her customer's preferences.
Studio Hours: None.
Telephone: (203) 847-0469.

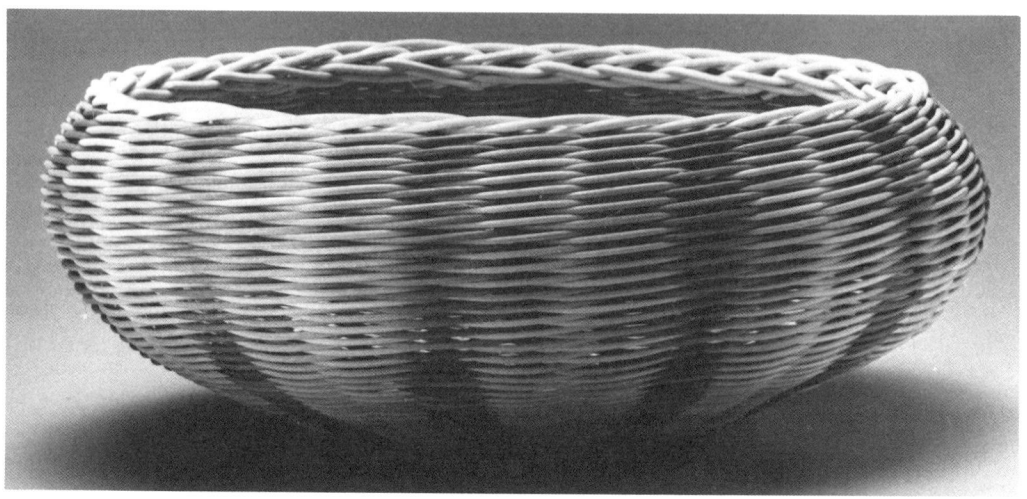

Round basket with hanging vertical design in blue and natural round reed. "Because of its strong design and shape, I like this basket as a display piece or with one group of items inside." The shape will vary. Maximum diameter 16 inches; $90.

THEODORE OTIS SOULE

Critters by Otis
75 Hartford Avenue
Old Saybrook, Connecticut 06475

Ted Soule creates whimsical sculpture creatures that he welds together from pieces of old farm equipment, old tools, springs and all types of scrap metal. These heavy metal creatures often resemble extraterrestrial beings, reptiles, insects, farm animals and other species both living and extinct.

Most of his critters move in some way; some have bobbing tails, others spinning necks or wiggling arms. Ranging in size from six inches to six feet, each critter projects its own captivating personality.

Ted works days in a machine finishing shop and creates his creatures at night and on weekends. Whenever he can get away, he combs the New England countryside looking for old metal equipment and parts found on abandoned farms. Since he rarely finds the same part twice, all his creatures are one of a kind, although they may sometimes share some similarities.

"My sculptures stand, squat and crawl as monuments of my teeming dreams and visions," says the twenty-six-year-old graduate of the Rhode Island School of Design. Ted is a member of the Connecticut Guild of Craftsmen, the New Canaan Society for the Arts and the Mystic Art Association.

Brochure: No.
Commissions: Yes.
Studio Hours: By appointment.
Telephone: (203) 388-3894.

"Knight Warmer" of welded metal in black and silver is a heater. "Holds my business cards in summer and keeps me warm in the winter." 5 feet 2 inches; $300.

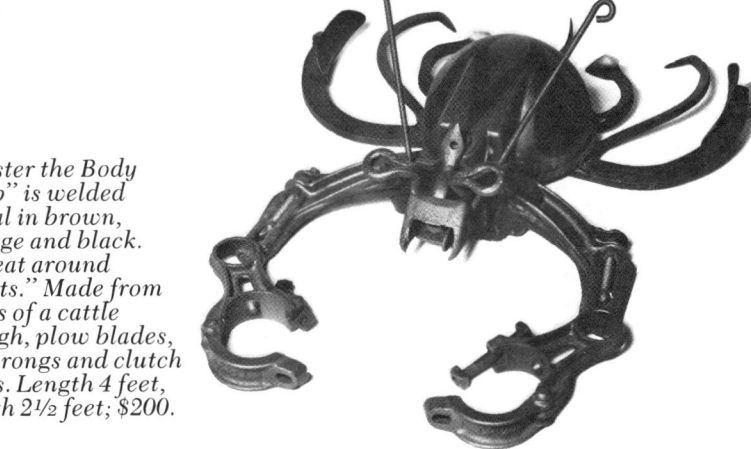

"Buster the Body Crab" is welded metal in brown, orange and black. "Great around plants." Made from parts of a cattle trough, plow blades, ice prongs and clutch arms. Length 4 feet, width 2½ feet; $200.

209 · MIXED

LORRAINE SCHECHTER

LS Graphics
PO Box 99
Roxbury, Connecticut 06783

As a longtime illustrator, Lorraine Schechter had been experimenting with a "more reductive" style in her drawings. It was a natural step to her first paper sculpture. "I wanted another dimension," she recalls. "A third dimension." Fortunately she was awarded a grant from the Connecticut Commission on the Arts, which gave her the time to experiment further, developing her concepts of paper sculpture.

Today, Lorraine's drawing has been relegated to second place as she devotes her time to the demands of her growing production line of hand-screened, die-cut gift cards that become small paper sculptures. These vibrantly colored objects project an uncanny sense of action and movement even though they're stabiles and not mobiles. "They're very expressive," observes the thirty-seven-year-old artist.

"The card gifts are going like crazy," Lorraine told me. "It's starting to require more time from me in a business sense, which I find exciting. My goal is to have the card business running smoothly and developing so that I can get back in the studio to make more one-of-a-kind sculpture."

When creating a sculpture, Lorraine first makes an artful and complex drawing of the subject. "Before I get anything simple, it's got to be complex," she says. Reducing the drawing to a few lines "that express the subject best," she makes a thoroughly simplified drawing ("which can take an hour or three weeks") and then cuts out the paper, creating a three-dimensional image of the original drawing. "People respond to my objects and feel nice about them and want to keep them in their homes," she notes. "That delights me."

Lorraine received her masters degree from the University of Pennsylvania Graduate School of Fine Arts in Philadelphia. Her work has been exhibited throughout the East in group and solo shows and is in several public collections.

Brochure: For 75 cents you will receive a brochure picturing nearly two dozen different cut-out gift cards and mailable paper sculptures.
Commissions: One-of-a-kind paper sculptures "representing personal objects and things that are part of your life" are welcomed by commission.
Studio Hours: None.
Telephone: (203) 263-0079.

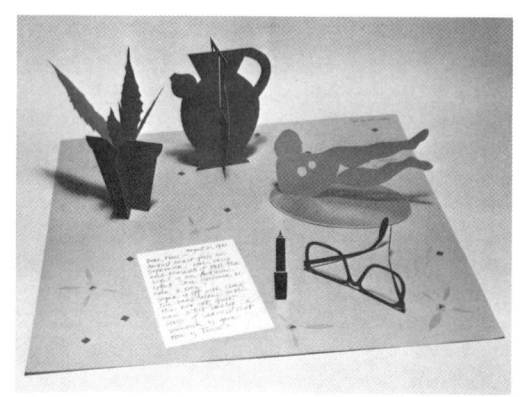

"Still Life with Nude" sculpture is cut, laminated, collaged, colored paper. It is one of a kind and measures 20 inches square; $350. A Plexiglass display box is available.

Paper sculpture card gifts are hand silk-screened in vibrant color in heavy-weight paper and cut from a hand-tooled die. Shown here are goldfish-in-bowl and stretching-cat designs. Individually packaged with an envelope, easy assembly instructions and a blank notecard to send personal greetings. Card size is 5-by-7 inches; $4 each postpaid.

Mary Blake

Mary's Applehead Characters
57 Douglas Hill Road
West Baldwin, Maine 04091

When Mary Blake made her first applehead doll in 1976 as a present for a little girl, she had no idea that she was embarking on a path "that would lead so far and reach so many people." Mary's craft is a continuation of one of this country's oldest craft traditions, which the colonists had adapted from the native Indians.

Mary, thirty-two, uses native Maine materials in her work whenever possible. She carves the face and hands from fresh Maine Macintosh apples. Each evolves into its own unique personality as it dries over her wood stove. After drying, each doll head is coated with varnish. "I have noticed, as have others, that many of the faces seem vaguely reminiscent of people we used to know, or wish we had known better."

Her dolls come appropriately dressed in gay prints and brightly colored all-natural materials. "I like to buy my cottons and wools directly from the old mills that are holdovers from nineteenth-century England. It isn't always easy to avoid polyesters and synthetics, but it's worth it to me."

Her character's expressions run from sly old grins to beaming, bemused looks but Mary says, "I will never make one with an unhappy face. After all, dolls are meant to evoke a fanciful, happy world.

"I feel especially fortunate to be able to work at home," she says, "to be with my son David as he grows up. My characters are always a part of our home during their creation and they always carry a bit of a small Maine town wherever they go." Mary is a member of Southern Maine Craftsmen and the Regional Artisan's League.

Brochure: Yes. Please send 25 cents and self-addressed, stamped envelope.
Commissions: No.
Studio Hours: Mary sells her dolls from a small shop in front of her house, daily from 9 A.M. to 5 P.M.
Telephone: (207) 625-3529.

Shopping-bag-lady applehead doll. "Here's grammy with her bags stuffed with goodies. Everybody knows someone just like her." She wears a bright red wool coat with a matching, pleated point skirt and, like all of Mary's dolls, is about 9 inches tall and free-standing; $25.

Man-with-pipe applehead doll. This dapper little gentleman has a pipe and cane and sports a bright green wool vest and matching shirt. 9 inches tall, $25.

211 · MIXED

ELIZABETH O'ROURKE

Handmade Paper Products
40 Rugg Road
Allston, Massachusetts 02134

As an undergraduate at Syracuse University, Elizabeth O'Rourke had intended to pursue a career in printmaking or paper conservation. However, after taking a course called "Book, Paper and Print," she became irrevocably hooked on bookmaking. "What really excited me was learning to marble paper," she told me. "Marbling encompassed everything I loved in art and I quickly developed my own personal and unique style."

After moving to Boston in 1981, she became aware of a local papermaking studio called Rugg Road that was about to open its doors. She offered her assistance and has been working there ever since.

"Usually I make five to six books at one time, but they are all different; some may be similar but each one is unique. The final product is always durable, long lasting and beautiful.

"My work appeals to almost everyone I have met," observes the twenty-four-year-old artist, "especially writers and other artists, since those are the people I have the most contact with." Many of her books have velvet spines with marbled covers and endsheets. Inside, the 100-percent handmade rag paper has been sewn in the traditional way.

"I try to coordinate the paper color with the marbling colors and with the color of the spine material." Lately she has been adding gilt gold to the marbling colors to give it a "rich, almost Renaissance look" to the book. "This is nice in those cases where the book is to be a special present, such as a wedding gift."

Brochure: No.
Commissions: All work is one-of-a-kind. Elizabeth is planning to incorporate handset type, linoleum cuts, silkscreen and other graphic techniques in her books. Commissions would be considered.
Studio Hours: By appointment.
Telephone: (617) 787-1371.

Handbound books containing from thirty to fifty pages of handmade paper with marbled covers and endpapers. They are suitable for writing or drawing, depending on the type of materials used. "They are very tactile pieces that need to be held to be believed. Handmade paper is a unique experience to write or draw on. These are books that you will keep forever as sketchbooks, diaries, albums and more." Japanese sidesewn books, shown on the right top and bottom, take about two or three weeks for completion. All other books take four to six weeks; $30 to $75.

212 · MIXED

Bernard Toale and Joe Zina

Rugg Road Handmade Papers
40 Rugg Road
Allston, Massachusetts 02134

Rugg Road Papers opened in 1982 as a fully equipped facility for the production of custom handmade papers. The studio is owned and directed by Bernard Toale and Joe Zina, who have created an elegant line of acid-free, custom-made bookpapers and stationery papers. They also make custom-made artist's paper for drawing, relief printing, lithography and watercolor.

The 1,200-square-foot mill can process a full range of European and Oriental fibers along with local plants, which are used for decorative effects. Custom papers can be produced in sizes of up to 22 by 30 inches and colored with a variety of natural and synthetic dyes and artist's pigments. Both artists also create large-scale, one-of-a-kind paper art pieces.

After successful careers as first a potter and then a textile artist, Bernie Toale, thirty-six, became entranced with the nature of paper about nine years ago. He has since been involved with handmade paper as an instructor, artist and production papermaker. "Paper can be a fast medium. I can see an idea finished in a day. It's very seductive. It allows me to have a physical participation similar to working with clay and a range of color and textures similar to textiles." A member of the faculty at the Boston University Program in Artisanry and the Massachusetts College of Art, Bernie is the author of *The Art of Papermaking* (Davis Publications, 1983) and is a member of the American Craft Council.

Joe Zina, thirty-four, became a papermaker following a ten-year career as a dancer with the Nikolais Dance Theater of New York. While touring and performing with Nikolais, he also assisted them with the development of visuals, costumes and prop construction. "Having left the stage, I am transferring that kinetic and visual imagery into paper forms as backdrops and scenic designs," he explains. "My motifs and themes reflect my experiences in movement and theater as well as with elements, forms and textures in nature." He is a member of the American Craft Council and the New England Letterpress Guild.

Brochure: Yes.
Commissions: Specially commissioned production work or artist's papers are welcomed. Large-scale decorative paper constructions can also be commissioned and special book projects can be arranged in conjunction with an associated letterpress facility.
Studio Hours: By appointment.
Telephone: (617) 787-1371.

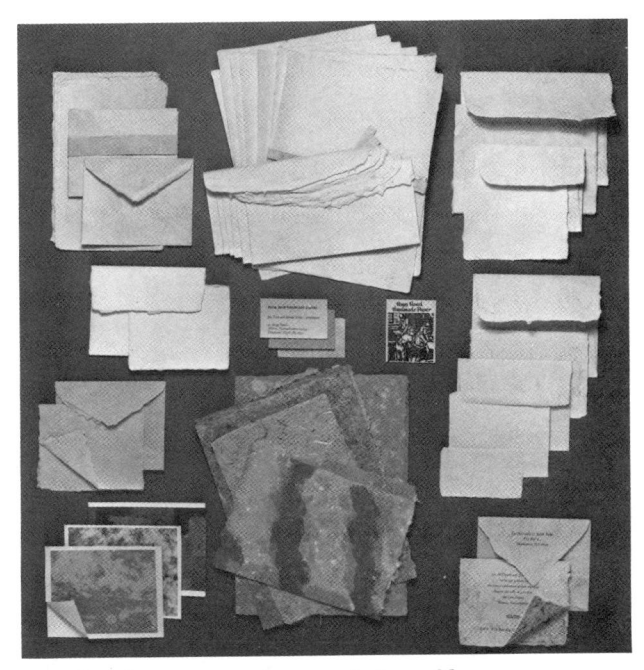

Handmade paper stationery of abaca fibers or hemp in assorted pigmented colors. Packages of eight sheets and six glued and folded envelopes. Sheet size is 8½ by 11 inches; $13.50. Stationery also available in 5½ by 8 inches; $12.00

Product line of handmade paper products also includes note cards, wedding invitations, business cards, greeting cards and specialty and custom handmade papers. Write for complete brochure for more information.

HAROLD T. HAYWARD

Leprechaun Sheepskin
RR 1, Box 246
Conway, Massachusetts 01341

It's a long way from planning for a career in geology to creating sheepskin apparel for a living, but that's the path that Harold Hayward has traveled.

While studying geology at the University of Massachusetts during the early Seventies, Harold started sculpting in soapstone, which led him to the discovery that he enjoyed working with his hands. He soon found himself making a pair of mittens out of the fur from an old coat. They promptly fell apart and he made another pair, this time from sheepskin. "Before I knew it, I was selling mittens," recalls the thirty-one-year-old craftsman. Today he has a line of sheepskin products that includes several styles of hats, moccasins, coats, mittens and headbands. He has also recently added auto seat covers to his line.

"I produce products that are not only functional and long-wearing, but beautiful and stylish as well," says Harold, who has been working full-time in sheepskin for ten years. He has found that his products sell well, even in this depressed economy. "I believe this is a result of their quality, durability and uniqueness of design," he says.

Harold purchases his raw materials in person rather than having them shipped. He selects about 1 out of every 150 pelts that he inspects. "I try to get sheepskins that are soft and dense on the fur side of the skin," he told me. On the leather (suede) side, he looks for uniformity of color and lack of weak spots or flaws in the surface.

Living in rural Western Massachusetts and being a devotee of cross-country skiing, hiking and bicycling gives Harold ample opportunities to "thoroughly field-test" his designs for maximum warmth and comfort.

He is a member of the League of New Hampshire Craftsmen, the American Craft Council and Celebrations, an artisan's collective.

Brochure: Yes. His expanding line of ten to fifteen items is fully described with complete ordering instructions.
Commissions: Yes.
Studio Hours: By appointment.
Telephone: (413) 369-4949.

Moccasin-style house slipper features 5/8-inch-thick cuffed upper with adjustable cowhide suede lacing. Matching cowhide sole and 1-inch-deep pile on the inner sole. The sole is strengthened by a 1-inch-cowhide welt on the sidewall of the upper. Available in many colors and all sizes; $49 a pair for extra small to extra large, $64 for extra-large size.

"Russian" hat with welted crown and roll-up brim of sueded shearling with 1/2-inch fleece pile. Hidden fold-down woven wool ear flaps help out during cold New England winters. Made in many different colors and sizes from small to extra large; $70.

Sheepskin mittens have separate inset thumbs for greater flexibility. Inside seams with 3-inch roll-up cuffs for extra warmth. All colors and sizes; $49 the pair.

Darius Strickler

At the Studio
317 Main Street
Great Barrington, Massachusetts 01230

Darius Strickler is trying to create the "contemporary mask" by combining the mask's psychological, ceremonial, theatrical and therapeutic nature with its historical universality. "The wearing of a mask is both powerful to the viewer and empowering to the wearer," he explains. "Masks appear to conceal the self but they are self-revealing. To mask is to unmask, visually unleashing the power of a greater life force."

By combining classic references with brilliant colors, inlays, embossing, illustration and electronics together with his sculpted paper mask forms, the thirty-eight-year-old artist succeeds in evoking feelings that contain a touch of political, social and artistic comment, even satire.

Darius says that his intent is to "replace one and one half of the two TV sets in every American home with at least three masks. Members of the family could choose from characters of beauty, saintliness, courage, joy, prosperity, wisdom, truth, understanding, forgiveness and so on." Darius thinks that this would soon bring the family closer together, and ultimately "reestablish neighborhoods, ally the world and maybe reduce the need for psychotherapy through an enhanced awareness of self-identity." Could be. But meanwhile, his mask forms make mysterious and evocative statements and are wonderful and decorative works of art.

In addition to his line of masks, Darius creates greeting cards, folders, bags, light sculpture, and large wall tapestries that incorporate variations of the images shown here. All his materials are "museum quality. Every precaution has been taken for these works to endure for at least 1,000 years."

Brochure: No, but slides will be sent on request.
Commissions: "I would like to contact theater companies, interior designers, corporate art consultants, galleries for shows, installations and commissions."
Studio Hours: By appointment.
Telephone: (413) 528-1866.

Masks are formed in clay or wax; no life casts are used. Handmade paper (usually abaca, cotton rag or synthetics) is pressed into the forms, which are then finished with dyes and paints by brushing, stenciling and embossing.

Cast paper mask in cotton fiber and acrylic paint. This is a limited edition mask that measures 17 inches high, 11 inches wide and 6 inches deep; $450.

Lifesize eyes and bigger-than-life lips in cast paper, finished with dyes and acrylics in bright colors. Eyelids and lips finished in metallics. Mounted on a 16-inch flexible rod. "Could be used in potted plants and flower arrangements." Lifesize eyes, $45. Lips 4 inches wide by 5 inches tall by 2 inches deep; $40.

Susan B. Mulholland

Cider Mill Road
Leverett, Massachusetts 01054

Susan Mulholland describes her hand silkscreened notecard designs as somewhere between abstract and representational, "using just enough detail to identify the object, but leaving room for the viewer's imagination to work."

Since most of her designs feature floral motifs, she uses a wide range of colors, especially greens, blues and purples, which have proved to be favorites. "While I do many shorebird and animal designs," she told me, "this seems to be the year for flowers, with my Iris series as the most popular." She usually adds about a dozen new designs each year to her line of more than twenty-five current designs.

Susan recently remodeled her house with her archaeologist husband who also works at home, which is a former summer cottage overlooking Leverett Pond. "My new studio will be large enough to allow me to eventually expand the business and purchase more advanced equipment," she says. "I hope the card production can become more efficient, allowing more time for designing and printing large, limited edition prints." Susan, thirty-two, is also planning to begin designing and silkscreening textiles. "It will be a nice change to work on large pieces after nine years of designing for greeting cards."

Brochure: A full-color sheet showing her line of designs is available.
Commissions: No.
Studio Hours: None.
Telephone: (413) 549-0797.

Thistle, daffodil and wild columbine designs from Susan's comprehensive line of silk screened note cards. These have three-color designs printed from hand-cut stencils. Thistle is in purple and greens, daffodils in yellows and greens, columbine in red with yellow and green. Cards are 4 inches by 9¼ inches; $1.50 each.

LISA BRAUER

5 Waldron Street
Marblehead, Massachusetts 01945

"The feelings I endeavor to evoke are not particularly lighthearted, but painful," says Lisa Brauer of her series of porcelain dolls and figures that she calls "Future People." Meant to represent either "earth's future generations or beings from another world," the strangely beguiling figures also effectively express for the artist a "statement of feelings of aloneness and the futility of human interaction."

Acknowledging that her creations raise emotions "that people would often rather not confront," Lisa has unquestionably managed to convey some gut-deep feelings through her compelling, limited-edition dolls. Among her creations are: Walkman Doll, ("isolates itself, headset cuts into scalp, skull bulges and cracks from bombardment of music; face is flat and expressionless with blank, staring eyes"); Munchkin Doll ("baby from another world"); Rod Man ("numb to everything, including rod running through head and man hanging beside him"); and Coma ("exists in space, is beyond thoughts and feelings").

"I can't think of a specific reason for why I make dolls," Lisa told me. "The ideas and feelings I seek to express seem best represented by figurative art. The dolls are more personal and approachable than traditional sculpture. They can be picked up and held. They can sit around your living room like friends."

Lisa, thirty-one, received her bachelors degree in art history from Syracuse University and her masters degree in ceramics from the State University College at New Paltz, New York. She is also an alumna of Penland School of Crafts and has been a practicing craftsperson for three years.

Brochure: No.
Commissions: Yes.
Studio Hours: By appointment.
Telephone: (617) 631-7829.

Walkman doll is a comment on high-tech society and its depersonalization. As with all Lisa's dolls, the heads, hands and feet are slipcast, unglazed porcelain from original molds. Airbrushed stains provide muted coloration. Bodies are stuffed fabric and clothed in handmade clothing. 18 inches high; $150.

Rod triplets. "The pressures of life have elongated these guys. They are numb to the rod through their heads." Suspended by a ring and can be hung on wall. 10 inches high; $70. Also available as twins ($50) and single ($30).

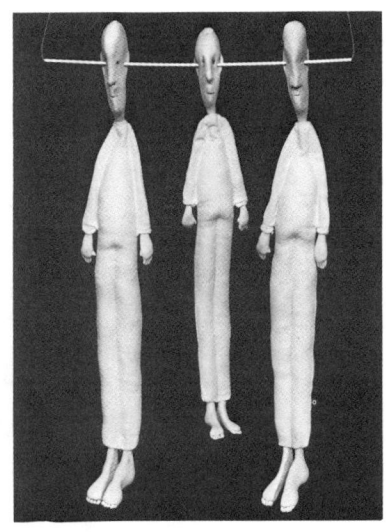

Richard E. Davis

*Adirondack Designs
Box 2094
Vineyard Haven, Massachusetts 02568*

Seeking self-fulfillment through creative work is one thing. Making a living at it is another. Richard Davis found this out when in 1979, after nine years of working part-time in leather, he decided "for personal and creative freedom" to become a fulltime leathercrafter. "I've discovered that I have to, as a maker of women's accessories, be far more fashion conscious than in the past," he explains. "This new consciousness results from my concern with design as well as function."

Trying to keep abreast of the latest fashion trends is something that the twenty-eight-year-old craftsman feels he has mastered. His line of graceful-looking handbags, wallets and portfolios shows a tendency toward geometric shapes, frequent quilting effects and bound or turned edges. Often incorporating exotic materials such as snakeskin or lizard skin as accents, he has striven for a "classical appeal" in his accessories through the use of popular colors and shapes. "The use of color and texture is extremely important to me as a design element," he elaborates, noting that his work appeals to people "who are interested in design as well as function and who appreciate the look and feel of top-quality leather."

Richard is a member of the American Craft Council and Americans Concerned for Artisanry and Craftsmanship. He received an undergraduate degree in environmental sciences and was in a masters program in regional planning before deciding to devote himself full time to leatherwork.

Brochure: Yes.
Commissions: Yes.
Studio Hours: None.
Telephone: (617) 693-2177.

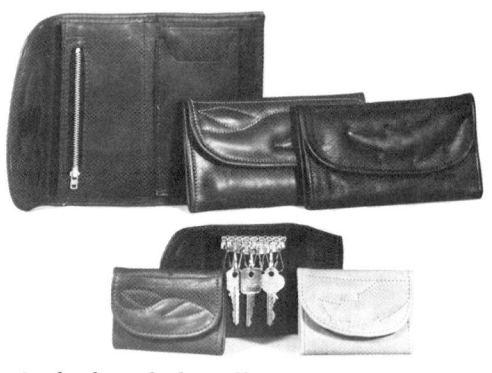

Quilted cowhide wallet, top. Size closed 7 by 4 inches; open 7 by 11 inches; $38. On bottom, key rings of quilted cowhide come in a variety of patterns and colors. Closed size 4 by 3 inches; open 4 by 7 inches. For six keyhooks the cost is $12; a 12-key version is $15.

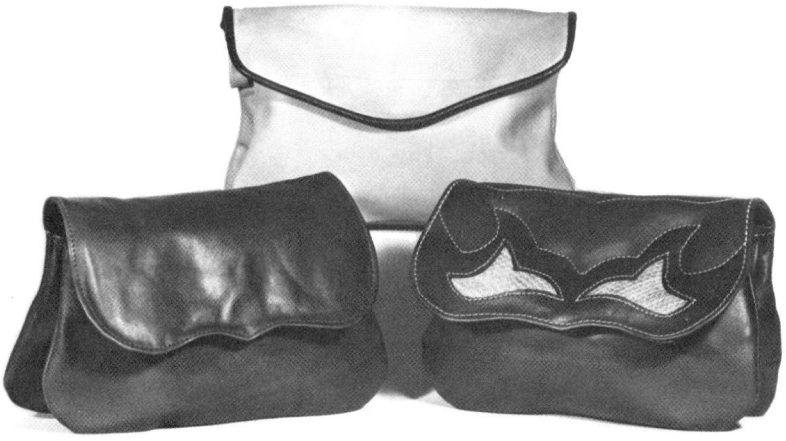

Top bag is cowhide with contrasting kid binding, $60. At lower right is a bag done in quilted cowhide and snakeskin reverse appliqué effects, $65. Lower left bag is cowhide, $55. All bags are 6 by 10 inches, have two zipper pockets, adjustable straps (not shown) and magnetic closure.

TED ARMEN

RD 1
Barre, Vermont 05641

The idea to build a fully functionally three-horse carousel didn't exactly spring full-blown from Ted Armen's fertile mind. Ted says that ideas like the one that resulted in the carousel can occur anywhere, "in conversation, in a book or simply as a thought that springs to mind, say, while eating a pear."

When an idea interests him, he begins to wonder about it, about the "technical problems, about the different variations possible and about how it would look and feel." At some point the casual thinking becomes the early planning for the project's actual undertaking. That's when Ted says the fun begins. "The thought that this thing—a carousel—might actually *be* fills me with a tremendous excitement," says the twenty-seven-year-old craftsman.

Ted had been doing some carving in wood, mostly relief and furniture carving, when he happened to come across a "marvelous" book, *A Pictorial History of the Carousel*. One thought led to another until years later he started carving the first horse, a seahorse, later joined by a vanilla-ice-cream pony and a palomino charger, at forty-nine inches to the withers the tallest of the three. A motorized unit beneath the steps drives the carousel, the horses leaping and landing twice with every revolution.

"I want the carousel to be more than a rotating stand for three carvings," Ted told me, "more than a ride for kids, more than a smallish replica of an industrial amusement machine. I wanted it to be a single precious object, large enough to climb onto, into and be a part of."

Ted recently completed the last work on his carousel, which has been exhibited at Goddard College in Plainfield.

Brochure: No. Slides and prints will be sent for serious inquiries.
Commissions: Yes.
Studio Hours: None.
Telephone: (802) 476-6719.

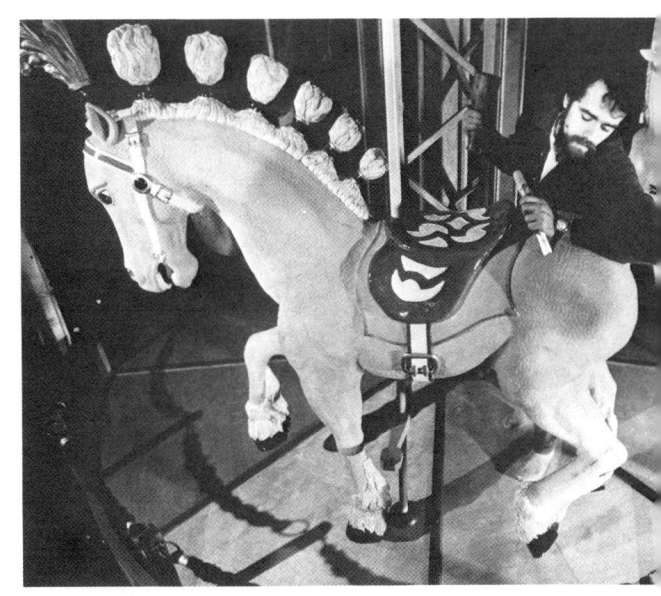

Ted is shown here putting the finishing touches on his palomino charger, one of three horses on his handcrafted operating carousel. The palomino, a seahorse and a pony are of laminated basswood construction and carved by hand. The horses prance with every revolution of the stage.

All work was conceived and carried out over several years by Ted except for the colorful decoration of the curved panels around the carousel base, which were painted by Sara Munro-Dorsey of Plainfield, Vermont.

The horses' saddles, ribbons and other trappings have been sanded very smooth and gessoed, then painted with a high-gloss enamel. The manes and tails are smoothly tooled and strongly stained with acrylic. The flesh areas have been tooled to an even, stippled texture and brushed with a thin coat of acrylic color. The asking price for the carousel is $50,000.

JACKIE SPEETER ABRAMS

Willy Hill Baskets
RFD 2
Groton, Vermont 05046

Jackie Abrams has been weaving baskets since 1975, when she was apprenticed to Ben Higgins, one of the last pounded-white-ash basketmakers, in Chesterfield, Massachusetts. "Baskets are an important part of my life," Jackie told me. "I weave them, I collect them and I use them. The baskets I weave are inspired by those used for generations in almost every culture, adapting the same basic techniques that have proven to be functional and lasting since 7000 B.C. I weave baskets for use, durability and beauty, for basket lovers and basket collectors."

Jackie, thirty-four, uses a variety of materials in her work, including imported natural materials and native Vermont fibers. Striving for "pleasing contrasts in color and texture" and using a repertoire of different techniques, she creates both a popular line of production baskets and one-of-a-kind pieces, enjoying the opportunity that this work gives her to explore new designs, materials and techniques.

Her work has been featured in national publications and invitational exhibitions and is available in shops and galleries throughout the country.

Jackie moved to Vermont in 1976 with her husband Steve, a potter. Their studios are in their home as are their two daughters, Dani and Rina Rose, "who keep all their toys in baskets."

She has taught several workshops in her craft and is a member of Craft Professionals of Vermont, the League of New Hampshire Craftsmen and Vermont Hand Crafters.

Brochure: A brochure is available for $2.50, refundable with first order.
Commissions: No.
Studio Hours: By appointment.
Telephone: (802) 439-6265.

Four baskets made of reed and seagrass. Reed, chosen for its strength and uniformity, is the inner core of rattan, a jungle vine, and is beige in color. Seagrass is made of twisted grasses and resembles rope, in shades of green and beige.

From left: Yarn basket with double handles for easy carrying. "This versatile design is useful for storing yarns, toys or magazines." Diameter is 16½ inches by height 7½ inches not including handle; $60. Hen basket was traditionally used to carry hens to market. This one is designed to hang on a wall to hold a plant. Height 12 inches, width 5 inches; $110. Knitting basket may also be used for needlework projects or carrying and collecting. Diameter is 12½ inches, height 6½ inches not including handle; $52. Shipping additional for all prices.

Jeremy Seeger

Box 117, Fassett Hill
Hancock, Vermont 05748

"All my life I have been surrounded by folk music," says Jeremy Seeger, "and have come to love and appreciate traditional instruments and their music." For the past fifteen years Jeremy has been building fretted dulcimers, a traditional American folk instrument native to the Appalachian Mountain region.

Jeremy says that the fretted dulcimer is one of the easiest instruments to learn but "for the more advanced player or professional musician, the dulcimer can also be played with quite sophisticated picking and chording."

The three- or four-stringed instrument, he adds, "offers a combination of versatility, simplicity and charm that provides a constant source of pleasure." Its unique "mountain sound" comes from the two drone strings that are strummed along with the melody strings. Jeremy's dulcimers are four stringed, with a double melody string "so that the tune stands out better against the drone strings." It is played just like a three-string dulcimer.

"The two most important features of every dulcimer I build," says Jeremy, "are its high quality of wood and its easy action, allowing it to be played with a light touch." He has recently begun building hammer dulcimers using traditional construction techniques to obtain a rich, vibrant sound.

Jeremy, thirty-eight, has been building, playing and selling dulcimers since 1968. His formal instruction in woodworking began in the sixth grade in The Netherlands, where his family lived for many years. He is a member of Vermont Handcrafters and Vermont Musical Instrument Makers.

Brochure: Yes.
Commissions: He builds custom dulcimers according to the customer's aesthetic choices.
Studio Hours: By appointment.
Telephone: (802) 767-3790.

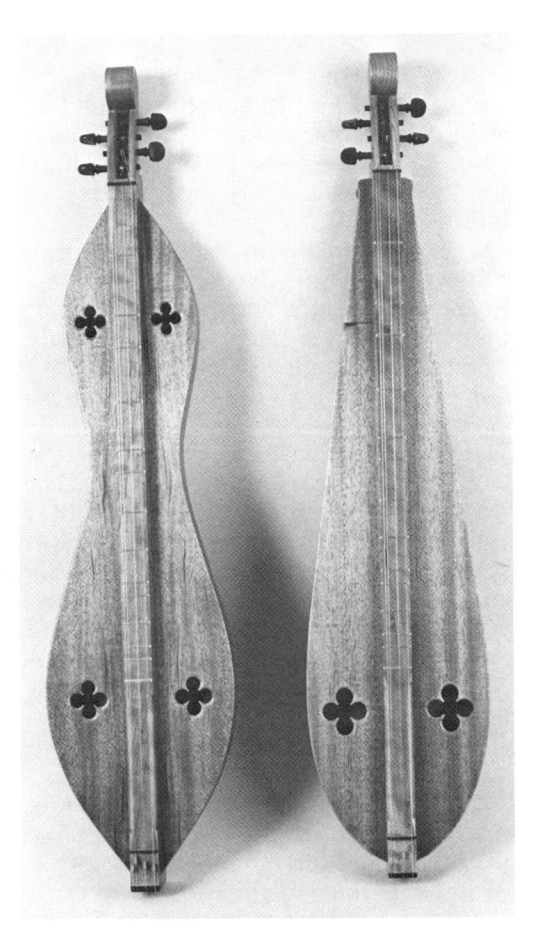

Fretted Appalachian dulcimers in hourglass shape, left, and teardrop shape. Made of mahogany and cherry wood, they feature cloverleaf soundholes and are 34 inches long, 8 inches wide and 3 inches deep; $280.

Detail of end of fretted dulcimer showing fine tuners of cherry and bridge of ebony.

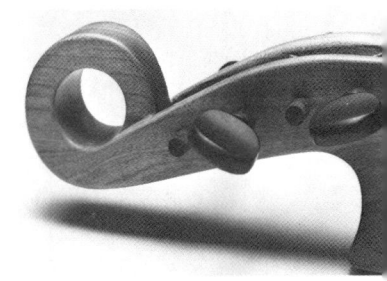

Detail of scroll on fretted dulcimer. Scroll is cherry with ebony pegs.

221 · MIXED

MAUREEN SHORT AND STAN KATZ

Feathertree Studio
104A Mount Philo Road
North Ferrisburg, Vermont 05473

"Feathers hold me in awe of their unique beauty," exclaims Maureen Short, who is one half of Feathertree Studio. "The beauty of just one shining feather is marvelous; but when combined with other equally exciting feathers, the effect is startling."

Maureen, thirty-one, began doing featherwork nearly five years ago when she decided to make a pair of feather earrings. Since then her work has slowly evolved to larger pieces that join the "softness of feathers with the smooth strength of wood."

Her partner in this endeavor is Stan Katz, a thirty-six-year-old woodworker who designs and builds wooden tables and frames that beautifully complement Maureen's featherwork. Their recently introduced line so far consists of end tables, shadowboxes, framed mirrors and wallpieces. Crafted from a variety of native hardwoods and combined with delicate pheasant feathers under glass, the pieces are both elegantly functional and unusually decorative.

Maureen lives on a hill in Charlotte, Vermont, with a "glorious" view of Lake Champlain and the mountains behind it. "Watching the sun set behind these mountains has often given me a real empathy for the Indians before me who saw other brilliant sunsets here long ago," she told me. "The uplifting from the feeling of gratitude for being a humble spectator of Nature's gift inspires me in my work."

Brochure: Yes.
Commissions: Yes. Either with wood and feathers combined or with either medium separately.
Studio Hours: Wednesdays and Fridays by appointment.
Telephone: (802) 425-3458.

This solid white-oak nightstand has a pheasant feather design under the ¼-inch glass top. Your choice of brass or porcelain knob. The drawer locks with a skeleton key. Also available in black cherry, maple and yellow birch. Height 27 inches, top is 14 inches square; $275 plus shipping.

A pleasant pheasant feather design on velvet and in a wood frame suitable for hanging. Designs will vary from that pictured. Choice of beige (shown) or brown velvet and woods as above. 14 inches square; $55.

Annie Sears

*East Hill Porcelain Doll and Marionette Co.
RD 1, PO Box 1360
Plainfield, Vermont*

The East Hill Porcelain Doll and Marionette Company is populated by numerous and varied character types—everything from joyful clowns, jesters and fools to saddened Lebanese women and aged farmers. And then there's Annie, twenty-four, who is the designer, sculptor, seamstress and marketing agent for this crew. "I am the worker of the crowd," she told me. "It's my job to create, clothe and embellish the dolls and find homes and entertainment centers where they may live and perform.

"It's their job as dolls and marionettes to help people laugh away scornful moods, give friendship to a child and at times speak out politically."

All dolls have individually sculpted and painted porcelain busts with cast hands and shoes of hydrostone for added durability. The bust, hands and shoes are sewn with carpet thread, the same way antique dolls were made in the eighteenth and nineteenth centuries.

Annie's studio is housed in the rolling beauty of the Vermont Green Mountains, which she finds perfectly suited for her creative instincts. "It is very isolated here. I'm at the foot of a mountain where wild animals hunt for food outside the shop during the late night hours, a time I find very quiet and peaceful for long hours of creating."

"I strive for excellence in the creating process," Annie says, "and do not hesitate extending production time for correct completion of the work. I work for the work and the work works for me." She is a member of the Art Resource Association in Woodbury, Vermont, and the Vermont State Craft Centers in Windsor and Frog Hollow.

Brochure: Available on request.
Commissions: Yes.
Studio Hours: By appointment.
Telephone: (802) 454-7871.

Three jesters. Each jester is individually produced. The faces are hand carved from porcelain and no two are alike. The hands and shoes are cast in hydrostone for added strength and durability. Height 22 inches; $350 each.

ELLIOT BURCH, FRED CARLSON, PETER FISCHER,

Vermont Musical Instrument Builders Cooperative
Box 147
Plainfield, Vermont 05667

This recently formed cooperative consists of five craftspeople who specialize in the art of musical-instrument construction. According to spokesman Fred Carlson, they have come together "to share some of the economics, play, work, joy, magic, dust and true grit" of the instrument-making process. With a variety of beautiful woods such as spruce, cedar, cherry, walnut, rosewood, maple, ebony and mahogany, they create a diversity of instruments from traditional to original, from beautifully simple to intricately sculpted and inlaid designs.

Ken Riportella creates free-formed, hand-hewn, acoustical instruments. Each one is a unique and original sculpture that produces a quality of sound that its creator says is "harmonious with the visual continuity of the design, creating in each instrument a three-dimensional presence and making the instrument seem alive." One of his instruments was included in an exhibition at the Smithsonian Renwick Gallery in Washington, D.C., and later toured the country. "There is something very special about a handmade instrument," he observes, "not only the looks of it but the sound."

Susan Norris' latest instrument has a sound all its own. The ten-stringed piece, called a "Suzalyne," has the range of a violin and a viola combined. "It contains the essences of waterfalls and mountains that sing to me on my walk to the shop," she told me, "and dream birds that flutter lightly above me in the early morning." The twenty-eight-year-old craftsperson loves the process of working a rough piece of wood "into something elegant and filled with its own magic song." She also makes fiddles, guitars and many other stringed instruments. Her work is entirely custom oriented. "I love the process of blending another's special energy with my own to create the perfect instrument for them."

"Instruments should entice you to play them by their look, sound and feel," says Peter Fischer, twenty-eight, who has recently developed an exceptionally light and elegant hammered dulcimer that's

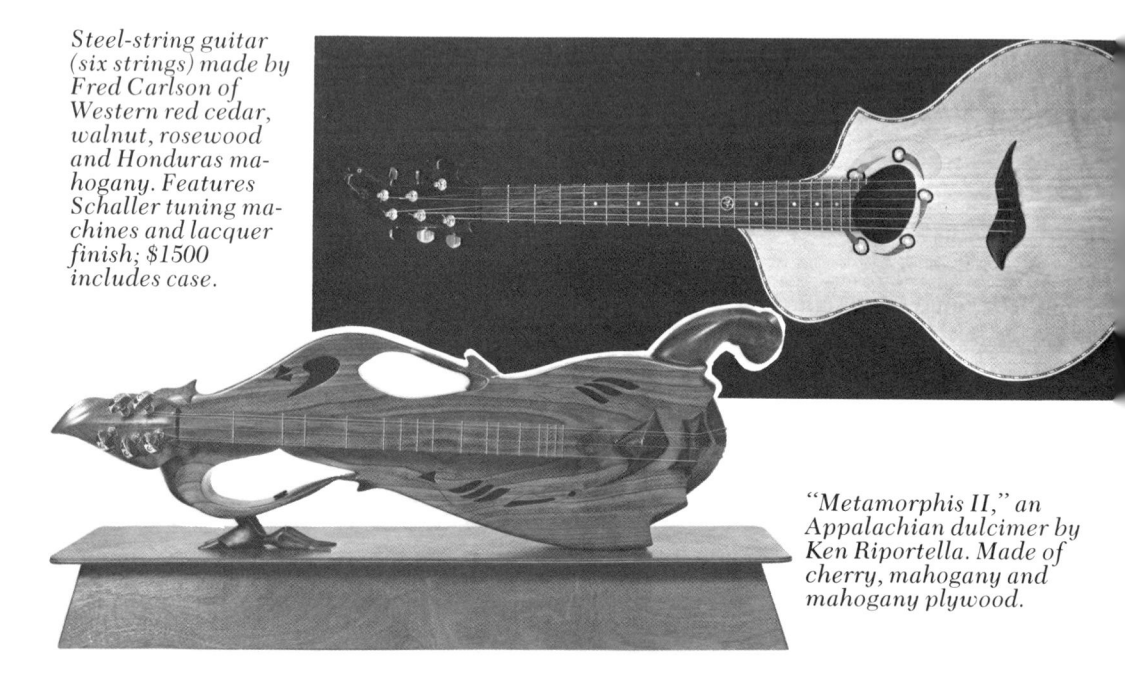

Steel-string guitar (six strings) made by Fred Carlson of Western red cedar, walnut, rosewood and Honduras mahogany. Features Schaller tuning machines and lacquer finish; $1500 includes case.

"Metamorphis II," an Appalachian dulcimer by Ken Riportella. Made of cherry, mahogany and mahogany plywood.

Susan Norris and Ken Riportella

"affordable and easy for the beginner to play. Nothing that's machine made has the special feel of a handmade instrument," he says. Peter started out doing guitar repair work and studying Renaissance stringed-instrument making. He makes violas da gamba, flutes, banjos and guitars as well as the dulcimers.

Elliot Burch, twenty-seven, made his first banjo from an "obsolete, hopefully unmissed, hardened pine rafter" taken from his family's attic. He learned to play it the first day it was finished and has since sharpened his skills to create the most delicately inlayed designs, graceful carvings and artistic shape in his work. "There needs to be more music in the world," he says. "Everyone should try to play some instrument. Hopefully I can contribute." He has constructed many banjos and hammered and mountain dulcimers as well as an occasional guitar, harp or mandolin.

Fred Carlson, twenty-seven, builds his instruments to "sing the songs of the dust of life. The magic of music begins with the dance of chisels on work bench, glue and clamps waltzing to the rhythm of sanding, scraping, polishing, writing the songs to be sung later." His guitars, dulcimers, violas da gamba and other instruments are of original designs, "based on tradition and built with love."

There is much sharing of the co-op members' different skills and knowledge among each other. "Sharing with a community of builders is very important in sustaining me," notes Peter Fischer. "What great sounds come from the shop around breaktime when somebody strikes up a tune! 'What's that tune, Elliot? I'll see if I can pick it out on this fiddle here.'"

Brochure: No.
Commissions: Among the co-op members, you can find virtually any type of acoustic stringed instrument that you could want. Write them, indicating either the person or type of instrument that interests you.
Studio Hours: By appointment.
Telephone: (802) 479-0862.

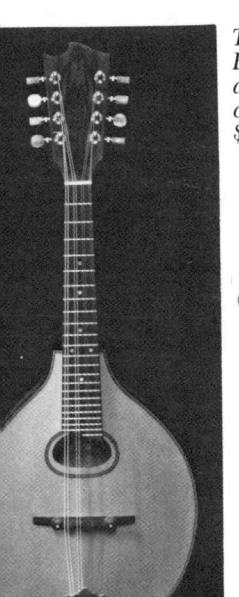

This mandolin is carved top and back by Elliot Burch. It features an oval soundhole and can be custom ordered with inlays and carvings as desired. Prices range from $500 to $900.

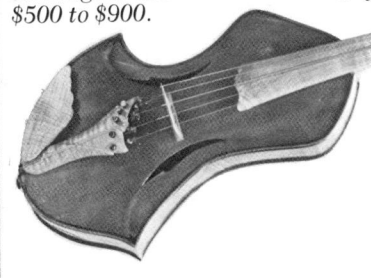

"Suzalyne" is Suzy Norris' ten-stringed bowed instrument. Five bowed strings have the range of a violin and viola combined and are augmented by five sympathic strings running under the fingerboard. The back, ribs, neck, fingerboard and tailpiece are made of curly maple. The top is sitka spruce and the pegs are ebony; $1800.

Hammered dulcimer by Peter Fischer weighs only eight pounds and is decorated with a graphic of the planet Saturn. Its back and side are maple, its top redwood; $400.

SUSAN ABBIE PETERS

*Pleasant Street
Saxtons River, Vermont 05154*

Mention macrame to most people and images of macrame hanging planters spring to mind. But, as Susan Peters observes, macrame can be developed on many levels. Susan has made everything from bags to baby hammocks, preferring to make intricately worked wall hangings, large room-divider planters or window treatments, many of which are commissioned by individuals or businesses.

"Trees are a dominant feature of Vermont and a continual source of inspiration for my work," she says. "Capturing the beauty of a tree, whether standing alone or in a group with branches intertwined, is to reaffirm its importance in our lives."

Susan initially plans most of her designs on paper but sometimes a piece "takes on a life of its own as it develops, which makes working on them more exciting." Her aesthetic concerns are with the "balance of open and closed space and the texture of the finished piece." She has found that the "response of the fiber to a particular knot" is integral to her work. For instance, the three-dimensional quality of the tree trunk is a "natural outgrowth" of repeating vertical double half-hitches. Susan uses primarily natural cotton and jute in her pieces, sometimes accenting them with color by knotting and wrapping.

The thirty-eight-year-old artist is a member of Frog Hollow State Craft Center and the Jelly Bean Tree Craft Co-op. She is a part-time Title One instructor in reading and learning skills and occasionally gives workshops in macrame.

Brochure: In progress.
Commissions: "I'm happy to collaborate with customers on planning."
Studio Hours: By appointment.
Telephone: (802) 869-2558.

This group of five macrame trees was done in fine natural two-ply jute and is mounted top and bottom on hardwood. You can commission any kind of tree to be depicted and in any number from single tree designs to small forests. Size, color and/or kind of string can be custom ordered and the dowels could be Plexiglass if desired. Prices vary but usually are around $35 to $50 per square foot. The design shown here measures 72 inches wide by 42 inches high and is $1000.

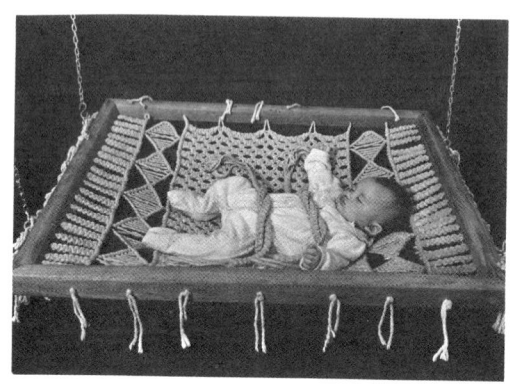

The baby hammock is made of soft white-cotton welting cord and blue-and-green soft wool wrapping on the outside of the diamond design. It is supported by a hardwood frame and a macrame safety belt is included. Details such as type of design, size and colors are individually arranged if desired.

Costs usually run from $35 to $50 per square foot. This hammock measures 30 by 42 inches and costs $320 with hanging hardware included.

SABRA FIELD

Tontine Press
RFD 2
South Royalton, Vermont 05068

"To celebrate divine creation by making prints my occupation," is how Sabra Field decribes what she does for her art and her living. With the landscapes of Vermont providing her with both inspiration and the subject matter for many of her prints, Sabra's woodcuts are colorful celebrations of her environment. "I need the peace and the green," she said, "but most of all, the mountains. I am moved by the interaction of the mountains and the sky."

One of the oldest forms of printmaking still in practice, woodcut prints are particularly demanding of the artist's skills. When producing a print, Sabra first generally cuts her images into the plank-grain wood blocks, one for each color. It is an exacting job; each carved block must perfectly register with the others. Inking the blocks by hand, she pulls each impression on either the proof press or on the faster large-etching press.

Sabra and her husband Spencer established Tontine Press in 1969 to market her prints to collectors. Since then, she has created more than ninety different limited-edition woodcuts. Her work has been shown in more than thirty one-woman exhibitions and in numerous group and invitational shows in Vermont and across the country.

Some thirty galleries in the Northeast, South and Midwest carry her prints, which can also be seen at Tontine Press in East Barnard.

Brochure: Full-color reproductions of her prints will be sent on request.
Commissions: Sabra has done special, limited-edition prints for organizations ranging from IBM's Burlington offices to the Vermont State Arts Council. Commissioned editions are welcome.
Studio Hours: Daily from 9 A.M. to 5 P.M. and by appointment.
Telephone: (802) 763-7092.

"The Mountain Suite" is a series of four woodcuts hung in sequence from autumn to summer. Framed in silver molding with Plexiglas, they portray the seasons of New England in a sweep of 63 inches. From left: "Mountain Autumn" depicts a blue-and-salmon sky, a smokey blue mountain, golden hillside and black-and-white cows. "Mountain Winter" has bright stars glittering against the velvet-blue sky while a deep-blue mountain looms above the farm. "Mountain Spring" exhibits a pale-blue sky, grey woods and red sugar house. "Mountain Summer" shows puffy clouds in a deep-blue sky, blue mountains beyond the green-forested hill and yellow windrows of hay in the green meadow. Each print is 15 inches wide by 20 inches high and is $100 framed and $60 mounted.

JAMES KELSO

Route 1, Box 5300
Worcester, Vermont 05682

Jim Kelso's first professional exposure to handcraft was in 1973, when he started to make and sell handmade banjos. Not able to make the living that he desired from the craft, he began to look around for something else. Having worked with inlays on his banjos he had become interested in the art of gun engraving, which also used some of the same materials and techniques.

"Although I had no previous interest in guns," he recalls, "I became fascinated with the intricate designs and multiskilled crafts used to decorate them." He perfected his engraving techniques and started selling his work to collectors right from the start.

Three years ago Jim began to work on custom-made knives. "I find that knives can embody many qualities apart from being weapons," he told me, "and that the best convey feelings of beauty, grace and power as much as any crafted object."

Jim's work tends toward traditional styles with some influence from his interest in Oriental art. He does all work except the grinding of the blade, which is done in close collaboration with a bladesmith.

"I do not make an arbitrary distinction between art and craft," says the thirty-three-year-old knifemaker. "It is not so important what we call our work as is the inspiration that we draw on and are able to infuse into it. The best works will always instill a sense of awe and wonder and draw our attention to the face behind the mask of physical appearance."

Jim is a member of the Guild of American Firearms Engravers, and Art Resource Association and the American Bladesmith Society.

Brochure: No.
Commissions: All work is one of a kind and commissionable.
Studio Hours: By appointment.
Telephone: (802) 229-4254.

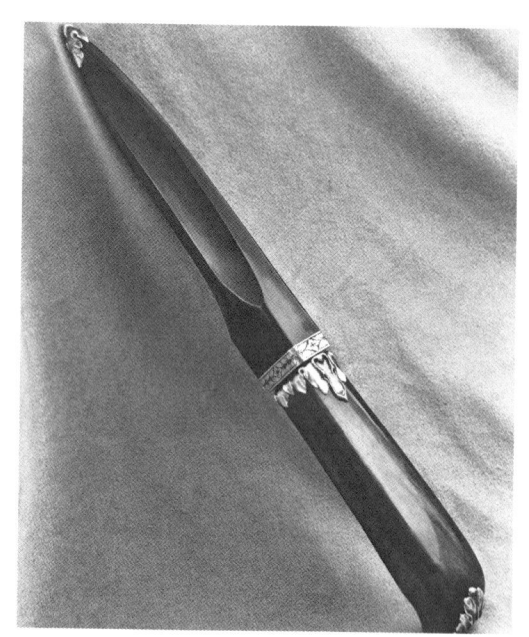

Victorian-style dagger has an ebony handle and sheath, cast sterling fittings and mother of pearl flower on the butt. Sheath throat is engraved. Length 12 inches; $1200.

Folding knife, top, with mother of pearl scales and cougar engraving. Knife was made by Phil Boguszewski, all other work by Jim Kelso. Length 7 inches; $400. Small hunting knife on bottom has a walrus ivory handle. Blade by Keith Davis, other work by Jim Kelso. Length 8 inches; $600.

Wood

Mary Kirchoff and Phyllis Wigham

Livestock Unlimited
30 Meetinghouse Lane
Madison, Connecticut 06443

Livestock Unlimited evolved three years ago from a Christmas project of Phyllis Wigham's and Mary Kirchoff's. These two friends, who had done various craft projects together for years, became intrigued with the images of some crudely carved antique barnyard animals they had seen in a book and set out with some wood scraps to recreate them in their own style, using a friend's horses as models.

A local exhibition of their work led to their first sales, which soon convinced the partners, both thirty-nine, that they could possibly make some money doing something that they both enjoyed.

"Working with wood was a new dimension we both found challenging and rewarding," explains Phyllis. "The horses, cows, sheep and donkeys led to giraffes, elephants, goats and more. We've also done special orders for a walrus, a milking goat and the Three Bears, fully dressed."

Mary has been making puppets professionally for twelve years. She enjoys the "change of pace" of woodworking. "She is the inspired designer who created the originals," notes Phyllis, "and makes many of the changes as we progress from the rough animals to those with personality and fine detail."

"We both feel that we've been successful thus far," Phyllis told me, "having learned a great deal about the business world while doing something creative that adds meaning and depth to the rest of our lives, family, jobs and our own living barnyard animals."

Brochure: A color postcard is available and a complete brochure is in the works.
Commissions: Yes.
Studio Hours: None.
Telephone: (203) 245-9308.

Examples of the menagerie of wooden animals mounted on stained-and-painted wheeled platforms by Livestock Unlimited:

African animals available include lion with a furry mane and tail and leather ears, 8½ inches long by 6 inches tall, $24; giraffe with painted spots and fur mane and tail, 15 inches tall, $36; camel with tufted humps and beard is 8 by 8½ inches, $25.

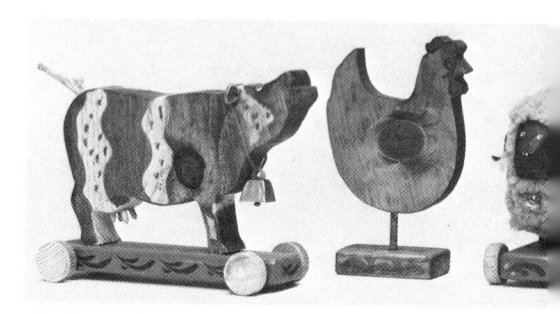

The barnyard group includes stained-and-painted mooing cow complete with bell, 9 inches long by 6 inches high, $30; chicken in the rough, stained with a painted comb and trim, 7 by 7 inches, $12; fleecy sheep with bell on an antiqued platform, 7 inches long by 6 inches high, $25.

230 · WOOD

Andrew M. Simon

Andrew Simon/Design Ltd.
Down on the Farm
Moodus, Connecticut 06469

"The most creatively satisfying part of my work is the act of observing," says Andrew Simon. "Like a camera, I record images and existing design elements, focusing upon details, motifs and the environment around us. This data is distilled and revitalized in my work."

Andy mainly designs and builds custom furniture and architectural woodwork for a variety of clients. Projects range from a simple coffee table to a makeover of a complete room. He has also developed a production line of items that includes clocks, bookends, vases, lamps and office and kitchen accessories.

"I enjoy wood as a medium," Andy told me, "but my focus is toward design." While an architectural student at the Rhode Island School of Design in the early Seventies, Andy discovered the joys of working with wood. "My work combines the design process with a material that can take many forms through careful handworking. It's also a sensory involvement—the smell of freshly cut cherry wood, the feel of a finished piece."

Andy works primarily in hardwoods, using clean, simple lines, soft, rounded edges and natural wood tones. Although any finish can be specified, his preference is to leave the wood unstained and finished with clear polyurethane to emphasize its natural colors and graining.

He enjoys the close interaction with his clients. "A close client/craftsman relationship and the information shared there is essential to the creation of a successful piece of furniture," he says. "My role is really that of translator."

"Basically," concludes the thirty-year-old woodworker, "the things that I build are made with lots of care and love."

Brochure: Yes.
Commissions: Yes, "from small pieces to interior landscaping."
Studio Hours: Tuesday through Saturday from 11 A.M. to 5 P.M.
Telephone: (203) 873-1059.

Wall-mounted cabinet in background is made of red oak with black-walnut trim and pulls. Features adjustable shelves, pull-out turntable storage, cassette drawer, smoked-glass doors and shelves. Finished satin smooth and sealed with polyurethane for a maintenance-free finish. Measures 84 by 84 by 18 inches; $3700. Coffee table with walnut top and oak frame and legs and oak and walnut nesting tables. Coffee table is 30 inches square and 17 inches high; $1100 for both coffee and nesting tables. Also available separately.

Mantel clocks in native and exotic hardwoods. Shown from left: Birdseye maple/mahogany, padouk/maple and zebrawood/walnut. Other woods available. All clocks have a guaranteed quartz movement. Square or rounded shapes measure 5 inches wide by 6 inches high and 3 inches deep; $60 to $80.

LAURENCE HENDRICKS

Pinnacle Designs
RFD 1
New Preston, Connecticut 06777

Laurence Hendricks has a clear sense of his mission as a designer and craftsman in wood: "It is my function to combine the elements of function and aesthetics in such a way that, together with technical expertise and sound engineering, a piece of furniture results that will do what it is designed to do, do it for many years and please the senses as well.

"Not for me the sculpture that is used as a table but the table that is sculptural in form," he told me. "Not for me the addition of modeling or inlays to enhance the beauty of a piece; I prefer to let the color and grain of wood and, sometimes, the raw shape of a board provide all its own beauty."

Calling his designs "less plastic than some of my contemporaries," the forty-five-year-old woodworker emphasizes that his work is more closely aligned with the "straightforward designs" of the Shakers than with "the organic and sculptural products of the more recent past."

Laurence started out as a woodworker following his discharge from the Navy in the late Sixties. When an opportunity arose for apprenticeship with a New Jersey woodworking couple, Laurence decided that it was too good an opportunity to miss. After learning the basics of the trade, he moved to Connecticut to work for an established woodworker. "After a few years," he remembers, "I was able to build a house and became self-employed."

Brochure: In preparation and should be ready by publication date.
Commissions: Yes, 95 percent of his work is custom ordered.
Studio Hours: By appointment.
Telephone: (203) 868-7018.

The baby cradle is made of ribbon-stripe mahogany and is cold molded over a form. Other woods are available. 35 inches long by 18 inches wide and 13 inches high; $850 plus shipping.

232 · WOOD

PETER M. PETROCHKO

370 Quaker Farms Road
Oxford, Connecticut 06483

"Although crafts are sometimes a difficult and frustrating way to make a living," notes Peter Petrochko, " I have found it to be a very creative and rewarding process. I am proud to be a wood craftsman and wouldn't trade it for any other career."

Peter concentrates mainly on creating beautiful wooden bowls and canisters, using an unusual process of his own discovery. About eight years ago, he bought his first bandsaw and started to experiment with different types of angular wood cuts. He continued to explore the process on and off until about three or four years ago, when he "became serious" about it. "I had done furniture and direct carving," he recalls, "and was looking for something to master and specialize in."

Starting with a flat board, he draws circular shapes and cuts them out with an angled band saw. For each piece, he cuts a series of from one to twelve tapered, concentric rings.

Carving a base to match the rings' contours, he stacks them precisely over each other and compresses them using a veneer-type clamp or a cement block. Each bowl then goes through three stages of disk sanding inside and out with one final hand sanding. Peter next rubs in from eight to twenty coats of Behlen's salad-bowl finish and finally completes the piece by buffing it to as fine a finish as he can achieve.

"I'm able to get pretty sculptural in my work and like to fool around with light, form, color patterning and texture," he told me. "I consider much of my work to be spontaneous and experimental in nature. This philosophy allows me more flexibility in the initial stages of design and has proved to be more fun, too."

Peter, thirty-four, is a member of the Connecticut Guild of Craftsmen, the Society of Connecticut Craftsmen, the Society of Arts and Crafts in Boston and the Greater New Haven Arts Council. His work is available in galleries throughout Connecticut and the Northeast.

Brochure: He hopes to have one by December 1983.
Commissions: Yes.
Studio Hours: Usually 10 A.M. to 6 P.M. Monday through Saturday. Call first.
Telephone: (203) 268-8462.

Assorted round bowls in various sizes and woods including both native and exotic hardwoods such as mahogany, walnut, yellow poplar, African zebrawood, oak and maple. Sizes range from diameters of 9 to 16 inches and heights from 5 to 11 inches. The largest bowl shown here has a diameter of 16 inches and is 11 inches high. Prices range from $50 to $1000 according to wood and size chosen.

Ian B. Edwards

10 Saugatuck Avenue
Westport, Connecticut 06880

Having been born and raised in New England, Ian Edwards suggests that he "could not help but be influenced by the talent and resourcefulness of the Yankee craftsmen.

"This long tradition of creativity and ability evident throughout New England has had an impact on my dreams, goals and accomplishments," says the thirty-five-year-old woodworker.

Beginning as an apprentice carpenter in a local Connecticut carpenter's union, Ian has been working with wood for eighteen years, the last two in business for himself. "My primary business goal and interest," he notes, "is in creating quality, hand-crafted furniture, fine antique reproductions and restorations." He also builds and installs bookcases, wall units and an occasional kitchen.

"The satisfaction of creating a beautiful piece of furniture, the pleasure of making a living doing what I enjoy and the independence of successfully operating my own business all combine to make this a happy and worthwhile experience," he says.

Ian's work is done mostly on commission. Most designs, he notes, are "a collaboration of what the customer wants and what I feel is proportionately more pleasing and practical." Much of his inspiration comes from Colonial craftsmen and an interest in classic furniture design.

"Although I derive great satisfaction from running my own business and working with wood," he told me, "my greatest satisfaction is when I deliver a piece of furniture and the customer tells me they love it."

Brochure: No.
Commissions: All work is on a commission basis.
Studio Hours: Monday through Saturday, 9 A.M. to noon and 1 P.M. to 6 P.M., but it's best to call first.
Telephone: (203) 544-8935.

Queen Anne lowboy is made of solid Honduras mahogany with the back and drawers of Southern yellow pine. Mortise and tenon and peg construction; drawers are hand dovetailed. Solid-brass hardware with a glazed stain-and-lacquer finish. Height 30 inches, width 36 inches, depth 20 inches; $1400.

This cedar armoire has four doors but it can also be done in a two-door version. Here it's used as a stereo cabinet but could be used for all-purpose storage. Unit pictured is honey-brown and can be made to order in any wood. Drawers can be added inside or below doors if desired. Height 84 inches, width 36 inches, depth 20 inches; $900.

ABBY MORRISON

Ace Woodwork
RR 1, Box 4058
Camden, Maine 04843

Woodworking has fascinated Abby Morrison ever since childhood. "My first knives were treasured and the curled chips they whittled had a magical quality," she remembers. She surmises that her love of woodworking probably is derived from her love of the forest. "Walking was our main family outing and in the rustic atmosphere of our camp, I made a connection between the inner calm resulting from time spent in the woods and the sensitivity and patience needed in woodworking."

Abby first studied woodworking in high school and later took a sixteen-month cabinet and furnituremaking course, learning traditional hand joinery while making American period pieces. Further honing her skills in furniture-restoration work, Abby works as an independent cabinetmaker, which allows her time for her burl work.

"Burl bowlmaking is a very intuitive process, from locating the burls to finish carving, scraping and sanding," she says. Looking to integrate her furniture-making background with her current work, Abby is presently experimenting with burl chairs. "On an immediate level, I wish to communicate my own sense of love of the woods through an ordinarily ignored tree deformity."

The twenty-four-year-old woodworker is clearly entranced. "There is something wholly absorbing in the total uniqueness of each burl and its transformation to the receptive gathering form of a bowl."

Brochure: No.
Commissions: Yes.
Studio Hours: By appointment.
Telephone: (207) 236-2408.

After carefully removing the bark and the cambium from the outside of the burl, the inside is roughed out with some delicate chainsaw work and further shaped by hand using adze and gouge. On smaller pieces, Abby uses a bandsaw on parts of the exterior. She finishes each bowl by first using burr and disc grinders to smooth and polish followed by several wet sandings. Olive oil and beeswax are used for a lasting, non-toxic, low-gloss finish.

A spalted beech burl vessel. "This burl was fairly symmetrical to start with, which is not usually the case." Native Maine burls of all varieties are used including maple, ash, birch, oak, pine and cherry. Textures range from spiny to blistered to smooth; color from highly figured, deep brick red to even cream, often with great contrast within one piece.

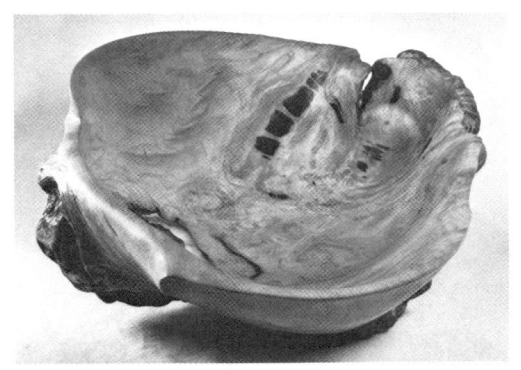

In this rock maple burled piece the series of darker markings are caused by the natural coloration of heartwood. Both these bowls are $275 each. Others range from $50 to $500.

DAVID AND SUSAN MARGONELLI

RFD 1, Box 84
Dover-Foxcroft, Maine 04426

Susan and David Margonelli were first attracted to furniture making as newlyweds back in the middle Sixties when they found a book on Shaker furniture. The Shaker style's simple designs and technical excellence inspired them to eventually teach themselves how to make their own furniture that "would last, function and age well, while fitting into a variety of settings without looking dated or contrived."

Their early work was derivative of Shaker design but more recently their production has grown to include additional styles such as contemporary tables and desks or Hepplewhite and Chippendale beds and chests. "We enjoy creating for a specific period or need," Susan told me.

"Making custom furniture for a living has allowed us many special experiences," says Susan, "from meeting all types of people, to working at home and having lunch together." Most exciting, however, is the "lack of boundaries or structure" in their professional lives. "We never know who the next customer will be or what they will want. In our future, there will always be another piece to build or a design or technical problem to solve. We are sometimes exhausted but rarely bored."

The Margonellis, both forty, have been making and selling their furniture in Dover-Foxcroft since 1971. "Our goal has always been to produce lasting, functional furniture suited to modern living." They are members of the American Craft Council.

Brochure: For a deposit of 5 dollars, you will receive a set of color photos of a sampling of their work, refundable upon return of the photos.
Commissions: Most work is done on commission.
Studio Hours: By appointment.
Telephone: (207) 564-7552.

This slant-front desk has a tiger-maple cock bead on the exterior drawers. The size and arrangement of the interior drawers and pigeonholes can be varied to suit your needs. Height 40 inches, width 40 inches, depth 19 inches. In cherry, $1950; walnut, $2100.

This walnut music cabin is a rounded, dovetailed case set on a frame with tapered legs. The doors have puffed panels and the interior has twenty sections for music books. It can also be ordered with a desk interior. Height 66 inches by width 34 inches; $2,100.

JOSEPH TRACY

Route 102
Mount Desert, Maine 04660

Joseph Tracy has been practicing his craft for thirteen years—six years of studying furniture design and woodworking at the School for American Craftsmen in Rochester, New York, and the last seven years as an independent woodworker.

Joe's furniture has a decidedly contemporary and light feel, which he attributes to several influences, including Japanese architecture, Shaker furniture and Scandinavian Design. "I try to keep my work visually simple, with a touch of grace and whimsy," he told me. "I often use straight and almost-straight lines to define my shapes and won't hesitate using materials other than wood if a piece calls for it."

For a piece of furniture to be successful, Joe feels that it must succeed in three ways: "It should be pleasing to the eye and hand. It should invite the viewer to step closer and examine it further. The piece must be sturdy but not overbuilt so as to appear heavy."

The thirty-six-year-old woodworker enjoys virtually every aspect of his work—from the first creative spark to the refinement of the rough idea, the selection of materials and the cutting into the wood—it's all a pleasure to Joe. After he finishes a piece, he'll invariably live with it for a while "to see how it feels" before presenting it to the customer.

Joe moved to Maine seven years ago with his wife Lucy. They have twin five-year-old sons and live in a house that he built over his workshop. He is a member of Directions, a state craft group.

Brochure: No.
Commissions: Yes.
Studio Hours: None.
Telephone: (207) 244-7360.

Maple serving cart with safety-glass tray and Plexiglas/rubber wheels. "A rather elegant piece that shows off anything placed upon it because of its simple lines and transparent qualities. It is 32 inches high by 24 inches wide and 36 inches long; $925.

Leather-upholstered side chair in oak; also available in any desired hardwood. "A lightly upholstered but extremely comfortable dining or desk chair that derives its comfort from the flexible ash slats in the seat." $600.

Jeff Kellar

10 Exchange Street
Portland, Maine 04101

"I make furniture that fulfills traditional functions and is constructed with traditional joinery," notes woodworker Jeff Kellar. "Within these boundaries, my aim is to invent new forms and in this respect my work is sculptural."

Using the simplest design elements—symmetrical curves, bevels, flat planes—Jeff "looks to the styles of the past" for inspiration, "not for direct quotation but in the hope of distilling some of the spirit that animates them."

Jeff enjoys doing custom work for clients who have specific functional requirements. "My clients are usually very concerned with their environment. They care about the objects they are surrounded with and usually enjoy work that is straightforward." He especially enjoys creating desks, collection cases and occcasional pieces.

Jeff, thirty-three, graduated from the University of Pennsylvania in 1971. A film maker and display designer before teaching himself to be a woodworker, he moved to Portland, Maine, in 1975 and set up his first and present workshop. He belongs to the American Craft Council.

Brochure: No.
Commissions: All work is custom.
Studio Hours: By appointment.
Telephone: (207) 773-6269.

Occasional table is constructed of East Indian Rosewood. The drawer front and panel for top are kingwood, a Brazilian rosewood. 30½ by 22½ by 16½ inches; $1250.

A collector's display cabinet made of East Indian rosewood and tulipwood with interchangeable drawers. The contents of the uppermost drawer are visible through glass in top of piece. The escutcheons and the frame around the glass are tulipwood. Drawers are lined with black velvet. Height 31 inches, width 22 inches, depth 17 inches; $2450.

Cliff Rugg

40 Pleasant Street
Portland, Maine 04101

"To make something that has meaning, that touches the heart and speaks from the heart is something that I strive for in my work," notes woodworker Cliff Rugg. Working in an old barn attached to a 175-year-old house in Gorham, Maine, Cliff creates contemporary hardwood furniture and other wooden objects that he describes with a chuckle as a "direct aesthetic assault" on the senses.

"Inspiration and its expression flow from ultimate sources, and require responses of ultimate choice and commitment," he told me. "For me ultimate sources are our natural environment; the human condition; emotional, intellectual and physical contact with the world, my work and the work of others; and my relationships."

In addition to woodworking, Cliff's passions are many, including gourmet Chinese cooking ("making beautiful food is no different than making beautiful furniture, except that furniture lasts longer"); poetry; and fly fishing.

Cliff points out, however, that nothing comes close to the creative satisfaction that he receives from working with wood. "It's the only thing that puts all my loves together in one place."

Durability, texture, form, history and human appeal are what draw him to wood. "Curves, forms, surfaces, scale, function—all combine to create objects which become more than what they do, more than what was intended."

Referring to the Japanese concept of kami—the spirit of nature that is in all objects—Cliff emphasizes that his woodwork has touches throughout that "show that you care." If he can't find appropriate brasswork, for instance, he'll strike it himself to get exactly what he wants. "I'm a spiritual person, grounded and centered. My work is one way that I express my feelings about the world and myself to and for other people that I know and care for.

"People need to have natural fabrics, woods, aesthetic stimulation, art and painting and things that are handmade to connect with other people and tap into that great flow." Cliff, thirty-nine, is married and the father of two children.

Brochure: Yes.
Commissions: Yes. Cliff promises that he will make you "furniture that has one step in the past and one step in your life."
Studio Hours: By appointment.
Telephone: (207) 774-5111.

This mahogany dropleaf gateleg table features mortise-and-tenon frame and legs. The skirt is cross dovetailed and acts in concert with the top. Petal feet on cabriole legs and a teardrop cutaway pad. Also available in cherry, walnut, curly maple. Measures 66 by 40 inches oval; $1100 in mahogany.

Standing chest is made of birdseye maple and cherry. Hand-wrought brass quadrants and nautical brasses, ogee feet, carved fan, dovetailed drawers. Each large drawer is 24 by 44 inches for full sheets and drawings. Also available in cherry or walnut. Chest measures 46 inches wide by 26 inches deep and 50 inches high; in maple and cherry $2600.

HOWARD HASTINGS

Old Stage Road
Barre, Massachusetts 01005

Howard Hastings builds custom-made cabinets for people's homes. Although he is perfectly capable of building traditionally squared-off cabinets, he's an advocate of a more flowing, easygoing style. "Many people's work has too much structure and not enough feeling in it," he notes. "My cabinets are easy to get close to emotionally and physically."

"Seeing what a breeze does to a field of hay or how a gentle snowfall can embrace a stone wall is the greatest influence in my style of cabinets," Howard told me. "The inspiration for my work is a response to my encounters with nature near my home on a small New England road." The thirty-eight-year-old woodworker will often carve a countertop to resemble a soft blanket of snow; other elements are apt to lean the way trees lean in the forest. "People want to rub their hands over the wood," he notes. "I encourage that."

When a commission is begun, Howard first gets to know the people for which he's working, "their inner vision of what they want and their personal needs and requirements." He then works to produce a solution that is beautiful, functional and that harmonizes with their environment. The relationship between the cabinet and the space around it, the light, colors and textures in the room, how it will be seen and used are all considerations in the design. "Through the design, I try to help people feel what I've seen, to enjoy the peace that I've experienced watching one season become another."

Howard received his fine arts degree from the Rhode Island School of Design. He has had fifteen years experience in restoring eighteenth-century New England homes and in custom woodworking. He is a member of the American Craft Council.

Brochure: No.
Commissions: All work is custom made.
Studio Hours: By appointment.
Telephone: (617) 355-2004.

This wall cabinet is made of cherry and birdseye maple. The refrigerator is behind the tall panels, appliances are behind the rolltop and on the side is a blackboard and a broom closet, 92 by 96 inches; $1400.

The corner cupboard is made of ash, butternut and pine and is a pleasing blend of concave and convex planes. It is slightly larger at the floor than at the top and it leans back slightly toward the wall. It is 89 inches tall; $1500

ALPHONSE MATTIA

*173 Durnell Avenue
Boston, Massachusetts 02131*

Alphonse Mattia has been making furniture since his days as an art student at the Philadelphia School of Art fifteen years ago. He had planned to go into industrial design but was lured by the "warmth" of the furniture shop, which at the time was a part of the Dimensional Design Department. "The objects I saw being made there seemed more personal and individual than the things I saw the industrial-design students working on," he recalls. He switched majors and has been at it ever since.

A few years after he decided to major in dimensional design, the word "crafts" came into vogue. He didn't particularly like being labeled a "craftsman." "People had been impressed and curious when I told them I was a dimensional designer," he says. "When I told them I was a craftsman, everyone had an immediate mental image of what they thought I did." Unfortunately, he says, they often had the wrong image.

"I consider myself an artist or designer," he told me. "As a designer I try to solve three-dimensional problems. As an artist, I try to express an idea or visual concept and hope to evoke a response. I think that contemporary furniture, while playing with our feelings and memories, should also redefine our notions of objects."

Alphonse, thirty-five, is an Associate Professor of Woodworking and Furniture Design at the Program in Artisanry at Boston University. He received his masters degree from the Rhode Island School of Design. His work has been exhibited in numerous group and one-man shows and has been featured in nearly a dozen woodworking magazine articles. He has taught workshops and lectures across the country and is a member of the American Craft Council.

Brochure: No.
Commissions: Yes. He spends most of his time on commissioned work while periodically creating speculative pieces for galleries and museums.
Studio Hours: None.
Telephone: (617) 353-2086.

The rocking chair is made of laminated vermilion (padouk) and upholstered in cotton velvet over down. Upholstery is almond green; wood is a rich red. "This chair is comfortable. It is a piece that I have always liked." Size 42 inches high by 24 inches wide by 42 inches deep. Similar chairs start at $1500. Chair shown is $2000.

Mirror in zebrawood, wenge, carved-and-lacquered birch and sandblasted glass. The lines are sandblasted on mirror and painted. "This piece is typical of my newer work — more color, more sculptural." 26 by 48 by 4 inches; $1800.

241 · WOOD

Jeffrey Briggs

17 Dalton Street
Newburyport, Massachusetts 01950

Jeffrey Briggs sells plants that have the distinct advantage of requiring little or no light and virtually no watering. "They do not get bugs," notes Jeff, "you do not have to feed or talk to them. All you need to make them flourish is an occasional featherdusting and some lemon oil."

His larger-than-life renditions of tulips, day lilies, daffodils, snowdrops and birds of paradise accurately mimic the real thing's gracefulness and beauty, their delicate floral essence rendered in wood sculptures that range in size to nearly 4 feet high. The line was inspired by Jeff's wife and partner Lindley, who thought that carved wooden flowers would be a nice addition to a sculptured garden she was working on. Jeff helped her out and "the idea just took off."

From 1971 to 1979, before Briggs' blooms had blossomed, his business was basically built on beautiful, carved butterflies and bugs. More than 5,000 butterflies made of carefully matched strips of pine, aromatic cedar and redwood have flown out of Jeff's studio to date.

The thirty-six-year-old woodcarver is also known for his one-of-a-kind and commissioned pieces, which have been aptly described as "amazing" in their artfulness, attention to detail and complexity. His work has included everything from a six-foot wooden chalice overflowing with lifelike, carved grapevines to a series of one-of-a-kind mirrors embellished by female figures handcarved from poplar and mahogany and elegantly styled with an Art Nouveau flair.

"My work is an expression of my love for the sensuous line, the flowing line, the line that bends and turns back on itself," he told me. "I find the warmth of wood and the gentleness of line in the female figure a natural extension of this love."

Jeff studied at the School of the Boston Museum of Fine Arts. He has shown his work at numerous exhibitions and shows throughout the Northeast.

Brochure: Separate brochures are available for his blooms, butterflies or custom-made work.
Commissions: Yes.
Studio Hours: By appointment.
Telephone: (617) 465-5593.

Large butterfly wall sculpture is made from carefully matched strips of pine, cedar and redwood. It is finished with two coats of Danish oil and is 34 inches high by 24 inches wide by 4 inches deep; $100 plus shipping. Small butterflies (not shown) are made entirely of carefully chosen pine strips. They are 24 inches high with a 21-inch wingspan and sell for $48 plus shipping.

The day lilies floor sculpture is constructed from poplar, mahogany, maple and butternut. They are first carved and assembled, then sanded, finished with two coats of Danish oil and lastly hand buffed with wax to a velvety smoothness. Size is 46 inches high by 30 inches wide by 40 inches deep; $1500 plus shipping. Others from $120 to $2200.

242 · WOOD

ROSANNE SOMERSON

173 Durnell Avenue
Roslindale, Massachusetts 02131

Rosanne Somerson designs and builds one-of-a-kind and limited production furniture that is clearly a successful fusing of ornament with function. "I try to establish a certain stance or character in the overall form of the piece," she says, "which I hope will become intimate company to those who live with it."

She especially enjoys designing "eclectic" pieces—vanities, night stands, entranceway tables, telephone tables, unusual storage boxes—"furniture pieces that have unique personalities." Much of her work has been tables or mirrors and often uses such materials as glass, leather, handmade paper or paint combined with the wood.

"Commercially available furniture has become so expensive that it is possible for the designer/builder to compete with what someone would buy in a quality furniture outlet," notes the twenty-eight-year-old designer. "A plus is that the handmade piece will most likely be better constructed and made with higher quality materials."

"The real advantage occurs," she says, "when you find someone whose imagination and aesthetic sense appeals to you. When you think that you can hire this person to make a special and unique piece for your particular space, the prospect of commissioning furniture becomes very exciting."

Rosanne received her fine arts degree in 1976 from the Rhode Island School of Design. She has been a self-employed furniture maker since 1978 and has held several teaching positions. She was an editorial staff member of *Fine Woodworking* magazine until 1981 and has had her work exhibited in numerous exhibitions throughout the East.

Brochure: No.
Commissions: Rosanne works primarily on a commission basis.
Studio Hours: By appointment.
Telephone: (617) 323-6320.

The "High-Heeled Coffee Table" is made of cherry and ebony with a glass top. The curved cherry rail that connects the legs is laminated and joined to the legs with a curved shoulder, multispline joint. These curved pieces support a double triangular form that sandwiches the round carved end disks. The corners of the top triangle that support the glass are cross-splined to add strength. Dimensions are 50 inches length, 19 inches width and 16¾ inches height. Similar work runs $1500 to $2400.

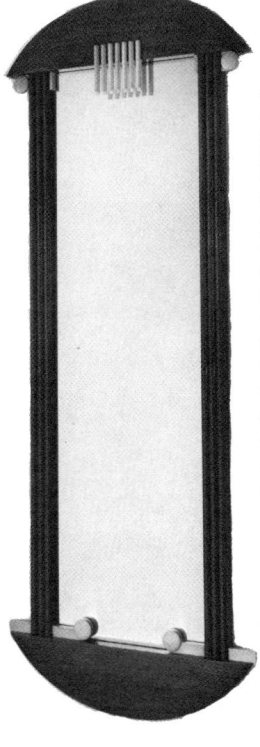

"Ever Wonder How You'd Look with Bangs?" is a full-length mirror made of Australian lacewood and holly. The holly splines at the corners are functional as well as decorative. They extend into mortises in each of the frame pieces, creating the joints, and are left oversized so that they can be carved and shaped to ornament the piece. This is a limited-production item and uses a variety of wood types. Dimensions are 62 inches high by 24 inches wide and 2½ inches deep. Price range is $795 to $1100.

Douglas P. Amidon

*Amidon & Co., Inc.
376 Route 130
Sandwich, Massachusetts 02563*

During Douglas Amidon's sixteen years as a professional woodcarver, he has built the growth of his craft business on three different activities, each of which has met with both artistic and commercial success.

First, there's his main occupation of handcarving wooden signs. Using traditional techniques coupled with modern design sensibilities, Doug carves elegant typography, logos and other embellishments into his signs, which are then finished with multiple coats of paint and often gold leaf. His distinctive signs attractively mark commercial and public locations throughout New England and especially his native Cape Cod.

The second leg of the business, his production series of "footstools," has met with widespread acceptance by people across the country who are amused by the silliness of this effective visual pun. As functional as they are whimsical, each stool has a plushly upholstered seat supported by a carved leg and foot encased in the shoestyle of your choice.

Third, his extraordinary one-of-a-kind and commissioned work has captured the fancy of numerous collectors and has included everything from sculptural woodcarvings to furniture pieces.

The thirty-eight-year-old woodcarver talks knowingly of his chosen medium. "It can be fickle or constant, surprising or dependable, beautiful or ordinary. Wood has a certain independence that requires that I work with it, adjusting my thoughts and techniques as a piece progresses.

"I know," he adds, "that the quality of my work will be the direct result of the skills, judgments and efforts brought to my workbench." Doug is a member of the Society of Cape Cod Craftsmen.

Brochure: Three separate flyers are available showing his one-of-a-kind work, footstool series and examples of signs.
Commissions: Although "volume is very limited," Doug welcomes inquiries.
Studio Hours: Summers only, 10 A.M. to 5 P.M. daily.
Telephone: (617) 888-0565.

The ultimate footstool is a production piece carved from pine and painted and plushly upholstered in varying fabrics and colors. "We can match most shoe and sneaker styles." Sizes range from 14 inches high (standard stool size) to 28 inches (bar-stool height); From $110 to $330.

This studio sign is carved of pine with gold leaf lettering and oil paints for other areas. The glass insert is by John Knight. It is one of dozens of possibilities in, and combinations of, type, shape, size, style and color of sign. Pictured sign is approximately $650.

David E. Friedline

6 Vernon Street
Somerville, Massachusetts 02145

"In today's world of mass production," says David Friedline, "the prevailing standard is 'good enough.' " Not so with David's furniture, where the term "absolute best" is more appropriate. "As I examine many fine examples of traditional furniture, I am in awe of what was routinely accomplished without the aid of woodworking machines," David told me. "I argue that with the machine at our disposal, our work today should be at least as fine."

In 1974, before he had started building furniture, David designed and built guitars and other stringed instruments. The work demanded that he use hand tools with a high degree of precision. "Stringed musical instruments must look and sound well," he explains, "as well as resist the self-destructive forces of taut strings."

It is this fine woodworking experience that he brings to his furniture. "A well-designed piece of furniture should fulfill its function," he says. " It should have sufficient strength for decades of service and should create a balanced visual effect compatible with both today's architecture and hopefully tomorrow's."

This philosophy has led the thirty-one-year-old furniture maker to explore a "more quiet approach" to style, which is in part inspired by the "timeless aspects of European, American and Oriental traditions." With a consistent mastery of detail, David develops each new design by building on a basic theme, which he then evolves into variations. Many of the final decisions on proportions and detail are made in the workshop during construction, adding a spontaneity to the finished piece. Says David: "My objective is to produce furniture which does not clash with or dominate its environment and remains visually interesting after first glance."

He is a member of the Society of Arts and Crafts in Boston, Concord Art Association and the American Craft Council.

Brochure: Yes.
Commissions: Custom inquiries for all kinds of furniture and modifications of present designs are welcome.
Studio Hours: Daily, 9 A.M. to 5 P.M. or by appointment.
Telephone: (617) 776-5200.

The writing desk and leather-upholstered chair are both made of American black cherry wood. Desk is 44 inches wide by 28 inches deep by 41 inches tall. The two pieces are $3200; chair is available for $575.

This time the desk-and-chair set is made of American black walnut and curly maple. The chair is upholstered in velvet. Desk is 46 inches wide by 25 inches deep by 29½ inches tall. The set is $2800; chair alone is $525. All work shown here is one of a kind/limited edition; design repeats are similar but not identical. Wood selection, overall dimensions and use requirements can be discussed. When ordering matched set of chairs discount 10 percent for two, 15 percent for three and 20 percent for four or more.

WILLIAM PATRICK AND LINDA GIVEN

Landscape Woodworks
272 Willow Avenue
Somerville, Massachusetts 02144

William Patrick discovered the wood lathe in 1973. He was, he recalls, "amazed" with the tool, having had many years of experience in woodcarving and constructing sculptural assemblages. He located one and bought it immediately. After overcoming some dubious initial instructions that had him trying to turn wood that was traveling in the wrong direction (away from him), he became hooked. He learned how to turn a rolling pin and, after much experimentation, how to keep a laminated rolling pin together while turning it. "Three workshops, nine years, a couple of hundred craft fairs and several thousand rolling pins later," he formed Landscape Woodworks with his partner, Linda Given.

To make their line of functional wooden objects, Bill and Linda first select and laminate unusual domestic and exotic species of wood into designs that suggest landscapes. They then form them into functional objects, such as cutting boards with the silhouette of a mountain under a full moon or rolling pins with contrasting moons and stars inlaid into the surface. Their series of six poem plates are graphically more complex. Each comes with a clear glass-plate insert and a poem by Bill relating to the title and design of that plate.

"We hope our work is at once stimulating and soothing," Bill told me. "Our landscape designs are meant as recognizable visual guides. The colors, varied grains and unique figures in the wood allow the viewer's imagination to amplify existing guides or to suggest whole new interpretations. It is this visual dialogue between our work and those who use it which gratifies us most."

Their landscape designs have been featured in national magazines and several exclusive mail-order catalogs and are sold in fine-craft and gift stores, galleries and museum shops around the country. Both Bill, thirty-three, and Linda, thirty-one, are members of the American Craft Council.

Brochure: A handsome and informative brochure will be sent on request.
Commissions: No.
Studio Hours: By appointment.
Telephone: (617) 628-1841.

The rolling-pin and cutting-board pieces are made from native woods as well as exotica — imbuya, a dark Brazilian wood is shown here. "The kitchen implements are designed to be used and when properly cared for will last a lifetime." Prices from $22 to $30.

"The Moon and the Lake" is one in a series of six poem plates. Laminations of curly maple, curly oak, imbuya, padouk and ebony are turned square on the lathe. Each plate has a poem to accompany it, written by Bill. Plate prices range from $75 to $150. Glass insert allows for convenient use as service plate. Pictured plate is $75; set of 4 for $260.

Ellen Mason and Dudley Hartung

Raccoon
20 Vernon Street
Somerville, Massachusetts 02145

The partners in Raccoon, Dudley Hartung, fifty-three, and Ellen Mason, forty, have been jointly designing and making one-of-a-kind and limited-edition furniture and accessories for more than ten years. They are both self-taught woodworkers who each spent fifteen years in other professions — Dudley an engineer and inventor and Ellen a research consultant — before they decided to do something "pleasanter for the mind."

Ellen and Dudley's studio is in a large old Somerville factory building, part of the Vernon Street Studios, which house about sixty other artists and artisans in two buildings. Most of their work is done to order. "We're often close and friendly with our clients," Dudley told me. "I enjoy most of my customers and like when they appreciate my furniture. It's an enjoyable experience when customers have made a commitment and we have fulfilled it."

Striving for "natural designs that are pleasing to the eye," they generally lean toward the curvilinear rather than the straight edge, often basing designs on the natural beauty of sine waves and the like. "We don't think of ourselves as sculptors," he says, "but we like to look at our work with a sculptor's eye." Much of their work is designed with a "purity and simplicity of line and design" that is their Western interpretation of time-honored Oriental principles.

Noting that the "grain determines the cut of the plane," Dudley explains that "materials should be used in a way that is compatible with the material. Wood is basically a linear material, gentle forms, lots of strength with a fair amount of bulk."

Dudley likes that nature of wood. "You have to force clay, glass and metal to do what you want. With wood you can only go so far. You make other materials flow; wood flows by itself and the design restraints should generally be incorporated and not fought."

Raccoon's work can be seen in their studio or in galleries and shows on the East Coast. They are members of the American Craft Council.

Brochure: No.
Commissions: "Whether you have a clear idea with many specifics or just need a fine table or whatever, we work with you to fulfill your needs."
Studio Hours: Open regular hours Monday through Friday but call in advance. Saturdays by appointment only.
Telephone: (617) 776-9110.

This Art Noveau inspired mahogany desk includes two file cabinets, two drawers and two open cubbyholes. There is also a secret compartment. 78 inches long; $4000.

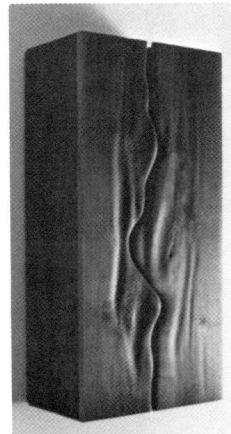

Wall-hung cabinet with carved front doors of highly figured American black walnut. The interior compartments are made of birdseye maple and house 265 tape cassettes. Height is 40 inches; $1500.

Gary Wright

Box 1661
Conway, New Hampshire 03818

Ask Gary Wright what he does for a living and he'll refer you to this definition from an 1839 issue of *"The Penny Magazine"*: "Marquetry is the art of assembling veneers from hundreds of species of wood, sometimes interspersed with gems, ivory, mother-of-pearl, etc. to collectively form a picture or design."

Gary, a fifty-three-year-old longtime woodworker and "deeply frustrated artist," is seeking to change marquetry's hobbycraft image. "Marquetry is an ancient art and craft, painstaking and difficult in its execution," he says. "It deserves a better consideration than it is now getting."

Landscapes form the bulk of his work as the woods naturally lend themselves to that, but Gary is intent on exploring the full capabilities of the medium. "I feel there are visual expressions that marquetry can enter outside the area of 'interesting decor.' I would like viewers to enjoy a work in its entirety rather than be fascinated by its construct of wood.

"In working with a piece," he explains, "I try to let the wood itself tell the story. The color and texture of the woods are always expressive and should be utilized to best advantage. Only natural woods, in their particular color, grain and figure are used to represent whatever the piece is to convey."

"It is an exciting craft and a fortunate juncture of interests," he told me. "It is my sincerest intent to be among the world's best." Gary is a member of the Marquetry Society of America and that of Great Britain, the League of New Hampshire Craftsmen and the Society of Arts and Crafts in Boston.

Brochure: Yes.
Commission: Yes.
Studio Hours: By appointment.
Telephone: (603) 447-2375.

"November Place" is a one-of-a-kind marquetry landscape and uses a variety of woods. "The old hill farms are lonely places and the people who carved them out are gone. The elms are dying and the apple trees and the barns, too." 28 inches long by 12 inches high; $750.

HOWARD HATCH

PO Box 281
North Conway, New Hampshire 03860

Howard Hatch began his career as a craftsman in 1972, when he decided somewhat abruptly that he wanted to go to school and learn to make furniture. To his great surprise, without the aid of a portfolio or relevant background, he was accepted at the Rochester Institute of Technology, where for the next three-and-one-half years, he "thrived on a diet of sawdust, 3-D design, art history and advice from a number of gifted teachers."

After graduation in 1974, armed with a fine-arts degree in woodworking and furniture design, and not much else, Howard struck out on his own. Soon he started doing locally commissioned work and selling through the shops of the League of New Hampshire Craftsmen. His career since then, he says, "has been a building process on many levels." Today, the thirty-three-year-old woodworker is kept busy with orders for residential and office furniture and retail items, all of which are designed to be "affordable, well made and personal."

Most of his work is commissioned, which Howard especially enjoys because of the nature of the client-designer relationship. When creating a new design, he first takes into consideration the client's special needs and the environment in which the piece will be used. During the refining process, he considers his own emotional reactions to the design of the piece, examining its proportion, grace, weight and strength before he finally settles on a final version. "My goal as a craftsman is to grow with each piece I make."

Howard's work has been featured in group and one-man shows throughout the Northeast. In 1981 he was commissioned to design and build two tables for the New Hampshire Governor's Council Chamber in the State House in Concord. He is a member of the League of New Hampshire Craftsmen.

Brochure: No.
Commissions: Nearly all work is commissioned and inquiries are welcomed.
Studio Hours: Monday through Saturday, 9 A.M. to 5 P.M.
Telephone: (603) 356-3929.

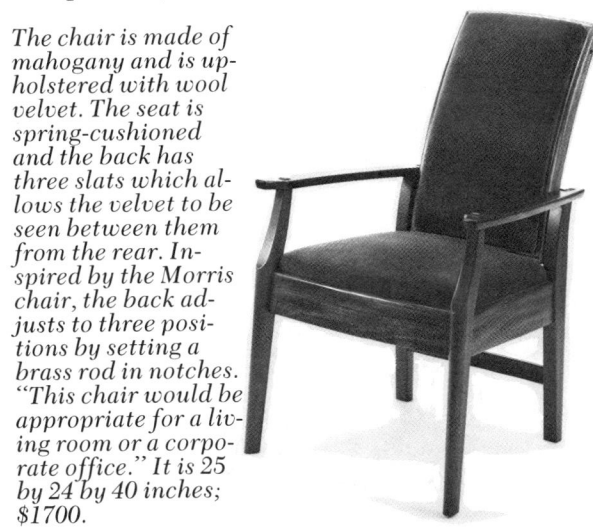

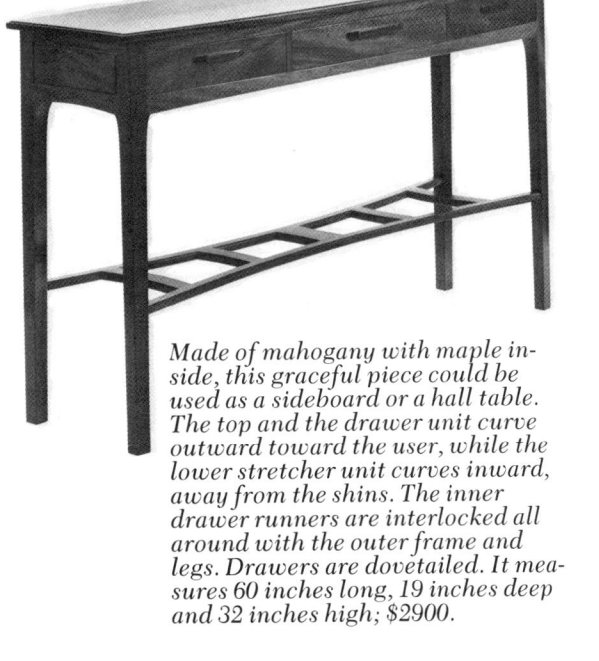

The chair is made of mahogany and is upholstered with wool velvet. The seat is spring-cushioned and the back has three slats which allows the velvet to be seen between them from the rear. Inspired by the Morris chair, the back adjusts to three positions by setting a brass rod in notches. "This chair would be appropriate for a living room or a corporate office." It is 25 by 24 by 40 inches; $1700.

Made of mahogany with maple inside, this graceful piece could be used as a sideboard or a hall table. The top and the drawer unit curve outward toward the user, while the lower stretcher unit curves inward, away from the shins. The inner drawer runners are interlocked all around with the outer frame and legs. Drawers are dovetailed. It measures 60 inches long, 19 inches deep and 32 inches high; $2900.

JAMES PRITCHARD

RFD 2, Boulder Drive
Petersborough, New Hampshire 03458

Before Jim Pritchard began woodcarving he had been a builder whose specialty was reproduction detail and millwork. Two years ago, during a lull between houses, he tried carving a pine figure in the manner of nineteenth-century trade figures. To Jim's great pleasure, somebody offered to buy it.

Encouraged by this early success, Jim continued to concentrate on his woodcarving. Today he carves many large, one-of-a-kind figures, including a series of rollicking satyrs, lighthearted and captivating figures with cloven feet. These creations are, he says, a fulfillment of one of his ambitions: "the portrayal of ugly people having a good time." He has also recently added a limited production line of smaller items, both figures and decorative accessories.

When Jim, forty, sets out to do a new project, he first develops the rough idea, maybe doing some sketches and patterns and then roughing out the figure. "During this stage," says Jim, "I feel I'm in complete control of the process." But about the time the final form begins to emerge, "the figure itself takes over and begins to dictate nuances of its own pose and expression. By the time the piece nears completion, it's the boss and I'm working for it."

In an effort to make his sculptures "rather relaxing to have around," Jim carves figures that are meant to appear "preoccupied with their own thoughts." "Even my still-life pieces have people implied in them, since most are articles of clothing meant to look as though they're about to be retrieved by its owner." After he carves the piece, his wife Laurel takes over, "contributing her considerable talents" to sanding, painting and finishing the work.

Brochure: A brochure of current designs is available for $2.00

Commissions: Half of his work is on a commission basis. Inquiries are invited. "I quote on commissions after receiving information on subject, costume, colors, etc."
Studio Hours: By appointment.
Telephone: (603) 563-8647.

"Cavalier" is the seventh large piece in Jim's satyr series. "They remind me of carnival animals in that they provide an opportunity for carved and painted decoration." This one-of-a-kind piece is representative of the series in size and price. Height is 64 inches including stand; $1500.

"New Shirt" is the first in a series of production items. "Struck by the similarity of a new, neatly packaged chamois shirt to a section of plank, I turned it into a box lid." The box is stained, the shirt is natural with a clear finish. 8 by 15¼ by 5¼ inches; $130.

AARON THOMAS BROWN

Wellspring Woodworks
Putnam Hill Road
South Lyndeboro, New Hampshire 03082

Aaron Brown makes three-dimensional wooden puzzles that he admits "can really frustrate people." But even though he's responsible for all those hapless souls, "it turns out well in the end, for they eventually get their puzzles back together again and a sense of order is restored to life."

One of the intriguing things about these hardwood puzzles is the amount of forms — up to thirty — that come out of one small space. "I have done a lot of abstract drawing," Aaron told me, "and cutting a puzzle on the bandsaw is quite similar; but instead of a pencil the saw blade is the drawing instrument." No templates are used in the process so the inner design of each puzzle is unique, containing pieces that often turn out to be small sculptures themselves.

When not making his puzzles, Aaron, twenty-seven, is a carpenter by trade. A sense of order and calm is what he seeks in life. "An important thing to me as a craftsperson and a human being is to be content with what I do and how I live; to accept life as meaningful. Recently I have come to see that I must stop questioning life, stop checking what I do and why I do it. With my mind cleared of such thinking and focused in the present, then even moving a dumptruck of sand from here to there, with a shovel, is no problem."

That sounds like good advice, coming from a man who makes truly exasperating puzzles.

Brochure: Yes.
Commissions: No.
Studio Hours: None.
Telephone: (603) 654-2933.

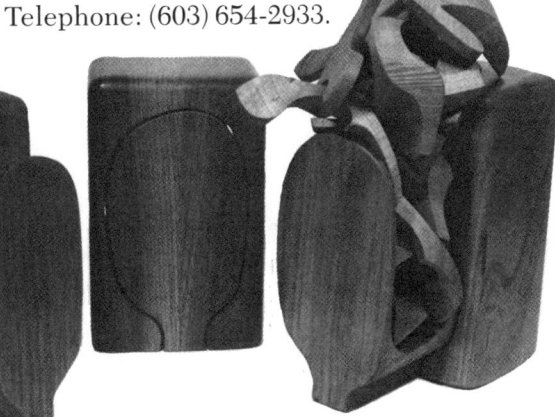

Tree-shaped puzzles contain about twenty interlocking inner pieces. Shown are red-mahogany partially opened puzzle on left; a black-walnut closed puzzle in center; and a cherry puzzle all mixed up on the right. Available in mahogany, oak, walnut and cherry. They measure 3½ inches high by 4 inches wide and 6 inches long; $38.

The flat walnut jigsaw puzzle is made of about thirteen interlocking wild animals. They all stand on their own as sculpture. The tray is made from a 1 inch-thick frame and a mahogany plywood bottom. Also in cherry. Measures 10 inches long by 8 inches wide; $36.

Lenore Howe and Brian Braskie

North Woods Chair Shop
RFD Province Road
Strafford, New Hampshire 03884

"Though I've always objected to the idea that one might be defined to any great extent by what one does for work," says Brian Braskie, "it is with some pleasure that I apply the term 'chairmaker' to my partner, Lenore Howe, and to me."

Lenore, thirty-five, and Brian, thirty-six, have been "life-partners" for nearly twenty-four years, sharing between them an array of business skills and artistic experiences. "It would be as difficult to define precisely when dawn becomes day as it would be now to clarify our reasons for believing that we could work wood into extraordinary chairs," Brian told me. There is, however, no difficulty in citing influences on their meticulously hand-turned and finished furniture. "It has been steadfast and simple," he declares. "It is Shaker."

Their preference for Shaker-influenced styles derives from the style's "honest joinery, the comfort of the designs and the 'intelligence' inherent in chairs that blend well with any decor." While noting that their appreciation of the Shakers has not been "particularly religious or academic," the partners point out that they believe, as did the Shakers, that "extraordinary things can be accomplished by ordinary people, who put their hands to work and their hearts to God."

Both partners are members of the League of New Hampshire Craftsmen and have their furniture represented in several exhibitions and museums. "We will continue to make furniture for the minority of individuals who still find quality within their grasp, and more, find it necessary in their lives."

Brochure: A free brochure showing their chair styles is available on request. Full-color photos and a handsome brochure with tape/stain samples is available for 2 dollars.
Studio Hours: Workshop is closed to the public, but a "pretty-well-stocked" showroom is open anytime by chance or appointment.
Telephone: (603) 664-9594.

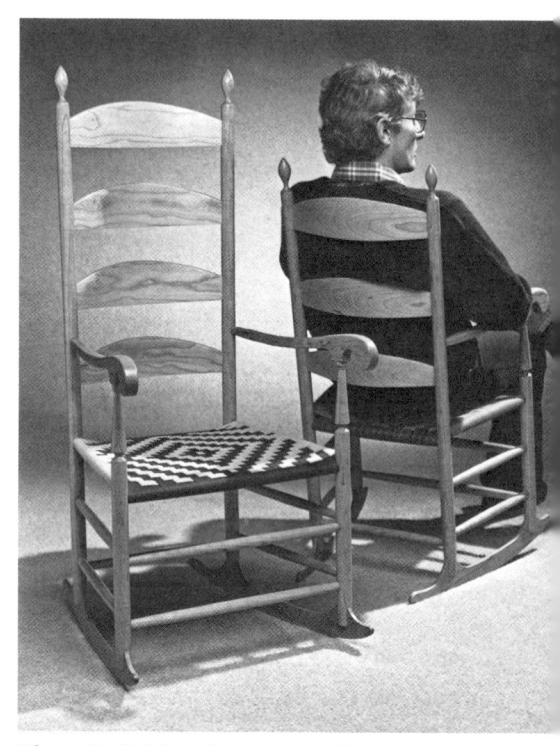

These Enfield rockers are made in both four-slat and three-slat sizes and are extremely comfortable. Made of either cherry or maple, the large rocker is 47 inches high, 23¼ inches wide and 15½ inches deep with a seat height of 16 inches. With a Shaker-style woven tape seat it's $350; with a caned seat, $385. The small rocker can also be made in either cherry or maple and is 40 inches high, 21 inches wide and 14½ inches deep with a 16-inch seat height. Taped seat, $295; caned $325. Shipping additional.

CAL AND RICK SCHNEIDER

RD 2, Box 238-6
Bristol, Vermont 05443

Rick and Cal Schneider's father was, in their words, "a man of tools," who taught his sons the proper use of and respect for tools. It is not surprising that the brothers, now thirty-three and thirty-eight, express a "reverence" for tools and their utility that has deepened throughout their many years of working with wood.

Both Rick and Cal started making their livings with tools first as carpenters and later as fine woodworkers. Each brother had followed his own path. In 1976, Cal was in Vermont finishing work on a sailboat of his design while Rick was in western New York making carved and inlaid furniture. One of Rick's major efforts had been the nearly 600 hours that he spent building an ornately turned spiral staircase made of oak.

Finally fate and shared interests brought the brothers together. "We had such common interests and had always enjoyed collaborating on projects," remembers Cal, "that in 1977 we built a shop together in Monkton, Vermont. It is a sunny, passive-solar building that is very conducive to good feelings about our work."

The Schneider brothers do primarily commissioned, one-of-a-kind design/build projects, including architectural woodworking, fine furniture and small personal items. Working either from their own measurements or from an architect's blueprints, they do woodworking that they stress emphasizes "detail, innovative problem solving, and sensitive, functional design."

Brochure: No.
Commissions: The majority of their work is by commission.
Studio Hours: By appointment.
Telephone: (802) 453-3651.

Oak circular stairs with second-floor landing. "We design and build staircases from simple to ornate in any shape and size." Pictured stairs are 4 feet wide and 9½ feet high; $7500.

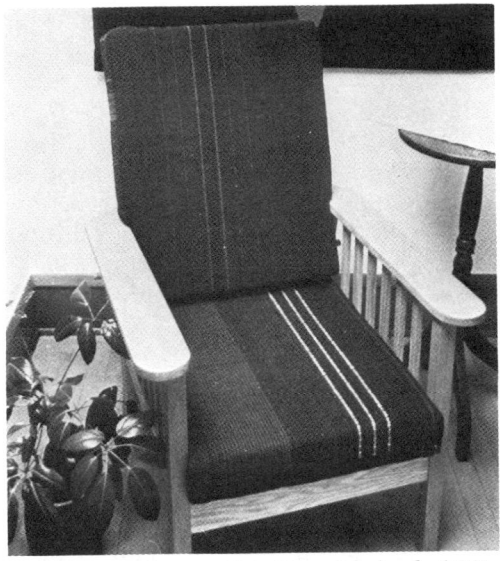

Oak Morris chair with adjustable back; $450.

TIMOTHY FISHER

RFD
Craftsbury Common, Vermont 05827

Tim Fisher has artfully joined both his interests in furniture design and sculpture into his carved-wood sculptural tables. The tables, which have handcarved sculptural bases and a smoothly finished wood or glass top, are made in a variety of woods.

"I prefer working with wood more than any other material," Tim told me. "It fits right in with my lifestyle. When you make maple syrup, you're always improving the sugar bush and cutting dead trees. I'm always looking for especially large or interesting stumps and logs for carving." Tim also arranges for the milling of the logs he cuts into boards for table tops and other furniture projects.

"I've always been attracted to sculpture," he says, "but making something that's both functional and sculptural is very appealing to me."

Tim's first professional experience as a woodworker was as an apprentice to a furniture maker in Putney, Vermont. He later studied furniture making, sculpture and architecture at Rhode Island School of Design, earning his bachelors degree in fine arts in 1977. While at RISD, Tim built his first sculptural table for himself. People saw it, liked it and started to offer him commissions to make others. His path was set.

"Most people don't have room for a sculpture in their houses," says the thirty-two-year-old woodworker. "But they do have room for a table that's also a sculpture in their dining rooms." No dining room? No problem. Tim also enjoys making sculptural furniture such as coffee tables or benches by special order. He works mostly in native New England hardwood—maple, black cherry, elm, birch, beech, ash—whatever's available in the area.

Tim especially likes carving elm, which he predicts will soon be a rare and coveted wood as more old elms succumb to disease. "It's a stringy, fibrous wood," he explains. "For the same reason that it's hard to split cleanly, it makes a good carving wood for sculpture." He also uses a lot of cherry, which is widely favored for its rich, warm color, but he will consider using any wood desired. "I'll use exotic hardwood or anything that the client wants."

Tim lives with his wife, Kathleen, a painter, in northern Vermont. In addition to working on his furniture, he teaches art, has written several books and tends to his maple-syrup farm.

Brochure: Yes.
Commissions: Yes. "The client specifies the size and often the materials to be used. I keep an inventory of logs and stumps for carving so a client is welcome to pick through them with me."
Studio Hours: By appointment.
Telephone: (802) 586-2216.

This coffee table is representative of Tim's sculpture but is unusual in that it is made of native New Zealand woods gathered during a recent stay. The oval top is made of rimu and is 27 by 39 inches diameter. The 19-inch high base is Tasmanian blackwood; $800.

DAVID SAWYER

RD 1, Box 107
East Calais, Vermont 05650

David Sawyer had been a mechanical engineer for many years until one day he realized that he wanted something more from his labors. "I found that I wanted to use my hands and heart as well as my head," he recalls. So he turned to woodworking and for the last fourteen years has made thousands of wooden pitchforks, hundreds of ladderback chairs and many other pieces including apple-picking ladders, tables and wood carriers. Windsor chairs are his most recent endeavor and one of the forty-six-year-old woodworker's most satisfying yet.

"I like the unity of making beautiful, comfortable chairs from trees that grow in the woods here," he says. "Each chair is a miracle." Except for a little powered-lathe work and sawing, Dave makes his chairs in the manner of the best old Windsors of some 200 years ago, using careful handwork—shaving, carving, turning, bending and fittings, then usually finishing his pieces with milk paint, which he rubs and oils to a fine finish. "The old chairs were painted and I prefer mine that way as it unifies the design," he says. Chairs can also be finished in clear oil or sold "in the wood."

The designs are traditional but not exact copies. "I don't try to be original," David says. "Inspiration comes from fellow craftsmen past and present, customer's needs and a continuous process of learning by doing."

David emphasizes that he strives for quality throughout his work. "I give a lifetime guarantee: The chair will outlast either myself or the original owner."

Brochure: A brochure with drawings and photos and a milk-paint color sample card will be sent for $1, credited toward your first order.
Commissions: Yes, custom Windsor chairs or reproductions of old Windsors.
Studio Hours: By appointment.
Telephone: (802) 456-8836.

Comb-back chair has a pine seat, maple turnings and a back of ash, ironwood and maple. The finish is milk paint, black-on-red, rubbed through and Watco oiled. 45 inches high; $480.

Balloon-back chair also has a pine seat with maple turnings and an ash back. It is stained and oiled. "This is a copy of an old Federal period 'bamboo' chair which I repaired." Height 36 inches; $275.

JEFFREY C. PARSONS

RD Box 130
Hinesburg, Vermont 05461

Jeff Parsons says that he first began to develop a strong interest in woodworking in the early Seventies while he was working for a company that made reproductions of gold-front-banjo and girandole clocks. In 1975 he applied, and was accepted, to Boston University's Program in Artisanry's four-year wood program. After graduation he held a couple of jobs before opening his own workshop in Shelburne Farms, Vermont, in 1982.

"Both my custom and production work represent an integration of initial concept, technique and joinery," says the twenty-six-year-old woodworker. "My concepts tend to be simple, clean-lined, direct and functional." To Jeff function is the primary consideration and affects everything else about the piece. "How the piece can fulfill its function most effectively dictates its design, the utilization of joinery and the materials used." As a result his work has fewer curves these days. "Things are a lot more direct today than they were several years ago. The process dictates how things are looking, all within the framework of functionality."

Most of Jeff's work is commissioned, but he is working to develop a production line that he hopes will develop into a solid and consistent area. "A production line expansion would allow the shop to support itself so that production items would happen without some of the pressures that now occur."

Jeff is a member craftsman of the Vermont State Craft Center at Frog Hollow and the American Craft Council. He received his fine arts degree in furniture design and construction from Boston University in 1979.

Brochure: No.
Commissions: Most work is custom ordered.
Studio Hours: By appointment.
Telephone: (802) 985-2913.

Plant hanger is a production item and is available in all domestic hardwoods. It has an estimated load limit of 80 pounds. It is 12½ inches high; $40.

Mahogany desk was designed to wrap around the person seated behind it, making more surface area accessible. It has six drawers and the top is in two pieces for structural as well as aesthetic reasons. It is 5½ feet long and 29½ inches high; $3750.

EDWARD LOEWENTON

Elwood Turner
PO Box 302
Johnson, Vermont 05656

Ed Loewenton is one artisan who doesn't like to use the word "craft" when describing his occupation. "Frankly, I stay away from that word," he says. "I practice an old-fashioned *trade* in the classical sense. After seven years of doing nothing but woodturning, I'm beginning to feel slightly competent. I might have learned faster but I was apprenticed to an ignoramus: myself." Today, he says, he can get his woodturning students to do in two hours what it took him three months to learn.

Ed, a thirty-eight-year-old dropout from a doctoral program at an Ivy League school, prefers to label himself an "industrial designer, a product engineer, a professional woodturner, and hopefully, always an artist." He produces a line of turned-wood objects that includes baby rattles, rolling pins, honey servers, lamps, folk toys, candleholders and a mortar-and-pestle set. "I try to make products offering an alternative to machine-made goods. Not that there is anything wrong with machine-made goods," he emphasizes.

Noting that he is not one for the "fashionable jargon used as space filler in the artsy crafts mags," he says that it would be irrelevent for him to discuss the motivating aesthetic principles behind his work. "The viewer might have another opinion," he explains. "You either like what you see or you don't.

"Ah, but functional! That's something else! How long will it last? How well does the piece do its intended job? How does it fit the hand? How well balanced is it? Does it become one with the user or is it put aside, reluctantly?

"A person should buy a few things, carefully, use them skillfully and with understanding and keep them," he says. "It is my hope that my products be so honored by their owners." Ed is a member of Hollow State Craft Center in Middlebury, Vermont.

Brochure: An eight-page brochure of his complete product line is available.
Commissions: Yes, "anything round and made of wood. Also product prototypes, working models, architectural work and patterns for ceramic and metal casting."
Studio Hours: None.
Telephone: (802) 635-7433.

Turned beer mugs are shown in cherry, left, and a one-of-a-kind walnut/spalted birch. Available in cherry or walnut/oak or special order woods, the porcelain-lined mugs hold approximately 13½ ounces. They come gift boxed and are 6 inches high by 4½ inches wide; from $60 each.

Wine goblets are walnut and maple and have a 24-karat gold overglaze. They are lined with porcelain and hold 5½ ounces. Attractively gift boxed either singly or in pairs, they stand about 10½ inches high; $45 each. Other woods from $40 each (without gold band).

John C. Sollinger

*Vermont Sled Co.
RD 1, Box 235
North Ferrisburg, Vermont 05473*

John Sollinger has been working wood in one form or another since he left college in 1970. His experience has encompassed everything from a nine-year stint as a professional luthier to building a post-and-beam barn from timber on his own land.

In addition to his current line of toys, mainly sleds and rocking farm animals, John, thirty-six, tries to do as wide a variety of custom woodwork as time permits. "I feel that a small shop such as Vermont Sled Company is better suited to building high-quality items in limited numbers for sale to select markets rather than trying to compete with more mass-produced toys from larger shops.

"I make every effort to keep my level of workmanship high and my designs unique, beautiful, functional and rugged enough to last for generations. Each reflects the fine woodworking skills and interest in historical tradition that led to the creation of the company."

John started his company in 1981. It became a full-time business in mid-1982. "I feel it is important to integrate my working life with my family life," John told me. "My home life includes my wife and daughter who give much assistance and inspiration, and a small farm that provides most of our food and is a good design source for the toys I build."

John is a member of the Frog Hollow State Craft Center and Vermont Handcrafters, Inc.

Brochure: Yes.
Commission: Yes.
Studio Hours: None.
Telephone: (802) 425-2536.

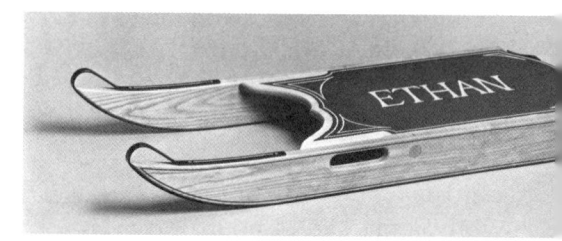

The Vermont sled can be personalized as shown with your child's name or with a snowflake. It is constructed of painted pine and steel-shod ash runners. "Rugged enough to provide years of hard sledding yet attractive enough to be used for decorating." Available in red, blue and green. Height 5 inches, width 13 inches, length 39 inches; $110.

Rocking holstein has a high-gloss enamel finish that is durable, child safe and easy to clean. Blossom, named after the Sollingers' cow, is large enough for children from 1 to 4 and sturdy enough for older kids. Height 21 inches, width 14 inches, length 38 inches; $300.

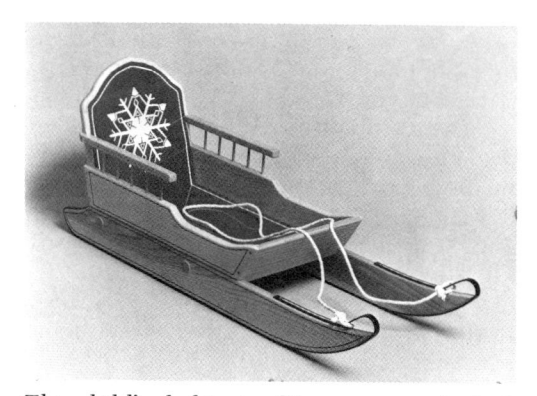

This child's sled is sturdily constructed of ash and painted pine with steel shoes on the runners. It carries children from infancy to about 3 years old and is available in red, blue and green. Height 15 inches, width 13 inches, length 39 inches; $220.

David I. Steckler

*Fine Woodworks
RD 2, PO Box 480
Plainfield, Vermont 05667*

David Steckler initially became interested in woodworking in the early Seventies while serving as a Peace Corp forester in West Africa. Stationed for two years in a remote part of Liberia, his job included overseeing several European logging companies. One of those companies employed a Liberian woodworker whose only job was to build furniture for the European employees' homes. David came to be a great admirer of the man's woodworking skills and shortly found himself spending more of his time after work in the shop. Eventually a close friendship was born and David began to design and build his own furniture in the shop.

After his Liberian assignment ended, David spent three more years in the Peace Corps, before deciding in 1979 to quit forestry and pursue woodworking fulltime. After attending a furniture-design school, David joined a small cooperative woodworking shop in Central Vermont, where he still builds his one-of-a-kind furniture and other craft items. "My formal training in woodworking has been rather traditional in the sense that we were drilled with developing an uncompromising eye for perfection—cutting sloppy dovetails would not do," says the thirty-three-year-old woodworker. "I would never compromise my construction ethics for the sake of form. They must both be in harmony before it leaves the drafting table."

David, who describes his furniture as "generally very linear, not too much sculpture, verging on Scandinavian," uses mostly local woods such as butternut, ash, elm, cherry, maple and mahogany. But he maintains a special fondness for exotic woods, having been exposed to more than 200 varieties of native hardwoods while in Liberia, and uses them whenever he can.

"My clients want something more in tune with their lifestyle other than commercially made furniture," he says, noting "I sell to young professionals a lot. They seem to enjoy the process." David is a member of the American Craft Council and Frog Hollow in Middlebury, Vermont.

Brochure: No.
Commissions: Most of his work is custom but he'll reproduce work with customer's specifications in mind.
Studio Hours: Monday through Friday from 9 A.M. to 5 P.M.
Telephone: (802) 456-7440.

Hotplate of walnut with a Vermont green-marble inset top is handcarved, sanded and then rubbed with four coats of tung oil-varnish. This one-of-a-kind piece could be reproduced on commission. It is 2 inches high, 16 inches long and 6 inches deep; $85.

This writing desk of walnut and cherry is one of a kind and has seventy handcut, decorative dovetails in both the desk and its small carcase, which is easily removed from the top. Dimensions are 32 inches deep by 50 inches long by 30 inches high; $3500.

ROBERT F. OLSON

PO Box 451
Putney, Vermont 05346

"Mankind has been building furniture for over 4,000 years and all of the good ideas have been tried," says furniture maker Robert Olson. "So the creativity usually means combining ideas and refining lines and profiles until you have it the way you want it."

Most of Bob's work is movable furniture from a portfolio of designs that he's developed over the past five years. His larger pieces are individually made; the smaller ones made in series of six to twelve. "When I design any piece of furniture I want it to be useful, sturdy and good looking." Usefulness is the primary consideration. "A good piece should perform a service," he says, "by providing a seat or a working surface, by holding a mattress level and off the floor or by storing goods.

"If after it has done that it also delights the eye, then so much the better," says the thirty-two-year-old woodworker. "And therein lies the art of furniture making: combining the functional with the beautiful."

Bob gets ideas from the furniture he sees in houses, in museums and from pictures in books. In particular, he likes the "cleanness of line and the simplicity of shape" of Shaker furniture.

"With limited care, a well-designed and finely constructed piece of furniture will be of use for many years and many generations. It is a sound investment, it will always please the eye and it is a reflection of your own personal taste." Bob is a member of Putney Artisan's League. His work has been shown at the Brattleboro Art Museum and has been featured in *The New York Times* Home Section and the Fall 1983 Bonwit Teller catalog.

Brochure: Sixteen items are illustrated in a foldout brochure.
Commissions: Yes. Custom furniture, built-in cabinets and interiors of his own design.
Studio Hours: By appointment.
Telephone: (802) 387-4288.

Cherry crib has mitered mortise-and-tenon joints and is easily knocked down for transporting. The front side of the crib folds up and down. This crib stands 48 inches high, 34 inches wide and 54 inches long; $750.

This hanging clock is of cherry wood with an enamel face and a fourteen-day "bim-bam" chiming movement. Other movements and chimes are available. Height 29 inches, width 15 inches, depth 6 inches; $395.

260 · WOOD

Gordon H. B. Bretschneider

Bretschneider & Bretschneider
Box 12, School Street
Shoreham, Vermont 05770

"I was going to be a bookbinder," recalls retired banker Gordon Bretschneider, "then I was introduced to the dovetail joint." That was in 1971 and Gordon, now seventy, has been making fine furniture ever since. Basing his work on "the great antiques of yesteryear," he creates classic furniture whose traditional designs have been adapted to "current living needs."

"I like certain proportions and forms," he explains. "If you clean up Chippendale decoration, you have something very nice." He designs, he says, "by theft and serendipity, interested suggestions and client input."

Gordon makes his furniture primarily from Honduras mahogany, which he favors for its beauty and versatility. Traditional fine joinery and a variety of colors and finishes are used throughout his work. "The finish we have developed is soft, warm and smooth and glows with four coats of oil." Each piece is wet-sanded before staining, producing a surface that's resistant to damage from hot and cold water or alcohol.

"We derive great satisfaction from knowing our furniture is well made and will stand the test of time," says Gordon. He teaches both in his shop and at Frog Hollow Craft Center.

Brochure: No.
Commissions: "We do like commission work. Our patrons are usually intelligent, interesting people. Each brings their own touch and wishes to the process."
Studio Hours: By appointment. Usually open Tuesday through Saturday.
Telephone: (802) 897-2621.

Tall case clock of Honduras mahogany with hand-painted dial. The wood is colored chemically, wet-sanded to a soft, warm and smooth finish and rubbed with four coats of oil. "This finish seems to be impervious to water and alcohol from all the tests we have given it." Eight-day movements with chimes are imported from West Germany with either chain or cable drive. Height of clock can vary; this clock is 7 feet 9 inches tall; $3950.

This slant-top desk is made of Honduras mahogany with oak and birch plywood as secondary woods. Large drawers have handcut dovetail joints. Drawer fronts have a cocked-bead edging. Desk is 36 inches wide, 20 inches deep and 42 inches high; the writing surface is 30 inches high; $3725.

Ronald Voake

R. Voake, Toymaker
Route 113
Thetford Center, Vermont 05075

Ronald Voake makes wooden toys that are meant to endure, not only because they are structurally sound, but because they are also a "pleasing thing of beauty to the child." His toys, he says, "are made for the child to experience 'value.'"

Ron constructs the toys entirely from hardwoods, using mostly cherry and beech. Working with one or two designs at a time, he builds a pair of each over two or three days, putting much care into the details and the finishing in an effort to create something "pleasing to the eye and touch but nevertheless exceptionally sturdy."

The thirty-seven-year-old craftsman began making wooden toys in 1970 while still employed as a school teacher. He began making the toys as a hobby, giving them to his wife to use in her classroom devoted to children with learning and emotional problems. "My first efforts met with disastrous results," Ron says, "as they were returned to me in pieces after one combat day in class."

Today he works full time to produce a line of about one hundred sturdy and well-designed toys, ranging from cars, trucks and trains to rocking animals and block sets. "I work alone in my shop and the continuity of the process is one which I hope is translated materially in the finished work."

Brochure: A full-color flyer listing his many designs is available for 60 cents and a self-addressed-stamped envelope.
Commissions: No.
Studio Hours: Usually 10 A.M. to 5 P.M. every day, but call first.
Telephone: (802) 785-2837.

The giant engine and coal car is constructed from select beech and cherry. "A riding toy that two children can enjoy together." For 2½ years old and up. It is 54 inches long, 12½ inches high and 9 inches wide; $110.

Bulldozer is also of select beech and has cherry treads. It rolls easily on concealed wheels and is for children 3 years old and up. 24 inches long, 12½ inches high; $95.

These rugged hardwood toys are carefully sanded to ease all edges and are covered with a natural nontoxic urethane finish. All joints are screwed and glued for durability.

The large rocking horse is made of select beech with cherry accents for the mane and movable tail. For riders 2 years old and up. It is 31 inches long, 28 inches high; $120.

Fairs

INTRODUCTION

There is no better way to experience the richness and diversity of the contemporary craft scene than to attend a craft fair.

I am not talking here about the typical charity bazaar or flea market. Although you'll occasionally find an emerging talent or a local professional who's helping out for the cause, most often these events are open to anyone who pays the booth fee. Consequently, there's a lot of "noncrafts" on display, along with the work of hobbyists — pressed and dried flowers, calico, decoupage, greenware and similar work.

I have also not listed the many commercially produced arts and crafts shows, which take place year-round, either outdoors or, often, in an indoor shopping mall or similar building. The crafts at these events can vary from flea-market quality to professional, depending on the popularity of the fair and the jurying standards used for participation. Many top professional craftspeople tend to avoid these events, which generally offer a wide mix of work from painters, hobbyists and mall-show crafters who specialize in highly commercial, often ticky-tacky work. Some commercial promoters do present consistently professional quality shows, but they are the exception to the rule.

What *is* listed here are seven of the best and most comprehensive juried craft fairs in New England. Most are sponsored by nonprofit crafts support organizations. They are serious and traditional craft fairs where the crafts themselves are the stars of the show.

I've also included two fairs that are not exclusively devoted to crafts. One is a well-regarded multi-arts event, the other a Renaissance festival. Both emphasize the participation of professional craftspeople as part of their attractions.

Some notes and advice regarding the listed fairs:

Each of these events is scheduled on an annual basis. Since the actual dates may vary from year to year, it is suggested that you call or write the sponsor of the fair for specifics.

All the fairs listed here are juried according to strictly professional standards of workmanship, design and materials. You will not find such things as kits, embellished items, stones or shells, at these events. All the fairs have a high ratio of applicants to booth availabilities — usually from two to five applicants for each spot. The higher the competition among craftspeople for a booth, the higher the quality of the crafts you will see at the fair.

If you've been to flea markets or antique shows, you know that haggling over price is an accepted practice at those events. Not so at these craft fairs. Craftspeople set their prices according to competition, market demand, cost of materials, time, and training. They have one price for all parties. By dickering over price, you are, in effect, adversely commenting on the craftsperson's ability and talent. Don't do it.

Craftspeople do, however, enjoy feedback from fair visitors on their work and will happily answer questions about process, technique, materials, or whatever. They are friendly folks and one of the nice things about these fairs is the interaction that takes place between craftspeople and fair visitors, so don't be afraid to ask away. Fairs are also a good place to ask about commissioned work created to your specifications.

You will find primarily functional work at the fairs. The reason is simple: They sell best. One exception is the American Craft Council Fair at West Springfield, where there is a wider range, although functional items still predominate.

Naturally, food is available at all the fairs. Depending on the imagination of the promoter, everything from franks and burgers to tabouleh and tacos can be found.

One final note: These fairs are excellent opportunities to find newly emerging talent. Many craftspeople, once their work has become popular, find that they have all the business that they can accommodate and so they cut down or eliminate fairs from their marketing efforts. Conversely, these fairs are often the first place a new talent will attempt to break into when trying to market their crafts on a professional level. Work by new craft professionals is often lower-priced than it will be once they're established and market demand spurs higher pricing.

CONNECTICUT

GUILFORD HANDCRAFTS EXPOSITION
Guilford Green
Guilford, Connecticut

The historic Guilford town green is the locale for this popular craft fair, which was established in 1957. Five hundred craftspeople from across the country compete for the 108 available booths, which are set up under seven large tents on the green.

The prestigious fair attracts 20,000 to 25,000 people annually. "Visitors know that the quality of crafts here is high, that what they buy will be something of value," observes Fernn Hubbard, the director of the Guilford Handcrafts Center. "It's an enjoyable, educational experience."

Fair applicants submit five slides, which are juried by a committee of craftspeople chosen from the previous year's exhibitors. One indicator of the fair's popularity with craftspeople is that generally all of the previous year's exhibitors apply again for the next year's fair.

Crafts exhibited here include wooden accessories, blown and stained glass, pottery, silk screening, fibers (weaving, quilts, soft sculpture and batik), toys, metals, jewelry and leather. Past fairs have usually included an herbalist and one exhibitor who does a brisk business in cut-paper silhouettes.

There are regularly scheduled craft demonstrations by Handcrafts Center students and faculty as well as periodic performances by jazz and folk musicians and other performers.

Guilford has numerous pre-Revolutionary houses that have been restored to their original beauty. During the fair several of the historic buildings are open to the public.

When: Mid-July on Thursday through Saturday.
Where: On the Guilford town green.
Hours: Noon to 9 P.M.
Directions: Take Exit 58 from I-95 and proceed south on Route 77 to the green.
Admission: Adults, $2.
For more information: Guilford Handcrafts, Inc., P.O. Box 221, Guilford, Connecticut 06437. Telephone: (203) 453-5947.

NEW ENGLAND ARTIST FESTIVAL
Arts Extension Service
University of Massachusetts
Amherst, Massachusetts

"We try to distinguish ourselves from a typical craft fair," says Pam Korza, director of the New England Artist Festival. "We try to show the artistic process in all the categories that we have, from traditional to progressive art forms. It's a real inside look at art form through process, and an overview of what's happening in New England in all art."

Established in 1976 by the Arts Extension Service, the New England Artist Festival is billed as the largest and most comprehensive multi-arts event in New England. An estimated 600 artists — including more than 100 craftspeople — display, sell and perform their art for the 15,000 people who visit the UMass campus over the festival weekend.

Besides the craftspeople participants, other visual artists, musicians, dancers, singers, filmmakers and writers participate in the festival, which takes place in tents, on performance stages, in permanent campus buildings and outdoors.

The exhibiting craftspeople are selected by a board of twelve expert craft artisans and professional craft program administrators who suggest exhibitors according to criteria established by the festival committee. The 100 invited craftspeople-exhibitors display their work under a large tent in traditional craft-fair style.

The distinctive crafts on display include furniture, turned and carved wood, leather cloth-

New England Artist Festival

265 · FAIRS

MASSACHUSETTS

ing and accessories, pottery (stoneware, porcelain, raku), weaving, quilts, basketry, soft sculpture, batik, silkscreen, glass (blown, stained, etched), jewelry, pewter, blacksmithing, musical instruments, dolls, knitting and crochet.

Throughout the festival, another half-dozen craftspeople demonstrate their work for fairgoers. Demonstrations range from musical instrument building to stagecoach restoration, from papermaking to boatbuilding and kitemaking.

Another festival component that spotlights New England craftspeople is the Living Art Treasures program. Six of the region's artists and craftspeople "whose contributions to their discipline have brought them respect and recognition by other artists, collectors and arts appreciators," give slide presentations and talks during the festival. In 1983, the first year of this program, four of the honored were craftspeople: a glass sculptor, a woodturner, a potter, and a wood engraver/bookmaker.

The work of the honored artists and craftspeople is presented in a special exhibit, which is part of an invitational gallery show of painting, printmaking, sculpture and non-functional craft by about thirty-five other artists.

Throughout the festival grounds, large-scale outdoor art pieces are displayed as part of the Major Works program. About ten projects are accepted from the more than fifty proposals submitted to the festival committee. In the past, visitors have seen forty-foot-high inflatable sculpture, and work made of neon, metal, Plexiglas, wood, and even one made entirely of multi-colored glucose.

There is also a Performance Showcase, which comprises a continuous schedule of performances by fifty professional, New England-based groups and individuals in music, dance and theater. About 200 to 250 performers present their acts on three stages — everything from classical guitar duos to opera, bluegrass to jazz and folk music, comedy and drama, and contemporary dance and ballet are presented.

The diverse roster at the festival also includes: The New England Neighborhood Program, exhibits and performances of the work of about 300 community-based artists; the New England Film Festival, a continuous screening of the films of seventy-five regional, independent and student filmmakers; a series of poetry readings; a small press exhibition; children's theater; and a popular-artist evening concert featuring nationally known performers.

When: An early weekend in June.
Where: In and around the Fine Arts building at the UMass campus in Amherst.
Hours: Saturday, 11 A.M. to 7 P.M.; Sunday, 11 A.M. to 6 P.M.
Directions: From I-91, take the Amherst/Route 9 exit. Follow the prominently posted signs to the UMass campus.
Admission: Adults, $4; children under 12, 75 cents.
For more information: Arts Extension Service, University of Massachusetts, Amherst, Massachusetts 01003. Telephone: (413) 545-2360.

KING RICHARD'S FAIRE
The New England Renaissance Festival
Route 58
South Carver, Massachusetts

About sixty craftspeople take part each year in The New England Renaissance Festival. But crafts are not the main attraction at this fair: An atmosphere of merriment and rollicking entertainments are what draw the crowds to this recreation of a 16th century English marketplace.

Fairs became popular during the Renaissance period in Europe when farmers, peddlers and townsfolk gathered periodically to barter livestock and goods. As these gatherings grew, so did the accompanying pageantry. Actors, minstrels and vagabonds of all kinds came to entertain, swindle and monger the large crowds.

It is the festive spirit of these gatherings — minus the swindling — that is so artfully packaged by the promoters of King Richard's Faire. More than 80,000 people visit the festival each year.

"Fun for all is not at a premium at our Faire,"

King Richard's Faire

MASSACHUSETTS

notes Robert Fox, crafts coordinator for the festival. The fair takes place over seven fall weekends on a wooded, twenty-eight acre site dotted with numerous medieval-style structures.

The craftspeople — known as merchants of the realm — sell their wares from permanent booths built to resemble 16th century Tudor craft shops. The structures, some of which are two stories with balcony and sleeping quarters, are a combination of both historically accurate and fanciful designs. All the fair's artisans and entertainers are costumed in Renaissance-style dress.

Craftspeople are juried into the fair for a period of three years. They must either build their own structure or purchase one from its previous owner. The number of craftspeople in any one medium is limited to three and craft items must be something that could have been made during the Renaissance.

Crafts offered include leather, jewelry, musical instruments such as flutes and dulcimers, pottery, batik, wooden toys, soft sculpture, stained glass, puppetry, macrame, quilting, doll making, silkscreening, blacksmithing, calligraphy, Renaissance clothing, and clay sculpture. Two especially popular items are clay jester's heads and beribboned lace crowns. Other merchants include astrologers, a face painter, an herbalist, a portraitist and a foot masseuse.

Although the style of crafts offered here is limited compared to contemporary fairs, the quality of craftsmanship is good and the spirit of fun is decidedly in abundance. Many of the artisans follow a Renaissance circuit around the country and are old pros at boisterously hawking their wares in a 16th century English dialect.

Demonstrations in such crafts as blacksmithing, pottery throwing, candle and wood carving, face painting and calligraphy are given during the festival.

The entertainment is continuous, both on the fair's three stages and off. There is jousting on horseback, swordfighting, gypsy dancing, Shakespearean plays, commedia dell'arte, storytelling, puppet shows and participatory games and events for both children and adults. Actors, jugglers, mimes, minstrels and magicians roam throughout the kingdom, to the delight of fairgoers. "You can't go ten feet without running into an entertainment," says fair spokesperson Carolyn Goodwin.

The forest is also full of colorful Elizabethan characters—mud-caked beggars, assorted

King Richard's Faire

scoundrels, urchins and peasants wander through the grounds, as does royalty, knights and damsels in distress — all drawing the fairgoer into a form of living theater.

When: Seven consecutive weekends from late August to early October.
Where: Off Route 58 in South Carver. The fair site is equidistant from Boston and Providence and just north of the Cape Cod Canal.
Hours: 10 A.M. to 6 P.M.
Directions: From I-495, take Route 58 North to Carver. The fair is on the left side of Route 58, approximately four miles from the exit.
Admission: Adults $7; ages 5 to 12, $2; children under 5, free.
For more information: King Richard's Faire, Inc., 710 Turnpike Street, Stoughton, Massachusetts 02072. Telephone: (617) 344-7998.

MASSACHUSETTS

ACC CRAFT FAIR AT WEST SPRINGFIELD
American Craft Council
The Eastern States Exposition Center
West Springfield, Massachusetts

Mention the word "Rhinebeck" to a working craftsperson anywhere in the country and chances are that the recognition will be immediate. It's a reaction that's indeed well deserved. In the ten years that the American Craft Council held its flagship fair at the Dutchess County Fairgrounds in Rhinebeck, New York, it became the largest — and preeminent — craft fair in the world.

It is likely, given the recent announcement of the fair's move to West Springfield in 1984, that in future years, "Springfield" will elicit the same reaction from craft professionals that "Rhinebeck" does today.

"We moved to get away from the tents, the limited access to population centers, and the (shortage of) motel rooms in the Rhinebeck area," explains Carol Sedestrom, president of American Craft Enterprises, the marketing subsidiary of the nonprofit American Craft Council (ACC).

With few permanent buildings at the Dutchess County Fairgrounds, more than half of the craftspeople there had to exhibit their work under tents or out in the open. At "The Big E" in West Springfield all the exhibitors will have display space under one roof. "Viewing the displays all under one roof will be much more comfortable than going from tent to tent to tent," notes Carol, "particularly on a rainy day."

Five hundred craftspeople-exhibitors display and sell their work to both the trade and the public at the fair. During the trade-only days, representatives of some 3,500 retail businesses place orders. The last three days of the fair are open to the public, which in 1983 totaled 50,000 visitors.

The exhibitors at the 1983 fair sold slightly more than six million dollars of their work during the fair's five days. This is inarguably big business — some craftspeople keep busy for a year or more with trade orders written at this one fair — and you'll consequently find highly polished displays, work of a uniformly excellent caliber and a great variety of styles for every taste.

It is not surprising that there is stiff competition among professional craftspeople to get into the fair. About 2,700 artisans apply each year for the 500 booth allocations.

A jury of eight or nine people — craftspeople, organization leaders, shop and gallery owners — are elected by the current year's exhibitors to pick next year's exhibitors from among the applicants. Over a period of several days, they view five color slides of each applicant's work, judging them on a point system of stringent guidelines established by the American Craft Council.

The work on display at the fair is generally innovative, stylistically diverse and among the highest quality in the nation. Although the percentages vary from year to year, a typical breakdown of the craft media represented at the fair is: pottery, thirty percent; fiber and jewelry, twenty percent each; wood and glass, ten percent each; and miscellaneous, ten percent.

About thirty percent of the craftspeople-exhibitors are New Englanders, twenty-five percent Californians, ten percent from the rest of the Northeast and the Mid-Atlantic, and the remainder from around the country.

One popular feature is the grouping of all exhibitors according to medium. With all clay in one area, all jewelry in another, and so on, it is possible for the visitor to examine and compare, say, the most recent work of 150 of America's best potters, all conveniently next to each other.

"One of the most exciting aspects of our

ACC Craft Fair

268 · FAIRS

MASSACHUSETTS

ACC Craft Fair

move to Springfield," adds Carol, "is that we are going to be able to offer our guests greater convenience, more comfort and still maintain the country atmosphere we had in Dutchess County." Possible activities being considered for future fairs include music performances, special craft exhibits, professional and public seminars, and children's activities. The main attraction at this fair, however, will always be the crafts on display.

The first ACC fair was held in 1965 at Mount Snow, Vermont. Results were encouraging and the fair moved into successively larger sites throughout the state until 1973, when it moved to the more permanent site at Rhinebeck. Shortly thereafter a paid staff of professionals was hired to replace what had been a volunteer operation.

Today, in addition to West Springfield, American Craft Enterprises operates three other renowned ACC fairs at Baltimore, Dallas and San Francisco. Each year 2,000 American craftspeople participate in the wholesale/retail fairs. About 10,000 businesses and 100,000 members of the public annually attend, spending a combined total of more than fifteen million dollars with the craftspeople-exhibitors.

"We definitely bring together the art and business of American craft," says Carol.

The American Craft Council is the country's leading craft support organization. Founded in 1945, the ACC today has more than 40,000 members. It sponsors two craft museums in New York City, publishes *American Craft*, a bimonthy magazine, and maintains various resource files and the country's largest library devoted to crafts. American Craft Enterprises is the marketing arm of the ACC.

When: The third week in June. The fair is open to the public Friday through Sunday.
Where: The Better Living Building of the Eastern States Exposition Center.
Hours: 11 A.M. to 7 P.M.
Directions: I-91 Northbound, take Exit 3 to Route 57. Exit at Route 159 North and turn right at Route 147 East. Proceed to parking area, Gate 9.

I-91 Southbound, take Exit 13 to Route 5 South and proceed to Route 147 West. Follow to fairgrounds.

From I-90 West, take Exit 6 and follow Route 291 to Route 91 South. Take Exit 7. Turn right over bridge to Route 147 West. Follow to fairgrounds.

From I-90 East, take Exit 4 and follow Route 5 South to Route 147 West, follow to fairgrounds.
Admission: Adults, $4; children under 12, free.
For more information: American Craft Enterprises, P.O. Box 10, New Paltz, New York 12561. Telephone: (914) 255-0039.

ACC Craft Fair

MASSACHUSETTS

WORCESTER CRAFT FAIR
Worcester Craft Center
Worcester, Massachusetts

There are no mountain, lake or forest vistas to behold at the site of the Worcester Craft Fair. But although the wonders of nature may be in short supply here, high quality crafts are not.

Held under a large tent in the Center's parking lot, the fair hosts 131 exhibitors who have been juried by a panel of craftspeople, educators and administrators. About 325 craftspeople vie for an exhibitor's spot.

"The fair has always been a professional and traditional crafts fair," notes the Center's executive director, Cyrus Lipsitt. "The work on display is excellent quality, marketable crafts — nothing hobbyish." The fair has been an annual event at the center since 1970. Approximately 8,000 visitors attend, traveling from a 100-mile radius around Worcester. Crafts on sale include pottery, wood, fiber, glass, basketry, metal, paper and fabric.

Studios at the Center are used for ongoing demonstrations in pottery, weaving, woodworking, stained glass and metal. Entertainment is provided by a local mime artist, who mixes with the crowd, giving impromptu performances.

When: A mid-May weekend.
Where: The parking lot of the Worcester Craft Center.
Hours: Friday 6 to 9 P.M.; Saturday and Sunday, 10 A.M. to 5 P.M.
Directions: From the Massachusetts Turnpike, take I-290 to Worcester. Follow Route 9 to Grove Street, which intersects with Sagamore Road.
Admission: Adults, $2; children, 50 cents.
For more information: Worcester Craft Center, 25 Sagamore Road, Worcester, Massachusetts 01605. Telephone: (617) 753-8183.

League of New Hampshire Craftsmen

NEW HAMPSHIRE

ANNUAL CRAFTSMEN'S FAIR
League of New Hampshire Craftsmen
Mount Sunapee State Park
Newbury, New Hampshire

The League of New Hampshire Craftsmen sponsored their first craft fair back in 1934, just two years after the League's establishment as a statewide crafts support organization.

Today, their Annual Craftsmen's Fair, held for six days in early August, is the oldest craft fair in the country. About 50,000 visitors come each year to beautiful Mount Sunapee State Park to view and purchase high-quality, exclusively New Hampshire crafts and to see the wide variety of exhibits, demonstrations and activities at the fair.

"The fact that the League's been doing the fair for fifty years allows us to do it well," says Richard Fitzgerald, Executive Director of the League. "We concentrate more on details, not so much on conceptual things."

The League's jurying system ensures that the quality and variety of the crafts at the fair remain high. "Visitors feel secure in that they know they won't be exposed to junk," says Richard. "There's nothing below a certain standard."

More than 100 League craftspeople, who have been specially juried into the fair, sell their work from booths sheltered by about two dozen brightly colored tents. "The tents lend a nice summer vacation touch to the fair that you don't get inside a building," notes Richard.

All media are represented, including stoneware and porcelain, weaving, wooden furniture and accessories, leatherwork, blown and stained glass, jewelry, apparel, pewter, iron, and graphics.

Continuous craft demonstrations are scheduled throughout the fair, often featuring unusual projects or hands-on participation by fair visitors. Among the craft demonstrations you're likely to see are woodworking, glassblowing, blacksmithing, weaving, basketmaking, pottery, ceramic sculpture, papermaking, cloisonné, and quilting.

The Main Building, a permanent park structure, houses the fair's major exhibit, "Living with Crafts." This imaginative display of some two dozen room settings is furnished entirely with crafts, most of them one of a kind.

More than 100 League craftspeople make the furnishings for the various rooms, which are designed by professional decorators. Motifs range from a Shaker room, several bedrooms and kitchens, a wide variety of living and dining areas, a modern office interior, a child's room and a bathroom. The exhibit is a special opportunity to see an unusually large display of handcrafted furniture.

Most pieces are for sale, and the staff on hand at the exhibit has portfolios and referral sheets for all the participating craftspeople.

Downstairs in the same building is another popular exhibit, The League Shop at Sunapee. This crafts "department store" offers a wide range of mostly production crafts by 150 to 175 juried League craftspeople not participating in the fair as boothholders.

A recent addition to the fair is a shop selling "handcrafted edibles." Fairgoers can buy such homemade goodies as maple syrup, honey, candy, cookies, herb mixtures, dried soups, breads, fudge, mustard and granola. All food has passed muster for excellence by a League jury.

Entertainment at the fair includes regularly scheduled musical performances, mime and folk dancing. A children's tent for ages four to eight is open for staff-supervised play with craft materials.

The fairgoer will also find much to do in the immediate area. Mount Sunapee State Park offers recreational activities that include hiking trails, gondola rides to the summit, a lakefront beach, and picnic facilities.

When: The first Tuesday through Sunday in August.
Where: At the foot of Mount Sunapee in the heart of the Dartmouth-Lake Sunapee Region.
Hours: 10 A.M. to 5 P.M.
Directions: From I-89, take Exit 9 and follow Route 103 West to Mount Sunapee State Park.
Admission: Adults, $4; ages 12 to 15, $2; under 12, free.
For more information: League of New Hampshire Craftsmen, 205 North Main Street, Concord, New Hampshire 03301. Telephone: (603) 224-3375.

VERMONT

SOUTHERN VERMONT CRAFT FAIR
Manchester, Vermont

CHURCH STREET FESTIVAL OF THE ARTS
Burlington, Vermont

MOUNT SNOW CRAFT FAIR
Mount Snow, Vermont

These three craft fairs are sponsored by Craftproducers Markets, Inc., a for-profit organization owned in its entirety by nearly 100 professional New England craftspeople.

The unusual ownership structure and the collective expertise of the stockholders has resulted in professionally run fairs that feature a balanced mix of high-quality craft items.

Each fair is juried individually by a committee of craftspeople elected by their fellow shareholders. To be eligible for ownership, a craftsperson's work must be of high enough quality to have been juried into one of the fairs.

Craftproducers Markets was started in 1973 by its present directors, Charley Dooley and Riki Moss. Originally a non-profit organization, the group converted to its present status in 1980. "It was in part an idealistic change," notes Riki, "bringing in the craftspeople to have a say and share in risk."

Each fair offers a full range of craft work, including clay, fiber, jewelry, glass, metal and wood. There are also some exhibitors in photography, graphics and sculpture. Exhibitors are primarily from New England with a few from New York State.

Southern Vermont Craft Fair

About 350 craftspeople compete for the 120 available booth spaces at this fair, which takes place under yellow-and-white tents in a beautiful valley setting. As with the other Craftproducer fairs, there are craft demonstrations and things like mime, music and juggling. About 9,000 visitors attend this fair, which was started in 1978.

When: First weekend in August.
Where: At the time of this writing, plans were to move the fair in 1984 to historic Hildene, the site of Abraham Lincoln's summer home in Manchester, Vermont.
Hours: Friday, noon to 6 P.M.; Saturday, 10 A.M. to 6 P.M.; Sunday, 10 A.M. to 5 P.M.
Directions: Hildene is near the intersection of Routes 7 and 30 in Manchester, Vermont.
Admission: Adults, $2; children, free.
For more information: Craftproducers Markets, Inc., P.O. Box 323, Grand Isle, Vermont 05458. Telephone: (802) 372-4747.

New England Artist Festival

New England Artist Festival

VERMONT

Church Street Festival of the Arts

A decidedly cosmopolitan ambiance is in evidence at this fair, which is held at the Marketplace, Burlington's award-winning pedestrian mall. One hundred twenty craftspeople (who were juried from about 300 applicants) set up their booths under small tents on the downtown mall. During the fair weekend an estimated 30,000 people come to the Marketplace to see and purchase the crafts and be entertained by many musical performances and other diversions.

"Someone coming to the fair can plan an entire day around the Marketplace, eating at one of the many fine restaurants or enjoying the afternoon at an outdoor cafe," notes fair director Charley Dooley. "One can even take in a movie or plan for an evening of music or theater, and all kinds of shopping is possible."

When: Third weekend in August.
Where: The Marketplace in downtown Burlington.
Hours: Friday, noon to 9 P.M.; Saturday, 10 A.M. to 6 P.M.; Sunday, 10 A.M. to 5 P.M.
Directions: Take Exit 14 off I-89. Follow the signs to downtown Burlington and the Marketplace.
Admission: Free.
For more information: Craftproducers Markets, Inc., P.O. Box 323, Grand Isle, Vermont 05458. Telephone: (802) 372-4747.

Mount Snow Craft Fair

When the American Craft Council decided in 1973 to move their eight-year-old Vermont fair to Rhinebeck, this fair was conceived as a "response" to the void left by that action.

"The first year, we held the fair in a space that was between two bars and a leeching field," remembers Riki Moss, one of the Craftproducers' founders. Things have improved considerably since that first fair.

Today, the fair is held on two consecutive weekends in the four-story ski lodge at the foot of Mount Snow. Each weekend seventy-seven exhibitors (chosen from 200 applicants) display and sell their crafts to 8,000 fair visitors. Only about ten percent of the craftspeople display on both weekends, effectively making each a separate fair.

When: First and second weekends in October.
Where: Inside the base lodge at Mount Snow.
Hours: First weekend: Friday preview, 5 to 9 P.M.; Saturday, 10 A.M. to 6 P.M.; Sunday, 10 A.M. to 5 P.M.
Second weekend (Columbus Day weekend): Saturday, 10 A.M. to 6 P.M.; Sunday, 10 A.M. to 6 P.M.; Monday, 10 A.M. to 4 P.M.
Directions: Mount Snow is in southern Vermont, about midway between Bennington and Brattleboro. Follow Route 100 to Mount Snow.
Admission: Adults, $2; children, free.
For more information: Craftproducers Markets, Inc., P.O. Box 323, Grand Isle, Vermont 05458. Telephone: (802) 372-4747.

ACC Craft Fair

Schools

INTRODUCTION

Here are twenty-one places—community centers, craft guilds, professional craft centers, and colleges—where you can find a variety of regularly scheduled craft classes taught by qualified professionals.

The list is by no means exhaustive. It is, however, a comprehensive sampling of the best courses of instruction available in New England. You'll find schools for children, teenagers and adults, places for serious beginners, centers for advanced amateurs and working professionals, and renowned university programs offering undergraduate and graduate degrees in craft media.

Class descriptions and fees are likely to vary over time. The listed information is meant to provide you with the flavor, depth and variety of the instruction being offered by each institution. Each of the listed organizations will send on request a detailed brochure listing their most recent schedules.

Most groups offer a yearly membership, which allows you to take a discount of about ten percent on the fees quoted here. Membership information is provided in the course brochure.

In addition to the listed places, other community organizations in your area are likely to offer craft courses. Check with your local college; most offer a few classes in crafts as part of their art curriculum. Also, many adult education groups and community centers offer instruction in craft media. And finally, many individual craftspeople give regular lessons independent of any organization.

The following statewide groups can provide you with more information about craft instruction in your area:

Connecticut Commission on the Arts
340 Capitol Avenue
Hartford, Connecticut 06106
(203) 566-4770

Maine Commission on the Arts
State House
Augusta, Maine
(207) 289-2724

Massachusetts Council on the Arts
One Ashburton Place
Boston, Massachusetts 02108
(617) 727-3668

League of New Hampshire Craftsmen
205 North Main Street
Concord, New Hampshire 03301
(603) 224-3375

Rhode Island Council on the Arts
312 Wickenden Street
Providence, Rhode Island 02903
(401) 277-3880

Vermont Council on the Arts
136 State Street
Montpelier, Vermont 05602
(802) 828-3291

Brookfield Craft Center

CONNECTICUT

BROOKFIELD CRAFT CENTER
P.O. Box 122
Brookfield, Connecticut 06804
(203) 775-4526

Brookfield Craft Center provides the serious student with a full spectrum of studio-level craft education.

The center, founded in 1954, is housed in four buildings on the banks of the picturesque Still River. Three of the buildings, including a restored 1780 grist mill, contain well-equipped studios for weaving, ceramics, woodworking, metalsmithing, stained glass and multi-purpose use.

More than 1,500 students attend about 175 classes annually, scheduled on a trimester basis. Classes are held days, evenings and weekends. During the summer session the center sponsors intensive one-week workshops, with instructors drawn from the ranks of the country's top master craftspeople.

Recently, weekly classes, which run from six to eight sessions of three to six hours each, have included basic and intermediate courses in stained glass, ceramics, basketry, jewelry, weaving, woodworking, leatherworking, botanical illustration and relief printing. Fees range from $85 to $160. Half-tuition scholarships are available.

The weekend workshops encompass an extraordinarily wide range of subjects. These sessions generally are six hours each on Saturday and Sunday with fees from $35 to $195. A sampling of one recent semester included the following: woodworking (cabinetmaking, marquetry, bird carving), metalsmithing and jewelry (stone setting, lost-wax casting, pave setting, jewelry mechanisms, pewter techniques, forging, reactive metals, cloisonné), ceramics (low-fired sculpture, colored clay, architectural tile), glass (stained glass design for architecture, conservation and restoration, hot glass, enamels and fused glass), fiber, fabric and weaving (tapestry weaving, rag rugs, wearable crochet, natural dyes, chemical dyes, lacemaking, painting on silk, uses of fleece), basketry (plaited baskets, rib baskets, basic basketmaking and basketry as an art form). There are also workshops in bookmaking, papermaking, puppetry, and on and on.

The one-week intensive summer workshops usually run six hours a day, although specialized workshops can run to nine hours daily. Fees are $75 to $250. Topics have included wooden boat building, chairmaking, jewelry making, cloisonné, airbrush techniques on porcelain, raku, introduction to wheel throwing, etched glass and sandblasting, a folding knife workshop, and weaving workshops in shaft-switching, and miniatures.

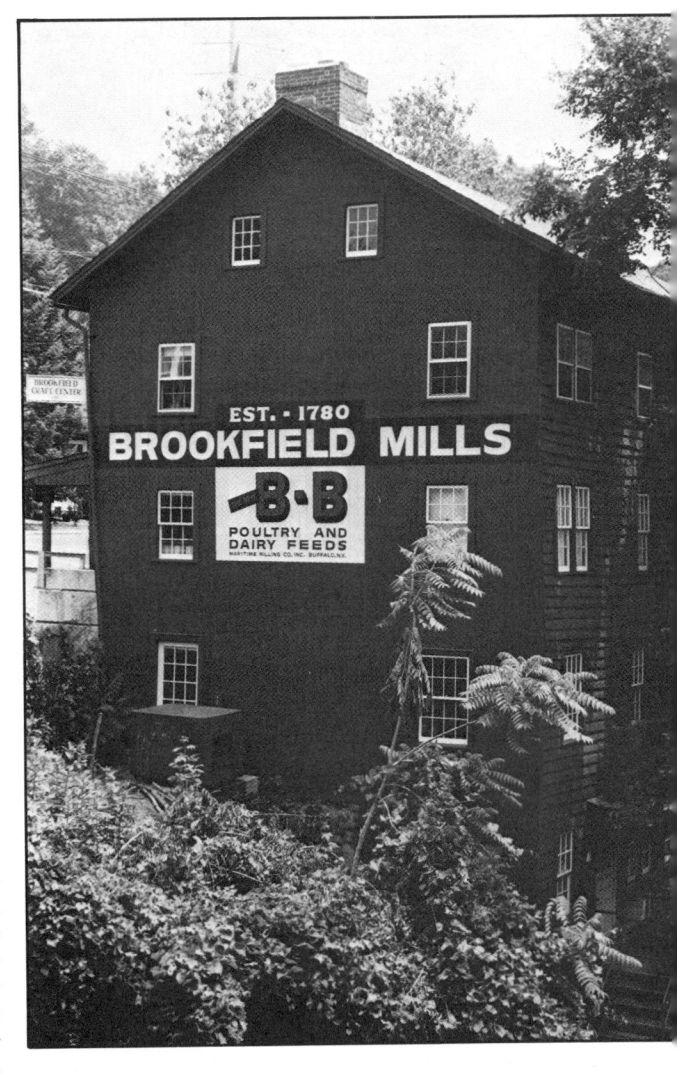

This is just a sampling. You'll find in a particular semester any number of basic, intermediate and advanced classes and workshops covering the gamut of crafts. Additionally, a children's program offers nearly two dozen courses in a variety of media.

The center also sponsors periodic lectures and seminars throughout the year on subjects like craft history, business management, and marketing. A retail craft shop occupies a nineteenth-century farmhouse where members' work is sold on consignment; there is also a library and a large gallery where six major shows a year are mounted.

277 · SCHOOLS

CONNECTICUT

FARMINGTON VALLEY ARTS CENTER
Avon Park North, P.O. Box 220
Avon, Connecticut 06001
(203) 678-1867

About 700 students enroll annually in this active center's year-round schedule of classes and weekend workshops. Classes are taught by working professionals in an environment where some forty artists and craftspeople rent studios and work. Classes are given in two all-purpose studios or in the individual artist's workspace with usually about eight students in any one class.

The center offers beginning to advanced classes in pottery, weaving, basketry, stained glass, jewelry, papermaking, quilting, woodworking, silkscreening, felting, calligraphy, printmaking, graphic and interior design, drawing, painting, sculpture and photography. Children's courses are also offered and there is a popular children's summer art daycamp. Nearly 200 classes and workshops are given annually.

Classes generally consist of from six to ten weekly sessions scheduled four times a year and costing $25 to $75. All students must join the center, which costs $15.

Workshops, which are scheduled throughout the year, are open to both members and non-members, run either one or two days, and are in the $10 to $30 range. Recent workshops have included a seminar on antique quilts, "eggs in the Ukrainian tradition," paper marbling, teapot design and construction, chair caning, and photography.

GUILFORD HANDCRAFTS CENTER
P.O. Box 221
Guilford, Connecticut 06437
(203) 453-5947

The mainstays here are regular courses of professional instruction in pottery, weaving and fibers, jewelry, metalsmithing, stained glass, and painting and graphics. Classes in these disciplines last ten to fifteen weekly sessions and are scheduled both days and evenings year-round. About 1,200 adults and children enroll annually with eight to twelve students attending any one class or workshop.

A typical schedule of classes at this restored old lumber mill includes basketry for the beginner or the experienced weaver (ten sessions, $78), floor loom weaving (fifteen sessions, $88), an intermediate weaver's study group (ten sessions, $55), introductory jewelry and metalsmithing (ten sessions, $50), basic stained glass (ten sessions, $70), oxidation pottery techniques (twelve sessions, $92), basic and intermediate pottery (15 sessions, $92 and $115), handbuilding in clay (ten sessions, $72). Scholarships are available.

There is also a wide range of painting and graphics courses that include such things as watercolor, oils, two-dimensional design, color theory, Sumi-e painting, portraiture and calligraphy. Tuition for these ranges from $69 to $92.

Hands-on workshops, which range from one to four sessions, encompass such areas as fiber (Seminole Indian patchwork, tapestry weaving, vat dyeing with procions, sash weaving); basketry (melon baskets, pine needle basketry, splint basketry); pottery (tiles, terra cotta); and special interest workshops (papermaking, bookcraft, folk art painting, Ukrainian egg dyeing). Fees run from $20 to $70.

In addition, special lectures, slide shows, demonstrations and seminars are regularly scheduled. There is also a series of children's classes (three to sixteen weekly sessions, $4 to $82) offered throughout the year.

SILVERMINE GUILD SCHOOL OF THE ARTS
1037 Silvermine Road
New Canaan, Connecticut 06840
(203) 866-0411

The Silvermine School is a fine place to go for a non-degree professional and comprehensive education in the visual arts, with an emphasis on non-craft disciplines.

The school, part of the Silvermine Center for the Arts, occupies a group of buildings on a beautiful six-acre rural site. Its excellent facilities include north lighted painting studios, separate buildings for sculpture, ceramics and mixed-discipline crafts, a printmaking studio, a photographic laboratory, an auditorium, an art supply store and an art reference library.

Professional instruction for adults is offered on a year-round, trimester basis in both day and evening classes. There are also children's classes held after school and on Saturdays. Special weekend and weeklong workshops and seminars are also scheduled. There is also a full-time, intensive two-year program leading to a Certificate in the Arts.

The fall and spring terms run fourteen weeks each; the summer term is eight weeks. Most classes are three hours duration and private studio time is available.

Typical offerings in a semester include

CONNECTICUT

Farmington Valley Arts Center

about sixty-five courses for novices to accomplished professionals. Craft-oriented classes include ceramics (four beginning and intermediate courses, $210 each); jewelry (hollow-forming, jewelry making, classical chain making, $210 each); introductory stained-glass design ($210); and weaving (five different courses from six to eight weeks and a weeklong workshop, from $85 to $100).

Also offered are nearly two dozen different painting classes, ten drawing classes, six sculpture courses, six printmaking courses, and courses in photography, graphic communications, art history and performing arts. Classes generally cost from $140 to $210, although certain specialized offerings cost more (a professional illustrator's class is $1,500). Membership in the Guild is required of all students at $25 a year.

In addition, many mini-classes and workshops are announced during the year, special youth programs are held, and a series of visiting artist's lectures are sponsored. There is also a respected chamber music series, started in the mid-Fifties.

The center also boasts a dramatic gallery complex totaling 5,000 square feet for the display of primarily two-dimensional work of Guild juried artists as well as invitational exhibits.

WESLEYAN POTTERS
350 South Main Street
Middletown, Connecticut 06457
(203) 347-5925

As the name implies, this group's forte is pottery and has been since 1948. From 600 to 800 students yearly take the pottery and other craft courses offered by the non-profit guild during its four yearly class sessions.

In a typical semester, there are some half dozen basic, intermediate and advanced pottery courses offered. There are also several basketry courses, weaving, beginning and intermediate jewelry, stained glass, silkscreening, calligraphy and graphics. Classes, which are taught by well-qualified instructors in spacious facilities, generally run from six to nine weeks, are two-and-one-half hours each, and cost from $30 to $66. There are usually twelve to fifteen students in each course. There is also a series of classes for children in pottery and general art.

One- or two-day special workshops are held throughout the year in such things as kitemaking, lampshade making, and photography ($20 to $50). Lectures, exhibits, demonstrations and films are also scheduled.

MAINE

HAYSTACK MOUNTAIN SCHOOL OF CRAFTS
Deer Isle, Maine 04627
(207) 348-6946

"Haystack," observes its director, Howard Evans, "is based on commitment." About 400 students annually come to this renowned summer crafts school to participate in what he calls a "strong interpersonal learning community for craftspeople at all levels."

Students enroll in two- and three-week sessions that offer a level of intensive study equivalent to a typical semester's university course. Novices and professionals, young adults of college age and retired people, all those "to whom craftwork is an important thread in their life," comprise the typical Haystack session.

"There's an incredible mix of people here," Howard told me. "In the university they tend to be homogeneous. Haystack tends to be wide open." The faculty, which changes each session, are all masters in their respective fields both in this country and abroad.

"Building a strong base of community as part of the working time" is an integral element in the Haystack experience. "We try to imbue the students wih the breadth and depth of the world and its relationship to crafts," Howard told me. "People talk about a 'Haystack magic.' They often make critical life decisions because of their work and experience here."

The center's brochure says the school has "an overall ambiance of sustained exhilaration as people pursue their work in crafts together." There is, it is pointed out, a "respect for individual uniqueness of all participants and sincere regard for the limits or potential of personal capacity. Within the basic philosophy, a wide challenge is posted for the advanced professional as well as the neophyte."

"We talk a lot about quality here," adds Howard. "Quality of lives, quality of crafts."

Courses offered include studies in clay, wood, metalsmithing, blacksmithing, glassblowing, stained glass, jewelry, weaving, fabric, graphics, papermaking, quiltmaking and photography. Fully equipped studios for each discipline are housed, along with accommodations, meeting rooms and offices, in about two dozen pitched-roof buildings designed by Edward Larrabee Barnes. The entire center sits on a heavily wooded slope overlooking beautiful East Penobscot Bay.

Most sessions are open to students at all levels of experience. However, certain selected sessions are offered only for experienced craftspeople. Admission to these sessions is by a jurying process that requires submission of five slides of recent work and a brief statement of intent.

Five sessions are held from June to September with enrollment in each limited to sixty-five resident and ten day people. Classes are generally scheduled from 9 a.m. to 3:30 p.m., five days a week, but the studios are open for use twenty-four hours a day, seven days a week.

Tuition is $115 per week and room-and-board rates run from $100 to $185 depending on accommodations desired. Scholarships are available both for technical-assistance studio monitors and work/study projects.

Although no degrees are offered, Haystack issues a certificate of completion that, according to Howard, is generally acceptable for course credit at most university art departments.

I can't say enough good things about this marvelous place — the beautiful environment, the intensity of study and commitment, the quality of the instruction, the sense of community — Haystack is, quite simply, a mecca for craftspeople.

Haystack Mountain School of Crafts

MASSACHUSETTS

HORIZONS
374 Old Montague Road
Amherst, Massachusetts 01002
(413) 549-4841

This newly established craft-oriented summer-camp program is held at Kents Hill School in the beautiful Belgrades Lakes district of Maine. An advisory board of professional craftspeople and craft administrators helped organize the camp's multi-disciplinary program, which offers participants studio-level instruction and hands-on experience in ceramics, weaving, woodworking, photography, batik and silkscreening. The camp is open to teenagers with all levels of experience.

In addition to the studio work, there are regular visits by leading master craftspeople who discuss and demonstrate their specialties such as raku firing, indigo dyeing and glassblowing. There are also field trips to artisan's studios, galleries, craft fairs, and suppliers.

Besides all this craft activity, there is the more commonplace camp stuff — swimming, hiking, informal sports, films, plays, music and so on.

Two three-week sessions are held in July and August. Campers may register for one session at $985 or both sessions for $1,875.

BOSTON CENTER FOR ADULT EDUCATION
Five Commonwealth Avenue
Boston, Massachusetts 02134
(617) 267-4430

This private, non-profit educational institution was established in 1933 to "reinforce the idea that education is a life-long process." In four terms of ten weeks each, Boston residents can choose from an eclectic catalog of some 200 courses that cover everything from Archaeology ("The Creatures of Tasmania") to Wine & Spirits ("Quality Jug Wines").

As part of this melange, there are about a dozen mostly beginning and some intermediate courses offered in pottery, weaving, stained glass and woodworking.

The classes, which normally are taken each term by about ten students per class (550 students per year take the craft courses), cost about $65 to $76 for a ten-week session of about two to three hours per week, depending on the course. Scholarships are available for many courses.

THE PROGRAM IN ARTISANRY AT BOSTON UNIVERSITY
620 Commonwealth Avenue
Boston, Massachusetts 02215
(617) 353-2022

The stated goal of this innovative university program is to "discover and develop the very highest talent among artisans today." Its multi-faceted curriculum is designed for students "who plan careers in working crafts media in their own studios, in businesses or in a variety of allied professions." Many graduates have gained nationwide recognition for their work.

Students undergo a rigorous concentration of studio work, majoring in either wood, ceramics, metal or fiber. Areas of concentration include jewelry design, holloware, metal sculpture, wood furniture design, historic stringed instruments, surface design, loom weaving, fiber sculpture, and traditional and non-traditional ceramics. These activities are enhanced by university courses in liberal arts, art history, business and design.

Additionally, there is a panoply of demonstrations, lectures and visits by renowned master craftspeople; field trips to galleries, studios and museums; a program of exhibitions; and opportunities for independent work/study programs.

Students are closely guided by a faculty of accomplished artists and craftspeople in "an individualized approach to the personal development of the artist/designer." About 100 students each semester are enrolled in the program, which is housed in its own three-story building on the university campus. Each student is assigned his or her own completely equipped studio for the duration of their stay at the program. Other university facilities, such as photography labs and engineering labs, are also available for special work.

Each semester runs approximately fifteen weeks with the average class of five to ten students meeting for a total of nine hours per week. Individual studios are always open to students, who range in age from seventeen-year-olds directly out of high school to mature adults who have studied in other fields or have solid, professional experience. The average age is mid-twenties.

There are three degrees and one non-academic certificate offered: a two-year associate's degree in fine arts, a four-year bachelors degree in fine arts, a graduate-level Certificate of Mastery (two or three years), and a masters degree in fine arts (two to three years). Evening and summer courses are usually also

MASSACHUSETTS

available for credit and non-credit.

Full-time tuition per year is $7,175; part-time tuition is $225 per credit, with most courses being four credits. There are student loans and scholarships available to qualified applicants.

In addition to general university requirements for admission, applicants to the Program in Artisanry must submit a portfolio of their work to be considered for admission.

CAMBRIDGE CENTER FOR ADULT EDUCATION
42 Brattle Street
Cambridge, Massachusetts 02138
(617) 547-6789

The Cambridge Center, incorporated in 1876 as the Cambridge Social Union, provides an array of courses for adults "who want to develop their best potential." Its historic classroom facilities include the Dexter Pratt House, built in 1808, where Longfellow watched the village blacksmith at work under the spreading chestnut tree.

I'm not sure if the tree is still there, but the center remains in good health, offering area residents hundreds of courses and activities in some sixty different areas of interest. Among these is a selection of about forty crafts courses, scheduled in day, evening and weekend classes. Courses are offered in three ten-week sessions and one eight-week summer session each year.

Crafts taught here, usually on a basic or intermediate level, include sculpture, pottery, stained glass, jewelry making, silk screening, textile design, spinning and plant dyeing, macrame, crochet, knitting, weaving, tapestry, needlepoint and bargello, quiltmaking and paper marbling among others. Courses usually are attended by about eighteen students and cost from $51 to $64 for the session.

DE CORDOVA MUSEUM
Sandy Pond Road
Lincoln, Massachusetts 01773
(617) 259-0505

Nearly 3,000 area residents annually enroll in the De Cordova Museum educational program of art, art-appreciation and craft classes. The museum offers more than 100 classes annually for adults, teenagers and children.

Although the De Cordova concentrates on two-dimensional art such as drawing, painting, printmaking and photography, there are sev-

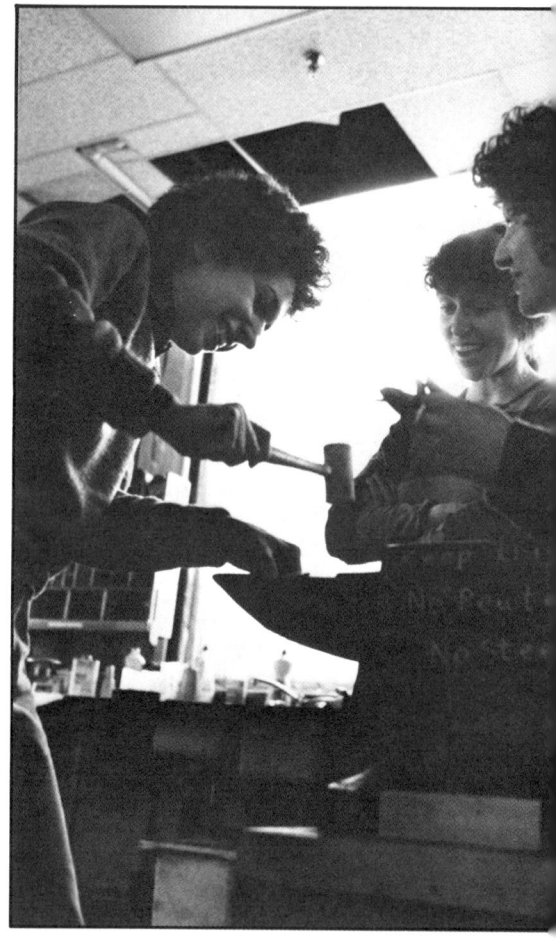

Boston University

eral courses offered each session in basketmaking, ceramics, jewelry and silversmithing, and stained-glass design.

There are three class sessions each year; fall and spring are fifteen weeks duration and summer eight weeks, with some intensive one-week workshops. Costs start at $85 for basketmaking and run to $130 for a stained-glass course. Proficiency levels range from basic to advanced and the average class size is about twelve to fifteen students.

ENDICOTT COLLEGE
Hale Street
Beverly, Massachusetts 01915
(617) 927-0585 extension 257

Ceramics, metal (jewelry) and fiber (weaving) are offered in the art department at this two-year college as both elective and major con-

MASSACHUSETTS

centrations leading to an associate's degree in fine arts.

Courses are given over two semesters of nine weeks duration each plus a week for final examinations. The two-year program also requires an internship or work experience in the student's major for four weeks each year. Students work as apprentices, teaching aides, in galleries or museums or craft shops and as therapy aides.

There are complete professional facilities for student use and classes average between twelve and twenty students per class. Tuition, room and board is $7,500 per year. Scholarships and student loans are available.

LEVERETT CRAFTSMEN & ARTISTS
Leverett Center, Massachusetts 01054
(413) 549-6871

This rural center offers classes taught by well-qualified instructors during three annual terms of about four to six weeks duration each.

There are courses in jewelry making, clay sculpture (handbuilding), basketry, woodworking, weaving, painting and drawing and silkscreening. Courses are generally for beginners and intermediate students. Fees range from $28 for basketry to $130 for jewelry making. There are usually six to fifteen students in each class, usually given in the center's professionally equipped studios.

Amy Shapiro, Leverett's director, told me that there will be an increased emphasis in upcoming terms on educational programs geared for professional artists and craftspeople and covering such topics as business management and marketing.

THE WORCESTER CRAFT CENTER
25 Sagamore Road
Worcester, Massachusetts 01605
(617) 753-8183

The Worcester Craft Center is the oldest non-profit educational institution for the study of crafts in the country, tracing its ancestry back to the mid-nineteenth century.

More importantly, however, today it is a thriving craft school with modern facilities and instructors drawn from the ranks of the area's top professional craftspeople.

The center, which occupies a 26,000-square-foot brick building, sponsors four ten-week sessions for adults; three ten-week sessions for children; a full-time, two-year professional craft studies program; and seminars and workshops throughout the year for both the community and the professional craftsperson.

About 1,200 to 1,400 people yearly attend the adult craft classes, which meet for three hours weekly.

A typical listing of classes includes: ceramics (seven courses from beginning to advanced, Japanese techniques, production methods, and colored clay techniques); enamelling (beginning and intermediate), fiber (basic to advanced weaving, batik, quilting, basketry, oriental rug repair), calligraphy (four courses from basic to advanced), photography (three skill levels), wood (furniture design, woodturning, design, traditional woodworking, functional and sculptural woodworking), folk art painting (country arts and early American decorating), stained glass, house designing and building, and metalsmithing (basic to advanced classes).

Most of the adult classes cost $85 for non-members and $65 for members; membership is $25 yearly. There is usually an average of ten to twelve students per class.

The center also sponsors an unusual two-year, full-time professional studies program leading, if desired, to an associate degree through Quinsigamond Community College. Students major in either clay, fiber, metal or wood, and study other courses such as photography, marketing, craft history and business management. Tuition for this program, which covers thirty-six weeks each year, is $2,800. Student loans are available. Each year about eighteen students at different ages and levels of skill enter this program.

Additionally, throughout the year, noted craftspeople conduct one- and two-day weekend workshops, lectures and demonstrations. Generally costing from $35 to $70, subjects have included such things as quilted containers, sculptural forms in raku, lost wax casting, advanced diamond setting, steam bending of wood, color and design for textiles, and textures on metals. There are also advanced crafts seminars regularly given for professionals.

In addition, the center posts a full schedule of two-hour classes for children in multi-media, clay, fiber, metal and wood. Classes are limited to twelve students and cost $85; $65 with family membership.

The center also houses large gallery spaces, a retail craft shop, a supply store and a reference library.

New Hampshire

ARTS & SCIENCE CENTER
14 Court Street
Nashua, New Hampshire 03060
(603) 883-1506

A year-round schedule of classes in crafts, painting and drawing, photography, dance, exercise, and computers for both adults and children are posted at this community-oriented center.

Craft courses are taught by professionals and include beginning and intermediate pottery, sawdust-fired sgraffito, raku, stained glass, jewelry, quilting, weaving and needlework.

Courses generally cover ten weekly sessions attended by an average of eight to ten students. Fees range from $50 to $75. There are also one-day workshops and six-week mini-sessions. The modern building contains large, bright classrooms with all equipment necessary to practice craftwork.

The center also sponsors about two dozen classes for children and teenagers in crafts, fine arts, dance and computers.

LEAGUE OF NEW HAMPSHIRE CRAFTSMEN
205 North Main Street
Concord, New Hampshire 03301
(603) 224-3375

The League has always emphasized the quality and the breadth of its statewide craft education program. "We are primarily an educational organization," notes League Director Richard Fitzgerald. Even the organization's ten retail outlets are thought of as a "subtle and profound educational tool," introducing many local people for the first time to a variety of fine craftwork.

Each of the ten affiliated shops is also involved in more direct craft education — hands-on classes, workshops and demonstrations in most major craft media. Schedules vary from seasonal to a comprehensive year-round posting such as that at the Sharon Arts Center, which is listed elsewhere in this chapter. For more details on each shop's schedule of classes, contact them directly. They are listed in the first section.

Arts & Science Center

NEW HAMPSHIRE

In addition to its retail outlets, the League also supports seven purely educational local groups around the state, each of which sponsors varying schedules of classes and demonstrations. These groups—in Colebrook, Pittsburgh, Warner, Littleton, Monroe, Bridgewater and Lisbon—may be contacted through the League's Concord headquarters.

Instructors for all sessions are drawn from the League pool of 500 juried professionals. Those who have expressed an interest in teaching and whose capability and experience lend themselves to the job are made available to the statewide local groups.

The average course session runs about six to ten weeks and costs from $35 to $65. Instruction is primarily on a beginning or intermediate level, although occasional advanced workshops are held for serious amateurs and professionals.

The League also sponsors an annual "Seminar" for about 100 professional craftspeople, who apply for acceptance by submitting slides of their work. The four to six day retreat, held each January, attracts craftspeople from across the country eager to participate in the six workshops of intense technical training given by a faculty of master craftspeople. Costs for the sessions are about $200 to $250 for tuition, room and board. Contact the League for further details.

The League also runs an active cooperative educational program with area schools and maintains for its membership an extensive library of craft books at its Concord headquarters.

MANCHESTER INSTITUTE OF ARTS AND SCIENCES
148 Concord Street
Manchester, New Hampshire 03104
(603) 623-0313

Manchester Institute, a private, non-profit continuing education center, offers two semesters of both college-credit and adult education courses in art, music, crafts, languages and dance.

Fifteen courses are offered in cooperation with area colleges that will grant college credits for successful completion. Typically there are about a dozen courses in this category offered in painting, drawing, graphic design and photography as well as courses in beginning and intermediate pottery and jewelry. These two-credit courses run fifteen weeks and cost $90.

Non-credit adult education courses meet weekly for twelve weeks and include classes in silkscreening, stained glass, pottery, weaving, jewelry and silversmithing and quilting, all taught on a beginning and intermediate level. Tuition fees for these courses, which generally have from eight to fourteen students per class, is $70 to $85.

SHARON ARTS CENTER
P.O. Box 361
Sharon, New Hampshire 03458
(603) 924-7256

The Sharon Arts Center offers the Monadnock region a broad range of professional instruction in crafts and various arts. Four sessions are posted yearly, each of eight to ten weeks duration.

Courses are primarily at beginning and intermediate levels and include pottery, printmaking, jewelry, graphic arts, photography, quilting, weaving, birdcarving, art history, stenciling, glassblowing, wrought iron, painting, drawing and fly tying.

Classes of about eight to ten students meet weekly for three-hour periods in the school's well-equipped studios, which are open twenty-four hours a day for student use. About 700 students yearly attend classes at the center.

Workshops of one-, two- and three-day duration are also regularly scheduled on all levels of skill and in such subjects as English smocking, paper marbling, fabric and wall stenciling, matting techniques, airbrushing and carbon dust drawing.

Classes generally cost $60; workshops $35. There are also children's classes offered in pottery, drawing and ballet. The complex also houses an exhibition gallery and a League of New Hampshire Craftsmen retail craft shop.

RHODE ISLAND

RHODE ISLAND SCHOOL OF DESIGN
2 College Street
Providence, Rhode Island 02903
(401) 331-3511

Rhode Island School of Design offers the serious and dedicated student a comprehensive four-year education in one of six craft majors, including wood furniture design, ceramics, glass, jewelry/metals, printmaking and textile design.

One of the country's premier art and design schools, RISD (pronounced riz' - dee) also offers thirteen other undergraduate degree programs in a full range of fine arts, architecture and design disciplines. Additionally, there are ten masters degree programs, including some in craft media.

"RISD is committed to giving students the skills, experience, and habits of mind which will enable them to compete effectively in the professional world," states Lee Hall, president of the school. "The fact is, we regard art not as a diversion or amusement, but as an essential part of the growth and well-being of our civilization."

It is within this environment of excellence and achievement in art and design that students pursue their work under the guidance of a full-time faculty of noted artists, architects, historians and designers.

All freshmen must enroll in the basic "foundation program," which is designed to help students "widen their visual perspective and strengthen their confidence in their own way of seeing and expressing themselves." As part of this curriculum, first-year students must take courses in two- and three-dimensional drawing and design, English composition and art history.

Students choose their majors during the second year of study. In addition to the six craft programs, undergraduates can major in architecture, industrial design, interior architecture, landscape architecture, painting, apparel design, graphic design, film/video, illustration or photography.

The programs in glass, ceramics and jewelry/light metals are all within the Department of Sculpture, with facilities housed under one roof. "Curricula cooperation" among the three disciplines frequently occurs.

The Department of Textile Design offers a broad education emphasizing a "thorough understanding of design process, structure, materials, techniques, and the interdependence of these elements." "Individual artistic expression" is encouraged "whether in design for industry or in functional or non-functional textiles."

The printmaking program, in the Department of Painting, offers basic and advanced courses in relief, intaglio, lithography and silkscreen. Students who want to major in printmaking must submit a portfolio at the end of their sophomore year and begin their studies in their junior year. Traditional and contempo-

Rhode Island School of Design

rary techniques are studied.

The wood furniture design program is part of the Industrial Design Department. "Each student is provided with the traditional values of industrial design, combined with an in-depth understanding of a visual language. Using this language, students analyze and solve diverse problems from both technical and aesthetic viewpoints."

RISD also offers two-year masters programs in ceramics, furniture design, glass, jewelry/light metals, and printmaking.

Students at RISD can organize an elective curriculum that benefits from the many artistic disciplines on campus. There are also numerous opportunities for exposure to an extraordinarily wide range of art and artistic points of view. For instance, the on-campus Museum of Art is one of the country's most extensive art teaching resources, containing forty-five galleries for the exhibition of more than 60,000 objects from every culture and period. Facilities are open to the campus community and there is an active schedule of exhibitions, concerts and lectures by guest artists given throughout the year.

About thirty-five percent of RISD students come from New England, forty-five percent from the central eastern seaboard region, and the rest from other areas of the country and abroad.

There is stiff competition for admission and students are required to submit freehand drawings and a portfolio of their work along with the usual application materials. Tuition is $6,700 per year and room and board $2,880. Financial aid is available in the form of scholarships, work/study programs and student loans.

Rhode Island School of Design

VERMONT

SHELBURNE CRAFT SCHOOL
P.O. Box 52
Shelburne, Vermont 05482
(802) 985-3648

Established in 1945 to teach crafts to community children, the Shelburne School has developed into a year-round craft education facility offering professional instruction to area people of all ages.

About 450 students register each year for beginning, intermediate and advanced courses, including regular sessions in woodworking (ten weeks, $80), pottery (eight weeks, $64), weaving (eight weeks, $70), stained glass (six sessions, $50). There are also courses in sculpture, painting, watercolor, and house design.

Four sessions are posted each year at the school's facilities, which include a woodworking building, a pottery building, several weaving studios, a jewelry workshop, a stained glass studio and a painting studio.

One- and two-day workshops are also scheduled throughout the year on topics such as basic rug making ($30), photography ($20), and clothes design ($45).

The school continues to run a strong program for the young people in the Shelburne area, offering weekly classes after school and daily classes in the summer to children from pre-school age to teenagers.

THE VERMONT STATE CRAFT CENTER AT FROG HOLLOW
Middlebury, Vermont 05753
(802) 388-3177

A modest program of community-oriented instruction is supported by Frog Hollow on a year-round basis. About 650 people annually attend classes and workshops, which are held in two lower level studios in the restored mill housing the center.

Twenty-five to thirty weekly class sessions are held each year, including pottery, calligraphy, drawing, stained glass, chair caning, batik, and quilting. Most courses are offered for beginning or intermediate students, run from three to eight weeks, and cost between $25 and $70.

The center also posts about fifty-five workshops yearly. These are usually scheduled for one or two days and include sessions on such things as cut-paper lampshades, stenciling, woodgrain and sponge painting, mixed-media jewelry, basketry, wreathmaking, and dried flower arranging. Fees run from $15 to $35 per day.

Frog Hollow

There is also a series of professional-level workshops — either hands-on sessions taught by master craftspeople or seminars on business matters like marketing or bookkeeping. Frog Hollow also conducts weekly pottery classes for students in local elementary schools.

VERMONT STATE CRAFT CENTER AT WINDSOR HOUSE
P.O. Box 110
Windsor, Vermont 05084
(802) 674-6729

Headquartered in a stately old inn, the second of Vermont's two craft centers sponsors three semesters yearly of crafts instruction for area children and adults. Professional instructors teach primarily beginning and intermediate classes, although occasionally an advanced or professional workshop will be held.

About a dozen classes are posted each session in such subjects as woodworking (eight sessions, $50), quilting (eight sessions, $45), upholstery (ten sessions, $40), puppetry (seven sessions, $28), weaving (eight sessions, $55), handspinning (four sessions, $28), fly tying (five sessions, $33), and interior design (six sessions, $40).

One- and two-day workshops are also scheduled each semester in a variety of topics. A typical semester will include workshops in wall stenciling, dried flower arranging, fabric picture frames, hammock making, chair caning, rag rugs, Seminole patchwork and batik. Fees range from $6 to $35.

Glossary/Index

GLOSSARY

CLAY

Ball Mill A grinding machine with a porcelain lining and small hard pebbles inside for grinding clay finely.

Bisque Preliminary firing to harden the ware for glazing.

Burnishing Dry polishing of hardened unfired piece to produce a glazelike surface which may be fired.

Casting A method of reproducing in quantity by using liquid clay and molds.

Celadon Glazes A gray-green semi-opaque-to-opaque glaze (reduction fired).

China Paint(ing) A low-fire glaze decoration applied to already glazed and fired whiteware or porcelain.

Clay Body A composite of various ceramic materials used to make pottery.

Coiling Building the walls of pottery with ropelike rolls of clay, then smoothing the joints.

Cone Thin, finger-length pyramid of ceramic material made to bend and melt at prescribed temperatures, providing a visual indication of temperature in the kiln.

Corian™ Dupont trademark name for a stonelike plastic that resembles marble.

Crackle Glaze One featuring minute, decorative surface cracks; sometimes accented by rubbing with color.

Crystal(line) Glazes Those featuring clusters of crystal-like shapes or colors within a more uniform, opaque glaze.

Earthenware Tan or reddish pottery fired at a low temperature. In an unglazed form, its porosity prevents it from holding liquids.

Engobe Another term for slip, usually containing very little clay and being largely composed of materials associated with glazes.

Flameware A flameproof ware, as distinct from ovenware.

Glaze The glassy surface coating of pottery; infinite variety available.

Hand Built The final object is assembled by hand. It may employ wheel-thrown, cast, coiled and/or slab elements.

Inlay A technique of decoration in which the object is incised with a design, a colored clay is pressed into the incisions, and the piece is then scraped to confine the colored inlay to the incisions.

Low Fired Clay fired at a temperature sufficient to fuse it into a solid mass, but too low to make it completely nonabsorbent.

Low-Fire Glazes Low-temperature finishes, usually associated with bright and shiny colors.

Luster A metallic or iridescent effect resulting from the application of a thin film of metallic oxide.

Mat(te) Glaze A nongloss or dull-surface glaze.

Millefiore Technique Used primarily to describe glass, it can also mean the process of cutting and inlaying pieces of colored clay.

Mochaware A type of pottery having a brown mosslike or treelike decoration produced by allowing colored slips to flow over the surface.

Neriage A Japanese technique in which a mixture of colored clays is thrown on the wheel, resulting in a marbleized product. (Pronounced "neh-ree-AH-gay")

Nerikomi A Japanese technique of handbuilding with colored clays, specifically using press molds. (Pronounced "neh-ree-KO-mee") This term is often confused with Neriage; the root words are neri—to mix, komi—to press into, age—to pull up.

Oxidation (or Oxidation Fired) Firing ceramic ware at high temperatures and without adjusting the atmosphere inside the kiln. It results in lighter, brighter colorations of glazes.

Oxide Metal oxides used as coloring agents, often dissolved in a glaze.

Porcelain A hardy clay body which is glasseous white and sometimes translucent.

Pottery A generic term for clay objects.

Press Mold A mold into which clay is pressed, as in dish molds, or a hollow mold, the sections of which are pressed together.

Raku Porous earthenware originally made in Japan and associated with the Tea Ceremony. It often has a scorched look which is a result of the rapid cooling in combustible materials.

Reduction (or Reduction Fired) Firing ceramic ware at high temperatures and in the presence of added carbon to reduce the percentage of oxygen in the kiln. This produces muted and subtle color variations.

Saggar A clay box in which pottery is fired to protect the ware from flame and ash.

Salt Glaze A hard, glassy glaze resulting from the vapors created by the introduction of salt into the hot kiln atmosphere. It frequently results in an orange-peel texture.

Sawdust-Fired A primitive firing technique in which slow-burning sawdust produces subtle gradations of color.

Sgraffito Decoration in which slip or other

Glossary

coating is scratched or cut away to reveal the clay body beneath.

Slab Built Ceramic ware formed from flat pieces or "slabs" rolled for the purpose.

Slip Clay mixed with water till it is almost liquid. It is used for casting.

Slip Glazes Watery clay used for decorative effects and applied by pouring, dipping, brush or spray.

Smoke Trailed A body or glaze discolored by a smoky reduction fire.

Stain Any oxide or prepared pigment used for coloring bodies, slips, or glazes.

Stoneware Natural clay, or blend of clays, which is fired over 2100°F for little or no absorbency. It differs from porcelain principally in color, being gray, tan or reddish.

Terra Cotta Hard, unglazed, brown-red earthenware clay, most often used for ceramic sculpture, including small figures and architectural ornaments.

Terra Sigillata Roman method of obtaining a waxy, semiglazed finish using only the finest particles of iron-bearing clay separated by flotation.

Thixotropic Clay A special-formula porcelain having a taffylike consistency which allows it to be shaped by draping and pulling until it sets up.

Underglaze Pigments applied to the raw clay or bisque and covered with a transparent glaze, having the advantage of permanence.

Wax Resist Decoration by applying warm wax to pottery or a layer of glaze so that a successive layer of glaze will not adhere to the wax-decorated area.

Wheel Thrown Forming of pottery by the action of the potter's fingers and hands against clay centered on the revolving platform of a potter's wheel.

Whiteware White clay body high in Kaolin, considered to be "pure clay."

FIBER

Appliqué Stitchery in which a design is created by sewing pieces of fabric or other materials to a fabric background.

Batik (1) A method of applying dye to cloth which is covered in part with a dye-resistant, removable substance such as wax. After dyeing, the wax is removed, and the design appears in the original color against the newly colored background. (2) The cloth itself.

Boumaki A kind of Japanese dyeing in which fabric is wrapped tightly around a pole for resist dyeing.

Cyanotype (Blueprint) A method of applying a silhouette or other design to fabric by coating it with a light-sensitive dye, covering it with a film negative or other object and exposing it to light.

Faille A woven cotton, rayon or silk fabric showing a slight rubbing.

Felting (1) Fabric made of unspun wool (sometimes with fur and other natural or synthetic fibers) which is matted together with moisture, heat and pressure. (2) A fabric resembling this, such as a highly napped cotton.

Hand Screened Stencil-printed cloth to which one or more colors are applied by hand through stretched, fine-meshed "screens" of silk or organdy. The mesh is blocked where color is not wanted.

Harness The frame of a loom upon which the heddles are placed. Warp threads are drawn through the eyes of the heddles, which move up and down as the shuttle with the weft yarn passes by. The movement of the heddles determines the pattern of the weaving.

Hmong A mountain tribe of the north of Laos.

Ikat Yarn which is either tie died or painted before being woven into fabric. (Compare "plangi.")

Overshot A distinct weaving pattern or the technique for achieving it. It involves a special loom threading and the use of heavy yarn (alternating with finer yarn) in the "weft," or narrow direction.

Plangi Woven fabric which is pattern-decorated by tie-dyeing; that is, by tieing or knotting parts of fabric so that they will not absorb the dye.

Resist (Resist-Dye) Patterning of yarn or textile by covering certain areas, usually with liquid wax, before dyeing.

Sprang A twisting pattern related to weaving in which warp threads are twisted around each other using dowels which are removed and replaced as the work progresses.

Tapestry A weft-faced fabric, often with slits here and there where colors meet.

Trapunto Decorative quilting in which the design is outline-stitched in two layers of fabric, then padded heavily between to form a high relief.

Warp The yarn which runs the long way in cloth made on a loom. It is under tension during weaving and is usually stronger

GLOSSARY

than the "weft" (or "fill") yarns which run across it.

Wax-resist See Resist.

Weaving The process of making fabric by interlacing a series of warp yarns with weft yarns at right angles.

Weft-faced A tapestry weave in which the yarn running the short way is dominant in the design.

GLASS

Aqua Silver See Surface Decoration.

Baluster A traditional English style of goblet with an air bubble in its stem.

Barley Twist A twisted, pulled stem or handle.

Batch A quantity of raw materials mixed in proper proportions and prepared for fusion in the glass furnace.

Cameo/Intaglio A technique in which the finished glass form is covered with another coating of glass of a different color into which is carved or etched a design that exposes the base color.

Cased Glass Glass completely covered (through blowing or dipping) by other, usually differently colored, glass. Outer layers can be partially cut away to reveal color(s) of the previous "casings" beneath.

Copper Foil Technique A process for joining glass by applying adhesive copper tape to each piece and soldering the copper together.

Crushed Glass See Surface Decoration.

Enameled Glass That decorated with particles of translucent, usually colored, glass or glasslike material, which fuses to the surface under heat. Multicolored designs as well as monochrome coatings can be created.

Etched Glass Glass decorated or otherwise marked by the use of hydrofluoric acid. The glass is first covered with an acid-resistant substance (wax or gum); the design is drawn through the resist with a point; and the exposed glass is etched by the acid.

Free Blown (Freehand Blown) Glassware shaped by air pressure, such as by mouth-blowing through a metal tube ("pipe") to which molten glass adheres.

Fumed Glass Glass with an iridescent surface.

Graal Technique Glass which is "blown twice." Glass is made with a color overlay which is then cut, etched or sandblasted with a decoration. The piece is subjected again to the heat of the furnace to impart fluidity and smoothness to the design and then encased in lead crystal.

Hot Glass Glass worked in its molten state directly from the furnace, usually in three dimensions. The term is used in opposition to "stained glass," which is usually flat and worked cold.

Lamp Work The technique of manipulating glass by heating it with a small flame.

Leaded Glass Glass containing a percentage of lead oxide, which increases its density and improves its ability to refract and disperse light. It is used for ornaments and for decorative and luxury tableware.

Off-Hand Blown Glass That which is shaped and finished by blowing and with hand tools rather than by using molds.

Powder Design See Surface Decoration.

Sand-Blasted Glass Glass whose surface is blown with fine sand under high pressure. It results in a roughened, nontransparent surface (commonly called "frosted"). Deeply engraved patterns can also be produced by using protective stencils.

Silver Nitrate See Surface Decoration.

Silver Veiled See Surface Decoration.

Slumped Glass Precast glass, such as plate glass, which is heat softened and molded over forms.

Soda-Lime Crystal A type of glass not particularly resistant to heat and used in windows and bottles.

Surface Decoration Many chemical and physical substances are applied to hot glass during the blowing process, often by rolling the hot glass over a table on which a substance has been sprinkled. Commonly used are powdered or crushed glass and silver nitrate.

JEWELRY AND METAL

Base Metal Any metal other than a precious metal, as copper, zinc, tin.

Cabochon A gem or bead with a smooth curved surface, highly polished but not faceted. (Pronounced "kah-ba-SHONE")

Casting The process of pouring molten metal into a hollow mold. The cast metal duplicates the object (wood, hard wax, etc.) originally impressed in the mold material. Some processes permit more than one reproduction.

Champlevé Enamel work in which transparent or opaque enamel is fired into etched or carved areas, leaving the metal partly exposed. (Pronounced "shahm-pleh-

GLOSSARY

VAY")

Chased Metal whose surface is patterned by striking with a hammer or other noncutting tool. The metal is worked from the front only.

Cloisonné Enameling in which the colors are separated by thin metal ribbons or wires to maintain the pattern and keep the melting colors from running together. (Pronounced "cloy-zon-NAY")

Constructed (1) Hand made in parts and assembled to form a whole.
(2) Not cast.

Electroformed Creation of a metal object by electrically depositing metal on a master form of wax. After the wax is removed, a metal shell remains.

Electroplated Coated with a thin layer of (usually precious) metal by passing an electric current through a chemical solution containing a source of the metal.

Enamel A usually opaque vitreous composition applied by fusion to the surface of metal, glass or pottery.

Epoxy A plastic coating applied to the surface of metal which may look like enameling.

Fabrication Making an object in parts and assembling it to form a whole.

Forged Metal shaped, usually by hammering, while at a red or white heat in blacksmithing, but usually cold in jewelry.

Granulation Tiny particles (as of metal) heat-fused to a metal surface without the use of solder.

Grisaille Enameling made by firing various thicknesses of whitish opaque enamel on an opaque black background. (Pronounced "grih-ZY"; rhymes with "sky")

Holloware Vessels, such as bowls and pitchers.

Lapidary The art of cutting, polishing and engraving precious stones.

Lost-Wax Casting A one-time reproduction process in which an object (as of wax) is impressed into sand or surrounded with a special plaster to make a mold. The wax is burned off, and molten metal takes the form of the "lost" wax.

Married Metal That featuring intricate (but sometimes subtle) patterns of different alloys, as of bronze, copper and silver.

Oxidize To cover with a coating of oxide, used on metal to darken it.

Patina (1) A surface coloring, usually brown or green, produced by oxidation of bronze or other metal. It occurs naturally or can be produced artificially for decorative effect.
(2) The substance used to produce the effect.
(3) A surface luster occurring from age or use.

Pave A style of setting in which small stones are placed close together in holes drilled in the metal, the burr of metal around the hole being pressed over to hold the stone in place.

Plique-A-Jour Enameling in which transparent enamels fill small openings in metal, suggesting stained glass windows. (Pronounced "PLEEK-ah-ZHOOR")

Raised Hammering a flat sheet of metal into a container-type form

Repoussé A design raised in relief on a metal surface, or the process of hammering (on both sides) to achieve it. (Pronounced "Reh-poo-SAY")

Resin (Polyester Resin) A plastic which may be bonded to metal or cast in molds.

Reticulated A metal surface delicately wrinkled by a special heating process.

Sand Cast To produce a casting by pouring molten metal into sand molds.

Scrimshaw Whalebone or similar material having intricate scenes or designs engraved on its surface.

Vermeil (Pronounced "ver-MAIL") (1) A descriptive term applied to orange-red stones.
(2) Gilded silver, bronze or copper.

Wrought Shaped by beating or hammering, often elaborately for decorative effect. Wrought iron is also a low-carbon metal which can be elongated without breakage; it is resistant to corrosion.

ASSORTED MEDIA

Case Binding Bookbinding done by gluing sewn sheets into a cover which has been made separately.

Serigraph A print made by the silk-screen process.

WOOD

Band Saw A power saw employing a continuous loop of toothed metal band.

Burl A dome-shaped growth on the trunk of a tree.

Holtzapffel Lathe A traditional wood-turning machine with carving attachments powered by the lathe instead of by hand; used for ornamental or decorative work.

Jig Saw A narrow saw mounted vertically in a

GLOSSARY

frame for cutting curves or other difficult lines.

Laminated Composed of layers bonded together for strength, thickness or decoration.

Marquetry Decorative patterns formed of thin layers of wood (and sometimes other materials such as ivory) inlaid into the surface, usually of furniture.

Mortise A notch, hole, groove or slot made in a piece of wood to receive a tenon of the same dimensions.

Renaissance Intarsia A form of wood inlay, especially of other materials such as ivory and metal, in which the material is inlaid into the solid wood instead of being glued on the surface as with veneer.

Router A machine with a vertical, drill-like cutter for cutting designs into wood or for decoratively edging it.

Spalted Naturally decayed wood with distinctive markings; used for its decorative effect.

Tenon A projection on the end of a piece of wood.

Turned Wood shaped by tools while it revolves about a fixed axis, as of a lathe. Cylindrical forms (dowels, rungs) and circular designs are made this way.

Veneer A thin layer of wood of superior value or excellent grain to be glued to an inferior wood.

LEATHER

Boiling A water-forming technique in which leather is immersed for a short time in boiling water, causing the leather to bend and pucker. When dry, the leather is extremely hard, though fragile.

Carving A decorative technique in which the surface of the leather is cut with a swivel knife and the background is depressed using modeling tools or stamps. Also called incising.

Chrome Tanning A tanning process using salts of chromium to make leathers that are especially supple and suitable for bags, garments, etc.

Cuir-Bouilli (kweer-boo-e) literally, boiled leather. A general term, from ancient usage, for water-forming.

Embossing A decorative technique in which a design is raised in relief, working with modeling tools on both hair (grain) side and flesh (inner) side.

Flesh Side The side of the leather that was closest to the musculature of the animal; the inner side.

Glue-Resist A decorative technique in which a removable glue is applied to the leather before it is glued. The dye cannot penetrate the glue-protected areas.

Kip A large calf skin, usually thicker than calf.

Laminating A technique of bonding layers of leather together under pressure for strength, thickness or visual effect.

Lasting A water-forming process in which the damp leather is forced over a mold and clamped or nailed in place until dry. When dry, the leather retains the molded shape.

Ounce A measure of the approximate thickness of leather. One ounce = $1/64''$.

Saddle Stitching A two-handed stitching technique using a needle at both ends of a single thread. It produces a uniform stitch on both sides of the leather.

Stamping A technique using handmade or commercial metal stamps on damp leather to create a pattern or to depress the background of a carved piece.

Split The inner layer of the leather cut from the top grain portion.

Suede A type of leather, either split or top grain, in which the flesh side is buffed smooth. Suede splits are buffed on both sides.

Tooling General name given to several related techniques of working vegetable tanned leather to create effects of low relief; carving, stamping, embossing, etc.

Top Grain The outer surface of the hide, still possessing the original grain surface; the hair side.

Vegetable Tanning (Oak tanning, bark tanning) A tanning process using extracts of tannic acid, that makes strong leathers suitable for belts, bags, etc., and that is able to be water-formed.

Water-Formed (Wet-Formed) A technique in which leather is dampened to make it more pliable, and worked freehand or over a mold or last. When dry the leather will retain its shape.

INDEX

Abrams, Jackie Speeter, 220
Abrams, Steve, 110
ACC Craft Fair at West Springfield, 268
Ace Woodwork, 235
Adams, Laurie V., 83
Adirondack Designs, 218
Alberetti, Mary Lou, 78
Alianza, 33
American Craft Council, 268
Amidon, Douglas P., 244
Anava Textiles, 134
Andrews, Beth, 88
Annual Craftsmen's Fair, 271
Armen, Ted, 219
Artful Hand, 43
Artifactory, 51
Artisans Cooperative, 33, 40
Artisans East, 53
Artisans' Hand, 62
Artist Express Depot, 49
Arts & Science Center, 284
Asylum Glass Studio, 172
Atelier Shadur-Maynard, 154
Atelier Studio/Gallery, 20
At the Studio, 215
A Touch of Glass, 18
Aufrichtig's, 12
Avon Place Glass, 175
Aylen, Peter, 185

Barber, Jillian K., 107
Barry, Monica M., 123
Bittersweet Handcraft Village, 12
Blake, Mary, 211
Blistein, Alice, 148
Bonnema, Garret and Melody, 82
Boston Center for Adult Education, 281
Boston University, 281
Boutin, David R., 164
Branfman, Steven, 94
Braskie, Brian, 252
Brauer, Lisa, 217
Bretschneider, Gordon H. B., 261
Bridgeport Balloon Works, 206
Briggs, Jeffrey, 242
Brookfield Craft Center, 12, 277
Brooklin Crafts Cooperative, 24
Broudo, J. David, 90
Brown, Aaron Thomas, 251
Brown, Deborah, 159
Brown, Judy and Steve, 183
Brown, Tafi, 139
Buechner, Matthew, 179
Bull's Bridge Glass Works, 162
Bunnell, Wayland, 104
Burch, Elliot, 224
Butler, Robert A., 195
Byron, James, 206

Caleb's Sunrise, 23
Cambridge Center for Adult Education, 282
Carlson, Anna, 138
Carlson, Fred, 224
Cary, Elisabeth, 190
Ceramic Choreography, 86
Chosen Works, 23
Church Street Festival of the Arts, 273
City Lights Glass, 168
Clark, Chris, 75
Cliff, Barrie, 198
Clifford, Linda, 156
Color Wheel, 104
Company of Craftsmen, 18
Compton, Robert, 109
Concord Arts & Crafts, 49
Concord Gallery, 49
Connecticut Commission on the Arts, 276
Connecticut River Artisans Cooperative, 13
Contemporary Crafts Gallery, 22
Corner, 42
Correll, Charles M., 176
Costello, Jeanne, 127
Craft-Haus, 63
Craftproducers Markets, Inc., 272
Critters by Otis, 209
Cummings, Brian, 202

Danforth, Fred and Judi, 203
Danforth Museum Shop, 38
Davis, Richard E., 218
Decordova Museum, 282
Deer Mountain Pottery, 92
Designers Circle, 60
Design Works, 46
Dickerman, Jennifer, 150
Different Drummer, 58
Diggs, Jo, 125
DJB Designs, 159
Dodds, Judy, 157
Dokus, Jack, 201
Don Muller Gallery, 42
Down on the Farm, 16
Drevich, Shirley, 187
Dring, Bebe Holland, 166
Drooker, Penelope B., 142
Dunwell, Anna, 130
Duryea, Lynn, 84

Eastern Bay Cooperative Gallery, 30
Eastern Maine Craft Co-op, 28
East Hill Porcelain Doll and Marionette Co., 223
Edwards, Ian B., 234
Elements, 13
Ellen Harris Gallery, 44
Ellis, Bob, 102
Elwood Turner, 257

295 · GLOSSARY/INDEX

INDEX

Endicott College, 282
Endleman-Kraus Galleries, 20
Epstein, David, 191
Erickson, Peter, 196
Ethel Putterman Gallery, 43
Evergreen, 14
Exeter Craft Center, 50
Extras, 202

Fantastic Umbrella Factory, 56
Farmington Valley Arts Center, 11, 278
Farrington, Lee, 131
Feathertree Studio, 222
Feher, Patri, 116
Fein, Randy, 87
Fellerman, Stephen, 162
Fiber Artistry, 118
Fiberworks, 136
Fiber Works, 122
Field, Sabra, 227
Fine Woodworks, 259
Fischer, Peter, 224
Fisher Gallery, 11
Fisher, Timothy, 254
Five Wings Studio, 103
Flynn, Jim, 137
Forman, Camille, 120
Fox, Susan, 74
Franconia League of New Hampshire Craftsmen, 50
Fretz, Marian and William, 184
Friedline, David, 245
Functional Fibers, 129

Gandelman, Roger, 165
Gateway Gallery, 25
Gervens, Lynn, 91
Giesmann, Gregor, 89
Gifted Hand, 46
Gilson, Nancy, 101
Given, Linda, 246
Glover, Mary, 172
Golden Toad, 52
Goodman, Sara, 149
Gordon, Helen M., 147
Grad, Andrew, 186
Greenwich Art Barn, 14
Griffith, Anita, 76
Grove, Edwin R., 194
Guilford Handcrafts Center, 15, 265, 278
Guilford Handcrafts Exposition, 265
Gutkowski, Karen, 153

Halibut Point Pewter, 197
Handcrafters Gallery, 29
Handmade Paper Products, 212
Hands On!, 26
Handworks, 32

Hanover League of New Hampshire Craftsmen, 50
Harrison, Vicky, 167
Hartung, Dudley, 247
Hastings, Howard, 240
Hatch, Howard, 249
Haystack Mountain School of Crafts, 25, 280
Hayward, Harold T., 214
Hawkins House, 59
Heilman, Barbara, 150
Heilman, Chris and Joyce, 174
Heminway, Frances Lee, 80
Hendricks, Laurence, 232
Hertzbach, Bobby T., 126
Hildebran, Diane, 204
Hirshberg, Lois, 92
Hollis Center Pottery, 85
Holsten Galleries, 45
Horizons, 281
Howe, Lenore, 252
Hurd, Lois D., 143

Island Artisans, Inc., 23
It's Only Mud, 76

J. G. Silks, 127
Journeyman, 37
Jubilation, 42
J. W. Graham, 58

Katz, Stan, 222
Kaye-Moses, Linda, 189
Kellar, Jeff, 238
Kelso, James, 228
King Richard's Faire, 266
Kirchoff, Mary, 230
Klara Simpla, 63
Klivans, Elinor, 122
Kohn, Judith, 141
Kovach, Drew, 159

Lacoste, Jan, 93
Landscape Woodworks, 246
Laughing Sun Design, 137
Laughlin, R. Bruce, 163
League of New Hampshire Craftsmen, 49, 50, 52, 53, 54, 55, 271, 276, 284
Leather Shed, 32
Lee, Barbara, 118
LEE-HEM Porcelain, 80
Le Jardin de Verre, 166
Leprechaun Sheepskin, 214
Leverett Craftsmen and Artists, Inc., 40, 283
Lightship Baskets, 207
Lily G. Iselin, 57
Limited Editions, Essex, CT, 13
Limited Editions, Newton, MA, 41
Livestock Unlimited, 230

296 · GLOSSARY/INDEX

INDEX

L. J. Serkin, 60
Loewenton, Edward, 257
Log Cabin Creations, 138
LS Graphics, 210

MacDonald, Elizabeth, 72
Magdanz, Andrew, 175
Maine Commission on the Arts, 276
Maine Potters Market, 29
Manchester Institute of Arts and Sciences, 285
Maple Hill Gallery, 28
Margonelli, David and Susan, 236
Marion-Ruth, 36
Marketplace, Inc., 30
Markiewicz, Gail, 81
Mary's Applehead Characters, 211
Mason, Ellen, 247
Massachusetts Council on the Arts, 276
Masseau, Jean Carlson, 155
Mattia, Alphonse, 241
Maynard, Paul and Tamar, 154
McIlvane, Edward J., 180
Meredith-Laconia Arts & Crafts, 52
Metamorphosis, 44
Milkhouse Pottery, 74
Miller, Jim, 172
Miller, Rosemary, 167
Minkowitz, Norma, 121
Morrison, Abby, 235
Mount Snow Craft Fair, 273
MPH Stained Glass, 167
Mudslingers Studio, 77
Mulholland, Susan B., 216
Mung Bean, 24
Munro-Dorsey, Sarah, 152
Murphy, Ellen, 77

Nadel, Lois Cassen, 73
Nanci Enamels, 200
Neely, Cynthia H., 119
New England Artist Festival, 265
New Horizons, 43
Newman, Rochelle, 132
Norris, Susan, 224
Northern Lights Glass Studio, 169
Northside Craft Gallery, 48
North Woods Chair Shop, 252

Old State House, 15
Olson, Robert F., 260
O'Neil, Nancy Gutkin, 171
Oppenheimer, Doris R., 129
O'Rourke, Elizabeth, 212
Ozereko, Frank, 98

Palmer, Dottie, 86
Parsons, Jeffrey C., 256

Patchwork Puffery, 147
Patrick, William, 246
Pat's Ceramics, 108
Pearce, Eve S., 145
Perceptions, 37
Peters, Susan Abbie, 226
Petrochko, Peter M., 233
Pewter Crafters of Cape Cod, 198
Pinnacle Designs, 232
Pincus, Katherine, 135
Plum Dandy, 27
Plumdinger Studio, 189
Plum Tree Pottery, 105
Polesny, Anna V. A., 134
Popovits-Rechel, Dahlia, 114
Potter, Leslie, 167
Potter's Shop, 41
Praxis, 27
Prints and the Potter, 47
Pritchard, James, 250
Program in Artisanry at Boston University, 281

Quaigh Design Center, 64
Quaigh Designs, 40
Quaking Aspen Stained Glass, 171

Raccoon, 247
Rainbow Glassworks, 164, 165
Rainbow's End, 52
Redfield, Janet, 170
Redwing Craft Cooperative, 47
Rhode Island Council on the Arts, 276
Rhode Island School of Design, 286
Rial, Nancy, 133
Richmond, Roger R., 173
Riportella, Ken, 224
River Valley Crafts, 32
Rizzo, Louis W., 85
Robbins, Judy, 117
Roberge, Roger, 111
Rosenquist, Marilyn and William, 207
Rowe, Nancy, 144
Rugg, Cliff, 239
Rugg Road Handmade Papers, 213

Salty Dog Pottery, 102
Samara, 62
Sand, Toland Peter, 177
Sandwich Home Industries, 54
Sawyer, David, 255
Scanlan, Cathleen, 178
Schechter, Lorraine, 210
Schnabel, Carol, 158
Schneider, Cal and Rick, 253
Schoolhouse Shop, 55
Scribner, Nancy, 208
Sears, Annie, 223

INDEX

Seavey, James, 197
Seeger, Jeremy, 221
Setzler, Bobbi, 77
Seymour, John H., 79
Shapiro, Dianne, 146
Shapiro, Susan, 175
Sharon Arts Center, 54, 285
Shelburne Craft School, 288
Shlien, Laura, 100
Shop at the Institute, 51
Shop at Wesleyan Potters, 16
Short, Maureen, 222
Sho-Shin Studio, 173
Shutt, Carol, 124
Signature, 34, 39
Silk Purse and the Sow's Ear, 59
Silo, 20
Silverman, Jean, 105
Silvermine Guild Galleries, 19
Silvermine Guild School of the Arts, 278
Silverscape Designs, 32
Simon, Andrew M., 231
Simons, Patricia Uchill, 108
Skera, 38
Small Axe Productions, 56
Snow-Eklund, Sally, 128
Society of Arts and Crafts, 34
Soft Sculpture, 146
Sollinger, John, 258
Somerson, Rosanne, 243
Soule, Theodore Otis, 209
Southern Vermont Craft Fair, 272
Spectrum of American Artists and Craftsmen, 36, 39, 41, 45, 57
Steckler, David, 259
Stoneham Pewter, 199
Strickler, Darius, 215
Strong Craft Gallery, 26
Stowe Pottery, 63

Tamsky, Eleanor Dole, 168
Taylor, Teresa, 102
Taylor-Parsons, Alison, 151
Ten Arrow, 37
Tenenbaum, Fred, 169
Terry, Diane Graham, 115
Terry, Ralph and Sandy, 97
Tewksbury's, 54
Thames Street Glass House, 179
Timeless Designs, 25

Toale, Bernard, 213
Tontine Press, 227
Tracy, Joseph, 237
Tree's Place, 44
Trillium Fine Crafts, 62
Turning Point Pottery, 100

Unicorn, 65

Vermont Council on the Arts, 276
Vermont Imports, 35
Vermont Musical Instrument Builders Cooperative, 224
Vermont Sled Co., 258
Vermont State Craft Center at Frog Hollow, 61, 288
Vermont State Craft Center at Windsor House, 64, 288
Voake, Ronald, 262
Voltaire's, 22

Walch, Barbara, 95
Weaving on the Wind, 145
Wellspring Woodworks, 251
Wesleyan Potters, 279
Whaler's Wharf, 45
Wheeler, E. H., 106
Whipporwill Crafts, 35
White, Cheryl and Ted, 199
White, Tom, 96
Wigham, Phyllis, 230
Wild Goose Chase, 36
Willy Hill Baskets, 220
Willy Hill Pottery, 110
Windfall Pottery, 88
Winston, Martha, 99
Wintje, Kim, 140
Winzeler, Nan, 200
Wise, Laurie, 188
WiseEye Photo Graphics, 116
Wobbly Land Patchwork, 156
Wonderful Things, 38
Worcester Craft Center, 47, 270, 283
Worcester Craft Fair, 270
Wright, Gary, 218

Yolen, Nancy, 182

Zax, Andrea, 136
Zina, Joe, 213

Photo Credits

Openers

Page	Credit
5	Courtesy Windsor House Craft Center.
67	Glenn Moody photo.
71	Marna G. Clarke photo courtesy Farmington Valley Arts Center.
113	Christopher Irion/Camerawork photo courtesy Frog Hollow Craft Center.
161	Jamey Stillings photo.
181	Lee Everitt photo.
205	Phil Zimmerman photo courtesy Farmington Valley Arts Center.
229	Ed Hewhall photo courtesy Rhode Island School of Design.
263	Courtesy American Craft Enterprises.
275	Courtesy Rhode Island School of Design.
289	Gary Gilbert photo courtesy Rhode Island School of Design.

Gallery

Page	Credit
11	David Gaynes photo courtesy Farmington Valley Arts Center.
12	Courtesy Brookfield Craft Center.
15	Copyright 1983 by Bill Tchakirides Photography Associates, courtesy Old State House.
17	K. A. Simon photo courtesy Down on the Farm.
19	Millie Rose Madrick photo courtesy Silvermine Guild.
21	Courtesy The Silo.
22	Courtesy Voltaire's.
24	Courtesy Brooklin Crafts Cooperative.
31	David Klopfenstein photo courtesy East Bay Cooperative Gallery.
35	Meryl Zassman photo courtesy The Society of Arts and Crafts.
39	David Photography photo courtesy Signature.
42	Courtesy The Potters Shop.
46	Courtesy The Gifted Hand.
47	Courtesy Redwing Craft Cooperative.
48	Courtesy Worcester Craft Center.
53	Copyright 1979 by Bob Raiche, courtesy The Golden Toad.
55	Andrew Bonatakis photo courtesy Sandwich Home Industries.
56	Courtesy The Fantastic Umbrella Factory.
59	Courtesy The Silk Purse.
61	Courtesy Frog Hollow Craft Center.
65	Courtesy Windsor House Craft Center.

Artisan

Page	Credit
74	Bill Tchakirides
75	Reene Shmerl
76	Tom Hopkins
77	Amy Radcliffe
78	John I. Russell
80	David Gaynes
82	Dennis Griggs
83	Brian VandenBrink
84	David Klopfenstein
87	Judith Berk
88	Tom Lang
89	Gina O. P.
90	Robert M. Aude
91	Richard Freierman
93	Susie Kushner
94	R. Arruda Studio
97	Industrial Photographic Service
103	Charley Freiberg
106	Northlight Photography
107	Jack Spratt
108	Chee-Heng Yeong
110	Andrew Klein/Afterimage
111	Bill Wasserman
114	David Rechel
118	A. Vincent Scarano
120	Michael Vesaker
121	Bob Hanson
126	Ed Judice
127	Tom Lang
128	Karl Eklund
130	Steve Dunwell
131	Roger D. Farrington
132	Richard Newman
136	Jon Zax
137	Allan Teger
138	Walter Carlson
139	Bob Gere
140	Frank Hagenbuch
141	R. B. Croteau
143	Cathy Carver
144	Roger Williams/The Luce Studio
145	Peter Crabtree
146	Hyam Siegel
148	Fred Hill
149	Erik Borg
152	Art Edelstein
153	Jill Noss
155	Erik Borg
156	Bill LaFrance/Mountain Mist Studio
157	Jim Dodds
158	Erik Borg
159	Harley Freeman
162	Stan Fellerman
167	Earl Colter
168	David Dodge
170	David Klopfenstein
171	Macomber Photography
174	Mark Rockwood
175	Jamey Stillings
179	B. Sterling Benkhart
180	Ric Murray
182	B. Ratensperger
185	deFeo, Mercy
186	Stephen Dapkiewicz
187	Ken Winokur
188	Paul Richeleau
189	Evan Soldinger
190	Susie Kushner
194	Andrew Haltof
195	Studio 11

Photo Credits

Page	Credit
199	Allan Teger
201	Chet Brickett
203	Erik Borg
206	K. Beland, M. J. Main
207	Gerard Roy
208	Ty Hyon
211	W. Marc Bernau
212	Debbie VanderMolen
213	Steven Stone
216	Studio Sergei Starosielski
217	Branoran, Harting
218	Christie Nevius
219	Chris Radcliffe
220	Andrew Klein/Afterimage
222	Paul Boisvert
223	Glenn Moody
224	Andrew Klein/Afterimage
225	Andrew Klein/Afterimage
226	Jack Peters, Esther Parada
227	Spencer Field
231	David Viens, K. A. Simon
233	Bill Tchakirides/Photography Associates
234	Carmine Picarello
236	R. Normand
237	Bob Zuckerman
239	Peter Macomber Studios
240	Chuck Kidd
242	John I. Russell, Allan Teger
243	Charlie Hogg
244	Ed Robinson
245	Barbara Hakim, Susie Kushner
246	Allan Teger
247	David Caras
249	Kennett-Rudnik Associates
251	Andy Paul
254	Andrew Klein/Afterimage
255	Jay O'Rear
257	Randolph Schnitzel-Peasey
259	David L. Ryan

Fairs

Page	Credit
265	Courtesy New England Artist Festival.
266-267	Courtesy King Richard's Faire.
268-269	Courtesy American Craft Enterprises.
270	J. Northrup-Bennett photo courtesy League of New Hampshire Craftsmen.
272	Courtesy New England Artist Festival
273	Courtesy American Craft Enterprises.

Schools

Page	Credit
276	Courtesy Brookfield Craft Center.
279	Marna G. Clarke photo courtesy Farmington Valley Arts Center.
280	Courtesy Haystack Mountain School of Crafts.
282	Copyright 1979 by Ted Polumbaum, courtesy Boston University Program in Artisanry.
284	Courtesy Arts & Science Center.
286	Ira Garber photo courtesy Rhode Island School of Design.
287	Gary Gilbert photo courtesy Rhode Island School of Design.
288	Courtesy Frog Hollow Craft Center.

To order additional copies of this book, see the next page!

Please send me _____ copies of The New England Handcraft Catalog at $14.95 each. Please include $1.50 postage and handling per book.*
(*Orders for three or more books are shipped postage-free!)
Connecticut residents please also add 7½% sales tax.

    Enclosed is my check for _____.
    Please charge to my _____ MasterCard _____ VISA
    Card Number _____ Expiration Date _____

Please ship to:
Name _____
Address _____
City _____ State _____ Zip _____

Your order will be shipped within 48 hours of receipt.

The Globe Pequot Press

The Globe Pequot Press, Old Chester Road, Box Q, Chester, CT 06412
  Telephone: (203) 526-9571

---8<---

Please send me _____ copies of The New England Handcraft Catalog at $14.95 each. Please include $1.50 postage and handling per book.*
(*Orders for three or more books are shipped postage-free!)
Connecticut residents please also add 7½% sales tax.

    Enclosed is my check for _____.
    Please charge to my _____ MasterCard _____ VISA
    Card Number _____ Expiration Date _____

Please ship to:
Name _____
Address _____
City _____ State _____ Zip _____

Your order will be shipped within 48 hours of receipt.

The Globe Pequot Press

The Globe Pequot Press, Old Chester Road, Box Q, Chester, CT 06412
  Telephone: (203) 526-9571

To order additional copies of this book, see the next page!

Please send me _____ copies of The New England Handcraft Catalog at $14.95 each. Please include $1.50 postage and handling per book.*
(*Orders for three or more books are shipped postage-free!)
Connecticut residents please also add 7½% sales tax.

 Enclosed is my check for _____.
 Please charge to my _____ MasterCard _____ VISA
 Card Number _____ Expiration Date _____

Please ship to:
Name _____
Address _____
City _____ State _____ Zip _____

Your order will be shipped within 48 hours of receipt.

The Globe Pequot Press

The Globe Pequot Press, Old Chester Road, Box Q, Chester, CT 06412
 Telephone: (203) 526-9571

---- ✂ --

Please send me _____ copies of The New England Handcraft Catalog at $14.95 each. Please include $1.50 postage and handling per book.*
(*Orders for three or more books are shipped postage-free!)
Connecticut residents please also add 7½% sales tax.

 Enclosed is my check for _____.
 Please charge to my _____ MasterCard _____ VISA
 Card Number _____ Expiration Date _____

Please ship to:
Name _____
Address _____
City _____ State _____ Zip _____

Your order will be shipped within 48 hours of receipt.

The Globe Pequot Press

The Globe Pequot Press, Old Chester Road, Box Q, Chester, CT 06412
 Telephone: (203) 526-9571